CONCRETE
BOXES

CONCRETE

BOXES

Mizrahi Women on Israel's Periphery

Pnina Motzafi-Haller

With a Foreword by Virginia R. Dominguez

WAYNE STATE UNIVERSITY PRESS
DETROIT

This edition is a translation from the original Hebrew publication *In the Cement Boxes* (Magnes Press, 2012) published by arrangement with the Hebrew University Magnes Press Ltd., Jerusalem.

ISBN 978-0-8143-4059-2 (paperback)
ISBN 978-0-8143-4442-2 (hardcover)
ISBN 978-0-8143-4060-8 (ebook)

Library of Congress Cataloging Number: 2018930305

Published with support from the fund for the Raphael Patai Series in Jewish Folklore and Anthropology.

Wayne State University Press
Leonard N. Simons Building
4809 Woodward Avenue
Detroit, Michigan 48201-1309

Visit us online at wsupress.wayne.edu

This book is dedicated to the memory of Dr. Vicki Shiran,
friend, mentor, and leader of Mizrahi feminism

Contents

Preface

AS I PREPARED to finally let go of the English version of this book, first published in Hebrew in 2012, I revisited French sociologist Pierre Bourdieu's insightful 1962 work "Célibat et condition paysanne." In it, I discovered the following statement, which (if one disregards the dated reference to "men") captures my goal in this book: "Sociology is not worth one hour of trouble if its aim is only to discover the strings that move the individuals it observes, . . . if it does not take as its task to restore to men the meanings of their actions" (108). *Concrete Boxes* is an attempt at such restoration. It aims to place the experience of Mizrahi women who reside in a small town in Israel's Negev Desert at the center of attention. It is an effort to document, using extended first-person narratives and life histories, how these women forge meaningful lives despite their marginalization on multiple counts.

The women featured in this book are the daughters of Jewish immigrants sent by the Israeli state to settle the country's remote desert regions in the 1950s and 1960s. In their starkly isolated locale, they survive the many powerful structural disadvantages it imposes, including limited employment opportunities, an inferior educational system, and a dominant Israeli discourse that patronizes and stigmatizes them. Their ethnicity, their gender, and other structural forces confine them within what I visualize as a *concrete box* that limits their own and their daughters' hopes for social mobility. How does it *feel* to be placed in such a box? How do these women experience their circumstances? Do they struggle to break free from them? In this ethnography, I document life on the Israeli margins from the perspective of women whose voices are seldom heard. Their stories offer a particularly revealing vantage point from which to grasp many of the contradictions inherent in Israeli society and culture.

Mizrahi critical discourse had blossomed by 1995, when I returned to Israel after almost two decades of living in the United States. I was excited to meet other Mizrahi activists like myself, many of whom also had acquired their PhDs in leading U.S. universities. Our academic work was stimulated by our social activism, which culminated in 1996 in our founding of a nongovernmental organization (NGO) we called HaKeshet HaDemocratit HaMizrahit (Mizrahi Democratic Rainbow). In the last decade two influential Mizrahi groups with somewhat different social and political agendas have emerged. One is HaMizrahit HaMeshutefet, a movement of left-leaning Mizrahi intellectuals who advocate joint Mizrahi and Palestinian political activism. The other movement, Tor HaZahav (The Golden Age), calls for a cultural revival of Mizrahi traditions. In the summer of 2016, the Israeli minister of education publicly endorsed policy guidelines proposed by the Bitton Commission (headed by the celebrated Mizrahi poet Erez Bitton), which called for expanding school curricula to include Mizrahi Jewish history and culture.

Israeli academia seems to have remained impervious to the recent Mizrahi florescence in the cultural and political spheres, as reflected in documentary filmmaking, poetry, and popular media. Regrettably, sociological research in Israel continues to use theoretical and analytical frameworks that fail to examine inequality through mutually constitutive class, ethnic, and gender lines. To date, there is no comprehensive academic documentation of the dire effects of rampant neoliberal policies on Israel's peripheries. This may be changing: in August 2016, supported by a Ministry of Science research grant, Sigal Nagar-Ron and I began a three-year study of employment patterns among Mizrahi women in the Negev. Our project continues the lessons begun in *Concrete Boxes* by seeking to examine multiple lines of social exclusions and explore the manner in which they shape social reality in tandem.

A final note about the process of reworking my original Hebrew book into the text you are reading now in English. I anticipated that issuing an English version of the book would be a simple work of translation. I even secured generous grants to pay professional translators for the task. But after English versions landed on my desk from a series of diligent translators, I could see how much more work I needed to do to produce an account that would make sense to non-Hebrew-speaking readers. Doing so, I felt, was not merely a matter of cleaning up syntax or explaining Hebrew expressions. Rather, I needed to rework large segments and write new sections to intelligibly convey the tone of the work in translation. I worked for months with my interlocutors' accounts, revising every phrase to preserve the flow of the original narratives. It felt like writing a new book to address new audiences.

So why did I go through this arduous process? Why did I insist on publishing my book first in Hebrew and then in English? After all, Hebrew publications get almost no professional credit in the Israeli academic system. Professional recognition and promotion hinge on publishing in recognized international, mostly English-language, journals. Furthermore, I was trained in an American academic milieu and had written my PhD and most of my earlier academic publications in English. Still, I chose to write *Concrete Boxes* in Hebrew, because I wanted to address Israeli readers within and outside academia. These are the audiences who are intimately familiar with the issues and reality I problematize in my work. This was a *political* decision, and it framed every element of my ethnographic work and the tone and style of my writing and analysis. I also wanted my interlocutors, their families, and their friends to be able to read my work. I made a real effort to write in what feminists call an "evocative" style rather than in dry, reference-filled academic jargon. I hoped that my book would be accessible to a wide readership and thus would enter public discourse rather than remain confined to narrow academic circles. As I send this English version of the book to press, I am glad to report that reception of the Hebrew version was indeed enthusiastic. Since that version came out in 2012, I have traveled between public libraries and prisons, NGOs and activist groups, cultural centers and college seminar rooms, meeting in each setting with people who had read the book and were deeply engaged with the issues it raised. I spoke with people about the meaning of Mizrahi identity in contemporary Israel and about the limited opportunities for social mobility of youth raised in Israeli "development towns"; I debated with my audiences the role of academic work in shaping social activism; I lectured in NGOs about grassroots feminism as articulated in my research in Yerucham and about the place of reflexivity in academic scholarship. This interaction was deeply gratifying. At one point, well-known Israeli actor and director Yiftach Klein called to ask whether he could use the book as the basis for a play. I was initially apprehensive, worrying that my insights would be flattened and reproduce rather than challenge familiar Israeli narratives about Mizrahi identity and peripherality. I worked closely with Klein and found his adaptation to be powerful and sensitive, and the play—*BeKufsaot HaBeton*—was ably produced by the Dimona Theater. For more than two years it was performed around the country, bringing the complex issues that concern me to audiences who might not have read my book.

My greatest hope is that this English version will introduce a wide range of readers to the seldom-discussed inner contradictions of Israeli society, as seen by those who live in its backyard.

Sde Boker
November 2017

Foreword to the Hebrew Edition

It could be argued that ideology, which determines that only momentous events should be written about, misses the point that it is impossible to understand the world without reporting on the incidents that take place out of the sight of those in positions of power.

Orly Lubin, *Women Reading Women*

MOTZA'EI SHABBAT. TIME is standing still. I step outside to see if I can count three stars so that I can tell Rina, who is hosting me this weekend, that the Sabbath is over and we can watch the news on TV. Rina is a widow I met at a senior citizens club in the southern town of Yerucham when I was just beginning my ethnographic work there.

During the long weekend in Rina's home, I feel as though I have returned to my childhood days in Migdal Ha'Emek. Rina cooks Iraqi dishes for me and warns me that I will have to respect her religious lifestyle. And so every time I inadvertently turn off the light in the bathroom (the only one left on for the whole Sabbath) and every time Rina expresses disappointment that I do not eat more ("Then why did I cook all this? What a shame. If you don't eat it, it'll be thrown out. Who's going to eat all this food?"), I am reminded of my parents' home. Rina does not agree to let me take notes during her detailed recounting of her complicated life story. It goes without saying that my suggestion to use a tape recorder is also ruled out. "You'll remember it all and write it down on Sunday," she insists. Without my professional gear, I revert to being "little Pnina," the one who doesn't eat enough, who forgets again and again not to turn off the Shabbat light.

When I finally manage to spot three stars, I walk out to the street with a feeling of relief. The Sabbath is over. And suddenly, as if drawn back into an old home movie, I reexperience the *motza'ei shabbat* of my childhood. Rina joins me and, wrapped in our shawls (she lends me one of hers), we cross the small park in front of her house, making our way at a leisurely pace to the main street. As in the Migdal Ha'Emek of my memories, the main street in Yerucham is not referred to by its official name but is simply known as "the center" (*ha-merkaz*). As I take in the scene, I am overcome by a feeling of déjà vu: The young men dressed in tight pants with gel in their hair. The teenage girls flaunting their perfect bodies in colorful trendy outfits that expose midriffs, tanned shoulders, straight backs. Young families ambling behind baby carriages. Warm smiles of acquaintances: How are you? What's happening? I feel a deep joy sharing this relaxed stroll down the main street with Rina. Sitting at the two cafés that overflow onto the sidewalk are those few who feel like shelling out 10 shekels for a cup of coffee or a mug of beer. Most of us are content to meander along. Rina and I nibble on sunflower seeds that we brought from home in a small paper bag. We buy a popsicle. Lemon flavored. Like the ones I used to buy as a little girl in Migdal Ha'Emek so many years ago. When we tire, we sit on the low stone wall that borders the sidewalk. Greetings come my way. How are you, Pnina? Where are you these days? We haven't seen you . . . Come over . . . Stop by . . .

I belong.

In January 2000 I begin spending more time in Yerucham, driving 20 minutes on empty desert roads from my home in the campus community of Midreshet Sde Boker to the homes of the women who enter my office as cleaners. I intend to write a research proposal over the course of that year in which I suggest an ethnographic field project focusing on the process of increasing religiosity among Mizrahi women in Yerucham. The three-year research grant I am seeking from the Israeli Science Foundation will provide necessary research funds and academic legitimacy for my project. My interest in conducting the ethnographic work in Yerucham is academic (I have found almost no empirical research documenting the reality of life for Mizrahi women in Israeli development towns), but at the same time it is driven by a critical political urge to challenge Israeli social prejudices about life in what is dubbed the *periferya*.

In an autoethnographic essay I published in 1997, I traced the intellectual and personal journey that led me as an angry young Mizrahi college graduate to pursue a doctorate in the United States, determined to study anthropology as a way to understand my place in Israel's complex social reality. I spoke about my emotional inability to study Israeli society at that time in my life and about the necessary detour I took into research in Botswana. So when I walk the dusty streets of Yerucham, I feel an emotional proximity to the place and its inhabitants as well as a deep sense that I can finally undertake the project that led me to choose anthropology as my life profession. There is nothing remote or foreign to me about the social space of this southern development town, so like the Migdal Ha'Emek of my childhood. My experience, I am aware from the start, stands in stark contrast to the negative portrayals one encounters in the limited academic literature and in Israeli public discourse of life in these peripheral towns.

"The ethnic concentration [of Mizrahi Jews], and the low socioeconomic background of most [development] town residents," writes critical social geographer Oren Yiftachel, "affected a rapid transformation of the towns into conspicuous pockets of deprivation and poverty" (2001: 123). In his book *A Shady Deal in the South*, Daniel Ben Simon offers the following description of life in southern development towns:

> Economic adversity, and remoteness from the Israeli experience, gave rise to a gloomy reality in the development towns—or more precisely, the non-development towns. Feelings of alienation, rage, and despair built up among the residents. They felt that an affluent society had become indifferent to their struggles, and related to them as leeches. It is therefore not surprising that instead of abating, the sense of deprivation perpetuated itself, seeping into the next generation. They were native-born Israelis, but they inherited their fathers' residual bitterness and were thus drawn into a bleak worldview. An ethnic identity built on strong feelings of discrimination was instilled in them, as it was in their parents. Instead of becoming full-fledged Israelis, a tendency developed to isolate themselves from the rest of society. They preserved the behavior patterns of their parents, and returned to the cultural values of their birthplace. The "Israeliness" offered to them when they arrived gave way to an ethnic perspective that emphasized their lack of integration into the surrounding society. (22)

The harsh assertions of this empathetic journalist (himself an immigrant from Morocco) leave no room for a more nuanced understanding of life in development towns. Are the lives of the residents in fact marked only by "hardship" and "a bleak worldview"? Who is it that represents life in these towns in terms of adversity and failure? What do residents have to say about their lives? What terms do they use to describe them? Are they aware of their image in the eyes of the "affluent society"? Do they ignore or fight, oppose or internalize, outsiders' perceptions of their lives? How do they really live?

Ben Simon, who was a Knesset member from the Labor Party when he wrote *A Shady Deal*, speaks out of genuine compassion for the residents of Israel's southern development towns and with a sincere desire to erase the marginalization and social disparities that he documents in his book. But he also clearly ignores the agency of the men and women who inhabit these outlying Negev communities, seeing them as hapless victims of neglect and discrimination. He does not hesitate to declare, "Of course the residents themselves, who developed a sense of dependency, are also to blame. They were unable to mobilize the inner strength to pull themselves out of their misery. They sunk into a paralyzing state of despair" (14).

Ben Simon is not alone in expressing this view. Israeli public discourse is rife with one-dimensional, reductive depictions of life in development towns. It is a public discourse that perpetuates stereotypes focused on poverty and unemployment, dependence on the welfare system, inarticulateness and lack of sophistication, intense religious observance, and membership in the Shas Party.[1]

Academic literature has done precious little to correct the prevalent perception of development town residents as victims rather than as agents who shape their own lives. Academic research, even more recent critical analysis, is centered on a liberal discourse that views external factors and policies as the determining forces structuring life in Israel's geographic and social periphery. Thus, whereas modernist sociologists and urban planners (Ben Zadok 1993; Efrat 1994) blame conditions in development towns on the "mistakes" of policy makers, critical scholars (Yiftachel 2001; Yiftachel and Tzfadia 1999) locate them in the nonegalitarian structure of Israel's social system, which produces weak populations at the nation's margins.

I do not disagree that external factors play a critical role in shaping the circumstances of life in development towns such as Yerucham. What I argue here is that the agency of those who live in these towns is also key to understanding local reality. More than a million Israelis reside in development towns today. How do they cope with the chronic unemployment that marks their lives? What do the anger and happiness, pain and joy, success and failure, of the men and women living in these "remote" towns look like? Scholarly empirical research into the lives of the working-class, ethnicized residents of these towns is scant, and studies of the Mizrahi women who call these locales home is almost nonexistent.[2]

Ten years ago, when I reviewed feminist Israeli academic research, which came of age in the late 1970s, I found that it focused exclusively on middle-class Ashkenazi women from the social center and that it ignored the experiences of Mizrahi women who inhabit the margins of Israeli society and Israeli territory. Mizrahi feminists have begun to publish critical work over the past decade[3] but have not yet addressed this lacuna. The Mizrahi-centered critical sociology that has emerged since the late 1990s has contributed little to our understanding of the day-to-day lives of the women who inhabit the Israeli periphery (see Aboutboul et al. 2005; Hever et al. 2002).

I wanted to learn what women in Yerucham have to say about the challenges of raising their children and how they balance child rearing and family life with work outside the home. I wanted to hear *how* they conceptualize their experiences, and, most critically, I wished to provide these women with a stage where their words can be heard.

An extended ethnography is the best tool for this purpose. For four years, I made frequent visits to Yerucham, meeting and speaking with many of its residents, participating in their daily experiences and their celebrations. The five women whose stories are recounted in this book were my key interlocutors. I accompanied them in their daily routines both in and outside Yerucham and took part in public and private events to which they welcomed me. *Concrete Boxes* tells the story of how I came to learn what I did during these long years of listening to and interacting with the men and women of Yerucham. It reveals the complexity of the process of knowledge production.

Foreword to the English Edition

CONCRETE BOXES: Mizrahi Women on Israel's Periphery by Pnina Motzafi-Haller is a tour de force, and I do not mean just with respect to Israel or even to sociocultural anthropology. It is a feminist ethnography that acknowledges Israel's social complexity, its ongoing social inequality, and its political-economic history while simultaneously showing us how and why it is important to see women making decisions and taking actions, even when we might not think these are in their best interest. That the original version was first published in Hebrew and in Israel was deliberate. It was meant to be read by Israelis of many different backgrounds, including those Motzafi-Haller interviewed and got to know in the course of her fieldwork. Although the Israeli academy has long valued the publication of scholarly work in English more than in Hebrew (and certainly Arabic), Motzafi-Haller chose to privilege readability in Hebrew over academic acclaim or career advancement.

I am honored to write this foreword and to think with and through Motzafi-Haller's work. This book has been noticed in Israel and debated and discussed in Israel's various publics. I am glad that it is now being published in English because it needs and deserves a far greater readership and because its translation has also allowed the author to do some updating and additional framing.

As I think of it, no other book accomplishes what Motzafi-Haller does here. Some articles and books, by sociologist Debbie Bernstein and social anthropologist Amalia Sa'ar, for example, come close, but they really do different things. Altogether, the work these scholars have done highlights the need for social scientists of Israel (of Israeli society, and of the State of Israel) to ask questions of all and not just of some and to take on topics that matter a great deal to people living in Israel who have not been encouraged or privileged in the study of Israel or Israeli society over the past several decades. The topic here is poverty and class, not framed as Jewish versus non-Jewish or Ashkenazi Jewish versus Mizrahi Jewish. And the focus is on the lives of women in what many Israelis (Jewish as well as Arab) tend to think of as "the periphery."

What this means to the lives of those who live there matters. Motzafi-Haller brings her university training to the field, but she also brings her own reflections on her family of origin and family of choice to her field and her writing. She is, in my view, a very courageous, principled, and committed scholar, who makes a point of sharing her feminist strategies as well as her mistakes.

Concrete Boxes is based on Motzafi-Haller's long-term anthropological fieldwork in Yeruham, a development town in Israel's south; the depth of the author's knowledge about poverty and development towns in Israel is to be noted and applauded. The book focuses on the lives and words (and actions) of five women the author got to know very well. She argues that they collectively say something important about the range of ways of being among low-income women in Israel during this neoliberal era. Neoliberalism is the background, of course, and here is where *Concrete Boxes* works well, in my view, with Amalia Sa'ar's ongoing work and recent book, *Economic Citizenship: Neoliberal Paradoxes of Empowerment*. But this book does something a bit different, making it as courageous as Sa'ar's, for it argues against taking those in development towns, low-income people, and, especially, low-income women as mere outliers or even as victims. *Concrete Boxes* presents a view of women in "out-of-the-way" places (as Anna Tsing would say) like Yeruham that is much more complex than standard Israeli government policy presents (and even more complex than the most dominant social science work in Israel presents).

Motzafi-Haller even argues against the "culture of poverty" approach (much critiqued in the United States since the era of Oscar Lewis and Daniel Patrick Moynihan) but still asks the question that remains to be asked in many countries or places, namely, to what extent do poor communities or households tend to reproduce poverty in children and grandchildren, and how and why does it happen? The focus on women (and the life choices they have made) allows for the question to be asked without falling into a blanket victimization of poor women or a blanket condemnation of their lives and values. I truly know of no other work that is as compelling. It is both very Israeli and, sadly, very relevant to many other settings.

As readers will no doubt discover, Motzafi-Haller's writing is also clear and engaging, and that is not something I take for granted. She is committed to writing clearly so that many people can understand her and her scholarly interventions. I think this book is so clearly and compellingly written that it could be used in both undergraduate and graduate courses, possibly becoming a widely read cross-over book. I imagine people interested in women, poverty, Israel, and North African/Middle Eastern studies wanting to read it. Indeed, I believe they ought to read it and contemplate its consequences. I have long thought of Alisse Waterston's *Love, Sorrow, and Rage: Destitute Women in a Manhattan Residence* as just such a book. Pnina Motzafi-Haller offers us a newer work, based on a different but equally fraught society that frequently presents itself as middle class and, largely, rhetorically and discursively relegates poverty and inequality to its racial or ethnic minorities.

Virginia R. Dominguez

University of Illinois at Urbana-Champaign

USA

References

Bernstein, Deborah. 2000. *Constructing Boundaries: Jewish and Arab Workers in Mandatory Palestine.* Albany: SUNY Press.

———. 1987. *The Struggle for Equality: Urban Women Workers in Prestate Israeli Society.* New York: Praeger.

Lewis, Oscar. 1966. *La Vida: A Puerto Rican Family in a Culture of Poverty—San Juan and New York.* New York: Random House.

———. 1959. *Five Families: Mexican Case Studies in the Culture of Poverty.* New York: Basic Books.

Sa'ar, Amalia. 2016. *Economic Citizenship: Neoliberal Paradoxes of Empowerment.* New York: Berghahn Books.

Tsing, Anna Lowenhaupt. 1993. *In the Realm of the Diamond Queen: Marginality in an Out-of-the-Way Place.* Princeton, NJ: Princeton University Press.

Waterston, Alisse. 1999. *Love, Sorrow, and Rage: Destitute Women in a Manhattan Residence.* Philadelphia: Temple University Press.

Acknowledgments

THIS BOOK IS the result of a collaborative effort. Over the course of a decade, I met with dozens of men and women in Yerucham who shared the little moments of their lives with me, opened up their homes and life stories to me, and agreed to be part of the book I envisioned writing. I thank all of them for their generosity and for helping shape the central message conveyed in these pages.

Five courageous women allowed their lives to form the centerpiece of this book. Two of them wrote essays that depict their lives in their own words. But all of them—those who wrote for themselves and those who allowed me to write for them—were active partners in all the thinking that shaped the analysis presented in this book.

I wish to express my gratitude to Motti Avisror, who served as mayor of Yerucham during most of my time in the field, and to Michael Bitton, the present mayor, who was director of the community center when I sat in on adult education courses there. Yair Mimran, who headed the local welfare department, always greeted me with a smile and allowed me to accompany women on their frequent visits to the Welfare Office.

Several students worked alongside me over the years to assist in the research. I especially thank Sigal Nagar-Ron, who read with great care many drafts of this book, and Reut Bendrihem, who experienced several ethnological encounters with me in Yerucham as part of her own independent fieldwork for her master's degree in anthropology.

Friends and colleagues read parts of or the whole manuscript at various stages, and their comments helped me see issues in a way that would not have been possible had I been working alone. I wish to thank Orly Benjamin, Shlomit Benjamin, Debbie Bernstein, Daniel De-Malach, Tamar El-Or, Michael Feige, Emanuel Marx, Uri Ram, Na'amah Razon, Ruth Tadmor, David Tarrash, and Nitza Yanai. Uri Ram helped me choose a title for the book, for which I am especially grateful. The publication of the Hebrew edition of the book was ably shepherded by Dr. Nurit Stadler, editor of Eshkolot Library of Magnes Press. Dan

Ben-Amos and Kathryn Wildfong of Wayne State University Press coached me in the long process of translating and revising the English edition. Special thanks to Linda Forman for her close final editing of the manuscript. This book was published with the support of the Israel Science Foundation. Additional support for the translation work came from the office of the President of Ben-Gurion University and the Bona Terra Department of Man in the Desert of the Jacob Blaustein Institutes of Desert Research.

Final thanks go to my two sons, Yoni and David, who love to cite my late mother's Arabic adage *l'tala' miniq-yialimik*, which means "the one who came out of you, will teach you."

CONCRETE BOXES

INTRODUCTION

WHAT DO LIVES that are "out of the sight of those in positions of power" (Lubin 2003: 17) look like in contemporary Israel? I take up this question in *Concrete Boxes* as I depict life in the small desert town of Yerucham from the perspective of its Mizrahi women residents. A major challenge for me in writing this feminist ethnography was to cultivate the ability to listen to my interlocutors and to hear them on their own terms and not through external discourses, patronizing or sympathetic as these may be. At the center of this book stand five women whose lives I came to know intimately in the course of four years of intensive fieldwork. During my research in Yerucham, I met and interacted with many more men and women than I depict in these pages, and I recorded, observed, or participated in a wide range of local social activities. But I decided that focusing on the lives of five individual women would enable me to better grasp the moral and emotional worldview of my research subjects and to gain an emotional affinity with them that is rarely achieved through more abstract sociological insights based on fragmentary quotes from a range of interlocutors. The women I chose to highlight were the more articulate among my interlocutors, and their words and actions illustrate local norms and conditions.

In centrist, middle-class Israeli discourses, lower-class Mizrahi women are often portrayed in negative terms; they are called *frechot* (sing. *frecha*), a demeaning term that connotes loud, vulgar, unsophisticated behavior and appearance. I wanted to paint as detailed and rich a picture as possible of the everyday struggles of my research subjects, in part to counter such prevalent demeaning images.

Cuban-born American anthropologist Virginia Dominguez captured this aspiration beautifully in 2000:

> Imagine it being okay to say "stop the silence" (or erasure or neglect of people we care about) or "stop the condescension" (in the way that someone we care about is treated by people both outside and inside the academy) and here's why: if you read my scholarly work, you will come to like

the people I care about not because they're perfect but because they are a whole lot more interesting, curious, quirky, dignified, and even more like you or your friends than you realize. (2000: 388)

Yet, over and above my desire to put an end to the condescension and paternalism that have produced a distorted image of lower-class Israeli women who live in peripheral areas such as Yerucham, I picked these five portraits because each allows me to explore a different analytical issue with broad social relevance. Each woman exemplifies in her social location and her choices a distinctive structural option for coping with the reality of life on the fringes. In other words, each woman's story is not merely an individual tale but an analytical entry point into a particular way of creating a meaningful life within a reality of multifaceted marginality. Thus, for example, the life story of a woman who has become more religiously observant sheds light on a social dynamic that characterizes the lives of other women, if perhaps less intensely than in the case in point. Likewise, the life of a welfare recipient who struggles to save money for her son's bar mitzvah celebration provides insight into the challenges facing other women who must raise families in an uncertain, financially unrewarding labor market.

Postcolonial feminist theorist Chandra Mohanty suggests that the lives and interests of marginalized women constitute a great vantage point from which "to access and make the workings of power visible—to read up the ladder of privilege" (2003: 511). I found this "reading up" strategy, with its concrete depictions of life on the margin, to be particularly rewarding as a means of exploring in a tangible way how social inequality is reproduced in contemporary Israel.

Five Stories within a Broad Analytical Framework

Ethnographic research is a labor-intensive project. Over the course of four years, I took part in almost 40 ceremonies and public events (Holocaust Remembrance Day ceremonies, Tu b'Shevat gatherings, community theater performances, evening entertainments in Yerucham's public square, Independence Day festivities). I was invited to and attended dozens of private celebrations (weddings, bar and bat mitzvahs, circumcisions, Jewish holiday celebrations). I interviewed key figures in the community (the then mayor Motti Avisror;

the director of the local welfare office, Yair Mimran; the principal of the local elementary school, Rachel Siboni). I listened to the life stories of some 50 men and women in Yerucham. I participated regularly in adult education courses at the community center, observing each class session and taking note of students' comments during class time and on their breaks. I attended a cosmeticians' nail-care course at the old Histadrut (labor union) center and volunteered to lead a course on Israeli film at the senior citizens center. I took part in several overnight field trips for local women organized by NA'AMAT,[1] and I accompanied women with whom I had developed a close bond to the Welfare Office, the open-air market, and PTA meetings at the school. But most important, I sat with women in their homes and listened to them, asked them questions, and laughed and shared hours of routine activities with them, day after day.

I recorded all of this meticulously. I took notes during conversations and immediately following events in which I participated, eventually filling up four thick notebooks. When I returned to my office, I used these handwritten jottings as a basis for my typed-up detailed field notes. I recorded and fully transcribed 18 of the life histories I collected. By the end of my four years of research, I had accumulated almost 2,000 pages of printed notes that document in detail various aspects of life in the town.[2] In addition to this raw material, I compiled hundreds of articles from the national press relating to life in development towns in general and Yerucham in particular, along with items from the local papers *Atid* and *Hadshot Hamakom*. I visited the local archive housed in the public library and employed a research assistant to summarize key documents I found useful.

Most of these data did not find their way into this book,[3] but they certainly informed my analysis. In fact, I spent almost my entire sabbatical year in 2002–2003 trying out different frames for presenting my accumulated data, only to return to the field for another year to follow up on the five stories I found most compelling, both for their human depth and for their theoretical poignancy. These stories illustrate five distinct paths for dealing with the concrete box of life in Yerucham: survival, religious strengthening, subversion, juggling of codes, and exit from the local scene by means of problematic "success."

The first chapter introduces us to Nurit,[4] a single mother who had been married to a drug addict. She is a welfare recipient and works odd jobs to supplement her income. Nurit's life story involves a desperate struggle for social recognition for herself and her children in the context of particularly dire material and social circumstances. Her story raises profound questions about the ability of single mothers to survive with dignity on limited state support. It speaks to the ways women face a reality of powerlessness and how they gain dignity and meaning in their lives. Nurit's young daughter Adi offers a glimpse into larger theoretical issues that stand at the center of my analysis: the intergenerational reproduction of class and the limited ability to imagine a future beyond the confines of local life.

The second woman to speak in this book is Efrat. Efrat's story (chapter 2) traces the choice for a life of increasing religiosity (*hit'hazkut*) that she, her five daughters, and her husband make, each in her or his own way. I argue that for Efrat, increased religious observance opens up pathways to employment and respectability that are closed to her sister, who has not taken that path. I argue that the *hit'hazkut* path is the most constructive of the five structural options I examine in this book. It leads to a stronger family life, greater economic stability, and social mobility that a secular education fails to provide.

In chapters 3 and 4, we hear the voice of Rachel, who navigates between various social and cultural codes. Rachel's family immigrated to Israel from Morocco. Although she comes from a low socioeconomic background, married before completing high school, and divorced after having four children, she is an outstanding local success story. Rachel makes use of her keen intelligence and exceptional energy to avoid dependence on welfare. She moves between middle-class codes and the lower-class milieu from which she emerged, and her story provides a rich platform for examining the theoretical question of hybridity and allows consideration of complex questions about the relationship between center and periphery, hegemony and marginalization. Rachel's juggling act defies any attempt to think in binary terms of a "center" that imposes its values on an isolated "local" reality. Chapter 4 makes explicit the inherent limits of Rachel's ability to juggle cultural codes, underscoring the importance of class position and material status in any analysis of hybridity.

At the heart of chapters 5 and 6 stands Esti, whom I call "the rebel." Hers is the story of a woman who refuses to comply with the local dictates of life in the town she was born and raised in. She refuses to marry, have babies, or keep a job, opting instead for gambling and financial irresponsibility. Esti's colorful personality offers a springboard for a discussion of feminist behavior on the fringe of society, a feminism that does not call itself by that name. Esti's subversive life choices come with a price. She is isolated, and financially she teeters on the brink of disaster.

The final voice we hear, in chapter 7, is that of Gila, who manages to break free of the limitations of life in Yerucham. She obtains a university education, works for many years as a schoolteacher and principal, and marries an Englishman. Her story speaks to her inability, successful as she is, to sever her emotional ties to the world she has left behind and to the price she has paid in attempting to create a meaningful self-identity outside Yerucham. The questions Gila's story raises have real implications for the ability of marginalized communities not only to attract members of so-called strong populations but also to retain native sons and daughters who have accumulated cultural capital. What happens when the most talented of Yerucham's children are sent to schools outside the town? Who stays behind? And what does the loss of successful residents say about the chances of creating a strong local community?

In my conclusion I trace the theoretical implications of my empirical data and ponder the power of reflexive feminist research and writing.

Writing a Mizrahi Feminist Ethnography

In 2002, as I was trying to come to terms with the ethnographic data I had recorded during the previous two years in Yerucham from the distance that a sabbatical year in Canada afforded me, I was asked by several Israeli feminist colleagues to contribute a chapter to an edited volume intended to make contemporary feminist theory available to Israeli students. Each contributor was asked to write a comprehensive review essay about one influential feminist theorist, pick one significant essay from that scholar's corpus of work to be translated into Hebrew, and discuss the relevance of the scholar and her insights to Israeli social reality in general and to local academic knowledge production in particular. I was asked to write about the prolific African American cultural theorist bell hooks.

The invitation to write the essay caught me at a turbulent moment. As Ottawa's steaming hot summer days gave way to freezing temperatures, which even years of life in Boston had not prepared me for, I wrote one draft outline of this book after another and read and reread my notes. Thinking about it now, I realize that the real impact hooks had on me as I struggled to define the structure and tenor of this book was not *what* she said (at the time I had already pored over more than two dozen books in the huge corpus of her work) but *how* she said it. She spoke directly to an audience that extended beyond (white, male) academia, and she did it with a brazen disregard for the imperatives of familiar academic discourse. Her essays were short, poignant, and exciting. Hooks did not write ethnography, of course, but I could hear her voice; I could feel her sincerity, her chutzpah.

Hooks is not the only feminist thinker whose style influenced me in my effort to find a comfortable theoretical and writing frame. Having followed debates in the United States in the late 1980s and the 1990s about the constitution of feminist research methods,[5] I realized that "giving voice" to my Mizrahi lower-class research interlocutors was not enough. In light of the absence of such research in the Israeli literature, I knew that the project was an important and urgent one[6] that I needed to undertake with epistemic and ethical honesty. But representing "them," making their/our voices heard was too simple. I wanted to speak openly about the problematic process of representation and to make space in my writing to convey the messy reality of long years of field research. I wanted not only to give voice to my interlocutors, as earlier feminists were so eager to do, but also to allow the women I met to emerge as full, complex human beings and to show how their lives were shaped by their ethnic, class, and gendered position at the margins of Israeli society. And, all along, I was deeply worried, like Ruth Behar, that "one does violence to the life history as a story by turning it into the disposable commodity of information" (1993: 13). I simply could not gloss over the confusion, the interruptions, and the digressions that characterized many of the stories I recorded. I could not cast the storytellers as my "research subjects" and myself assume the roles of "author" and academic analyst that a conventional realist style of presentation dictated. As the opening scenes of each of this book's chapters show, I wrestled with the ethics of representation. Although, as a Mizrahi woman born and raised in a development town, I felt a fundamental kinship with my interlocutors, at the same time I recognized that our encounter was never one between equals. In fact, I came to realize that what I was struggling with was not merely a matter of choosing a style of presentation; depicting the ongoing dialogue that I carried out with my interlocutors was itself the arena where class and ethnic categorizations played out and were enacted.

At the end of my sabbatical year, I decided to go back to Yerucham. I reentered "the field" with a determination to locate my unfolding relationship with my key interlocutors at the heart of the analysis. After two more years of intensive work in Yerucham, the structure of this book became clear to me. My position within the research, as a Mizrahi academic woman straddling the lines between ethnic belonging and class borders, took center stage. I developed my own writing voice, which insisted that there were no objective anthropological truths and that the best I could do was to convey incomplete, situated perspectives on reality.

The awareness that there is no naive knowledge and that the process of knowledge creation is complex and full of contradictions underlies the way I generated and then depicted the narratives presented in this book. At the heart of my analysis, then, is an effort to cultivate a more nuanced, humble, and less deterministic understanding of a particular social reality. Various strategies in feminist writing seek to represent a social reality that has no ultimate "truth," one for which the researcher is not an unquestionable interpretive authority. These strategies include reflexive writing, with the researcher revealing her place in relation to the interviewee; the introduction of subjects' voices unmediated by the researcher/author (e.g., personal diaries, letters, or texts composed by research subjects to describe their lives); submission of the written text to the interviewees for their reaction; communal writing by a number of people at different points in the project (multiple voices); and shifting between interpretation and questioning of the boundaries of that interpretation.

In this book I make use of several of these strategies, discussing each as I apply it. For example, I interpret Esti's life but at the same time take a step back to ponder the limits of my analysis; I make explicit the power dynamic underlying our interaction during a recorded interview and provide a space for Esti to lay out her own interpretation of her life in her own words.

Two conceptual points are central in my methodological approach and interpretation. The first is the distinction between an *encounter* and the standard understanding of an *interview*. The second is the location of the researcher in a Janus-faced position, both "within" and "against" the social setting being depicted.

Encounters, Not Interviews

I do not provide full, authoritative, cohesive summaries of the lives of the five women at the center of this book. Instead, in each chapter I offer a description of encounters, conversations, and shared moments as well as a range of interpretations. This writing strategy, in which I present fragments and do not speak in the name of the subject, is designed to make space not only for what the woman says about herself but also for what she says about me, alongside my own thoughts and my hesitant partial insights. I insist on not obscuring the power dynamic embedded in the research encounter. I refuse to play the role of the "professional," the "expert" who "knows" and thus has the authoritative say about the lives of these women. I place myself and the research subject on the same level: Both of us possess incomplete knowledge, and both of us have the ability to interpret and explain what is said between us. The purpose of this attempt to consciously and actively reduce my authorial voice, to avoid the claim that I know more about their lives than they do themselves, is to open the stage for alternative understandings of the situations depicted.

This process, which aims to give the subjects a "talking space" (Lather 2006: 208), involves a complex navigation between my various roles in the process of research and writing. I am, at one and the same time, a participant in the research situation, a partial member of the social group I am investigating, and the person writing the overall framework of the story being recounted. Indian feminist anthropologist Kamala Visweswaran suggests that such tacking between roles produces a text that "is marked by disaffections, ruptures, and incomprehensions" (1994: 20). Like Visweswaran, I believe that this approach "replaces the ethnographic goal of total understanding and representation" and, most critically, enables "respect for the integrity of difference" (1994: 21).

The "Within/Against" Position

My methodology also draws on Visweswaran's (1994: 15) idea that a feminist ethnographer is a "trickster," an acrobat or juggler. My position in relation to my interlocutors can be characterized as Janus-like, as I inhabit the setting I depict in my writing and I also stand outside it.

Throughout the book I constantly shift between the anchoring of the women's voices in the specific contexts in which they are articulated and my interpretive commentary, which interrupts the smooth flow of the story. Feminist scholar and theoretician Gayatri Spivak (1990: 35–50) holds that such a writing strategy does not confine itself to giving voice to the research subjects but strives to redefine the boundaries of discourse, to enable the creation of a counterknowledge.

Concrete Boxes was written against the backdrop of these tensions. It is the product of my constant working within and against conventions that assume I have the power to interpret and represent and at the same time of my attempt to construct a framework for thinking and writing that allows for the *creation* of Spivak's counterknowledge. Ethnography itself is a social process; and in the words of feminist theoretician Donna Haraway (1997), it should be read as a cultural practice, as something that enables thought, and not as a project of absolute knowledge that asserts certain truths. I thus offer this ethnography not as a statement of absolute scientific truth but as a basis for thinking about social and cultural processes in Israel.

Portraying Yerucham: A Quintessential Development Town

"If we were to divide the number of words written about Yerucham by the number of residents, we would apparently reach an Israeli record for number of words per capita," wrote one keen Israeli observer about the town's unique place in centrist Israeli public discourse. "There is something about this town that has turned it into a symbol for [all] development towns," he concluded (Rapoport 2005). Most Israelis would agree with this observation. When I toured with the Hebrew version of this book, speaking to students, public officials, youth groups, and members of the general public who gathered in local libraries in Yerucham, Arad, Migdal Ha'Emek, Be'er-Sheva, or Ashkelon, I was often asked why I had picked Yerucham as the site for my intensive, long-term ethnographic research. People pointed out that Yerucham represents an extreme case of neglect and failure. Not all development towns are like Yerucham, they asserted—some are successful, some have thriving high-tech industrial parks. Others heatedly argued that there are people in Yerucham who are not locked into the debilitating cycle of intergenerational poverty depicted in my book. I was glad to engage with this internal Israeli discourse. It was the main reason I insisted on writing the book in Hebrew. I told my Israeli audiences that I worked in Yerucham because it was close to my home, because the women who entered my university office as cleaners were from Yerucham, and, more broadly, because the book is not *about* Yerucham. It is a study of a specific social process: the reproduction of ethnic- and class-based inequality in Israel over three generations. To anthropology students, I cited Clifford Geertz's famous adage: "Anthropologists don't study villages (tribes, towns, neighborhoods . . .); they study *in* villages" (1973: 22).

There are ample statistical data to suggest that Yerucham is indeed one of the most poverty-stricken Jewish localities in Israel. Its remoteness and the history of colossal failure to rescue it make it a perfect place to explore the questions I pose in this ethnography. At the time of my research in 2002, 2,586 (27%) of the town's residents were welfare recipients. The unemployment rate stood at 13% of the local workforce.[7] By 2006 the unemployment rate in Yerucham was almost double the national average.[8] Before I turn to a short history of the many efforts made to change this reality and provide an update of that history since 2012, when the Hebrew version of this book was published, it is important to highlight a second critical element in this local scene of entrenched inequality: selective migration out of the town. In this ethnography I show how the concrete box locks in the most vulnerable segments of the local population and effectively funnels people with more cultural capital out of the community. The five paths I trace through the chapters of this book culminate with a story of success—the success that comes of leaving a town whose residents are locked into a cycle of dispossession.

One of the most obvious indicators of residents' dissatisfaction with life in town is the rate of out-migration. In 2000, the rate of out-migration from Yerucham was the highest of any development town in the south.[9] At the beginning of my research, in 2000, Yerucham was home to 8,900 residents. By 2007 the population had shrunk by 5.62%, to 8,400. By way of comparison, during this same period, Israel's population rose by 13.7%.[10] These figures are particularly meaningful in light of the relatively high local natural birthrate[11] and the deliberate channeling of people into the town, primarily immigrants from the former Soviet Union (FSU).[12] FSU immigrants made up 25% of Yerucham's population in 2000. Their numbers gradually declined over the course of the following decade. In 2001, FSU immigrants made up 23% of the local population, and in early 2005 their relative proportion dropped to 21%.

What do these data mean? They speak to a process of mass flight from town. "The greatest aspiration of many of the young people is to leave town," wrote *Haaretz* social affairs correspondent Ruth Sinai (2007), who moved to Yerucham in 2007 to report on daily life during the turbulent local election campaign. Those who leave town are young people, Sinai noted. The shrinking number of FSU immigrants in town also marks a kind of population selection—only the most vulnerable segments of the population remain. A brief local history sheds some light on this process.

History of Isolation and Exclusion

In 1951 the site on which Yerucham is located was known as Bir Rahme ("well of compassion" in Arabic). Its total population consisted of 269 Jewish immigrants from Romania, who were brought to the site straight off the boat. They were slated to work at Hamakhtesh Hagadol (the Big Crater, an erosional landform in the Negev Desert) and in the nearby quarries. But the difficult living conditions, isolation, and institutional neglect caused most of the early settlers to leave. Shlomo Tamir, who was sent by the Jewish Agency in 1952 to run the remote camp, writes in his memoirs, "The state institutions had no plan to develop the place. They saw it as a way station that would [later] be destroyed" (1978: 173).

Tamir led an effort to turn the labor camp into an agricultural village by developing small farms in the surrounding area. The name of the locality was changed accordingly from Tel Yerucham (drawing on the original Arab name of the site) to Kfar Yerucham (Yerucham Village). Between 1954 and 1957, 5,000 new immigrants were sent to Kfar Yerucham. The overwhelming majority of these immigrants soon left the village. By late 1957 the number of permanent residents in Yerucham stood at only 880.[13]

The next few years saw an influx of immigrants, predominantly from North Africa. Oral histories of these immigrants speak of forced settlement in the remote Negev town, which was slated to be officially recognized as a development town. Throughout the following decade, however, economic underdevelopment and perpetual dependence on government-sponsored public works projects continued to plague the struggling settlement. Its isolated position became a serious factor when the Arava Highway was completed in the late 1960s, dashing hopes that traffic to Eilat would pass through Yerucham. Another road completed at the time, connecting Be'er-Sheva and Mitzpeh Ramon, meant that Yerucham was effectively cut off from every major transportation artery. Remote, isolated, and without any sources of employment, the town's residents voted with their feet, leaving Yerucham in droves. Those who remained protested loudly, feeding the enduring image of the town in the mainstream Israeli press as a center of social delinquency, unrest, and destitution.[14]

Subsequent efforts to stop the hemorrhaging of the population included initiatives to attract impoverished *haredi* (ultra-Orthodox) families seeking cheap housing and, in the late 1970s, the absorption of religious-Zionist families who formed a *garin torani* (community-based outreach group). But neither these groups nor the Nachal (army community service) units of the Bnei Akiva youth movement that settled in Yerucham during the 1980s compensated for the flight of those who could afford to leave town.

In the mid-1980s the newly elected mayor, Baruch Elmakias, used the term "the State of Yerucham" in a provocative critique of the government's chronic neglect of the town and its continuing isolation from mainstream Israeli society (Rapoport 2005). Elmakias's vocal resentment of the central government and his colorful, unconventional personality did not win him much support in the centers of power, and his failure to balance the municipal budget met with a drastic response: intervention by the Ministry of the Interior to dissolve the elected municipal council and appoint its own local management team. Such intervention by the Israeli state has occurred several times in the history of the small town.

In 1992 Motti Avisror was elected mayor. Avisror, who was still in office when I began my research in Yerucham, brought in a new, less aggressive style of management. He surrounded himself with a small group of young educated leaders and was supported by the elite *garin* people who made their home in Yerucham. Avisror succeeded in substantially reducing the town's deficit and earned national admiration for what was depicted as an "educational revolution" in Yerucham. The Israeli press reported with enthusiasm on the town's matriculation rate, which soared from 17% in 1995 to 73% in 2003. Journalist Daniel Ben Simon hailed "Avisror's social revolution" as a turning point in the history of the failing town and a triumph of optimism over despair. The success story of the local education system attracted a great deal of attention, and the Ministry of the Interior awarded the young mayor prizes for successful administration.

But in 2003 Avisror lost in the municipal elections (by only 50 votes) to Baruch Elmakias, the previous mayor who had been removed from his post. Following Avisror's defeat, his signature legacy of educational revolution came into question. Critics argued that the improved matriculation rates had not benefited Yerucham's townspeople, because the number of residents had not risen, whereas unemployment had.

In his second, and deeply emotional, election campaign, Elmakias had lashed out against the people who opposed his candidacy, depicting them in clear racial and class terms as overeducated and economically well-off—in brief, a "white elite." Elmakias articulated a deep resentment that had been brewing for decades within the economically stagnant veteran population that supported him and that objected to the presence of privileged outsiders in town. I visited Yerucham often during Elmakias's campaign and recorded the deep visceral support he attracted from the group of unemployed and welfare-supported women with whom I associated daily. They cheered Elmakias's combative rhetoric, which spoke of the "sons of law professors" who had come "to steal Yerucham."

When I left Yerucham in 2005 to write this book, the town was mired in a crisis of governance and was the site of deep social unrest. In what follows I trace the main events in local history to the present day.

Elmakias's second election as mayor of Yerucham and his flaming rhetoric isolated the town nationally. The municipality once again sank into massive debt, and when it stopped paying its workers' salaries, the state intervened again. In 2005 Ofir Pines, the minister of the interior at the time, dissolved the elected local council and appointed Amram Mitzna, former mayor of Haifa and former head of the Labor Party, as acting mayor.

Mitzna was given two years to solve the crisis. "When I came to Yerucham, all its welfare, educational, and cultural institutions were at a standstill," Mitzna recounted on his personal website.[15] "The community center was closed, the Nitzan Center for the Advancement of Learning for Disabled Children was not functioning, the After-School Club for At-Risk Youth was shuttered, and the adult day care centers were facing closure due to millions of shekels in debts." Mitzna was confident that his connections in the central government would be useful in remedying small Yerucham's problems quickly and effectively. His name indeed opened doors. "It's doubtful whether any mayor would have enjoyed the same treatment as the former Labor candidate for prime minister," reported *Haaretz* journalist Ruth Sinai (2007). The cost of the projects he developed went beyond what the central government could budget, so Mitzna led an aggressive fundraising campaign among Diaspora Jews. Two years, however, were not enough for him to accomplish all the changes he had hoped for. Despite adamant local protests, Mitzna secured a controversial second-term mayoral appointment from the Knesset's Committee of Internal Affairs.

When Mitzna's imposed tenure finally ended in late 2010, local elections were held. Motti Avisror, who ran for mayor again, was quoted as saying that "Amram Mitzna's arrival halted the breakdown of the town's systems" and that the return to democratic elections in town signaled "the true test of Yerucham." Avisror was denied a second term by voters, however; 40-year-old Michael Bitton won 44.5% of the vote. Bitton, former director of the local community center and founder of the Youth in Yerucham association, beamed as he stated in his acceptance speech, "This is a victory for Yerucham. We ran a clean campaign that brought great honor to the city, and Yerucham is headed toward a new future."[16]

Yet, contrary to both Avisror's and Bitton's expectations, it soon became clear that Mitzna's celebrated tenure had not succeeded in changing the situation in the municipality. Mitzna had not simply failed to balance the budget despite lavish state and donor support, but when he left office the municipality was in fact in the throes of a severe financial crisis. A dismayed Bitton told *Maariv* in 2011, "Not only was the budget not balanced or Yerucham's problems solved but the solution that was adopted [by Mitzna] is one that I do not accept—loans." In 2014 Bitton, this time running as a Labor Party candidate, was elected to a second term in a landslide victory, winning 70% of the vote. In an interview he granted the Israeli financial daily *Globes*, Bitton admitted that his first term had not changed local reality, bitterly citing the persistently high rate of local unemployment, which then stood at 10%, and the fact that some 1,000 out of 3,000 families in town were registered with the local welfare office. Sounding less exuberant than in his acceptance speech, Bitton lamented, "One cannot fix social neglect of sixty years in five years, not in ten, nor in twenty," and he combatively asked his interviewer, "How do you people over there, in Tel Aviv, live with such an outrageous state of social inequality?" (Lieber 2015). Proud of the construction of a new middle-class neighborhood in town and boasting about a new, elegant café serving Italian coffee, Bitton stated that the real challenge was to break the cycle of second- and third-generation poverty in town.

This book focuses on that challenge. Liberal and neoliberal efforts to break Yeruchams intergenerational cycle of poverty and social isolation have not produced results. I raise questions about received models of modernist development by listening to what those who experience multiple forms of marginalization think about their lives and how they act within this set of limitations.

1

NURIT

Surviving Social Marginality

SHE ENTERS MY office with downcast eyes and asks, "May I clean your room now?" I give her a big smile. "Are you the new cleaner? But, um, what happened to Rachel?" She shrinks back, hesitating, still not looking at me directly. "Who's Rachel?" she asks. I regain my composure and extend my hand for a formal handshake: "I'm Pnina. What's your name?" She looks at me carefully and for a long moment does not move to shake my hand, which remains suspended in midair. Then she says the expected: "Pleased to meet you. I'm Nurit." She accents the second syllable, "Nu-*reet*," as the name "should" be pronounced, as you would say it to a schoolteacher. Maybe because I had said "*Rachel*" in the way that only teachers say that name. Her *r*'s roll off her tongue, like mine, sabra style.

"Rachel is the woman who worked here until yesterday," I explain to Nurit after my polite *na'im me'od*—pleasure to meet you. "So, did they fire her too?"

"Not that I have anything against you, Nurit," I hurry to explain. "But it drives me crazy that they fire the cleaning staff so often. Rachel was here for about four months. So, are you new here?"

I study Nurit. She appears to be in her forties. A small woman, maybe five feet tall, with a sunken face and dark circles under her eyes. Beneath her buttoned blue uniform, I detect a sagging stomach, suggesting a woman who has gone through multiple pregnancies. Her shoulder-length hair is dark brown and thin. When she smiles, her face lights up. She has a mischievous smile, full of life. But her body language communicates remoteness.

She walks over to the wastebasket next to my desk, pulls out the plastic bag that contains a few scraps of paper, and replaces it with a new bag. I watch her with sad amusement, observing what has become a familiar ritual. Every few months, a new woman appears in my office, her predecessor disappearing without warning. And each time, I introduce myself to the new woman and explain my inquisitiveness, my interest in her life, and the long breaks I take from typing on my computer so that I can listen to her words.

In my office, Nurit learns quickly, she can take a break to talk, rest, relax, hide from her boss. In my office she can lie down on the narrow bed I've set up in one corner and put her tired feet up on a small pillow. She can use the phone to call her family or take care of business, help herself to the crackers and candies I keep in a small jar, and enjoy a few laughs with the other cleaners who stop in for a brief respite from their hard work routines. Nurit quickly learns that my office is a haven and makes use of it often. She sometimes appears with one or two other cleaning women, but more often she comes alone. I always have time for her. But my conversations with Nurit are awkward. They do not flow easily, naturally. I have a feeling that she never relaxes in my presence, at least not in the way other cleaners before her have.

The uneasiness I feel when I am with Nurit does not subside, even after she has visited my office many times. When she tells me about herself, or about the other women cleaners at the Ben Gurion University campus in Sde Boker, where my office is located, I have the feeling that she is accentuating the negative. She has a tendency toward gossip of the unpleasant kind, the kind that incriminates others, that finds faults in them: This woman got her job because she's the manager's sister-in-law, and that one doesn't know how to clean. This one, poor thing, her husband is cheating on her, and the one who was fired recently was suspected of stealing. Nurit always prefaces her words with a warning: "But Pnina, don't tell anyone about it!" I have the uncomfortable feeling that she does this to capture my attention because that is how she interprets my interest in her life and in other cleaning staff's personal, mundane stories.

Like all the other cleaners, Nurit knows, from the moment we meet, that I intend to write a book about the lives of women from Yerucham. And like all the others, she expresses her enthusiastic desire to be part of a book that tells her story. As several other cleaners have, she invites me to her home, where we can talk at length without pressure. She rejects the option of conducting an interview in my office or home. Again and again, she tells me that I should come and record her life story and that it's a *really* sad one. "Forget about it! [*khaval al hazmaan*]."[1]

But our attempts to schedule an appointment at her home always come to nothing. And then, one day, Nurit stops visiting my office. A new woman has been hired to clean.

An Interview with Nurit—Finally

"Come. For Real. No Problem. Whenever You Want. Call."

I meet Nurit again in Yerucham, a few weeks after she stops working in Sde Boker. I bump into her in the square next to the Hyper Neto, the only supermarket in town. We make polite small talk and then Nurit repeats her invitation: "Come. For real. No problem. Whenever you want. Call." She makes sure I have her updated cell phone number and adds in a half whisper, indicating her words are meant only for me, that she will explain *everything*. With these words, she hints that the termination of her employment in Sde Boker is a story full of intrigue that she wants to reveal to me. She repeats again and again that she will tell me everything but only in a proper meeting at her house.

Over the next few weeks I try several times to contact Nurit by phone to schedule a visit to her home, but I am not able to reach her. A few times, when I pass by the gray apartment building where she lives (across the street from a small bakery where I buy fresh rolls whenever I visit Yerucham), I glimpse her apartment window and wonder what is going on in her life. I am very busy this spring of 2001. I spend three to four days a week in Yerucham, visiting several locales that I am documenting. I routinely participate in adult education classes held in the local community center, where unemployed men and women are encouraged to complete the matriculation exams to increase their chances of finding employment. I attend religion classes offered in the evenings by local rabbis or their wives, and I accompany Rachel and Esti, my two main research interlocutors, during their day-to-day activities. Several times I walk up the stairs to Nurit's apartment and knock on the door, but I get no answer. Even so, every time we bump into each other—in the Welfare Office, outside the bank, in line at the supermarket—Nurit pushes herself on me. She stubbornly and enthusiastically invites me to her home: "Come over, Pnina. What's with you? Whenever you want. It'll be fun." At some point I begin to understand that the source of my repeated failure to schedule an interview with her is a power struggle forced on me by Nurit, a struggle that makes me feel deeply uncomfortable and anxious to escape the unfulfilled connection with her.

The feeling of unease and the desire to get away from the strain that Nurit induces in me persists not only during my subsequent tense research encounters with her but also during the long months I spend planning this book's structure and as I read, over and over again, my notes documenting my relationship with her. On the one hand, I keep asking myself whether I really want to devote a whole chapter to Nurit's story, and, on the other hand, I wonder whether her story might make an effective opening chapter for the book.

Nurit, more than any other woman whose story I tell in this book, confronts me with the stereotype of the oppressed, downtrodden Mizrahi woman: a woman in distress, a woman who lives in poverty and subsists on scraps from welfare, a single mother who has been married to a drug addict. Nurit's life story seems to exemplify the social and personal pathology of marginalized Mizrahi women that is often portrayed in Israeli public discourse. I finally decide to open this book with her story precisely to deconstruct these familiar stereotypical frames and challenge these worn-out discourses of Mizrahi womanhood. By allowing Nurit to speak for herself, I expose the reader to parts of her life that are not limited to these "sad elements." Through her words, uttered in a range of settings, she emerges as a complete, complex human being who struggles to achieve dignity and make a meaningful life for her children and for herself. Her complex story flies in the face of the shallowness of Israeli public discourse, revealing a humane, multifaceted struggle for social recognition in trying circumstances.

Seeing Nurit beyond the stereotypes of Mizrahi welfare recipient and single mother is not easy. Her manipulative, brash behavior, which I have only begun to describe here, feeds into and reinforces the negative imagery of women of her class and ethnic background. In my early notes I call her "the fallen one." At first glance, she stands out for her failure to display the kind of warmth, resourcefulness, creativity, and steadfastness that other women I meet in Yerucham do, women who gain my admiration for their ability to sustain families, maneuver between pregnancies and part-time jobs, and care for their homes.

I ask myself whether Nurit exemplifies an inability to cope, whether she in fact represents the classic image of the woman victim. I read and reread my notes about her as well as the critical literature that explores the lives of women in poverty, and I come to understand that Nurit's story is no less one of initiative and courage than other women's. I realize that what *I* need is to develop the ability to see her courage and creativity, and what *she* needs is a safe space where she herself can discover and articulate her life story in all its complexity. Thus, only at the end of a long process of documentation, writing, reflection, and analysis am I able to grasp and begin to depict the distinctive ways in which Nurit fights extreme marginalization.

But I place Nurit and her story at the center of this opening chapter for another significant reason. I feel that my relationship with her represents my most resounding failure in Yerucham. Despite all my sincere efforts, I was not able to get her to open up to me. We achieved a few momentary breakthroughs, but on the whole, I never felt accepted, truly welcomed by Nurit. She did not allow me to sustain the illusion, which I set out to create during my long years of field research in the community, that we were friends, that we knew one another as whole persons, as women, as mothers, as Mizrahi. Nurit forces me to face the different social positions that define our relationship, never allowing me to forget that I am the woman "working in the office" and that she is the woman cleaning that office, that I am the academic documenting the life story of "the other woman"—her story. Nurit compels me to acknowledge the gaps in our respective positioning more than any other woman I know in Yerucham. Her behavior makes real the politics of class and cultural capital that stand at the center of our encounter and thus shape the act of its representation.

Through the story of my unresolved relationship with Nurit, I demonstrate the approach that shapes my writing throughout this book. My aim is to show that every story, every interview excerpt, every quote from a research subject is always a product of the unfolding relationship between that subject and the researcher. I am never an objective researcher, nor do I simply record the authentic words of my research subject and thereby document that person's clear, original, too-often-silenced voice. My writing in this chapter and in the rest

of this book is underlain by the assumption that knowledge is always copro-
duced. From this perspective, the story of Nurit and her struggles must center on the dynamic process that brought us together and on the many varied
encounters between us—between a Mizrahi woman of lower socioeconomic
status and a middle-class Mizrahi academic woman. In the following pages it
will become clear that I am not observing *her*, the welfare-dependent woman.
Rather, I am observing *us*, two Mizrahi women. One of the critical analytical values of such an expanded, contextualized, and deeply reflexive arena of
observation is that it enables us to grasp the pivotal role that class and class
position play in such encounters in contemporary Israel. It makes explicit the
centrality of class within shared ethnic positions and the pivotal role such in-
tra-ethnic class difference plays in shaping such interactions and thus the kind
of self-knowledge and interpretive analysis each of us has developed. More
critically, it underscores Nurit's unshakable conviction that class position su-
persedes and nullifies ethnic and gender affiliations.

From this perspective, the power struggle that Nurit coerces me to engage
in is not merely a logistical prelude to the "real" ethnographic breakthrough.
It is a telling example of the way Nurit deals with people who have power over
her and is therefore a key to understanding her mode of survival in a world she
sees as inherently hostile.

"She Thought You Was a Social Worker"

One day when I am in Yerucham and none of my interlocutors are available, I decide to try my luck with Nurit again. I call her cell phone and am surprised when
it is answered by an apparently elderly woman with a heavy Moroccan accent.
This woman, it turns out, is Nurit's mother. When I ask, "Where is Nurit?" the
mother launches into a long, shrill monologue that does not allow any interjection
on my part. She enumerates all her daughter's trials and tribulations. She repeats
the words "poor thing" (*miskena*) again and again and explains that Nurit is "sick,
poor thing" and "not working, poor thing," that her husband is a "useless junkie,
the poor thing," and that there is "nothing to eat in her home, the poor thing."

I listen to the mother's litany of woes in wonder and finally manage to bring
it to a halt when I insist she inform Nurit that "Pnina called" and I quickly

hang up the phone. Two days after this conversation, I meet Nurit on the main street of Yerucham. "What happened to you?" I ask her. "Your mom scared the hell out of me. Told me you were fatally ill and that you have nothing to eat and . . . don't ask . . ." To my surprise, Nurit bursts into loud laughter and says, "Oh, it was you? My mom told me someone called. She thought you was a social worker from Welfare." Nurit looks really amused. She smiles at me, and her expression tells me she knows I do not belong in the category of social service bureaucrats to which her mother has mistakenly assigned me. For one brief moment, I feel that the heavy curtain Nurit has placed between us has been pulled aside. For one short moment I am accepted; I have temporarily stopped being the woman from the other side.

The situation reminds me of the classic story American anthropologist Clifford Geertz tells of wandering around a Balinese village for days, his existence ignored by residents. A turning point came the day he and his wife fled the village square alongside locals—everyone having gathered to watch an illegal cockfight—when the police raided the area. Following this episode, the barriers that had made him invisible broke down and the villagers accepted him.

This time, when Nurit prompts, "So, when are you coming for a cup of coffee and a chat?" I hear a new decisiveness in her voice. "Come over tomorrow. After work. OK?" she adds in a tone that feels more sincere and suggests that I have a tangible invitation here.

I arrive, as agreed, at seven the next evening. But her apartment is dark. I knock on the door for some time, but no one answers. I am furious. Nurit's ongoing game has managed to upset me. This time, I will not keep silent, I decide. I tear a page from my notebook and begin to write Nurit a note, but the light in the stairway turns off every half minute and I am forced to press the switch again and again. As I am struggling to complete my note, a young woman enters the stairwell and politely offers her help. It turns out that she is Adi, Nurit's daughter. When Adi realizes I have come to see her mother, she invites me into the apartment and insists that Nurit will not be long: "After all, where does she have to go at this hour? She probably went to get something from her sister-in-law and she's sure to be right back," she promises me.

Adi plays the role of the perfect hostess. She offers me coffee and serves slices of homemade cake. I tell her about myself, about meeting her mother in Sde Boker, and about the book I am planning to write. "Are you only interviewing older women?" Adi asks with increasing interest. "What about us young women? What about the youth in our town?" I accept Adi's challenge and say, "I'd love to hear your story. Is it OK if I record our conversation?" Adi is extremely pleased with the idea. I put the little tape recorder between us on the coffee table, and we speak for almost three hours. Adi's story appears at the end of this chapter, in the section titled "An Office of Her Own."

Throughout the evening Adi periodically tries to call her mother but gets no response. "Her phone was probably disconnected again. She never pays her phone bill," Adi apologizes. The young woman behaves in the way one treats an important guest. "How can you write a whole book?" she beams at me in open admiration. "I write one page for an essay in class and get exhausted," she says. At the end of a long evening, I thank Adi for her hospitality and her willingness to share her thoughts with me and answer my many questions. She is pleased and urges me to come back tomorrow, at the same time, to meet her mother. "She'll be here, I'm telling you. Where can she go? I'm really sorry about this evening. I'll let you know as soon as I can about my mom." And indeed, Adi calls a few minutes later, when I am in my car and on my way home. "No problem. Sure thing. Come over, like we said, tomorrow at seven in the evening," she tells me repeatedly.

The next day I call Nurit's work number to tell her that I will not be able to keep our date, as I had promised Adi, because I will be busy. Nurit is surprised that I have managed to catch her on her work phone. It is clear to her that she is not the one who gave me this number. And when she realizes that it was Adi, she bursts out, "Don't ask what Adi did to me:[2] 'What kind of woman are you? Shame on you! What do you mean not staying home when such a quality lady comes to your house?' Listen Pnina, I . . . I'm embarrassed. I apologize. Look, Adi totally let me have it. She's crazy about you. So, please, come over, Pnina. For real. Any time you want. I'm home."

An Important Guest

A month passes before I find myself again at Nurit's place. I do not schedule an appointment with her this time. I happen to be passing through the neighborhood and see her sitting in the yard of her apartment building with a few of her neighbors. Nurit calls me over with open enthusiasm. She introduces me to the other women—"She's, like, a writer"—and tells them that I have come to write her life story and that I have already interviewed Adi, her daughter. She suggests that I interview all the other women in the building "because it's a building full of single mothers, like you wouldn't believe. Everyone here has a real story to tell. Just come and write."

"She's all right," she tells the women, who sit on discarded boxes or on the low concrete wall that frames the neglected yard, sipping the coffee one of them has brought down from her apartment. "She's a single mother too." Nurit is full of life, openly outspoken. She tells stories loudly, and we all laugh at her turns of phrase. She tells us about her work that morning for a local catering company that is providing food to a film crew shooting on location in Yerucham. She mentions the names of several famous actors and jokes, "I was serving them real quick, and Ze'ev Revakh [a well-known Israeli actor] says to me, 'You 20?' And I go, 'Yeah, sure. My one leg is 20.'" The neighbors make a warm, supportive audience. But Nurit chooses not to spend much more time with them. She excuses herself and leads me with great fanfare to her apartment. As we walk up the stairs, Nurit apologizes for her unkempt appearance and explains that she is dressed in "shabby clothes [bgadim zrukim] because I just got home from work."

In the apartment Nurit makes a big fuss over preparing a proper cup of tea for me, and, insisting that I have fresh mint in my tea, she rushes to her neighbor to get mint leaves, leaving the front door open. I hear her explain to the neighbor that she has a guest right now and invite the woman to "drop in later." When she comes back, she inquires if I am hungry, and without waiting for my reply, she invites me into her kitchen. I am happy for the invitation and follow her into the spotless space. She opens the refrigerator door wide, revealing an assortment of pots containing food. She takes out one after another, offering me chunks of beef, roasted red peppers marinated in vinegar, and large olives stuffed with ground beef. She scoops this food onto small plates that she carries to the living room table. As I peek into Nurit's pots and help myself to bites of the sumptuous feast she is dishing out to me, I wonder whether in this small, immaculate kitchen we have departed from the frozen, formal nature of our relationship and if she is going to be more open and relaxed with me from now on.

But this momentary feeling of closeness quickly dissipates when Nurit inquires if I eat spicy food. I awkwardly try to explain to her that I am not "some kind of Ashkenazi," and I declare, "Hell yeah, I eat spicy." But her question makes me feel as though I am positioned once again as the Other, as someone who does not belong. I go back to the living room and continue playing the role of the (non-Mizrahi/upper-class) "important guest" that she has defined for me. Nurit keeps on bringing out food, filling up every space on the small table. She serves pickles, fresh rolls, soft drinks, and plate after plate of her home cooking. I respond with the customary courtesy, saying, "Come on now, Nurit. What . . . I didn't come here to eat. Enough! . . . This is amazing!" Nurit encourages me to try each and every dish and explains that I have to eat because her children will not touch any of this food. They "only want schnitzel and scrambled eggs," she sighs in mild frustration. When she sees that I am openly enjoying the food she has placed in front of me, she returns to the refrigerator and pulls out yet another pot, presenting me with a steaming plate of meatballs in a creamy mushroom sauce. "You haven't tried this one," she insists. "Taste this. Eat."

The change in her attitude toward me is obvious. From someone to be avoided, to be toyed with by promising to tell her a life story, I have turned into a coveted guest, a person she can boast about to the neighbors, a guest to whom she can offer an enormous spread of food. Replacing the story of misery, poverty, and distress—the kind of story one tells a social worker—is a proud story of abundance, domesticity, and generosity. In this alternative narrative, I am placed in multiple positions on the spectrum of closeness and remoteness. I am a respected guest "who is, like, a writer," a person with a tape recorder who documents her host's words and thus turns them into formal, valued texts, and at the same time I am a single mother, like all the others in the building. I am a Mizrahi woman, but my class position makes me a questionable Mizrahi, one who might not enjoy spicy Moroccan home cooking, one who, like Nurit's children and the hegemonic Ashkenazim, is expected to prefer bland food like schnitzel or scrambled eggs. Similar contradictions stretch along the line of my relative power position, for although I am not a social worker and therefore hold no formal power over Nurit's welfare payments, I am nonetheless a resident of Sde Boker, a person who "works in the office" and who speaks correct, formal "high" Hebrew. Throughout the evening, Nurit swings between the positions of closeness and distance that link us and cut across our respective ethnic, gender, and class backgrounds.

What has caused this change in Nurit's behavior toward me? I am convinced that the turning point was my interview with Adi. Since I spoke with her daughter, Nurit has perceived me differently. I have been transformed from a player in a fierce power struggle that has entrapped us for many months into a respected guest who is offered food and stories—not only Nurit's personal story but the "sad stories" of *all the residents* in the building as well. The interview with Adi has opened up a new way for Nurit to see our relationship. Instead of the power she gained by *withholding* the interview she had promised, she has discovered the power that lies in giving the interview and showing off her connection to the interviewer. Since Adi defined me as "such a quality lady," Nurit has become convinced of the advantages of participating in an interview, which confers respectability on the interviewee.

Adi enters the apartment and smiles at me shyly. "Come, Adi, eat something?" Nurit tries to tempt her daughter. But Adi looks at her mother with open resentment and blurts out, "Yeah, right." "You see, I told you," Nurit says to me. "Them [the kids]? Just scrambled eggs and that's it." Adi sits next to me on the sofa. "What, she used the tape recorder for you too?" she asks her mother with open pleasure. Nurit too looks pleased. "But she didn't start the interview yet," she shares with Adi. I smile and turn on the tiny recording device, which I place on the low living room table. But even as the little red light flickers, indicating that recording has begun, we continue our small talk. I keep waiting for Nurit and Adi to relax, hoping we can begin a more natural conversation. I fill my mouth with the wonderful food that is laid before me, compliment Nurit for the wonderful flavors, and confide that I do not really know how to cook. But the two women do not relax. Their conversation is forced. Nurit's laughter is high-pitched; she repeatedly glances at the recorder and speaks loudly. The red light has been flashing for several long minutes, and still I have not initiated the much-anticipated interview.

"I Was Real Pretty"

A few minutes after I switch on the recorder, without so much as a knock on the door, a skinny, dark, somber-faced man walks into the apartment. He wears low-cut jeans and a synthetic-fabric buttoned shirt that hugs his lanky body. A red and white Marlboro cigarette pack sticks out of his shirt pocket. Nurit points at the small recorder and explains in a loud whisper that we are "recording here," checking again to see that the red light is on and giggling awkwardly. The man flops onto the sofa across from me and introduces himself. His name is Shmuel, he says, and he has been a friend of Nurit's for many, many years, since before she was dating Shimon, her ex-husband. He has a deep voice and a heavy Moroccan accent. He says *Nu*-rit, accenting the first syllable, and then apologizes and says he is used to calling her Nicole and not *Nu*-rit.

"What's with you . . . and with that 'Nicole'?" Nurit scolds him and explains that he is "a friend from a real long time ago, so he is stuck with that 'Nicole.'"

"Where do you know him from? School?" I ask her.

"What school? Who went to school?" Nurit laughs wildly. Shmuel smiles shyly. Nurit looks at Shmuel but speaks to me: "I know him even before he met his wife! We were 15 or something, and we'd go out to the road and stuff, and just hang out. We'd walk and stuff, me and him and his wife. Then there was this guy I had a real crush on. Poor thing, he's dead today. Some blood clot in the brain. He was a junkie and it got complicated. But I loved him. He was my first man. And this screw-up [pointing to Shmuel], he was my cover. So that I'll get close to that Herzl. And everyone thought I was Shmuel's lover. But Shmuel's like my brother. He's not my style." Nurit chuckles, looking straight into Shmuel's embarrassed face.

"And your husband, Shimon, how did you meet him?" I ask.

Nurit laughs loudly again and says something in rapid Moroccan to Shmuel. "Hey, I don't understand," I protest, and she turns serious. "Shimon? I met Shimon . . . when we were neighbors. Our houses were next to each other. Until today my parents and his parents live there, in the same neighborhood. And I was pretty. Real pretty . . . and there were many electric power shortages then. It was dark a lot of the time. And anyway, everybody was in jail. So I stayed with Shimon. He was an OK man. He's older than me by, like, six years. I rolled with it. Yeah, I dated Shimon . . . and my parents . . . they didn't want him. And so . . . I had an abortion . . ."

A knock on the door interrupts her narrative. "Who's there?" Nurit yells without getting up from the sofa.

"It's Schtigel," a voice declares.

"Schtigel . . . ha . . . ha . . . the cashbox is empty today," Nurit yells in an amused tone toward the closed door. Then she gets up and walks to the door, opening it halfway.

"This one is a yeshiva student," Shmuel whispers to me. I get up from my seat and follow Nurit, only to see Schtigel's departing back. He is dressed in a black jacket and sports a round-brimmed hat. Nurit returns to the room with a big, naughty smile.

"This Schtigel, every time he comes around I tell him, 'I don't have any money.' He says to me, 'What did you do?' I tell him, 'I bought cigarettes.' [She laughs at length.] I always get a good laugh with him. I tell him, 'You, you got dollars. Don't you have any to lend me?' He goes, 'You're kidding.' [She laughs again.] Every time he comes, that man, he pushes a donation box on me. But seriously [still laughing], me . . . every time I have some change, I place a few coins in his box."

Schtigel supplies Nurit with comic relief as she embarks on a hard, reflexive process, facing me and my small recorder. She enjoys the attention she is getting in her role as narrator, but her story is not a happy one. Sarcasm— "everybody was in jail, so I stayed with Shimon"—is not an easy way to deal with the pain that this kind of self-scrutiny brings to the surface, especially when a critical daughter is listening in. Nurit constructs a life story that, by her own criteria, is not one to be proud of. She had to hide her attraction to her first love, a junkie who got into trouble and died as a result of his drug habit. She then married a man who, by local standards, was not a good choice for a mate. She ended up with this "OK" man more or less by default, because he was there. She simply "rolled with it" (*mitgalgelet*), not in control of her life, even though she was pretty, even though she might have been able to attract a worthier man. Nurit notes in her sarcastic, humorous way that her decisions might not have been the best ones but that the reality she grew up in did not offer her better options, because, after all, "everybody was in jail."

Amidst this painful self-deprecation, the relation of a story constructed in terms of personal failure, the momentary ability to laugh at the expense of "this Schtigel" endows Nurit with power, shaky as it may be. This Ashkenazi, to whom she smirkingly attributes possession of dollars (as opposed to shekels; i.e., foreign currency that expresses power), needs a donation *from her.* This Ashkenazi man endows her with the power to decide what to do with *her* money. By choosing to use her money to purchase cigarettes and not necessities such as bread, she exercises that power

The comic relief afforded by the exchange with Schtigel, with all its reversals of power and powerlessness, of kidding and seriousness, of giving and taking, provides Nurit momentary escape from the humorless drama she is narrating. Her life story is a saga of sad events: of an unwanted pregnancy, of a failed relationship with a man she describes only as "OK," a man her parents did not approve of. Shimon was not a romantic choice even in local terms, and her relationship with him, the man who became the father of her children, is a story of failure that seems hard for her to face.

"I Do What I Feel Like"

Schtigel leaves, and I try to steer Nurit back to the story that his arrival interrupted. "So Nurit," I ask her, "I didn't understand, about the abortion . . ."

"Ai-ai-ai, you're taking me back so many years. I need to take a deep breath for that. And that nobody will interrupt me." She looks worriedly in Adi's direction. Adi is quiet, her eyes on the floor.

"Listen, if you don't want to talk about the abortion in the presence of Adi, I understand that, so let's leave it alone," I hasten to add.

"Forget about it, I don't hide anything from them. Feel free."

Nurit's face becomes grave. She stares into midair for a long, quiet moment and then seems to decide to face up to her bitter story. She focuses her gaze on me and continues in a serious tone: "The truth? The truth is I had an abortion before I got married to Shimon because my parents didn't want him."

Nurit's narrative is interrupted again, when the cell phone rings. Earlier, Nurit told me that she does not have a landline—it was disconnected because she did not pay the bills—and that her son, Shahaf, had bought her a new Star-Tech mobile phone as a birthday present. Adi answers the call and passes the phone to Nurit, but not before she snaps at the person on the other end of the line with open hostility, "What, I'm not good enough? You don't want to talk with me?" The person on the line turns out to be Shimon, Adi's father, Nurit's ex-husband, who is calling for the second time this evening. Shimon senses Nurit's high spirits and insists on joining our gathering. Nurit tells him that she is here "with my friend from Sde Boker, Pnina. You want to come over? Come over. Take a shower and come."

"What business does he have coming here?" Adi asks, without trying to conceal her rage. Then she drops any semblance of polite conversation and begins to imitate her mother, using a ridiculing, high-pitched voice: "'You want to stay? Here are your clothes. Take a shower. Why not. Here, the bed is ready . . .' And that's how he stays," she concludes, speaking to no one in particular.

"I do what I feel like, not what you feel like," Nurit says to Adi, and then, turning to me, she states emphatically, "I listen to them. They live here too. But first thing, I do what's in my head [*ma barosh sheli*]." Adi is furious. She loses all interest in the interview session, ignoring my presence and that of Shmuel. She demands in an impatient tone that her mother give her 100 shekels, insisting that she must leave right away.

"What do you need a hundred shekel for? I gave you 50 just yesterday," Nurit replies with great embarrassment, giggling nervously.

"Great . . . do me a favor. What's 'what for'? I need the money! It is how it is. I'm asking you for a miserable hundred shekel and all of a sudden you're out of it [money]. 'I gave you 50 shekel yesterday,'" Adi imitates Nurit, repeating the last phrase in a shrill voice. "All I am asking for is a hundred. What's your problem? Do you have it or not?"

Nurit stops giggling. She looks at me in embarrassment, and I pause the recorder. Nurit and Adi continue to argue, ignoring Shmuel and me. I keep silent. Shmuel stares at the floor.

Stopping the tape does not resolve the highly charged scene unfolding in front of me. What began as a proud consent to tell a life story has developed into a complex event during which Nurit faces the task of examining her life, not merely for my recorder but also for herself. As she struggles to construct her life story—the story of the pretty girl who chose badly, despite her parents' objections—Shmuel acts as a pillar of emotional support, but Adi becomes a source of distress and social anxiety. Adi's behavior links the story of the past to the present and highlights the difficulties of parenting in circumstances of poverty.

Nurit emphasizes that she is an independent, strong-willed woman, who does not bend to external dictates—either her parents' or her children's, both of whom try, in turn, to break up her relationship with the man she has chosen to marry. "I listen to them, they live here too," she says about her children. But Nurit insists that she makes her own decisions. In her narrative she has agency; she is a subject and not a victim. In her story she is a woman who controls her own life: "I do what I feel like [*ani osah ma barosh sheli*]." In Gayatri Spivak's (1988) terms, Nurit acts for herself, placing herself and her interests center stage. She rejects the terms of a discourse that defines her choices as wrong. But facing her young daughter's fierce criticism is not simple. Adi disrupts the space of reflection that her mother is creating with her story. With her belittling imitation of her mother, Adi charges, "You're a failing parent." And she does so precisely at the moment Nurit insists, "I do what I feel like." Adi violates all polite, conventional rules of discourse to undermine her mother's narrative of independence and self-definition and replaces it with her bitter claim that her mother is an inadequate parent, one who is unable to fulfill her children's emotional and material needs. In her violent interruption, Adi forces the rest of us to give up our speaking positions: Shmuel, Nurit, and I are rendered silent.

"I Need to Become a Decent Human Being First"

After an embarrassed silence that seems to stretch on and on, the door swings open without warning. A skinny man, about 40 years old, slightly bent, and holding a lit cigarette in his hand, walks into the room. This is Shimon, I assume. This is what a junkie looks like, I tell myself as I gaze into his sad, lost eyes. Shimon enters in small, slow steps. He scans the room for a long moment before he sits next to me on the sofa. His dramatic entrance intensifies the atmosphere in the room. Nurit's discomfort reaches new heights. Her laughter becomes more frequent and shrill. Adi's hostility is now palpable. "Here's the foot cream you wanted. Take it and scram," she shoots at her father.

Shimon ignores Adi. He directs his attention to me and asks where I am from. I answer that I am from Sde Boker. "And where were you from *before* you came to Sde Boker?" he persists in a sluggish, low voice.

"From Migdal Ha'Emek."

Shimon shakes his head and says in a deliberate halting rhythm: "Ahh . . . Migdal Ha'Emek . . . I was there . . . once . . . for a few months . . . I was there. It was a long time ago. We were there . . . in some . . . some . . . agriculture farm."

I fire a burst of short, embarrassed, and confused questions at Shimon. "What was it? An agriculture farm? What did you do on an agriculture farm? In Migdal Ha'Emek of all places? They took you there . . . in what framework? School?"

"No . . . it . . . it . . . is . . . 'cause . . . I . . . I was screwed up . . ."

"So . . . what . . . hmm . . . they sent you there . . . so . . . Migdal Ha'Emek . . . would . . . fix you up, kind of?" I clumsily try to jest.

"Me? I was done screwing up Yerucham, so I went to screw up all of Migdal Ha'Emek!"

Nurit and I laugh, and Shmuel claps his hands cheerfully. Adi twists her lips bitterly: "Great. Very funny." Shimon ignores Adi and continues speaking slowly, directing his words at me, pausing for long breaks: "No . . . the truth is . . . I have . . . an uncle . . . there . . . in Migdal . . . Ha'Emek." He tries to find out whether I know who his uncle is. I tell him that the family name sounds familiar but that I do not know the person he's talking about, because I left Migdal Ha'Emek many years ago.

A long silence follows. Shimon's arrival has dramatically changed the balance of power in the room. Nurit's story has been cut off. The attention has moved to Shimon, who, in his efforts to define himself in relation to me, the important guest, manages to upstage Nurit. He is able to jest, to present himself as a subversive protagonist, I think, the kind of person who "screwed up all of Yerucham." For this one short moment, Shimon is surrounded by a warm, sympathetic audience: the loyal Nurit, his good friend Shmuel, and me, an important guest with whom he can forge shared experiences.

Faced with his daughter's obvious hostility, he is afforded a moment of grace when Shmuel turns to him to remind him, with much ado, that they are both invited to an "event" (eru'a). Shimon takes a long time to respond. He slowly and laboriously informs his good friend, "I'm not sure I'm going," and then quietly adds, staring at Nurit, "I need to become a decent human being first." Shmuel gives Shimon an affectionate nod, as though to confirm his friend's statement. Shimon then stands up and heads toward the corridor leading to the bedrooms. His pace is slow, and he seems to have trouble keeping his balance. Nurit follows him. He asks for clean clothes, and she says something about not having had time to do the laundry. After a few more words, Shimon walks slowly to the apartment door. Nurit accompanies him. Shmuel, Adi, and I remain seated. Just before taking his leave, Shimon turns back to me and says in a dreamy voice, "It is a pleasure meeting you." I mumble the polite *na'im me'od* as Nurit closes the door behind him.

His statement "I need to become a decent human being first" and his heart-rending attempt to take part in a social setting where a code of polite conduct applies, in which one might say, "It is a pleasure meeting you," suggest that—for the few brief moments he spends in the apartment—Shimon shares in the reflexive mood dictated by the situation. Like Nurit, who is facing the need to sort out the choices she has made in her life, articulating her decisions, analyzing them, explaining them to herself and to us, Shimon too engages in a moment of self-scrutiny. "I'm not a [decent] human being," he says about his state of being in the world. I cannot appear in public in my condition, he admits in the safe space created by Nurit's and Shmuel's open support of him. He tries to make a social connection with me, the honored guest, joking with me and attempting to find common ground in our respective pasts. But his entry into these discursive relations also forces him to define himself as unworthy, as someone whose behavior is inappropriate. To enter into polite discourse, he must acknowledge his position at the margins of "proper society." He does so by ridiculing his marginalization and by extending it to all the social spaces he enters: When he states, "I was done screwing up Yerucham, so I went to screw up all of Migdal Ha'Emek," he surrenders to the rules of the discourse that have turned him into something less than "a human being."

"My Name Is Not Nurit"

After Shimon's departure, the atmosphere in the room calms down a bit. Nurit relaxes somewhat, her nervous, shrill laughter subsiding. Loyal Shmuel sits on the edge of the sofa in somber silence. I ask Nurit if she wants to continue telling her life story, and she seems happy to do so. She stares at the flashing recording light, leans back in her seat, and, newly resolute, says, "Listen,

Pnina . . . the truth? The truth is . . . my name is not Nurit. The truth? Everybody calls me Nicole. Even my kids, them, you won't hear them say 'Mama,' just 'Nicole.' Them? You only hear them say 'Mama' when they want money." Adi makes a face but does not say anything.

Nurit looks at Adi but speaks to the open space of the room, to the recorder. Her face is solemn and her words careful.

"Me, look, I'm used to him. He is my first guy. I never cheated on him. I was always loyal to him. I want him to take his time and come back like a decent human being. You heard him. He said it right here that he wants to be a decent human being. At some point, I understand him . . . but . . . I can't accept him. You want to be a decent human being? Then you need to take it on yourself. You need to pay the electricity bills, pay the water bills. But him? When he gets stressed out, he always goes back to the drugs. He . . . any stress . . . you can't put pressure on these kind of people. He runs to the drugs for comfort . . . and now . . . he's at his mother's. She adores me, actually . . ."

Nurit sighs and looks at me. I am silent and listen to her with deep attentiveness. She continues:

This, this is a rough life story. Look Pnina, it's . . . can you call this a life? I'm a single mother. I'm divorced. Since Adi was a year and a half, I've been divorced from him. And he would go to rehab and return. And I provided for the kids. What can we do? But I would take him back. And that's how I got pregnant from him again and again. And I needed to get terminations [abortions]. Because forget about it. Me? I had an IUD for 14 years and it shriveled up in my uterus. So one morning, I couldn't get out of bed. What do I know? IUD, no IUD! What am I, a gynecologist? So they took me to the emergency room, did an ultrasound and found this IUD. And they scratched and cleaned my uterus. So, this procedure was in December. And Shimon was in rehab that whole year. And when he got back from rehab, I was clear. My uterus was healed, healthy. It was clean, clear for conception. It was Passover. And I didn't lay with anyone. God forbid, I would never cheat on him. And he came home and I slept with him. And it was Passover and I was busy with guests all during the month of March. And it slipped my mind. I said, "My period didn't come, probably from all the Passover mess." But me, I had a feeling. I went to Shimon and I told him, "I'm pregnant." He went, "What?! You're too much! What, from the one time we slept together? You conceived from that one time?!" And I, I didn't ask anyone. I went to the gynecologist and told him, "Check!" He says to me, "Lady, you got twins!" When I heard this, I started crying. I told the doctor to immediately get me to an abortion committee. I told him, "Look, I'm not married and I was with someone and it slipped and stuff. Me, I don't have the means to feed these children. My situation is bad as it is." I was so deeply depressed, forget about it. It was a Wednesday. On the following Monday I was told that the committee has approved the termination [of the pregnancy]. He, Shimon, he actually wanted it. He said, "I didn't raise the first ones. I'll raise these new babies." And she [looking at Adi], she also wanted it. But there was nothing to do. It's a matter of honor. It's a Moroccan family. I'm divorced. How will I tell people that I'm pregnant? So I did it.

Nurit looks at me, and I can see enormous pain in her eyes. Adi sits quietly, sinking into herself in the corner of the room.

Nurit continues: "Listen, this isn't easy . . . to be a single mother. Sometimes I'd take him back because the kids wanted it. But he wasn't working. Maybe a few days. And that's it. And I always worked. I needed to provide for my children. I wouldn't deny anything to my kids."

Nurit abruptly goes silent. I tell her it is obvious that she does not deny her children anything. I say that her apartment is very nice, well kept, and she smiles with satisfaction. She describes how she moved walls in the tiny apartment, so that each of her children could have a nice room. And I express my admiration. She invites me into the bedrooms to see the walls painted with bright colors, the pictures hanging on them, the brightly colored curtains, and the handsome bedsheets. The whole apartment feels pleasant, clean, and airy. I repeat how much I like everything.

It is only after Shimon leaves that Nurit is able to tap into her pain. She stares at the small machine recording her words, but, in fact, she is talking to herself. Her long monologue, in which she analyzes her relationship with Shimon, reveals her deep compassion for her husband's difficulties. "You heard him," she tells me. "He said he wanted to become a decent human being." Her words make me a witness to Shimon's declaration, perhaps uttered for the first time. Nurit makes it clear that she has no one to rely on and that for many long years she alone has provided for her two children, without expecting her partner to support them. But she is not bitter or accusative toward her ex-husband. He tries his best, she says. He really wants to be a decent human being. And when she offers to show me her home, she is full of pride.

In her influential study of poverty, British sociologist Ruth Lister (2004) writes at length about sacrifices poor women make to protect their children. Lister notes that women in single-parent families pay for their altruism with physical and mental fatigue, but in return they gain pride. When Nurit declares, "I was always working," she expresses this combination of pain and pride, fatigue and decisiveness.

The Nurit who speaks at such length about her pain is very different from the woman I first met, who tried to draw my attention to her sad life story and who used the allure of that tale to wield power over me. Nurit is revealed here in all her humanity and kindness. Only during the intimate scene in her small living room do I see this other side of her—a complex, compassionate, and loyal person. I realize that the different spaces in which we have met have produced different narratives of self. Only in her home, where she is surrounded by the people who are significant in her life, can Nurit articulate the pain that underlies her many struggles to break the cycle of poverty and marginality in which she is trapped. Only in this safe space can she allow me to see her capacity for self-sacrifice and pride, loyalty and generosity, a single mother trying to create a better life for herself and for her children.

Nurit presents a different self in public spaces, where she encounters people who wield power over her. In these spaces she acts decisively and strategically to derive whatever benefit she can from such people. The manipulative self she revealed throughout our early encounters is indicative of her survival strategy, and that is why in this account I have insisted on depicting the power struggle she forced on me in our initial interactions. Like her mother, who assumes from my speech pattern that I am a social worker, Nurit performs the kind of behavioral pattern that highlights the victimhood of her life.

New research about women who live in poverty in Israel presents empathetic stories of women who, like Nurit, must deal with material deprivation and social marginalization. This new research breaks away from the more familiar tendency in academic and public discourse to ignore the voices of women who live in poverty and thereby to contribute to and reproduce narrow, stereotypical interpretations of such lives. Feminist scholar Michal Krumer-Nevo, one of the leading critical poverty researchers in Israel, notes perceptively that "middle-class people find it very hard to listen to life stories of people who live in poverty because such stories stir feelings of guilt and unease" (2006: 22). She asserts that "those who don't experience such distress blame the poor for their poverty" and tend to argue that poor people "don't take responsibility for their lives" or that "they are lazy" or "have no ambition."

The different spaces in which Nurit's story unfolds suggest that the voice of a research subject can be muted or can take a particular, narrow track in one setting and reveal itself in all its complexity in other, enabling circumstances. I hear more about Nurit's great effort to craft a sense of self-pride during another visit to her home, when she suggests that we watch the video of her son's bar mitzvah.

The Event Economy

Nurit's son's bar mitzvah video is not the first recording of a family celebration I have been invited to watch in Yerucham. By the time I view it, I have already accumulated many notes on what I come to call the local "event economy." In Yerucham, I have learned, the term *eru'a* (event, pl. *eru'im*) refers mainly to a family celebration, such as a wedding or a bar mitzvah, whereas in wider Israeli public discourse, it can refer to a variety of social, political, or health-related events. In Yerucham, when one speaks of having to attend an *eru'a*, one never refers to an event in this wider sense. The narrow use of the term seems to be a lower-class, mostly Mizrahi pattern. In Yerucham, the *eru'a* is an arena where social position within the community is played out, as reflected in who comes to your *eru'a* and who doesn't; how much time, energy, and thought you invest in the *eru'a*; where it is held, whether in a local hall or a venue in Be'er-Sheva (the regional capital); whether it is a grand event that draws in hundreds or even thousands of guests or a modest celebration held in one's house or garden. These parameters are central to local gossip in the isolated, small community.

People spend huge sums of money to produce such events. Expenditures are not limited to the catering hall's per-meal set price, a price often quoted in

U.S. dollars.³ They also include the costs of photographic services (video recorder rental, one or more still photographers, a photographer equipped with an instant camera to provide guests with souvenir pictures), music (live music, perhaps by known performers, or recorded music played by a DJ), fireworks, and even professional dancers to draw guests onto the dance floor. In addition, hosts spend inordinate amounts of money on the several outfits they wear throughout the event and on elaborate professional hairstyling and makeup.

A strict system of expectations defines who you invite to these events and whose events you must attend when invited, and an elaborate calculation determines the size of the check you give to the host (no one gives nonmonetary gifts anymore, a practice I remember from my own childhood). Family distance between the guest and the host is a key criterion determining the amount given. The closer your relation to the host (e.g., a sibling rather than a distant cousin), the fatter the check. But the relative social standing of the host and the guest also plays a part; if the host is the guest's boss or a local personality who is influential in town, the amount of the check has to be higher than the amount the guest would give to a neighbor or a colleague. When the host and the guest are from the same social class, it is important for the guest to give an amount at least equal to (and preferably a little more than) that received from the host when their positions were reversed.

People go into enormous debt, not only when they host their own *eru'a* but also when they participate as guests in a seemingly endless chain of events, say, a bris (a ritual circumcision) followed by a bar mitzvah and then a wedding. People cannot avoid this cycle of visitations and gift giving. During the summer months, when most weddings are held, people speak about the necessity of attending yet another nuptial event as an *onesh*, a punishment, because of the debt they incur to pay for another round of *eru'a* expenses. Despite the open grumbling about the need to attend all these expensive events, people who have paid their dues and attended all the *eru'im* hosted by family, friends, and neighbors expect a large attendance at their own *eru'im*. The larger the *eru'a*, the higher a person's social standing in the community. The expectation that once I attend your *eru'a*, you will attend mine is strictly construed, and few can avoid paying their dues. I was taken aback at the ferocity of the anger and humiliation endured by one person who was expected to attend an *eru'a* and failed to do so. By the same token, those who do observe the proprieties are spoken of approvingly. "Her *eru'a* was packed because she went to all the *eru'im* she was invited to," I heard more than one woman say with open admiration after a particularly successful, well-attended event. When one of my key interlocutors in Yerucham invited me to an *eru'a*, she promptly asked how old my sons were and promised me that she would not fail to attend my elder son's expected bar mitzvah.

In the following account of Nurit's event, both the material and the social calculations that precede an *eru'a* are made poignant. Financially, as I have stressed, the costs for hosting such an event are huge. As we will see, to finance her *eru'a* Nurit saved for many years and also took out loans that she then spent more years paying off. More significantly, her story shows that the *eru'a* can do more than reaffirm one's social standing; it is often a space where social positioning is crafted anew. Nurit's *eru'a* was a social setting where she fought her multiple exclusions and social isolation.

"People Haven't Forgotten My Event!"

Five years after her *eru'a*, Nurit is happy to show me the video that documents her son's bar mitzvah. She pulls the thick VHS cassette out of a deep drawer at the bottom of her TV cart and begins rewinding the tape on her old VCR. As the reel turns with a monotonous whirring sound, Nurit declares with pride, "People haven't forgotten my *eru'a*! They told me, 'Bravo for what you did.' You gotta see the pictures of the Moroccan cookies . . . the flowers, the food. Forget about it!" The way she is glued to the TV screen and the intensity of her comments as we watch the tape tell me that she has seen the video many times before and speak to the formative place of this event in her life. The *eru'a* constituted the single most important public setting in which this divorced woman, a single mother of two, could declare that she has a functioning family and that she is an excellent provider for her children.

Nurit talks about the many long years during which she saved and carefully calculated to produce her bar mitzvah event. She tells me, "I always worked and earned my money. And when I was stuck and had no income, my sister would help me. She's actually doing well, my sister. She's an art teacher and all that. And she would buy me food. Whole supermarket carts she'd bring me. And, yes, even the bank didn't give me trouble for not paying the electricity bill and stuff in my hard times, until I got some work. And, you see, even in my bad years, I'd put money aside for my kids' events. I had a plan, so that when my son is 13, I will be prepared."

Nurit goes on to describe the details of that long-term plan.

"You should see the bar mitzvah I made for Shahaf. I didn't hold back any expense from him. Years I saved for him. Put it aside. Knowing that when my son turned 13, I'll need this money. So after all these years I told Shimon from the bank, 'Shimon, I have my *eru'a* now, get me my money!' Get it? I had a saving plan of about 10,000 shekel. But it wasn't enough. What do you know? Just the band cost like 3,000 shekel. That was then! Who knows how much you pay for a band today! And the photographer too, like, 2,000 something. I also paid for studio shots. He made for me a huge photo of Shahaf that people [guests] came and signed their names on. The photographer came with me to the synagogue and made a video."

Nurit emphasizes the surplus of people, of food, of expenses. "You see," she tells me, "I invited 250 people. And I had another 50 reservations extra, just in case. I had a surplus, you see. All in all, I paid the hall owner 18,000 shekel. He worked it out with me. Discount here and there. A different man would have paid $17 for a plate. I almost broke even, you see. The whole thing that came in was like 15,000 shekel. Checks, everything, I gave him. And I took a loan, to pay what was left."

Nurit cites these numbers and the precise price she paid for each item with great emotion, and I react in the way I know she expects of me. I express my admiration for the amounts of food, the cookies, the balloons, and the fireworks. I ask about the guests. I say again and again how impressed I am with her *eru'a*. Nurit nods her head, only half-listening to my approving comments. She is completely engrossed in the videotape. "Listen," I say at one point, "You didn't try to save here at all." But something in the way I phrase this comment incenses Nurit, who replies heatedly, "What? Why didn't I what? *Save?* Why should I save? You mean, like, hold back? Like, because I'm a single mother? I, get me, Pnina, for years, years, I'm telling you, I put money aside for this."

I do not expect her angry reaction. Trying to mollify her, I explain, "Of course, Nurit. Look, no doubt, I can see that you made this *eru'a* the biggest possible." Nurit's eyes return to the glowing TV screen as she mumbles, "For sure! For sure I'd make it the biggest! I wanted it like that. Each one goes according to their own pocket. Each person does his own math. Whatever works for you." I am aware of her displeasure, so I continue trying to explain my comment: "No, really . . . don't get me wrong. What I'm saying is . . . just . . . that . . . people, they all know you're a single mother and that you don't have any financial support from the father of your kids, so that, I mean . . . maybe . . . people would have accepted it if . . . maybe . . . you had done something more . . . *tzanu'a* [humble] . . ."

But my clumsy effort to appease her produces the opposite effect. Upon hearing me say "*tzanu'a*," Nurit loses interest in the rapidly changing scenes on the TV screen and focuses on me in anger. "Are you crazy? *Of course*, I'll do the maximum! What *tzanu'a*?" she spits the word out with disdain, "I made *the* richest dishes. And because I work for the hall owner, I got several extra bonuses that others couldn't."

I am silent. The video continues to play, but Nurit shows no interest in it. She is deeply offended. "What *tzanu'a*? I work and I don't want my kids to feel *deprived*. I work and I provide for them . . . everything . . . so they will never say, 'Why, Mom, he got that and I didn't.'"

After a long while, she seems to calm down, and she says in a reflexive, quiet tone, "You see, Pnina, if I hadn't done it like this, I'm telling you, I would feel that something . . . like . . . bothers me."

"Why?" I regain my courage and dare to ask her directly. "What would bother you?"

But Nurit does not want to continue this conversation with me. She is not going to answer my question. "I don't know. I don't have answers. I really don't have any answers," she replies impatiently as she refocuses on the screen.

Reading my notes, I realize why Nurit is furious with me and my middle-class, conservative logic that suggests she did not need to spend beyond her means, a logic that offers criticism of her overexpenditure. People in the community know about her limited resources, I have reminded her, and thus she could have made do with less. But Nurit will have nothing to do with this simple instrumental logic. She declares again and again that she has invested *more* rather than less in her *eru'a* because she does not wish her children to "feel deprived."

The Hebrew term for deprivation is *kipu'akh*, which social workers and educators often use in relation to children from lower socioeconomic, often Mizrahi, backgrounds. *Mekupakhim* is an adjective used as a euphemism for humiliating deprivation, for impoverishment, a state of permanent helplessness. Nurit passionately rejects these terms and what they suggest. She insists that she has worked hard all her life to provide for her children so that they can gain self-dignity and *not* feel *kipu'akh*, deprivation. She has worked hard to avoid the material deprivation her children might feel because of their dysfunctional family but also out of a need to restructure the social isolation a label of deprivation implies. To secure her children's sense of belonging, of being like any other child in their community, she has felt the need to overcompensate—thus, her son's bar mitzvah required particularly rich dishes, the investment in every service the town photographer had to offer, balloons, and so on. She needed to make sure that people would *not* forget her *eru'a*. When I challenge her by asking her to explain *why* it would bother her *not* to have made this great investment, Nurit impatiently rejects my question and its implied logic. "I don't know," she repeats, effectively telling me that she has reached the limit of her reflexive ability. At this point, I am pushed out of what Nurit defines as a proper conversation. I need to stop asking my judgmental questions. She is not going to respond.

Studies that explore the experiences of women who live in poverty, whatever the context, emphasize that the feeling of social isolation is sometimes more tangible and painful than the material deprivation itself (Lister 2004: 74). Women in poverty, especially single mothers, exert tremendous amounts of energy to escape social isolation and stigmatization. Their active agency is directed at building a feeling of self-worth for themselves and for their children (cf. Narayan 2000; Scott 1994).

Shimon "Didn't Pay"

The bar mitzvah video has been frenetically edited. Each scene cuts quickly to the next as stars roll away into the background. The first long segment focuses on the colorful trays loaded with food, the champagne glasses stacked in a tall fragile pyramid, and the flower arrangements. These still-life close-ups documenting the abundance of food and the spectacle of the hall are interspersed with shots focused on the bar mitzvah boy's face. After this long, frenzied opening, the pace changes, and the camera captures a seemingly endless stream of arriving guests. Each guest walks into the hall and shakes hands with Nurit and her two children, who stand stiffly at the entrance. After this formal greeting, the guests are ushered to their seats at beautifully set round tables. After watching a long series of such greetings and handshakes, I notice an elderly man standing half a step behind Nurit. The man smiles at the incoming guests but does not shake their hands. "Who's this man?" I ask, and Nurit explains, "Look, look at my daddy, Pnina. What a sweet soul [*neshama*]. He stood with me at the entrance the whole time, so I won't be standing there alone."

"Your father? Aha . . . Where was Shimon? He didn't come to the event?"

"Shimon? Why? He didn't pay. Why should he stand?" Nurit fumes with repressed anger. I realize that this is a sensitive issue, so I keep quiet as we continue to watch guests walking into the hall. Nurit makes comments about the people who appear on the screen. She asks me if I know them. She introduces them by name: "This is my sister-in-law, and here is my neighbor Rivka, and that's my cousin." But then she returns to the issue of Shimon: "He didn't even come at the beginning," she says, reliving her aggravation at her ex-husband's behavior. Then she adds, "My daddy, a dear soul, he was there with me the whole time. [He] kept saying, 'Do you need anything?'"

The image of Nurit standing "alone" at the entrance of the hall to welcome her guests emphasizes the deficient family structure she has struggled so hard to overcome in planning her son's bar mitzvah. Shimon, the father of the bar mitzvah boy, is physically present in the hall, but he is not entitled to welcome the guests, to act as a proper host, because, as Nurit insists, he "didn't pay." Shimon's missing support is not simply material; it is also social. Shimon is not a proper father to his children, and therefore he cannot declare his status as a host of this grand event. Nurit's father can articulate his emotional support of his daughter in this important moment in her life, but he cannot take on the role of a host. Thus, he does not shake hands with the incoming guests.

The staging makes it clear to everyone that this is Nurit's event. And as though to remove any doubt about such an interpretation, Nurit declares, "This Shimon, he, coming like a guest."

When the video finally ends, Nurit stands up and, without a word, walks to the bedroom and comes back with a batch of photo albums. She sits next to me on the sofa and continues reliving the important event, this time through the photos that are organized in the albums, wrapped in shiny, rustling clear plastic.

"I Cried, I Cried throughout the *Eru'a*"

The photographs arranged in these albums show Nurit wearing three different outfits. In one set of images she wears a short-sleeved black evening gown, a necklace of large fake diamonds glittering down her chest. In another set of photos she is wearing a sky blue pantsuit with a long-sleeved silk blouse. In the third she wears an embroidered Moroccan outfit. Nurit's hair is dyed light blonde and is arranged in a tall, impressive beehivelike style. I enthuse, "Nurit, you look really gorgeous here," and she is pleased. I notice that Shahaf, the bar mitzvah boy, is wearing an elegant tuxedo. "Listen, Shahaf's tuxedo is amazing," I say.

Nurit seems much more relaxed now that we have watched the video together and I have stopped making annoying comments questioning her need to produce an event that everyone would talk about. And perhaps that is why, only after she is secure in my supportive, appreciative comments, she allows herself to express feelings she has not previously articulated. As we turn the pages of the photo albums, Nurit begins to speak about her pain, about the emotional price she has paid for the glitzy event she has produced. In reference to my comment about Shahaf's tuxedo, she tells me, "This tuxedo you're looking at, Pnina, let me tell you. It's from the beauty salon owner. You see. I did not pay for it. I came to the salon to do my hair, and he says to me, 'Listen, Nurit, I see that you're a hell of a woman [*isha a'l-ha-ke'fak*]. I hear that you are a single mother and such. So I want to take part in this mitzvah of bringing a boy to mitzvot. So allow me to give you Shahaf's suit free of charge.' It's like, get this, Pnina, it's a rent-a-suit, but he gave it to me until the next day free of charge!

It made me cry, I am telling you. I was so moved. You'll see me in the pictures, my eyes are red. I cried, I cried throughout the *eru'a*."

"Why did you cry?"

"Why did I cry? Look, seeing him like this. Raising him on my own for 13 years, and making him this bar mitzvah on my own, it's very hard."

And then she recalls the generosity other people showed her.

"Listen to this, Pnina, this beauty salon owner? He made me feel like a bride. They made me up . . . it was something . . . and then he says to me, 'It's all paid for!' Go figure it out: the glued-on nails they made me, the hairdo for me and for Adi, and the professional makeup for both of us. It was all paid for by the hall owner [Nurit's employer]. I was blown away. I did not know what to say. So I, I gave them 50 shekel each. Tip! Each one got his tip! You get it? He [the hall owner] made me this gift without me knowing about it. His wife likes me and she knows I've worked for him for eight years. And not only this, they also ordered a cab to take me back to the hall and everything. They really pampered me. And I gave them 50 shekel each one, and also I left a whole tray of these specially made Moroccan cookies for them to share."

Only after we have watched the whole video and leafed through the many albums is Nurit able to admit how hard it was to produce this large event and how much her act of sacrifice (her being a "hell of a woman" in the words of the beauty salon owner) was appreciated by people both in and outside the community. The salon owner's generosity is an articulation of his desire to take part in a mitzvah, not an act of charity. In this way his generosity toward her does not humiliate her. It is she who gives him the opportunity to gain Jewish blessings by performing a mitzvah, a noble act. In the same way, Nurit insists that the generosity of her employer and his wife is an expression of their love for her, an act of pampering. Unlike an act of charity, pampering is a privilege enjoyed by a person who has it all. Nurit could accept these acts of generosity because she could frame them in ways that did not diminish her. Her reciprocal position in relation to these generous gifts is emphasized by her own acts of giving. The woman who subsists on welfare and at times is dependent on donations of food from her family, gives generous tips. The tips paid to each of the waiters and to the workers in the beauty salon make her a giver, a donor, not just a person on the receiving end. But this cycle of giving and receiving is not restricted to the single day of the *eru'a*. As it turns out, it is a state of affairs that pertains to Nurit's life in general. A gray economy shadows the means by which Nurit makes ends meet in her fragile social circumstances.

Saving for the Bar Mitzvah

Nurit worked for eight years for the same local celebration hall owner. But the arrangement was never open or formal. She worked unreported hours, and most of her salary was paid in cash. The arrangement suited both the employer and Nurit, who did not want to declare this irregular income to the Welfare Office. Her welfare payments were barely enough to cover her daily needs, but Nurit made do with them; she "rolled with it" (*mitgalgelet*), as she put it. Exceptional expenses, however, could not be paid for out of her government stipend. The *eru'a* needed to be paid for with funds from unofficial sources in the gray economic sphere.

Nurit's relationship with her employer enabled her to save for her son's bar mitzvah because she never dipped into this undeclared income for ongoing daily needs. The feeling of gratitude she felt toward her employer is articulated in her detailed description of the way she managed her expenditures during the months that preceded the bar mitzvah.

> I came to him [the hall owner] and told him, "I want you to reserve for me the hall for this and that date. I don't have a deposit." All in all, get this, he always takes a deposit of like 200, 300 shekel, at least. It depends on who the person is, depends on everything. Now, what did I do? I told him, "Listen to me, I'm asking, don't deposit the money you pay me in the bank. I want it in my hand, in cash." And so, I was working like that in his place for many years. And every month I'd do overtime and everything and I'd balance with the welfare money. And when my son was like 12 or so, and I know I will need to make him his bar mitzvah, like, I'd take the cash and pay for the balloons, the band, the photographer . . . you get me? Like, months ahead of the *eru'a* I started paying directly for everything in cash. Balloons, I paid up like 200 shekel; printed invitations, something like 350. The cookies, I'm telling you, it cost me, then, who knows how much it cost today, like 2,500 shekel. It's not just plain cookies. These are special Moroccan cookies. There is a particular lady who made them for me. And jams! Great homemade Moroccan jams. Are you

kidding me? It's something special. But what can I tell you, it's all about the depth of one's pocket. We each make our own account. I was afraid people wouldn't come. It was my first event.

Detailing how she managed the many payments testifies to long-term planning. Nurit speaks of "balancing with" the social welfare payments. In other words, she lived frugally on these payments and used the cash she received from the hall owner to pay the many service providers she hired. But the undocumented payment for her many hours of work in the hall exposes her to gray labor-market arrangements; she works with no social rights or employment security. Nurit does not complain about the long, undocumented working hours. She does not feel exploited by the hall owner. On the contrary, she is grateful for the generosity he shows in helping her produce her event.

And the event, as it turns out, is not limited to the single evening celebrated in the rented hall, lavish as it is. Nurit tells me with great pride about a series of related events, each celebrated with a different, well-defined circle of family and friends.

> You think it's just the event in the hall? No way! I did a *Shabbat chatan* [literally, "groom's Sabbath"], and for that I bought a different set of clothes for me and the kids. Each of us needed a different outfit for the hall and a different outfit for the *Shabbat chatan.*
>
> You see this elegant black evening dress I wore in the rented hall? I bought it in Dominique [an evening-wear shop in Be'er-Sheva]. It cost me something like 1,500 shekel. And for Adi, I also needed to buy her several new outfits—one for the *Shabbat chatan*, one for the bar mitzvah evening in the hall, and one for the *aliya la'torah* [the event of Torah reading in the synagogue]. And as for me, I ordered two tailored suits. I was skinny back then, a model! And I got Shahaf suits for the *Shabbat chatan* and for the studio, each one separately. It was lucky that my daddy bought him the tefillin [phylacteries] . . . only that cost something like 2,000 shekel. And where's my mother's gold?

"What gold?" I ask.

"The gold they dressed him with at the *henna.*[4] My mama made the *Shabbat chatan* for me. In her house. She did everything. So after that comes the *aliya*

la'torah, always on a Monday. And in the evening it's the bar mitzvah celebrated at the hall, and before that on Friday and Saturday there was the *henna*
at my mama's. She invited only our families. His [Shimon's] parents barely
came. Him [Shimon] . . . he came like a stranger. They [Shimon's family] gave
me 500 shekel at the party. *Ya bki a'lek* [Arabic for 'cry over it,' i.e., it was a
pitiful nothing]. That's it. So you see why I was crying?"

"Why did you cry? About Shimon? Because he . . . ?"

"Forget it. Forget it. I did everything. Don't need anything from him. My
mama, she did the *henna* for me too. That same night, after the main course,
when we did the *henna*, we all wore traditional Moroccan caftans. These traditional clothes you see, they are all from my mama, she brought them herself
from Morocco. Yeah, she has these friends that bring her these outfits. It's, like,
people rent these outfits for a lot of money. Me, my mama, she brought me
everything."

Nurit falls silent for a long moment. She is looking at the photographs as
she recalls more expenses she has neglected to mention.

"The photographer alone took like 2,000 and something [pictures]. Made
me the studio shots. He also made me a huge picture that people signed . . .
came with me to the synagogue . . . and the video in the hall and everything.
And don't ask . . . I ordered whiskey and champagne. It was poured there like
water. Just the Moroccan cookies I ordered cost me . . ."

The *eru'a* is celebrated in stages in several spaces—the synagogue, Nurit's
mother's home, a rented celebration hall. In each of these spaces a different
crowd is invited and an organized system of rights and obligations, one of
which is the need to wear different outfits, is observed. The extended family
is invited to contribute to different segments of this extended event. Nurit's
mother supplies imported outfits from Morocco for the *henna* and invites the
family to her home for a *Shabbat chatan* meal. Nurit emphasizes the absence
of any contribution from ex-husband Shimon and his family, despite their attendance of the *henna* and the *Shabbat chatan*. In one of the photographs, the
bar mitzvah boy is seen sitting in his tuxedo between two elderly women. Both
women are holding boxes of jewelry. "This is what I was telling you about the
gold," explains Nurit. "The grandmas bring the gold to the boy. Here, Shimon's

mother is showing a *gourmet* [a thick, coarsely made golden necklace] and a bracelet, and my mama, she holds a necklace and a gold watch."

"So Shimon's mother did contribute something," I point out.

"What contributes? This is called contributing? This miserable *gourmet? Ya bki a'lek*," Nurit responds to my observation with clear displeasure, and then she adds, "Where is it now? Only the watch is left. He [Shahaf] lost all of it, here and there. It's like 3,000 shekel, it's all gone. Who knows."

Shimon's family is present, even though Shimon, the father of the bar mitzvah boy, "didn't pay." Nurit cannot erase their presence, as it is documented in pictures. But she insists that Shimon's mother barely fulfilled her part and emphasizes that she expected a more substantial contribution from her in-laws. And, to undermine the value of the contribution they did make, she notes that the pitiful present has already been lost. The only remaining jewelry still used by the bar mitzvah boy is the gold watch Nurit's mother supplied.

The wish to produce a special event that "everyone will remember" calls for plenty, for overabundance—champagne and whiskey, the most expensive beverages, must be poured "like water." Only through such overabundance can Nurit feel at ease, that nothing can bother her. The fact that people show up to her event, dress up for the night, greet her, and observe and enjoy the delicacies and the expensive beverages confirm that she has succeeded—she is accorded the social acknowledgment she craves. The fear that people will not attend, that she will be exposed as an empty shell, and the relief she feels when they arrive help explain Nurit's passionate urge to invest all her resources in this public ceremony. She is driven to host an event to which people of the community come and "give her respect." When the hall owner and his wife, who are aware of her vulnerable financial and social situation, discreetly offer to shoulder part of the expenses that she has taken on herself, she is grateful.

Even though she declares, "We each ride by our pockets," Nurit stretches her pocket beyond its limit. And the stress shows. She arrives at the hall exhausted but happy. For 13 years she has been preparing for her first event, and the effort bears the fruit she has expected: She reaffirms her connections to people in the local community, takes pride in her achievements, and gains respectability. The event is the epitome of social acknowledgment, in which sadness, happiness, pain, and joy combine.

"Understanding the phenomenon of poverty," writes scholar Yosef Katan, "is anchored in the premise that the economic resources that are available to individuals and families are not the only factor that determines their concrete life circumstances" (2002: 11). Sociologists Sarit Sambol and Orly Benjamin write, "The poverty-stricken working poor single mothers who participated in the study [we conducted] reported a constant feeling of social isolation. Their loneliness is a result of the constant demands of motherhood in circumstances where no alternative care is available as well as by their need to save expenses. The outcome is their systematic absence from social events" (2006: 59).

The link between social isolation and economic deprivation among single mothers has been recorded in a series of studies documenting the shrinking role of the Israeli welfare state (Stier and Levin 2000; Swirsky et al. 2007). Nurit's story validates their findings and makes visible the price paid in the struggle to escape social isolation. However admirable her struggles might seem, the question remains: Is Nurit successful in extracting her children from the same cycle of poverty and dependence she is locked into? In other words, how successful are Adi and Shahaf, Nurit's children, in structuring lives that are not restricted by the boundaries that have defined their mother's struggles?

The Israeli literature that poses this question in more general terms speaks about the process of "intergenerational transference of poverty" (Katan 2002; Salzberger 1995; Shayo and Vaknin 2002). The following section, in which Adi talks with me about her life and her aspirations, broaches these broad questions.

Adi's Story: "An Office of Her Own"

After placing a cup of coffee with milk and two slices of chocolate cake on the table before me, Adi sits erect on the edge of the sofa. She stares at the voice recorder that I have placed on the table between us, and it is obvious that she is enjoying the role of interviewee, one whose every word is being recorded. At 17, Adi is a plump young woman in her tight jeans and short, bright-pink T-shirt. Her brown hair has fashionable bright blonde stripes and is cut just below her jawline. She projects both a sweet childishness and a maturity beyond her years. She looks at me, expecting my direct questions, and answers each question briefly and concisely, as though making sure she provides the "correct" answer each time. I cannot get her to relax. The situation seems scripted: I am the important interviewer, and she is playing the role expected of her vis-à-vis such a personage.

"So tell me, Adi, your mother told me that you're studying for your *bagrut* [final matriculation certificate necessary for college entry] and that you're working hard at it."

"Yes, I'm studying hard and I do what's needed. I'm not in the *Iyuni* [academic] track, though, but in the *Ometz* [literally, 'courage'] classes."

"Ahhh, what is *Ometz*?" I smile, emphasizing my ignorance of the term, allowing her to explain.

"It's like . . . less academic. They help the pupil more in this track. Help one more in preparing for the exams." And then she adds with determination: "I'm doing the real *bagrut*, you see."

"What do you mean 'real'? What, there are 'not real' matriculation exams?"

Adi does not smile at my joke. "No, look. I am in the vocational track in high school, where you are supposed to get a profession and stuff. I'm not in the academic track. So the *Ometz* is a special program that is . . . how to explain it . . . going to . . . to improve us, to give us a better chance."

"And you want this? I mean the matriculation and such. I understand from your mother that you're really serious about it."

"Yeah . . . the truth? Ahhh . . . the truth is I want to succeed. It's on my level. Some girls they went to the *Iyuni* track, but there they don't get any special help. They don't get the extra exercises, the special marathon studies. You know about these marathons? It's, like, in our track, there are marathons twice a week, between 4 and 8 p.m. We do our assigned homework there and we go over the studied material. The students in the academic track get none of this."

I nod in approval, and Adi continues. "I want to finish school, I want to graduate, I want to develop. See? I don't want to be like my mom. What, I'll grow up and have kids . . . and then what? They'll have such a screwed-up mom . . . who doesn't know shit in her life?"

"Aren't you exaggerating a bit? What do you mean screwed-up mother? You really think your mom is screwed-up?"

"Ehhh . . . I . . . what can I tell you? I don't want to say bad things about my mother . . . but . . . still . . . how could I tell you . . . I want . . . I want to *succeed* in my life! To pass my finals, to *succeed in everything*. That's my aspiration."

"I wish you success from the bottom of my heart, Adi. Just tell me something, so, I mean, why . . . why do you think your mother didn't succeed in her life?"

"Because she's . . . what can I tell you? She was wrapped up in something else. She, her life was . . . she was very disturbed. She was . . . she got married young . . . she was maybe 17 when she was already pregnant with Shahaf. No way. No way. I don't want to go the way she went."

"So how will you do it?"

"I'll succeed! I'll put all my effort into it! I'll study. Work good, study good, and then something will come out of me. Me, how can I explain . . . I won't throw my future away!"

"And what about marriage and stuff? I heard you have a boyfriend. Is it true?"

"Of course I have a boyfriend, but I'm not into that . . . marrying young and stuff. Even after we date a few years, we wouldn't marry young like that. I want to go to the army. The army [service] is fun. It's the experience of a lifetime. My mom didn't do that. I don't want to repeat her way."

"I understand. Yes. So you'll go and get drafted into the army . . ."

"For sure. Look, I want her to be proud of me. Shahaf, he's never done anything with himself. He only got up to ninth grade. From there he went on to a boarding school and he left that too. He didn't want to work hard. From the boarding school he went the wrong way and started smoking and messing up. Him, his whole life is playing with beach buggies."

"And you? What will you do?"

"I'll succeed! Where there's a will, there's a way! I'm studying. With the tutors, with everything. And it'll work."

"So you're, like, determined to complete all your finals and all that . . . yes. So, how do you imagine your future?"

"My future? I, first of all, am not staying in Yerucham!" Adi stares at me with a determination I have not seen in her until that moment. When she continues, I feel that she is finally speaking her mind, not reciting what she thinks are the correct answers. She says, "I tell you the truth. You see . . . I see people here who took their finals and got their *bagrut* and all that . . . everything, yes? Everything . . . and I tell you . . . they got nothing out of it. You see them living in Yerucham and they do nothing. No job. Nothing. If you know what's good for you, you leave!"

I am taken aback by this new determination. "Tell me, Adi," I ask her pointedly, "what's wrong with life in Yerucham? Why is it so bad?"

She seems confused at my question. She says, "I don't know what's wrong. Everything is *not right*. It's the people, the fact there is no work."

And then she regains her voice and repeats with passion, "I wouldn't like to see myself in, say, 10, 15 years without a job here. I'd like to have a steady job. I want to be a secretary, something, something . . . *I want to have my own office one day!*"

"So, like, you don't want a cleaning job or a job in a factory?" I try to help her articulate her desires more precisely.

"No way. No way. I don't want to end up like this. I want an office of my own. I'll work hard. I'll try very hard and it'll happen. I know some girls who made it like this. They studied, they served in the army, and today . . . today, they live in Tel Aviv."

"What do they do there?"

"It doesn't matter. It doesn't matter what they do. The point is *they found their future*. I want what's best for me and my kids too." Adi's eyes sparkle. She concludes with a resigned declaration, "*There's nothing here in Yerucham!*"

"But your mother set you up a great home, here. No? Such a well-kept apartment you live in."

"I know. I know," she says slowly, "But . . . a house is not everything!" Adi's voice softens as she adds, "She, my mom, she buys us everything, and she cooks . . . out of this world. Come over, Pnina, one Saturday, you'll see what good food is. Forget about it."

Adi examines me and blurts out, "And what about you? Are you married? Do you have kids?"

"No, I'm not married and yes, I have two kids. Boys. We live in Sde Boker, on the campus."

"What is it like to live in Sde Boker?" Adi inquires.

"I think it's boring. There's nothing there, but my kids love it. They like the school, their friends."

"And did you get a chance to write a book about Sde Boker too?" she asks with a half smile.

"No. Not really. I wrote about my work in Africa. I was there for more than a year and I learned their language and everything. And now I work and do my research here, in Yerucham. But it will take me a long time until I finish writing my book about life in Yerucham."

"You're really writing a book? That's a lot of work," Adi enthuses.

"Yes, it's a lot of work. I'm planning on working for two to three more years before I write this book. And I'm glad I met you. Tell me, what do you say, Adi: Are the young people happy here, in Yerucham? I remember us complaining that we're really bored and there's nothing to do, when I was young, about your age, in Migdal Ha'Emek."

Adi looks at me with new interest. I am becoming more real to her as I mention my own experience in a development town not very different from the one she lives in. I say my life in Sde Boker is boring, which is not at all how she has imagined life in a middle-class community. When she speaks again, her response is less formal, less rehearsed.

"It's actually not too bad here. There is a pub, we take walks. I have a boyfriend. Not too bad." Then she giggles and recalls, "But you see, my cousin, she came from Tel Aviv and she's like, 'What's all this walking up and down the main road? Don't you have anything better to do here?' But I like it. Seeing friends. Talking. And the drugs they tell you about here in Yerucham? It's a matter of what you want. I'll tell you this: If you're looking for it, you'll go for it. It's the simplest thing. It's not like the people are a bad influence. You want it? You'll go for it. It doesn't bother me! I never touch this stuff. And . . . I have a lot of family here. I just came back from my aunt's house. I have an aunt who's an art teacher. I'm really attached to her family. I'm in their house a lot. Their house is like my house."

"That's interesting. Did you think about it, Adi, how is it that your aunt, the teacher, was able to study and your mother was not?"

"I don't know. She studied. She has patience for kids. Her husband owns a trucking company. Of course she succeeded. I know that she's even still studying. Every Tuesday she's heading off to some college."

"So do you want to be like her?"

"Not exactly like her," Adi says disinterestedly. She starts pressing buttons on her mobile phone. "Me, I don't have the patience for kids. But I want to succeed. I don't know in what." Suddenly she shakes her head and says, as though to end discussion of this issue, to conclude, "I want to have money. A job with a good income. Maybe, after school I want to work in makeup or something."

"In makeup? You like makeup? I thought you wanted something with an office."

At this Adi becomes openly agitated. She blurts out, "Why? Makeup is such a great profession!"

"And what about the *bagrut*?"

"For sure. For sure. Why not. I'm working on it. Why not."

It is getting rather late. We have been talking for almost three hours. I see that Adi has lost interest in the interview so I stop the recorder. I put the small machine in my bag and thank Adi for the interview, but I do not get up to leave. And it is then, when the recorder is already in my bag, that Adi seems to regain her interest in our conversation. She returns to the issue of the book I am going to write and asks me with real interest, "How do you find the patience? To write a whole book like that? Me? Books? I look at them, I can't take it. It bores me to death."

This direct, unexpected confession surprises me. After a whole evening in which she has repeated the mantra "I'll work hard, I'll study well, I'll succeed," Adi reveals herself as a young person for whom the world of books and studies is repulsive, a boring world, unpleasant and foreign.

Throughout the interview, Adi moves between two narratives that she is not able to reconcile. Only in an after-the-interview moment of candor does she try to make sense of these disjointed, somewhat contradictory narratives. She seems enchanted by the middle-class narrative she must have heard from her teachers, who suggest that study, academic scholarship, and hard work are the basis for a successful life. Adi reproduces this logic during the first part of the interview, when she tries to respond "properly," to give me expected answers. She identifies me as a "quality woman" and assumes I share her teachers' social milieu.

But Adi is left with the need to define, for herself, the meaning of this promised success. Success, as she understands it, means a job in an office, which has more status and pays better than a job as a cleaner or a factory worker. Adi is not quite clear what one does in this office. She assumes she'll be "a clerk, a secretary" and not someone who cleans the office or serves food. Success in this academic track produces, she guesses, "someone who knows shit."

There are two serious problems with the academic model of success that Adi references during the course of the interview. First, adopting it requires her to reject what her mother stands for. From the perspective of this model, her mother's life is a complete failure, and Adi is adamant that she will do everything she can to avoid repeating her mother's life course. But the initial articulation of disrespect for her mother makes her uncomfortable, because at a deeper level, Adi does seem to have a lot of appreciation for the warmth and support her mother provides, and she admires her mother's homemaking skills, particularly her cooking. And there is also a nagging doubt about whether the "study and you will succeed" scenario can actually deliver on its promise when put to the test in the everyday reality of Yerucham. Adi's doubt draws on her firsthand knowledge of people who have made it in academic terms, people with "diplomas in their hand" who stayed in Yerucham but were not able to break into the local circle of limited opportunities. These people end up, just like those without diplomas, doing cleaning or factory work. Adi's street smarts have taught her that the key to success is to escape the local arena, to disengage from Yerucham and its social stigma and limited opportunities. She sees the young women who have left Yerucham for life in Tel Aviv as alternative models of success. But then again, success in the big city is not a result of academic achievements. It does not matter what these young women are doing in the big city, Adi tells me. They are successful merely by having escaped the local arena.

But there is another narrative, a third option, albeit one Adi articulates less clearly. It is a hidden, denied, silenced narrative. This third option (academic "study hard" being the first and "leave town" the second) emerges only when I share with Adi my own negative personal experience of life in a development town and tell her that, when I was her age, I was bored with my life in Migdal Ha'Emek. Upon hearing my story, Adi seems to claim that she actually *likes* her life in Yerucham—the family, the friends, the walking up and down the main street, and the steady boyfriend. She rejects outsiders' perceptions (exemplified by the comments of the cousin from Tel Aviv) of life in her hometown and is able to connect to her warm feeling of contentment, safety, and love for the community. Yerucham becomes a positive space, a home where she can see herself building a future family, rather than a negative space she must escape in order to succeed. Success is redefined in this third narrative. In the future afforded by this option, there is no need to move to a big city to make a life of meaning and emotional security. In this scenario, building a secure home for your children and passing the time among friends as you walk up and down the main street are not necessarily perceived as failure. In this scenario Adi regains her respect for her mother even if she makes a clear decision not to repeat her mother's mistakes.

Why does Adi need to silence this third scenario, to reject it as illegitimate? Why does she begin the interview by voicing the "I will study hard and I will succeed" logic before she connects to this other, hidden option for a possible desired future? The dynamics of our long interview suggest that Adi is never completely convinced of the premise behind projects such as *Ometz*: success will follow if she just manages to pass her final exams and get her diploma. Even if she were tempted by the promise that a diploma will indeed enable her to escape blue-collar jobs and open a path to her dream of white-collar office work, Adi knows all too well that the local Yerucham economy has few white-collar positions, even for those with academic credentials. The rare story of her art-teacher aunt, who travels once a week to "some college," does not inspire Adi, who seems convinced her escape from blue-collar jobs lies, at best, in becoming a professional makeup artist.

This stunted professional aspiration reflects a solid, realist evaluation of the local economy that is not unique to Adi. I heard similar views from the women who attended a beauty arts class. The women paid almost a month's salary for this private course, hoping that it would provide them with skills that might earn them some income in the bleak local economy. Some of the women had a *bagrut*; others had vocational certificates qualifying them as dental assistants, kindergarten aides, or secretaries. They could not secure paying jobs in the small town's faltering economy. They took the beauty arts class, they told me, hoping to acquire another set of marketable skills. Yet, as Rachel, whom we will meet in chapter 3, asks, "How many hairdressers can a small community like Yerucham support?"

What these women suggest, and what 17-year-old Adi makes clear once she shades the "correct answers" during the interview, is that the liberal idea of "just get your academic *bagrut* and you will succeed" scenario has limited resonance in the local economy of Yerucham. Adi questions the premise that the hard work required to earn a high school diploma or even a *bagrut* certificate will set her on a path toward social mobility, will prepare her to "sit in an office" rather than clean one. Is Adi's analysis more accurate than the liberal modernist scenario stubbornly pushed by social reformers who invest money and resources (often for only a short while) to encourage Adi and her classmates to pass their final exams? Or maybe the meaning of success for Adi and other third-generation immigrant children like her has yet to be defined.

Adi's story raises troubling questions about the liberal model that locates the only path to social mobility in formal education. Adi states outright (and the story of Gila, explored in chapter 7, makes even more explicit): The few young people in Yerucham who manage to gain the required formal educational credentials are forced, or simply opt, to leave their home community. Adi's words, when listened to closely, reveal an alternative route, one in which Yerucham might become a desired space where one can build a home and a family. In such a community the negative experiences that have shaped Nurit's life can be avoided. Adi is clear that she does not wish to be married at a young age, divorce early, and depend on welfare. She declares her strong conviction that she can avoid drug addiction, the path her father fell into. She expresses a desire to serve in the Israeli army because she believes that doing so will expose her to new and exciting experiences that will make her feel part of the Israeli mainstream. She wants a stable job and a local communal life.

When I meet Adi again, 10 years later, she tells me she is proud to be included in this book. She reports that she did indeed serve in the army and that she delayed her marriage until she was 24. But, she admits sadly, her youthful dream of having an office of her own has not materialized. She tried to get better-paying jobs in Eilat, the southern tourist town, but, unable to do so, returned home. She now works at a local factory. She and her husband live in public housing in Yerucham.

Adi's story does not offer systematic documentation of the reality of life for the third generation in Yerucham, but it does open a space for rethinking the larger received wisdom about the social mobility of the sons and daughters of the women I focus on in this book. What her story asks us to do is problematize the modernist narrative that would "save" Israeli development towns by denying the validity of life lived in these marginalized spaces. In the following chapters, rather than focus on how local residents should be "rescued" from their multiply marginalized communities, I shed light on how specific women and their menfolk deal with the multiple constraints imposed on them, how they actually live within the concrete boxes of their lives.

2

EFRAT AND HER DAUGHTERS

The Road to Religious Observance

EINAT, A PLUMPISH woman in her early twenties, arrives at my office from her regular cleaning job in a building at the other end of campus. She enters the room without knocking, grinning from ear to ear: "Rinat told me you're doing a study on people who become religious. Listen, don't waste your time. First thing, you've got to talk to my mother, who got *really* religious! She covers her hair and everything. And afterward, to my downstairs neighbor."

I am caught off guard by Einat's unsolicited, wholehearted invitation and her eagerness to accept me as a "researcher." Is it really that simple? Why have I been so worried? I have been toying with the idea of embarking on a study of Mizrahi women from Yerucham for many months, but I have not yet had the courage to take the first step. I have not dared to present myself as a researcher to the women I have been meeting with daily in my office, women who have been informally sharing the details of their lives with me. I have been afraid that once I identify myself as a "researcher" who is interested "in them," I will be boxing them into the category of the weak, marginalized Other. I have been deeply concerned that despite my own Mizrahi background, they will feel like objects of an anthropological gaze that proclaims their multiply marginalized position as blue-collar Mizrahi residents of one of the most stigmatized development towns in Israel. Aware of the complex politics of ethnographic research, I expect them to flatly refuse to take part in my study.

From Einat's enthusiastic reaction I learn that it is my stated interest in documenting the process of *hit'hazkut* (literally, "strengthening"; used colloquially to mean becoming more religiously observant) that makes the difference. Most of the women I get to know in Yerucham, including Einat, feel pride and a sense of self-worth connected to their *hit'hazkut*, making my wish to document the experience acceptable in their eyes. My desire to record the strength and empowerment—as opposed to the marginalization and stigma—of living in Yerucham is rendered legitimate and thus welcome.

Einat displays considerable know-how in organizing my first interview with her mother. "You're going to record the interview with my mother, right?" she half-asks, half-states. And when I confirm that I would in fact be happy to record the planned interview, she declares, "Listen, it's OK. No problem. But there's no way my mother can come here, to Sde Boker. You should come to my place. I'll cook you a meal, my mother will come, and you'll interview her there. OK?" We agree that I will come the following Wednesday evening.

At the appointed time, Einat greets me at the doorway of her tiny apartment. The place sparkles. A table heaped with food awaits us in the eating area. She has prepared homemade chicken nuggets, a huge salad, and Israeli-style home fries. Soft drinks and snacks are set out on the living room table. She has sent the children on an outing with her younger sister so that they will not disturb us. It is obvious that my visit has been planned carefully. A young woman in her early twenties, whom Einat introduces as her "downstairs neighbor," has been invited to join us. Einat tells me excitedly, "She also has an interesting story to tell about her own transformation. Her parents are from Bnei Brak [a city known for its largely ultra-Orthodox population] and she married here in Yerucham." But we have little time to hear the details of the neighbor's story because Efrat, Einat's mother, arrives a few minutes later. After more introductions and greetings we are invited to eat.

During the meal we make small talk, which I do not record. I notice that Efrat's language is more "proper" than her daughter's. Her pronunciation is precise, and she makes a point of using correct Hebrew grammar. I learn that Efrat runs a private kindergarten from her home. Before starting her business, she had worked with children for many years at a NA'AMAT day care center. Efrat is dressed with understated elegance. A linen dress in a light olive color covers an almost boyish figure, and her hair is carefully hidden under a stylish velvet hat in a darker shade of green. Efrat's low-key style only underscores the eye-catching appearance of her daughter. Every morning, Einat comes to her campus cleaning job heavily made-up: bold blue eye shadow and strong red lipstick. Her long curly hair is bleached to a bright blonde. Her vivid hair and makeup, proud expressions of her individuality, emphasize the drabness of her blue work uniform. When she takes off her smock at the end of the day, she reveals tight, stylish, colorful street clothes that show off her full figure to best advantage. But today, in her home, Einat is wearing a comfortable dark pink sweat suit, and her long hair is gathered into a bun held in place with a simple black string.

After the meal, we move into the small living room and finally get down to the real point of the evening, the event we are all so excited about—the recorded interview.

Efrat's *Hit'hazkut*

"You Can't Say 'Became Observant' Because I Was Always Religious"

"So," I smile at Efrat, who is sitting opposite me, "I understand from Einat that you became religiously observant."

Efrat immediately corrects me, stating carefully, "I . . . did . . . not . . . become . . . observant. You can't say 'became observant,' because I was always religious."

"Ahhh! So what would be a better way to say it, to refer to the process you experienced? *Hit'hazkut*, right?"

Efrat nods her head.

"OK. So let's talk about that. I'd like you to tell me about your *hit'hazkut*."

Efrat takes a deep breath. She has anticipated the question, prepared for it, and is happy to tell her story. She is particularly proud that her remarks are being recorded. Smiling pleasantly, she begins.

"So, from a young age, I attended a religious boarding school. Very religious. I chose to go there. The boarding school was in Hadera. Today, it no longer exists; this was something like 30 years ago. So they came to my parents' house and asked if my parents consented to my living away from home. So I . . . well . . . it sounded good to me. I said they should let me give it a try. My parents agreed, because they knew it was a religious school and that the girls studied separately, so this was already a good sign. Because, you see, leaving home and being together with boys . . . it would have been rough. We had a dorm mother who was conscientious and hardworking, but it was still hard to leave home at age 12, and say good-bye to your mother at a point when you really needed her advice. But all in all, it was fun there. I was there for three years. I returned home every second weekend. We learned sewing along with the standard high school subjects. We studied everything. We learned a lot of religion, and it stayed with me, that foundation of maintaining a certain feeling in the home. Of being a believing person."

"Wait a minute. Your family, they weren't 'believers'?"

"My parents always kept Shabbat [the Jewish Sabbath], but they weren't—how should I put this—they were *masorati* [literally, 'traditional']. I'm more . . . um . . . more of a believer than they are."

Already, in her introductory remarks, Efrat locates herself on a scale with her *masorati* parents[1] at one end and the directors of the distant school she was sent to as a young girl at the other. She makes clear that this continuum has a hierarchical dimension that positions her parents on a lower level of religious commitment than those who advocate a rich religious curriculum. In her view, moving along the continuum in the direction of the educators had transformed her into more of "a believer" than her parents had ever been. It was the boarding school staff who instilled in her the foundations for being "a believer." But the process of diverging from her parents' religious practices was not easy, and Efrat paid a considerable price for this transformation. While at school, she was cut off from a loving mother and from the warmth and protection of her family, whom she saw at home only every two weeks.

Efrat does not claim that she is more knowledgeable today as a result of her education ("We learned a lot of religion") or that the training at the school equipped her with skills to help her progress in life. Classes in sewing and what she refers to as "standard high school" subjects did not turn her into a seamstress or provide her with the tools needed to enter the broader workforce. Paradoxically, what she was left with after three long and difficult years of separation from her home was, in fact, the "foundation of maintaining *a certain feeling in the home*." The woman who began her remarks by stating that she had always been religious came home from the religious school with a *different* definition of what, for her, constituted religiosity. The religiosity had always been there, rooted in her *masorati* home. What changed was the strengthening of her faith (*emunah*): "I'm more of a believer [*ma'amina*] than [my parents] are."

This emphasis on the centrality and power of religious belief, rather than on the observance or nonobservance of specific religious practices, is a recurring theme in Efrat's and other religiously strengthened women's accounts of their process of *hit'hazkut*. Efrat made the distinction between belief and religious praxis even more explicit upon her return home following her years at the boarding school. Once back in Yerucham, she gradually discarded the modest style of dress she had worn during her time at the school, and she began dating a young Moroccan man whom she describes as someone who "didn't keep Shabbat, didn't keep anything." She explains her decision to go back to wearing immodest clothing as a natural need to conform: "Since I'd left the boarding school, I needed to fit back into Yerucham. You can't be different."

Einat brings out an old photo album. "Look at what a 'hottie' my mother was back then," she laughs delightedly. In the photos the young Efrat is dressed in a fashionable miniskirt, her black hair cut in a boyish style. In other pictures she is seen dancing at a family wedding, her hair streaked, a stylish, sleeveless minidress revealing her slender figure. In one of the photos Efrat smiles into the camera as she embraces a short, dark young man. This is her husband, Moshe. As we look at the pictures, Efrat comments, "Look, when I met my husband back then, he was . . . a little . . . he wasn't religious at all. We met at a friend's house. He was only passing through for a day. He's from Tel Aviv, from Bat Yam [an economically depressed, then largely Mizrahi town on the outskirts of southern Tel Aviv]. Since he wasn't religious, I abandoned religion a little. But at the same time, there were things that were ingrained in me. It's not like I gave them up. Like Shabbat, for instance, or a warming plate [used instead of lighting a stove]. And I didn't turn on lights in the house."

Efrat's reintegration into life in Yerucham involved adopting the accepted style of dress in her hometown. Under the influence of her nonreligious husband, she "abandoned religion a little." Efrat's terminology makes fine distinctions regarding religiosity—the nonreligious husband, her partial abandonment of religion, the boarding school where she learned "a lot of religion." Her heavily religious rhetoric aside, her self-definition as a religious person fundamentally derives from the fact that she is the daughter of *masorati* parents.

Efrat's narrative suggests that although *masorati* Jews might not dress modestly, they are truly and deeply religious. By contrast, those who "learn a lot of religion" and keep the Jewish religious laws more stringently than *masorati* Jews are not necessarily more committed believers. Efrat makes clear here the distinction between those who declare their religiosity in an overt fashion (e.g., keeping a strict, modest dress code) and those, like herself, who have an unshakable deep faith (*emunah*) that does not need to be demonstrated by outward practices.

But differences in dress codes are not as meaningless as Efrat suggests. In fact, when Einat recommended her mother to me as an ideal interviewee for my study of *hit'hazkut*, she emphasized her mother's practice of covering her hair as a sign of her deep commitment to her *hit'hazkut* process. As we will see, Efrat's five daughters mark their respective places on the *hit'hazkut* spectrum by adopting different styles of dress. One insists on wearing a hat but without tucking all her hair inside it; another makes a point of wearing clothes that cover her knees and elbows but do not completely conceal her figure. The public statement a woman makes through the dress code she adopts builds a set of expectations about "proper" behavior. Thus, for example, the woman who covers all of her hair with a hat declares that she has attained a higher moral position than women who dress the "regular" way. This woman is then obliged to meet a set of expectations that fit her declared moral standard, such as avoidance of gossip or idle chatter.

In her story Efrat distinguishes between two periods in her *hit'hazkut*. When she speaks of the early stages of the process by which she became "more of a believer" than her *masorati* parents, she refers to her boarding school days. But when she describes the process that led her to adopt her current modest style of dress, she refers to a much later turning point in her life: the birth of her youngest child, Omer. Omer is the only son in a family of five daughters. Efrat's longing for a son began immediately after the birth of her first daughter, Vered.

> After Vered was born, I became pregnant again. I was around my fifth month, and one night, what did I dream? That I saw my uncle. He came toward me wearing a white robe, with a sack in his hand, and I ran to him saying, "Uncle, I've been waiting for you." I kissed him. And as I was kissing him, I saw that it was not him but a rabbi with a gray beard, dressed

head to toe in white. And he says to me, this rabbi, "Why did you kiss me? I don't kiss women." And I say to him, "I don't know what happened to me. I was kissing my uncle, and suddenly . . ." Then he says to me, "Take my hand so I can help you." And I hold his hand, and suddenly it's my uncle again. So he, my uncle, two tears fall from his eyes, and he says to me, "I was supposed to come to you, but I'm not coming." I woke up frightened, and said, "What's happening to me?" I ran to my mother's, and I saw that I'm bleeding. That's it. Two days later, I miscarried. Again and again—four boys. Each time, I cried, and each time, I had dreams.

Now, another time, I was pregnant again and I see myself standing on a high cliff, and I see an abyss and a kind of a river and my baby falls into the water and he's caught in an undertow, spinning around . . . and I scream, "God, save him!" And then I see a rabbi next to me and he says, "You have nothing to worry about. You're going to be all right, with God's help." And I ask him, "Are you going to save him?" And he says to me, "Tell me, your husband, does he still smoke on Shabbat?"

Efrat experienced the loss of a male fetus four times. The miscarriages frightened and saddened her, and she gradually came to the conclusion that they were connected in some way with religious observance. She knew she was not to blame. Her failure to give birth to a male child was not linked to any misconduct on her part. Her dreams confirmed this self-knowledge. The graybearded figures who appeared in them did not point to failings in Efrat's life. They did not call on her to change the way she observed Shabbat or question her status as a worthy woman. They pointed to the weakest link in her life—her husband, who smoked.

When asked to recount the later stages of her *hit'hazkut*, Efrat focuses on the main challenge she faced during that time: her struggle to change her husband from someone who has explicitly and provocatively declared himself to be nonreligious into a person who takes on religious practices. Efrat does not recount the stages of her own transformation. She simply insists that she has always been a believer. Her *hit'hazkut* is not centered on personal introspection, on her own individual transformation, but rather on the familial space, within which power relations between spouses play out. Not all women manage to include their partners and their families in their attempt at *hit'hazkut*

(Rachel, whom we will meet in chapter 3, is such a woman). The failure to include the husband in the process often leads to marital breakdown. A married woman cannot undertake the process alone, acting on a personal, individual decision. She needs to transform her husband as well to make her own *hit'hazkut* into something that has meaning and power. Efrat's *hit'hazkut* is therefore not merely a personal transformative experience but a restructuring of power relations in the family. Her dreams provide her with a new and influential position of power in the family dynamic. As she puts it, "I would say to my husband, 'Look at these dreams I'm having, about your smoking, and about what's happening to me. Maybe we're getting this from heaven . . . and you're not taking it seriously.'"

The *hit'hazkut* process, as we will see, unfolds as a struggle within the family structure and provides Efrat with a legitimate foundation for her growing influence as a wife and mother.

Hit'hazkut That Engulfs the Whole Family

When the children were born, my husband and I had such a separation of powers. On Friday nights, he was in one room and I was in another room with the kids. But it never bothered me. I said to him, "I want to raise my children my way. You can live however you want . . . to each his own." Because, to tell the truth, it didn't bother me. So, on Friday nights [at the onset of Shabbat], I would ask him, "You want to watch TV? Do it alone! Inside the room." And I would lock the door behind me, and he would watch television in the living room by himself.

Let me tell you, today I say that everything comes from above, from heaven. Believe me, my husband, he's something else! A proper project! And that's what I did, little by little, without pressuring him. Today, he does everything. I think back to the days when . . . he didn't keep Shabbat, and, yes, he smoked and . . . he didn't keep anything. Not a thing! I remember those days when I had to wake him up for work: "Moshe, Moshe, Moshe!" Five in the morning I would start, so that he'd make it to his bus at twenty to seven—an hour and a half! And then he'd get up at the last second, shoelaces untied, his belt in his hands [she stretches out the last syllables, emphasizing how much effort it took him]. You know what it's like? He would make it out the door by the skin of his teeth to catch his bus.

And now [Efrat relaxes, pauses for a moment, softens her tone], now that he's gotten stronger religiously . . . you should see how he wakes up, at 5 a.m., takes pita breads out of the freezer and puts them in the sun to warm up. He boils the water in the kettle. He says his morning prayers. He drinks his coffee. He arranges everything on the shelf so that it will be ready for me and the children when we get up. It lifts your spirit.

"So how did it happen? When did he begin keeping Shabbat?"

"The truth? It wasn't easy. It's hard when the husband doesn't keep things and the wife does. We would go to my mother's on Shabbat, and sometimes it would rain. And I'm holding on to the kids, and he's going by car. And I'm on foot with little babies, and he's screaming at me, 'C'mon, you moron! Put the kids in the car! It's raining! They're getting wet!' And I'd say to him, 'It's nothing. You go the way you want, and me and my children how I want.' I didn't give in. I was very strong when it came to this. I didn't agree to have them follow in his footsteps."

With these words, Efrat makes a connection between *hit'hazkut* in religious terms (taking on such practices as wearing a *kippah* [the Yiddish term is "yarmulke," a head covering for Jewish males] or no longer desecrating the Sabbath) and an overall personal strengthening of the husband as an individual, a husband, and a functioning father. The processes are intertwined. When her husband stops violating the Jewish code of behavior on the Sabbath, Efrat suggests, he becomes stronger in other aspects of his life, aspects not directly related to religious practice. He wakes up in the morning more easily, and thus his workday starts off better. He is able to participate in the care of the children and to show them love and attention (defrosting the pitas for them), in contrast to his passivity and haplessness in the mornings before his *hit'hazkut*. Efrat believes that the process of becoming stronger religiously "lifts the spirit." It makes a person more relaxed and frees time not only for once-neglected family needs but also for prayer. Efrat, who is concerned about the influence of her weak, nonreligious husband on her children ("I didn't agree to have them follow in his footsteps") enables him to create a new space in which he is strong enough to do his share in raising the children. Her husband changes from someone who uses offensive language (calling his wife a moron) and is unwilling to give up his comforts (riding in a car while his wife walks in the rain with the children) to someone who is part of a functioning family.

Efrat does not waver. She is certain that hers is the right path. Her connection with a religiosity rooted in Sabbath observance and modest dress affords her great power in the struggle with her husband. "I was very strong when it came to this," she admits. Although the process is not easy, Efrat demonstrates tenacity and determination. She insists on raising "her" children her way, while Moshe is adamant about driving and watching television on the Sabbath. In Efrat's narrative belief confers strength on the believer. It can overcome the personal weakness that has prevented her husband from waking up as he should in the morning, a weakness that has marginalized him in his own family. Efrat contrasts the moral authority and determination that her belief has bequeathed her to the feebleness of her husband, who has been unable to overcome his destructive smoking habit. Efrat recounts: "I'd say to him: 'Do anything, don't pray . . . whatever you want . . . but this smoking . . . Because the truth is, it's also for your health.' He was like a chimney. He smoked a lot in those days. I'd say to him, 'At least on Shabbat. One day a week, for heaven's sake!'"

According to Efrat, her husband is a true believer, but he needed to overcome his personal weakness to articulate his faith. She relates: "And he'd say to me, 'The reason I do it [smoke] is not because I don't believe in God. It's just hard for me. Understand, it's like when you say to a drug addict, "Stop with the drugs!" That's how it is with the cigarettes. I can't.'"

Efrat's husband draws the same distinction that Efrat does between *emunah* as a deep personal faith and the act of upholding religious practice. "It's not because I don't believe," he apologizes. From this exchange, as depicted by Efrat, it is obvious that her husband struggles not only with his own willpower but also with Efrat's growing authority in the family. When he finally manages to quit smoking, he makes a point of doing it outside the bounds of his relationship with his wife. As Efrat recounts:

> And then he was called up for reserve duty, and he met very religious people there. Very religious. And they said to him, "Come with us to synagogue," and he said, "No, I don't want to come. It's not that I don't respect

the place, God forbid, but it doesn't seem right to me to go and pray and then smoke on Shabbat. I prefer not to go." A couple of weeks later, he calls me up and tells me, "Look, I'm not coming home this Shabbat." I say to him, "Why?" "They didn't give me time off," he says. Understand, Pnina, he did have time off. Anyway, that Shabbat, he said, "Screw it!" He went to synagogue with his friends, grabbed the package of cigarettes and tore it up: "Even if I wanted a cigarette, I won't find one." He went with them, prayed, came back, went to sleep, and the whole Shabbat went by. Another Shabbat, he didn't come home. And another Shabbat. On the fourth Shabbat, he came home. I said to him, "What, so much time without a break?" He tells me, "No, I preferred to stay there, and . . . thank God, I haven't smoked in weeks." I was so happy! And he kept it up for a few months.

The "strengthening" (mit'hazek) husband is able to quit smoking when he is separated from family in a masculine space—away on reserve duty. Not only is this a male-centered space that lies outside the sphere of marital power struggles (and Moshe insists on not returning home during the entire period he struggles to quit smoking) but it is also a national space. Thus Moshe's critical act of hit'hazkut (at least from his wife's perspective) links his growing religiosity with his desire to be part of the community of men doing reserve duty. The difficult process of freeing himself from his smoking habit makes him stronger both as a husband and father and as a citizen. Efrat has no doubt that his efforts at hit'hazkut will be rewarded. She informs her husband that the message of yet another dream is decisive—she will give birth to a boy.

"And listen to what happened! I wasn't pregnant or anything. And I had this dream that I'm at the gravesite of the Baba Sali [a revered Moroccan rabbi and kabbalist], and there's a table set with all kinds of delicacies. And I see him, my uncle, among the crowd. And I run over to him and say, 'Do you know me?' He tells me, 'Yes.' And I ask him, 'Do you remember that I always wished for you to come to me?' And he says, 'Yes.' 'And are you coming to me?' And he says, 'In the merit of this holy gravesite, I am coming to you this time.' And I say to him, 'Really?' And I am filled with joy, and then I wake up."

Efrat admits that by this time she is beginning to doubt the message emanating from her dreams.

"The truth is, I didn't believe it so much. I said: Thank God, I have five daughters! If this is my lot in life, I'm grateful to God! There are those who don't even have daughters. Or sons. I thank God that at least I have daughters. And daughters are a good thing. A son, you need only one or two, not more. And then I got up and said to my husband, 'This month, I'm getting pregnant.' And he said to me, 'How do you know?' A month went by. My period was late. I did a urine test. They told me it was positive."

Efrat is acting from a position of strength and is therefore not worried about making prophetic statements to her husband. His reaction reflects her growing power in their relationship. When they receive the results of the pregnancy test and it turns out that she is right, her husband says, "Wow, I'm starting to be afraid of you!"

Efrat recounts their conversation with delight. "I said to him, 'It's a boy. No matter what anyone says.' And he said, 'How do you know?' I answered, 'You'll see.'"

And, she sums up, "I didn't want to do any ultrasounds. Nothing. And I knew, this time for sure it's a boy. And then my son, Omer, was born. And my husband, he got so much stronger—stopped smoking, began saying the daily prayers. Only a *kippah*, he wasn't yet willing to wear outside. [He'd wear one] only on Shabbat."

Efrat's process of *hit'hazkut* provides her with a power base in the family. She is the engine that drives the entire family toward a specific lifestyle. After years of accepting her husband's obvious lack of religiosity, she leads him to adopt the religious practices that she has maintained separately from him, on the basis of which she has brought up "her" children. The turning point in this struggle within the family unit comes when she is granted her heart's desire and gives birth to a son. The power base that Efrat develops is feminine. She cannot prevent her husband from driving or watching TV on Shabbat. But as a mother entrusted with the education of the children, she can insist that they walk with her in the rain and not desecrate the Sabbath by riding in a car with their father. Her husband makes his decision to become stronger religiously after long and patient encouragement on her part. And as a result, he is always one step behind her; while he still feels uncomfortable wearing a *kippah*, she has already started covering her hair—a public statement of her devoutness.

Moshe is not a man of many words. When I ask him on one of my visits to their home about the process he has undergone, he states simply, "It wasn't easy," adding, "I'm still getting stronger all the time."

Hit'hazkut as an Ongoing Process

Moshe's statement that he is still getting stronger underscores that *hit'hazkut* is not an abrupt transition but an ongoing process that must be embraced, cultivated, and sustained. *Hit'hazkut* is a lengthy form of personal growth that must be experienced individually. It cannot be rushed. When I ask Efrat's eldest daughter, Vered, if she is getting stronger religiously, she responds, "I'm taking it very slowly. Not overdoing it." In her judgment, people who overdo it—those who make a public statement that they have gotten stronger by taking on new practices such as donning a black and white outfit or a large felt hat—tend to crash quickly. Vered has heard many stories of women who tuck their hair under embroidered hats and of men who appear in public with black *kippot* and even *peyot* (sidelocks) but are unable to maintain the lifestyle expected of them and rapidly fall back into their old ways.

The varied paths to *hit'hazkut* taken by Efrat's five daughters substantiate Vered's observation. Their stories speak to the individual ways they have transformed their respective family practices and forged new patterns of friendship, employment, and leisure.

Intergenerational *Hit'hazkut*: Efrat and Her Daughters

The first interview I record in Einat's home leads to many more encounters with Efrat and her family. At these subsequent meetings I do not record our conversations. I drop by Efrat's home for unscheduled visits and am always welcomed with open arms. As I grow increasingly familiar with Efrat and her daughters' daily lives, Efrat also invites me to join her at special evening classes on religious topics, which she attends regularly. (I discuss my impressions of these classes later in this chapter.)

I begin my examination of the processes unfolding in the lives of Efrat's five daughters with the narrative of the youngest daughter, Rakefet. A shy girl of 13 when I first meet her, Rakefet wears long skirts and long-sleeved shirts, as one would expect of a student at a *haredi* (ultra-Orthodox) girls' school. At one of our early meetings, while I am waiting for Efrat to join me to attend a religion class, Rakefet shows me a certificate of academic excellence that she has received from her school. A few days later, however, she is less enthusiastic about her studies. She tells me that despite her success at the ultra-Orthodox school, she has decided to continue her high school education at the less Orthodox school of the Zionist religious movement, located in Dimona (a larger development town about 30 kilometers from Yerucham). At the *haredi* school in Yerucham, she complains, the "Sephardi" students are taught "Ashkenazi" customs, even if the teacher herself is "Sephardi." The teachers at the school also pressure the girls to continue their studies at a boarding school in Bnei Brak, a city in central Israel known for its ultra-Orthodox population. Rakefet refuses, but several of her friends transfer there.

I am impressed by this young girl's determination, wondering privately what her parents have to say about her decision.

"Why did you refuse to continue your studies in Bnei Brak?" I ask.

"Why should I go to a *haredi* school?" Rakefet responds. "I'm like my mother. I'm not *haredi*."

"You're not *haredi*," I repeat. "So, what are you?"

"I'm just a regular religious person [*datiya*], like my mother," Rakefet says firmly.

Rakefet's choice to define herself using her mother's terms, not those imposed on her by her teachers at the *haredi* school, and her open resentment that only Ashkenazi (European Jewish) and not Sephardi (North African and Asian Jewish) practices are taught and legitimized there highlight the ability of each of Efrat's daughters to choose her own path. In fact, the experiences that are shaping Rakefet's religious identity parallel those that influenced her mother 30 years earlier. Both Efrat and Rakefet have firsthand knowledge and are keenly aware of the differences between the religious practices of their Mizrahi home and those imposed in schools, where the emphasis is on religious studies and more stringent behavior and dress codes than those accepted in their family. Although Rakefet's school is located in Yerucham and she can continue to live at home, the disparity between the school and her family setting is similar to that experienced by Efrat as a boarding-school student. Rakefet withstands the pressure exerted on her to transfer to the Bnei Brak high school, perhaps because her mother provides the kind of positive role model that she herself had been denied a generation earlier. Efrat's immigrant *masorati* family offered little resistance to her attending the distant school where she was sent to study "a lot of religion." It is also critical that, at the time, Efrat had no option for continuing her high school education locally. Rakefet is able to resist the pressure of her teachers because her mother's *hit'hazkut* and her own pride in being *datiya* provide her with a viable rationale for doing so. Rakefet's older sister Vered later explains that Rakefet "absorbed religiousness more than my other sisters" because she was born and raised *after* their mother "had already become stronger religiously."

How are we to understand the significance of Efrat's *hit'hazkut*, in light of its influence on her youngest daughter, Rakefet? And why is Rakefet, who is said to have "absorbed the religiousness" of her mother in a deeper fashion than her sisters, sent to an local ultra-Orthodox school, where she feels she is taught in a manner that rejects her Sephardi religiousness?

To begin to answer these questions one must realize that religious education that is built around Mizrahi practices is almost nonexistent in Israel today (Leon 2009; Yadgar 2011). The ultra-Orthodox school that Rakefet attends is not unique in foregrounding Ashkenazi religious practices and ethics while aggressively rejecting Mizrahi-style heritage and praxis (Tzabari 2015). Raised in a family of Mizrahi *mit'hazkim*, Rakefet rejects the other locally available educational options—public secular and religious schools—and, in line with her family's enhanced religiosity, opts to attend the ultra-Orthodox elementary school. But when the school pushes its female graduates to continue their studies at an ultra-Orthodox high school in Bnei Brak, Rakefet feels that the disconnect between her family's style of religious identity and the Ashkenazi ultra-Orthodox educational approach is too great. She chooses to attend an all-girl high school (*ulpana*) in neighboring Dimona. Years later, I learn that Rakefet's educational choice prepares her better academically than Yerucham's secular public high school does its graduates.

Rakefet's four older sisters have absorbed their mother's religious commitment in their own ways, and examination of their varied practice sheds light on the individual dynamics of the process of *hit'hazkut* within the family and in the larger community. Each daughter's religiosity represents a different point along a continuum of intensity. Ra'aya, who is three years older than Rafeket, engages in the least intense practice, Vered, the oldest daughter, the most intense.

I meet Ra'aya for the first time at the local beauty parlor, where she works as a shampoo girl. Ra'aya, like Einat, wears stylish clothes that are definitely not modest. She attends the local public secular school, has a boyfriend, and is hoping to join the army when she graduates from high school. Ra'aya states simply, "My mother is the one who's religious, not me."

One day I notice that Ra'aya has changed her eye color. She tells me that her mother bought her a pair of blue-tinted contact lenses on a recent trip to the United States. Efrat also came home with a fancy makeup case for Einat. These items are clearly not associated with a modest, religious way of life, and the fact that Efrat bought them for her daughters demonstrates her acceptance of their chosen lifestyles. Efrat herself does not use elaborate makeup, but she does not impose her standards on her daughters. On the contrary, she openly supports their choices. After Einat is dismissed from her office-cleaning job Efrat relates, "It was all out of jealousy. Einat would always put on elaborate makeup and dress nicely for work, and that's why everyone was jealous of her." Efrat is not merely tolerant of her daughters' varied choices; she is convinced that *hit'hazkut* is an individual process that takes place at one's own pace.

Efrat's second oldest daughter, Chen, a dental assistant and the mother of a two-year-old, makes this tolerant perspective explicit when she describes her own gradual process of *hit'hazkut*. She began covering her hair only after several years of marriage, she tells me, when her son was born. Chen emphasizes that even through she wears a hat, she does not tuck all her hair into it, like her mother, because she does not feel ready for such an outward statement. "I am doing this at my own pace, slowly and gradually," she reflects.

Both Chen and Vered have developed a unique style of dress. Although they make a point of wearing long skirts and shirts that cover their elbows, they display an elegance and stylishness not typical of members of the *haredi* community in the town. The skirts Vered and Chen wear extend to midcalf but are tightly cut and made of thin fabrics that highlight their slender figures. The materials and colors of their shirts point to a personal aesthetic that refuses to accept the more stringent dictates imposed on *haredi* women.[2]

Vered openly proclaims her unwillingness to look like a *haredi* woman, even though she works in the local *haredi* community. The following account underscores the sisters' mutual acceptance of one another's choices, an acceptance that sees each version of the *hit'hazkut* process as the right one for the woman experiencing it. It also illustrates the fluid nature of the Mizrahi approach to *hit'hazkut* and its unorthodox mixing of spaces and practices that might appear at first glance to be contradictory.

Vered's Story

A Beauty Queen's Deep Faith

About a week after the first interview I record in Einat's home, I visit Efrat. She speaks excitedly about her upcoming trip to the United States with her husband to attend Vered's wedding. Vered, she tells me with undisguised pride, had followed her boyfriend to America less than a year earlier. The boyfriend comes from a religious family; however, he had abandoned religious practice over the years and become completely secular. But in America, of all places, as a result of his ties with the *haredi* community in Los Angeles, the future son-in-law has returned to religious observance. Vered, who, according to Efrat, has always been a "strong believer," is happy to go along with her boyfriend's decision to "live a religious life."

Efrat sends Ra'aya to fetch pictures of Vered, and she comes back with several giant albums featuring shots of a beautiful, doe-eyed young woman, tall and slender, with flowing black hair. The photos, taken by a studio photographer, show Vered in the kinds of poses typical of professional models. Dressed in a variety of stylish clothes, she gazes into the lens with a seductive yet impassive look. It turns out that, years before, Vered had been a finalist in a local beauty pageant, and her picture once graced the cover of southern Israel's local weekly *Kol Hanegev*.

To illustrate Vered's strong innate belief, Efrat recounts the following: "You know, when she took part in an evening organized for the finalists in the southern beauty pageant, she didn't want to desecrate Shabbat, since the event took place before sundown Saturday night. So she walked the entire way to the event. And once she got there, she told them to do her hair last so that she wouldn't violate Shabbat."

"Did she wear a bathing suit and model all the outfits like the other contestants?" I ask.

"Of course," Efrat and Ra'aya both answer.

Efrat looks at Ra'aya in puzzlement, trying to understand the underlying meaning of my strange question. Ra'aya, 16 at the time, interprets it for her mother: "Look, mom, some people would say, 'If she's religious, then why would she take part in a beauty pageant?'" But Efrat is unwilling to accept the implied criticism in the question. "What do you mean? She's not some *haredi* woman. She just didn't want to desecrate Shabbat. That is her belief."

Efrat reacts to my questioning of Vered's decision to don a bathing suit and walk down a runway after the Sabbath has ended with a lack of comprehension, and Ra'aya needs to clarify it for her. In the world Efrat and her daughters inhabit, a clear distinction exists between their self-perception as strong believers and behavior *haredi* women define as acceptable. As a strong believer, Vered makes an individual choice to participate in a beauty pageant. She sees nothing wrong with parading in a bathing suit so long as she makes an effort not to desecrate the Sabbath. The strength of Vered's faith is not dependent on outward indicators of religious identity or on what people might say, as implied by my question. In keeping with this same logic, the revealing dress favored by the extroverted Einat and Ra'aya's desire for blue contact lenses are not inconsistent with their respective levels of religiosity. As Ra'aya declares, "Maybe when I get married, I'll dress more modestly. For now, it doesn't feel right."

In the summer of 2002, almost three years after my initial meeting with Einat and Efrat, I meet Vered when she returns to Israel to live. The interview I conduct with her reinforces several key insights I have developed as a result of numerous interviews with *mit'hazkot* women in Yerucham. In addition, it confirms the sisters' mutual acceptance of one another, their recognition that each is at a different point on the continuum of *hit'hazkut*. And it also confirms the observation I make above regarding the distinctions they all draw between faith (*emunah*), religiousness (*datiyut*), and ultra-Orthodoxy (*harediyut*). Vered's story expands beyond the small spaces of Yerucham and Dimona, Bnei Brak and Jerusalem. Her process of *hit'hazkut*, which began and gathered momentum in the United States, encompasses a young Israeli gambler and a community of Mizrahi *mit'hazkim* in Los Angeles. Vered's story offers a broader temporal and spatial perspective on the process of *hit'hazkut*, which is rather different from her mother's experience almost 30 years earlier. Vered's story illustrates the changing circumstances, both historical and spatial, of the *hit'hazkut* process.

Yerucham—Eilat—Los Angeles—Yerucham: Vered's *Hit'hazkut*

I meet Vered in a small, old house located at the edge of the cloistered *haredi* neighborhood in Yerucham. When I comment politely that the house is special, Vered remarks that she prefers it to a larger apartment and that it is her choice to live close to but not quite in the ultra-Orthodox area. Vered is wearing a long dark skirt and a cream-colored blouse. Her hair is gathered under a simple hat, and her face is free of makeup. Her young son, who plays next to us throughout the interview, wears a *kippah* and holds a doll that recites the Shema prayer when he presses a button.

"Your mother told me that you became a lot stronger religiously in the States," I say, opening my interview when the red light of the recorder begins to flash discreetly. I use the verb form *hit'hazkut*, as her mother has instructed me. My words hang in the air for a long moment. And then I add with a smile, "I also saw your photos from when you were in Eilat."

Vered smiles back at me and says softly, "Oh, that's so embarrassing! Forget it. I'm going to cut out those pictures."

"Why? What's wrong with them?"

"Because . . . they say that if you leave pictures like that, it says something about you . . . and better that nothing should show anything bad about you."

"Why? What's so bad? I actually remember that you looked great in those pictures."

"The photos . . . they're immodest . . . really bad. But don't get me wrong. It's not like, when I see someone dressed like that, I think they're a bad person. For instance, let me tell you, I have another sister, Ra'aya, who dresses now like I used to dress then."

"Yes, I know Ra'aya. She worked as a shampoo girl at Yaron's and would come in every day with different colored hair and even with different colored eyes. And of course I don't have to tell you that your sister Einat also doesn't dress so modestly."

"Einat's like that. That's her personality. She's such a pure soul. There's no one like her. She's getting stronger [*mit'hazeket*] with God's help, but she's doing it her way. Slowly. Look, not everyone has to do everything. Everyone has their own personality."

Vered stops speaking. There is a long moment of silence, during which I pose no questions. She is pensive. Then she adds with a soft sigh, "Ra'aya will also get stronger. Wait and see. She'll get married, and you'll see her then. I pray for her . . . that she'll follow the road to *hit'hazkut*."

Vered, like her mother, accepts each of her sisters as individuals who are making their own way, at their own pace, in the process of *hit'hazkut*. She is convinced that the potential to grow stronger religiously has always existed in both Einat and Ra'aya but makes it clear that they should not be rushed into it.[3] She prays for them but is never critical of their current lifestyles.

"Look, I Always Kept Shabbat"

I ask Vered to describe her own process of *hit'hazkut*, and she offers the following narrative.

> Look, I always kept Shabbat. [Laughing] Not Shabbat like I keep it today. For instance, I would go down to the beach on foot. I lived with my husband when he was my boyfriend. He actually came from a religious family and left religion, and I met him [when he was] secular [*hiloni*]. I met him in Dimona. He was my first boyfriend. We went out for about two years, and then moved down to Eilat. He was in a group. He was a dancer. He danced at special events, discos. And in Eilat, he really made a living doing that. He was a real performer. And me, I ran a clothing store called Café. I graduated from high school in the business administration track, and right away I went down to Eilat. Why did we move there? My husband's best friend died in a work accident, and then my husband left everything and moved down to Eilat. I left home at 18 and a half. The only one who left home. I got out of the army in two seconds. No problem. I put on a long skirt [to qualify for a religious exemption], and that was that.
>
> The truth is, I didn't really want to get out of the army, but he didn't want it. He was afraid he'd lose me. And I didn't care that much [about the army], so that was it. We moved down to Eilat. Both of us worked. I earned a lot of money. I was a really good saleswoman. And then the manager left and I replaced her. I was earning really good money. But I didn't save anything. For no good reason. Nothing. Just clothes and more

clothes and perfume. And we didn't have expenses. We slept at the hotel, ate at the hotel. We wasted money on stupid things.

Vered calls attention here to the distinction that her mother and sisters also make between inner faith (*emunah*) and outer manifestations of religiousness (*datiyut*). Her hassle-free release from the army underscores this difference. Vered ridicules the simplistic, outward demonstration of religiosity (the long skirt) that the army accepts as qualifying someone for a religious exemption. She herself knows that she has always been *datiya*, religious, and in her value system, going to the beach on foot on Shabbat rather than wearing a long skirt is a truer expression of her faith.

Vered's assessment of her earlier life does not focus on her immodest dress or her practice of going to the beach on Shabbat but rather on her wasteful lifestyle and lack of purpose. As the interview unfolds, Vered states more than once that today she feels a sense of financial well-being, even though she is earning much less than she did when she managed the clothing store in Eilat. She contrasts the emptiness of her former life as a consumer of perfume and clothes with her present feeling of calm and inner peace.

"I Was More Religious than Him Then"

In an echo of her mother's experience, Vered is clearly the driving force behind the process of *hit'hazkut* in her marriage, even though her husband comes from a religious family. Early in their relationship, the couple lived in largely secular circumstances in Eilat, and Vered asserts that it was she, not he, who insisted on maintaining practices of Sabbath observance there. Vered also emphasizes that she made her move to the United States contingent on the couple keeping the Sabbath in their new location.

> You should understand, Pnina, I was more religious than him then [in Eilat]. And it was really hard. He would do a show [on Shabbat] and then take off for the disco. But I was against this. It was too much. To *walk* to a disco [in order not to drive to it on Shabbat]? So I wouldn't go out on Shabbat. He went out with his friends, and I stayed home.
>
> And then my husband and his friend wanted to go to America. And I was running the store and couldn't leave. I was supposed to fly out about

a month after them. He took a few things and put together some money. We had a laptop, and he sold it. They went to Vegas. His friend really had a lot of money. Together they had forty-something thousand dollars, and [to avoid losing it] they taped it to their legs, like this . . . under their pants. They were really excited. They started to gamble. In the beginning, he won. The hotel saw that they were winning and gave them a complimentary suite, free food—everything. And that's how they [the hotel] got them, until they'd lost the money. My husband went into a real depression. Their money was almost gone and they started to fight. They spent four months in Vegas. They were down to their last hundred dollars. The friend went back to Israel, wiped out. And my husband stayed because another friend of his suggested that he join him in Los Angeles. So he moved to L.A.

I heard all this, what happened to them in Vegas, and I started to have second thoughts. He was calling me every day. He begged me to come. But I said to him: I'm coming only if you start keeping Shabbat. So he promised and I flew over to the States. When I arrived, he rented this place for us. He and his friend worked together cleaning carpets. They bought a machine and did well for themselves. I quickly found work there. At first I was a babysitter, and they loved me. After that, there was this former Israeli woman who had a jewelry business. A girl, from Yerucham actually, told me to go there. And that's how I started to work there. A great place to work. Really great.

Vered agrees to move to the United States on the condition that her partner promises to keep Shabbat. She feels that Sabbath observance will preserve the quality of life of the young man she intends to marry. The money lost to gambling in Las Vegas and the emotional price that her partner pays as a result cause her to hesitate. She is already unsure if she wants to join him and live in the States. His promise to keep the Sabbath reinforces her sense of power, of control over a life that has gotten out of hand.

"Most of Them There Were Moroccans, Sephardim, Who Had Come Back to Religion"

Vered's insistence on keeping the Sabbath is reinforced by the community of Israeli ex-patriates in Los Angeles. Connecting to a community of *hozrim bitshuva* (newly observant), most of them of Moroccan origin, gives added impetus to Vered's *hit'hazkut* and, eventually, her husband's.

We had a good life [in L.A.]. What can I say? We went out a lot. At that point, I was still wearing the clothes I had brought with me from Israel. I came from Israel with suitcases filled with new clothes I had bought for the trip. I spent almost 10,000 shekels on those clothes. They were immodest clothes, the kind that expose your body. But on weekends, when we went to synagogue . . . You see, when you're there [in the United States], you look for a feeling of closeness to religion. There were tons of Israelis there. Most of them *hozrim bitshuva*. There were some who were moving in the opposite direction, going out with non-Jewish girls and stuff like that. But most of the Moroccans, the Sephardim, there were *hozrim bitshuva*. And there were some families there of former Israelis who started inviting us for a meal on Shabbat, and I was ashamed to go to them, like that, dressed in my immodest clothes. So I would wear long-sleeved tops, and that's how I started dressing more modestly.

One day, the rabbi of the community came to our house. Rabbi Chaim Luk. He was Israeli, Moroccan, a *paytan* [composer of liturgical poems]. And there in America, he had become a rabbi. He has 12, 13 children there. So he came over and said to us, "Listen, you're here in our community, and it's not so good that you're living this way. You've got to get married." At first, we were offended. What, if we don't get married, we can't stay in the community? Because the truth is we wanted to get married, but we didn't have the money, and we thought, "Who from the family would come to our wedding?" So we told him we didn't have anything, and he said he would arrange everything. With the money we had, we sent tickets to my future husband's parents. And my parents took out loans and came. You wouldn't believe how the people there arranged everything for us! Everyone in the community contributed—some $500, some $100. And there was also this organization that helps with wedding expenses, and they put out a few thousand dollars to cover all the catering. The only thing we paid for was the rings. They arranged everything: the photographer, the band, everything we needed. I sewed a simple wedding dress. A modest one. After the wedding, we went with my parents to Vegas and traveled around for a month. My parents wanted to have a good time. They took out a really big loan.

And that's it. Two months later, I got pregnant. My husband started going around with a knitted *kippah* the day after we got married.

And six months later, he had already switched to a black *kippah* [considered a symbol of greater religiosity] and started really getting stronger. He began working as a limousine driver. When we got married, he bought a car. We made money, but we didn't really take full advantage of the car because he didn't work on Shabbat. And later on, when he began going to synagogue in the early morning hours, he ended up missing trips then too.

I also got stronger. I stopped wearing pants—only skirts. And on Shabbat, I would wear a hat. With my hair showing. Later on, I started tucking my hair inside. And I would go to the religious classes of our rabbi. My husband would convince me, though he didn't have to try very hard because I wanted to. But he's stronger than I am now. He's a real yeshiva student. From morning 'til night he studies Torah. Already over there he decided to enter a *kollel* [yeshiva for married men] in Israel. In America, he began wearing a suit and growing a close beard. And then little by little he began to grow his beard longer. A limousine driver's suit is like the suit of a yeshiva student . . . [She laughs.]

The community of Israeli *hozrim bitshuva* in L.A. takes the young couple under its wing and encourages Vered to dress in accordance with its standards. Vered undergoes a gradual process of taking on the external markers of *hit'hazkut*. Following her marriage, she stops wearing pants and begins to wear a hat—at first with some hair showing and eventually with all of it covered. At the same time, her husband shifts from a knitted *kippah* to a black one. Throughout her narrative, Vered emphasizes the element of free choice. As she tells it, her husband tries to convince her to attend religious classes and thus become more observant, but he does not have to try hard because she herself wants to go. She *chooses* to take on the signs that "proclaim" her *hit'hazkut*. But Vered reiterates her view that these external markers of a deepening faith are shallow when she jokes about the resemblance between a limousine driver's uniform and a yeshiva student's style of dress. Her narrative speaks of a slow, incremental process whereby she adopts modest clothing or covers her hair only when she feels stronger.

"Just Like That, We Came Back to Israel"

The young couple's return to Israel introduces them to several new spheres of religious life that give deeper meaning to their *hit'hazkut* process.

First we went to Netivot [a development town in the northern Negev known for its community of religious Mizrahi Jews]. We signed a lease [for a house], but then we changed our minds and moved to Yerucham. We wanted to be near my parents. In the beginning, my husband worked with my father for a couple of months. Then he decided that he was going to study full time at the local yeshiva. I wasn't so keen on him entering the yeshiva world. I had begun working here at the preschool in the religious neighborhood. Our child was with me—not in the same nursery school but near me. Later, my husband felt that he wanted to commit more strongly to his Torah studies and that the local yeshiva was not serious enough, so he started attending a *kollel* in [neighboring] Dimona. He gets a small stipend. I'm earning around 3,000 [shekels] a month. And you wouldn't believe it! Suddenly . . . it's amazing! I'm starting to save! This is the good life. All of a sudden, there's enough for everything. I'm here for five months, and I'm saving really well. It's so incredible! Look, I'm going to a wedding, and the whole clothing thing doesn't interest me. I'm still dressing nicely and modestly, but clothes aren't everything. Once upon a time, I would spend 800 on an outfit. Now I know that it's all foolishness. Instead of throwing away money on clothes, I'll invest in my child's education. Once, you wouldn't have caught me shopping at a bazaar. Now, what do I care? If I find something nice, I'll buy it there. There are more important things in life. I used to be that way, but no more. Now what's important to me is my child: which preschool he'll be in, what type of education he'll have.

During the interview, Vered's little boy is running around us, and she gives him continuous attention in a patient, loving way. Every time he asks her to press the button on the "Shma" doll, she stops talking and does so.

"So that's it? You're part of the *haredi* community here? That's how you see yourself?" I ask her.

Not at all. I'm not like them. I don't wear a wig. I wear a long-sleeved shirt and everything, but I wear my clothes tight, not like them. They're something else. They came here from Jerusalem, and they have their own separate neighborhood. It's some special arrangement with the deputy mayor, Betito. The truth is, they came because life is good here. In Jerusalem, they wouldn't be able to rent an apartment half the size of what they have here. They're isolated and don't mix with people in Yerucham. Today, if someone's already living in this part of town for 40 years, of course they won't drive him out. But if someone secular wants to buy a house in their area, he's got no chance. Even us. I work in their preschool all day. It's hard. From 8 a.m. to 4 p.m. It's 24 kids. You come home exhausted. I'm not used to this.

To tell you the truth, my husband is dying to get into the *haredi* community. But I'm not crazy about the idea. I'm not so anxious to live in an apartment building. They should live and be well . . . they have a lot of kids, and it's noisy. I prefer the quiet here. But it's our child's education that we're thinking about. I want our son to study in a *cheder* [ultra-Orthodox elementary school for boys]. It's not just a religious school. It's a terrific place to learn! The kids in first grade here in the *haredi* community had a test with 101 pages that they had to learn off by heart. These kids are real geniuses! That's what my husband does now. He convinces parents to take their children out of the secular school and transfer them to the community's religious school. Listen, it's good. It saves the children!

Their time in Netivot, which they choose because of their close relationship with the community rabbi there, does not last long. Vered wants to reestablish her ties with her family and urges her husband to return to Yerucham. Connecting with her husband's family of origin, however religious, is not even an option for her. In Yerucham the young husband is eager to become a full-time yeshiva student. Vered prefers to maintain her independence. She lives frugally and emphasizes the gap between her wild spending habits of the past and the new values she has acquired. Since returning to Yerucham, she appreciates education and spiritual peace instead of clothes and jewelry.

Vered defines herself in apposition to two groups at this stage in her life but feels connected to neither. On the one hand, she lives on the fringes of but not in the local *haredi* community; on the other hand, she no longer feels part of her native *masorati* community. Although her husband wants strongly to belong to the *haredi* community, she refuses to move into the neighborhood, even though she works in the community's preschool and admires its educational system, which, she says, "saves children." As a local, Vered faults the circumstances of the *haredi* community's arrival in Yerucham and rejects living in the separate neighborhood its members have created for themselves in the town. But she also rejects the consumerism of her former life—a consumerism that her own sisters and other members of the *masorati* community still embrace. She chooses to send her son to a *haredi* school and supports her husband's new role as a "savior" of children who remain in what she sees as Yerucham's inferior public education system.

As our interview progresses, Vered justifies her lifestyle choices to an audience that subscribes to the dominant secular worldview. I become the representative of that perspective, as I present Vered with questions often posed to *mit'hazkim*. Although some of her responses to my questions are predictable, Vered also reveals a politically critical outlook toward the *haredi* community that her husband is so eager to join.

"What Does Religion Really Ask of Me?"

To challenge Vered and spur her to define her religiosity, I ask her if she really thinks the religious school "saves" children.

She answers, "Look, someone said to me: Let's say that one day you find out that this whole story about the World to Come is a bunch of crap. You won't be sorry that you lost out on things [in this world]? And I said to her: What did I lose? What does religion really ask of me? To honor my parents? What did I lose by honoring my parents? It only made things better. What else? Going out? There are *haredi* hotels. And education? I want my child to learn better things than *Little Red Riding Hood*, things that make him wise, like the Mishnah [part of the oral law of Judaism]. I don't want him to be an engineer or a lawyer. Lawyers are crooks. I want him to be a great rabbi."

"And what," I ask, "do you say to someone who tells you that science is important? Or who asks you who will develop the state? And who will run the stores?"

"God said: 'If you will follow my commandments . . .' If we all walk in His ways, we won't need the army, we won't need anything. We won't need lawyers. Because there won't be any need for their lies. Look, I know these are things that secular people don't accept. That's why I want to live in a place where my child won't be dragged down. I learned this from my husband, who grew up in a religious environment and 'fell.'"

"So everything about religion is good?" I ask.

"Look, I don't accept everything about religion. Ashkenazim, for example, go according to their rabbi, and Sephardim, according to theirs. Who decided this? Why is there a separation? My husband, look at him now, he's a real Ashkenazi. At the *kollel*, he has Ashkenazi teachers. He says to me: 'Ashkenazim are calm. Moroccans are a little hotheaded.' But if you notice, there aren't many *hozrim bitshuva* among the Ashkenazim. It's actually the ones who were born *haredi* and lived that way all their lives who leave religion. The Sephardim are the ones who come back to religion. The ones who helped me in Los Angeles were Sephardi women. They love to help. The wife of the rabbi would sit with us until two in the morning. They did us a real kindness."

Vered has developed a coherent, critical perspective on the reality of her new life in Yerucham. Unlike her husband, who is "dying to get into the *haredi* community," it is clear to Vered that that community is a closed society that is not integrating into the town. She does not hesitate to expose the *haredi* racism internalized by her husband, according to which Ashkenazim are calm and Moroccans are hotheaded. The members of the community, she stresses, only come to Yerucham because they can find spacious homes at a much lower price than in Jerusalem. Although Vered emphasizes that she does not want to be part of the local *haredi* community, she nonetheless chooses to adopt several of its key values—in particular, its patterns of consumption and focus on children's education.

The secular world is reduced in Vered's eyes to *Little Red Riding Hood* and crooked lawyers, which she contrasts with the religious world of educational texts like the Mishnah and behaviors that express respect for one's parents. But Vered's frame of reference is broader than the local tensions dividing the secular and religious communities in Yerucham or even in Israeli society as a whole. The community in Los Angeles, where she became stronger religiously, made her aware of the oppressive nature of *haredi* Ashkenazi practices in relation to the community of Sephardi *hozrim bitshuva*, to whom she feels more connected. Her model for a fulfilling, modest religious life does not come from her new *haredi* neighbors in Yerucham, who close themselves off and articulate explicitly racist intra-Jewish views. Vered's world is larger than theirs, and she develops her own life as a religious woman, mother, and wife through individual decisions and practices that draw from multiple sources.

Hit'hazkut in Yerucham

The journey of Efrat and her five daughters must be understood against the backdrop of the growing religiosity I document more generally in Yerucham. Efrat invites me to join her for religious classes held specifically for women in varied locales around town. Through these classes I get to know many women at various stages in the lengthy and intricate process of *hit'hazkut*. In the following sections I describe the dynamics of these classes and the insights I develop over the many months I attend them. During this period of intensive participation in the classes, I also become deeply involved in conversations about the meaning of the *hit'hazkut* process with a group of women from Yerucham who routinely gather in my office to enjoy the safe social space I offer in the midst of their tiring workday as campus cleaners. I call the group my "council of wise women" because its participants serve as a sounding board for my observations and budding analysis.

Religion Classes as a Site for Shaping Identity

Efrat speaks with great pride about the religion classes she has been attending for years. She tells me that these classes are offered by different teachers on different days of the week in various settings around Yerucham: private homes, public spaces, and synagogues. I learn that on Sundays the *rabbanit* Tami Wolf gives classes at the Tiferet Yisrael synagogue, and on Wednesday evenings *rabbanit* Sima Bitton teaches classes at the same location.[4] On Tuesdays, two rabbis teach a class at Hatse'irim synagogue. I attend several classes on an irregular basis before ultimately deciding to accompany Efrat to a class she regularly attends, taught by Rabbi Buskila. The rabbi, Efrat tells me, is the son of one of her elementary schoolteachers in Yerucham, a man who is also well-known in

Morocco as a *paytan*. As a young man, the son was not particularly religious, but he eventually got stronger, studied in yeshiva, and became a rabbi.

Rabbi Buskila's classes are held in a former private home. After the occupant's death, her daughters converted it into a space for women's Torah study. A hedge surrounds the small house, hiding it from view. The first time I attend Rabbi Buskila's class, I am alone. I had arranged to meet Efrat on-site, but she does not show. I enter the class several minutes after it has begun, feeling somewhat awkward. The walls of the small rooms of the home have been taken down, creating an open space that accommodates a table, several chairs, and a sofa. Hanging on the walls are framed pictures of rabbis. Among them I notice three studio portraits of wedding couples, like those seen on many household walls in Yerucham. A student later tells me that the women in these pictures are the daughters of the woman who once lived in the home. Holding Torah classes in the home is a way of "elevating the mother's soul," the woman explains to me in a whisper.

The rabbi sits at the end of a long table. He is about 30, has a black Herzl-style beard, and is dressed in the black-and-white outfit often worn by *mit'hazkim*. I sit in the only place left in the room, on the sofa close to the rabbi's seat at the end of the table. Next to me sits a young dark-skinned woman of about 25 with a child of about four on her lap. She wears a long, dark-colored skirt and a long-sleeved blouse. Her hair is gathered with a simple elastic band and is not covered. Opposite us, on a bare wooden bench, sit three Indian Jewish women. I am later told that they are sisters. The youngest of the three, a thick-set woman, wears tight black pants and a red sweater. Her two older sisters wear long skirts and shirts with elbow-length sleeves. None of the three covers her hair. They smile at me pleasantly.

On the other side of the room, opposite the rabbi-lecturer, sit three Moroccan women in their midtwenties. Two of them wear long dresses and brightly colored head scarves. The third is bareheaded. She wears long black pants and a blue cotton shirt with long sleeves. On chairs crowded together along the wall sit three other buxom Moroccan women in their late fifties or early sixties. Their dresses strain over stomachs bloated from numerous pregnancies. In the style of immigrant Moroccan women, their heads are covered with colorful kerchiefs tied loosely at the back of the neck.

At this lesson, as at all of Rabbi Buskila's classes, refreshments are offered. The table is laden with plates of roasted almonds and pistachios, seasonal fruits, chocolate-coated wafers, and bottles of soft drinks. During the class, none of the women touches the food or drink. It is only at the end, when the hostesses urge the women to enjoy the refreshments, that they hesitantly partake. This polite, restrained behavior on the part of the women is noticeable throughout the class. They listen to the rabbi's words with expressions of courteous respect but largely refrain from touching the photocopied pages arranged in colorful folders on the table. I assume that these materials are for the use of the students and take one of the folders lying nearest to me. I make use of "my" photocopies throughout the class, writing notes in the margins of each page in accordance with the rabbi's explanations. Only then do I notice that I am the only one taking advantage of these pages. From time to time, one women or another lifts a folder and leafs through it. Most of the time their faces are turned toward the young rabbi, who speaks energetically. He quotes several times from the pages in the folders but does not ask the women to follow along. I am the only one who takes notes during any of the classes I attend.

The subject of Rabbi Buskila's first lecture is the laws of ritual purity. We learn from him what steps a woman should take to determine whether she is ritually pure after menstruating. In subsequent sessions, he discusses the laws of separation between husband and wife and the laws concerning bloodstains on clothing, linens, and so on. The young rabbi shows no trace of embarrassment as he speaks, though he deals with intimate feminine matters. He does not refer directly to his audience but to women in general, always speaking in the third person. Thus, for example, he states, "If *a woman* saw blood . . . or if she felt an accompanying sensation but did not pay attention to it . . ." "The woman" is not expected to decide whether or not she is ritually pure, the rabbi asserts. The point of the lessons, he explains, is to guide "the woman" so that she will know when to consult a rabbi to receive his ruling and what indicators she should bring to him to enable him to decide for her in this matter. The number of details and minute directives that the rabbi conveys is staggering.

I attend Rabbi Buskila's classes on a regular basis, even when Efrat does not accompany me. Each of his lessons lasts an hour and a half without any break. The rabbi often uses quotes to support his religious teachings, but he seldom notes their sources or refers us to the printed sheets, which I examine during each lecture. Most of the religious instruction is based on examples drawn from everyday life. Little time is devoted to questions. The impression I have is that queries from the attendees are unwelcome and would be seen as interrupting the flow of the rabbi's words. Two instances illustrate the general tone of listeners' mutual silencing of one another.

In one class Rabbi Buskila describes in great detail the importance of the size of a bloodstain and the type of surface it appears on in determining whether it indicates ritual impurity. A young Indian woman of about 20 is attending the class for the first time. She periodically whispers to her older sister, who sits next to her, her face impassive. The sister silences her several times and continues to regard the rabbi with a serene, courteous expression. The younger woman, however, insists on disrespecting the rules of the game and eventually interjects an impatient question: "How can I bring to a rabbi the object on which the blood fell?" she asks embarrassedly. "What if it's a seat or a heavy armchair?" The young lecturer pauses in his monologue and responds in a tone of gentle amusement that he has just finished explaining that there is no need to bring the actual object ("because it's obvious that if it's a heavy piece of furniture, you're not going to drag your sofa on your back all the way to the rabbi's house"); rather, he tells the young woman, she should place a piece of wax paper over the stain and bring the paper, cut to the size of the stain, for the rabbi to pass judgment.

"But if it's paper, it will absorb the stain," insists the young woman.

"No, wax paper does not absorb things," the other women cut her off impatiently.

The rabbi allows the women to answer in his place and continues his lecture from the point where he had left off.

At a different class the rabbi explains at length the religious laws regarding different sizes of bloodstains, repeatedly using the expression "like a *gris* or more." He explains that a *gris* (a single grain of wheat) is 19 millimeters long, noting that this is roughly the diameter of the old phone tokens in use at the time (approximately the size of an American dime). One of the women removes a ring from her finger and hesitantly asks if it is the size he means; she holds up the ring to show him and the other women. Giggling awkwardly, the woman explains that she does not have a phone token, and where would she find one, and that her son has a collection of tokens but go ask your son to give you a token . . . and if he should ask why . . . The rabbi cuts off the embarrassed woman, nodding his head to confirm that the ring is in fact the size he is referring to. The other students react with anger to the woman's question—"A ring is like a phone token . . ." "What does it matter . . ." "The important thing is that that's the size"—as though to say, "What a pointless question!"

The rabbi does not acknowledge these comments but continues his detailed explanation by citing a complicated midrash (Jewish religious commentary). In a slightly singsong voice, he recites, "If it's less than the size of a *gris*, then she is ritually pure; if more, then she is impure. And why? [He answers his own question, continuing in a Hasidic cadence.] Once, in every Jewish home there were these little bedbugs, and women would turn over in their beds crushing these bugs, whose blood would spatter onto their clothes or body. The bloodstain from this bug when it exploded was found to be the size of a *gris*, and thus was established the size of the bloodstain that determined if she was ritually impure."

Aware of the complexity of the material he is presenting, the rabbi often provides illustrative examples using contemporary language laced with a bit of humor. If the blood falls onto a woman's "flesh," it is important to check where it fell: If below the belt, she is impure; if above the belt, not. Unless she is in a gym class, he jokes, and standing on her head or, he suggests, becoming a little more serious, unless she bends over to clean the refrigerator or is in any other inverted position. There is a fleeting spark of mischief in the young rabbi's eyes when he tells us that the woman must first check to see if there is an injury on her body or on one of her children's bodies to verify that the blood is in fact menstrual.

During another class, the rabbi explains the laws regarding the surfaces on which the blood falls. After a long series of examples of materials and objects that are or are not polluted by staining (anything that grows in the ground can become ritually impure; paper is not susceptible to impurity, unless it is a paper bag, in which case it belongs in the category of receptacles, which *are* susceptible to impurity), he moves on to a detailed discussion of women's undergarments: Cotton underpants absorb impurity, but synthetic ones do not;

however, if the synthetic underpants have cotton stitching, a rabbinic ruling must be sought. Sheets must be white during the seven clean days following the end of menstruation, after which a colored sheet (red, blue, green, but not flowered) should be placed on the bed. "And why not flowered?" he asks with a broad smile, as though testing whether we are following the logic of his examples. After a long silence, he answers his own question: Because if the blood falls on the white part of the pattern, it will render the woman impure.

The notes that I take so assiduously convey the level of detail in the presentation. I record that apart from the size of the bloodstain, other factors that affect impurity include the type of cloth the stain appears on, its color (red, black, and brown are the most likely to render the woman impure, but most colors require consultation with a rabbi), and the nature of the object on which it falls (most receptacles absorb impurity; a floor, for example, does not absorb impurity—a woman can wash it and all will be well—but a chair is a receptacle and thus absorbs impurity). I also take notes on a detailed exposition on sanitary napkins. In a style that reminds me of my army instructors describing the parts of a rifle, the rabbi explains that there are three parts to every sanitary napkin: the pad itself, the layer covering it, and the adhesive strips. I am astonished to hear such an impressive analysis of the structure and composition of sanitary napkins and to discover that there is learned discussion of their halakhic significance. And so I write: Pads are not made of cotton (which does not absorb impurity) but of shredded cardboard. But the synthetic material that forms the adhesive strip is made of polyethylene, which is a product of crude oil. And if the woman adds toilet paper to the pad, it must be folded over several times so that no blood comes in contact with the pad. There is no need to check the toilet paper even if the stain is larger than a *gris*—just throw it away and that's it. Do not insert the toilet paper deeply when wiping. Wipe externally. Because if you wipe internally, this requires consultation with a rabbi.

In another class, the rabbi presents the legal fine points concerning immersion in the ritual bath, taking pains to avoid confusing his audience. We learn that there are clear religious laws governing the permissibility of artificial nails (if the woman always wears them in public and is never seen without them, she is not obligated to remove them before immersing). We are also introduced to the complexity of halakhic rulings regarding shampoo. Shampoo (whether combined with conditioner or not) leaves a shiny film on the hair. Such a film is considered a *hatzitza*, or obstruction, and because immersion is forbidden in the presence of any obstruction, immersing with shampooed hair that leaves a film is problematic. The rabbi notes that "this is now being studied" and that the issue has not yet been resolved. But so as not to confuse us, he suggests simply, "Forget all the laws here. Either come to the *mikvah*[5] without shampooing your hair or just use a regular conditioner that helps untangle the knots but does not leave a shiny film." It is clear that he does not want to confuse his listeners. He obviously has a great deal of empathy for the women who are obliged to grapple with these complex arguments and regulations. At the end of one of the classes, he warns, "Next week, it'll be even more complicated," and smiles. "Just don't get all confused on me."

Only once do I witness the rabbi attempt to test whether his audience understands his explanations. With a hesitant smile, like that of a teacher who does not expect much of his students, he asks a simple question relating to an issue that he has explained at length in his previous lectures. If a bloodstain is smaller than a gris and is found on a colored item of clothing, asks the rabbi, is the woman ritually pure or impure? The women are caught off guard by the fact that he is asking them a question and smile uncomfortably. Then, giggling like schoolchildren, they throw out different answers: "Pure." "Impure." And again, "Pure." The rabbi smiles indulgently and briefly repeats the response that he expects. The women are embarrassed. A round-faced woman in a head scarf who sits to my left asks me in a whisper if I know the answer. I whisper back to her, "I'm totally confused." The rabbi continues with his lecture, as though the exercise has been nothing more than a mischievous diversion.

And so, as the classes go on, we are exposed to a growing number of facts and intricacies. In one of the rare breaks allowed by Rabbi Buskila, I ask some of the women, "Do you manage to remember everything? It's not too complicated?" They smile at me politely and offer comments along the lines of "Of course it's complicated. It's a Torah class." Hearing their responses, I begin to realize that their way of relating to the lessons differs from my own set of expectations about learning. Over and over again, wherever I go, the women I meet tell me, "These classes are so great! It's holy stuff." One woman says to me, "I go to a lot of religion classes. Torah makes you smarter." The reasons given for attending the classes differ from person to person, "It's fun; it's like going out." "It's good; it improves your marriage." "Of course it's good; it improves both you and society. When you're a good person, you get along with everyone. If you're always looking for drama, you're unhappy and everyone ends up fighting."

The women who come to Rabbi Buskila's classes vary in age and have reached different stages of *hit'hazkut*, as shown by their styles of dress, but everyone is welcomed with a smile. They all come to listen. There is no expectation that they will understand, remember, or internalize the knowledge presented to them. The very fact that they come, that a respectable number of women attend, is what makes the gatherings significant.

When the rabbi leaves the room, as they nibble on the expensive refreshments, the women speak repeatedly about the joy they derive from attending his classes. They also note with pride their participation in religion classes other than those taught by Rabbi Buskila. One woman tells me about the classes she attends in a private home belonging to someone "who has really gotten stronger religiously and brings rabbis to her house to give lectures." Each time, she relates, someone new comes to speak on a different topic. She states proudly, "I already know all the stuff. But I go there because I'm getting stronger all the time. It's good." Someone else mentions the *rabbanit* Sima Bitton. Another talks about the four days a week that she attends religion classes, noting the names of the rabbis who lecture at each of them. "I go to as many Torah classes as possible," states a young, bareheaded woman who is wearing pants and a long-sleeved shirt, "because it's a treat for the soul." "Yeah, because you don't work," Efrat says to her. And the young woman responds, "That's got nothing to do with it. At eight in the evening, you go to sleep, right? So I go to classes then, winter or summer." There is a great deal of pride in her words.

I come to realize that the very act of getting out of the house for such an important, worthy purpose is a source of enjoyment and pride for the women. The reason they listen for an hour and a half to the finer points of interpreting bloodstains and other minutiae is not to familiarize themselves with these details but to be part of the space where the classes take place. The act of participating in religion classes marks them as serious, respectable women with high spiritual aspirations, not gossips who spend their evenings watching shallow soap operas on television. The food and drink on the tables adds to the atmosphere of a pleasant evening out, a respite from their exhausting daily responsibilities in the home. The women here are doing something for themselves.

My overall impression is that the women in the classes are not especially interested in the complicated material itself. Their main goal is to engage in the admirable act of listening to Torah lectures.[6] Their very presence in the room places them on the continuum of *hit'hazkut* that is shaping their new identity. By entering the respected space of a religion class, they are accumulating cultural capital.

The Council of Wise Women

Over the months that I participate regularly in Rabbi Buskila's classes, a group of women office cleaners, most of them from Yerucham, coalesces around me. In my notes I call this group the "council of wise women" because its members react to my ongoing reports about my observations and emerging analysis of the process of *hit'hazkut*. I describe the class I have attended the previous evening, and they reinforce, contradict, and shape the questions and partial conclusions I develop each day. The women openly enjoy these get-togethers and the fact that I type their words directly into my office computer. They seem to have a good time.

The gatherings become a regular event, with unspoken rules. The women come to my office at about 11 a.m., after they have finished the first part of their daily cleaning rounds and before their lunch break. Sometimes only one woman comes to steal a few moments of quiet, stretching out on the bed in the corner of my office and treating herself to the candies or crackers I offer. Most often, they come in pairs. And sometimes the room fills with five or more women. Because the watchful eye of their work supervisor is a constant concern, we close the door, trying to keep our gatherings quiet.

We speak about a broad range of subjects, but my participation in Rabbi Buskila's religion classes, which none of them takes part in, becomes a major topic of conversation. One day, Yaffa (a married woman in her early thirties with two young children) tells me that the previous day, in the midst of washing the floor in her home, she had realized something important that she needed to make clear to me about "our being religious."

"Listen, Pnina," Yaffa says, "you need to understand that being religious is not just dressing a certain way with long clothes, or going to religion classes."

Yaffa is one of the most active commentators in my advisory forum. She is not merely aware that I am conducting a study but seems to deeply appreciate and become personally engaged in the research process, not only by sharing her personal experiences but also by insisting on helping me grasp things "properly."

Yaffa's commentary often triggers a lively debate. In this case, the others agree with her statement about the gap between dress codes and a deeper process of *hit'hazkut*, and they talk about women who wear modest clothing but are actually "faking it." In their remarks, they distinguish between "fakers" and those who are "truly religious." One of the women speaks about her sister, who is "religious like you wouldn't believe!" She describes her sister as perfect, so I ask her, "But what does your *perfect* sister do? In what way is she different from you?" The woman, who is less articulate than Yaffa, is at a loss to respond to my challenge. She tries: "How can I say it? Well . . . she likes things to be honest and clear." And then she concludes, "She's a person of quality." I persist: "But I don't know what you mean by 'quality.' What makes her more worthy than you?"

"Look," she tries again, "she's not like me. She loves religion . . . she was always like that. She's such a modest person."

Another woman chimes in: "Look, Pnina, religious women . . . how can I put it? They're . . . calmer. They act dignified." And someone else volunteers, "They're not wild like us. They're quieter. Everything by them is 'thank God,' 'with God's help' . . . How do you say it? They live a life that's serene."

But between the much-admired position of the "truly religious" and the opposite extreme of "wild women," as they label themselves, there is a range of possibilities.

Along the *Hit'hazkut* Continuum

Each of the members of my council of wise women locates herself at a different stage in the process of *hit'hazkut* that she is experiencing or aspires to experience. None defines herself as secular. Even those who declare that they themselves are not *mit'hazkim* insist that they are still believers (*ma'aminot*), and none counts herself among those who do not believe in anything at all.

One day I learn the meaning of this last category, when one of the regular contributors to my council shares her frustration with people who "don't believe in anything." She describes her conversation with an Ashkenazi male faculty member whose office she cleans regularly. She tells him that she had taken the previous day off to visit the "graves of the righteous" and offer donations of *tzedakah* (charity) because she wished to give thanks for narrowly avoiding a serious traffic accident. The man listens to her story and tells her that there is no connection between donations to charity and being spared from accidents. Although she does not see herself as a *mit'hazeket*, she is careful to specify, she could never understand the reaction of this person, or people like him, who "don't believe in anything."

One morning, I learn something that expands the range of categories on the *hit'hazkut* continuum. I ask one of the regular council members—a woman who dresses immodestly and who has stated more than once that she smokes and travels on Shabbat—if she observes the laws of ritual purity. "Of course!" she exclaims. "What do you think I am? A *meshumada*?" From the lively debate that develops out of this exchange, I learn that *meshumada* is a Moroccan word based on the Hebrew term *shmad* (forced conversion). *Meshumada*, in this context, problematizes a woman's Jewishness even if she can claim biological Jewish origins. Not observing the laws of ritual purity undermines a woman's identity as a Jew, for it means she believes in nothing. Those who do not observe the laws of kashrut or Shabbat do not fall into this fringe category. The wise women in my council fall within an acceptable continuum stretching from the *masorati* (traditional) at one end through the *dati* (religious), *ma'amin* (believing), and *mit'hazek* (actively getting stronger religiously) to the *haredi* (ultra-Orthodox) at the other end. None of them defines herself as *meshumada*.[7]

Efrat and her family make this scale more tangible. Efrat insists that she has always been a *ma'amina* (believer), though the boarding school she attended taught her "a lot of religion" to make her more *datiya* (religious). In the same vein, her husband is considered *hiloni* (secular, nonreligious), but his status as a *ma'amin* is never in doubt. Efrat's husband attributes his failure to stop smoking not to a lack of *emunah* (faith) but to his own personal weakness. Vered, as we have seen, does not see a contradiction between her participation in a beauty pageant, where she was required to wear a bathing suit, and her insistence on walking to the pageant so as not to desecrate the Sabbath. As her mother makes clear, that insistence demonstrates her deep *emunah*, her identity as a strong believer. In contrast to this discourse of *emunah*, the army grants Vered an exemption from service based on a simple dress code—wearing a long skirt—because that practice demonstrates that she is a *datiya*, a religious woman.

At one end of this complex, multilayered self-definitional spectrum stands the category of *haredi*, of ultra-Orthodox identity. The young Rakefet rejects her school's imposition of this label on her, insisting that she is *datiya* or, in her words, "a regular religious person, like my mother."

Hit'hazkut Takes Place within a Community

To position herself on the continuum between "those who don't believe in anything" and ultra-Orthodoxy, a woman must make a coherent public statement whereby her adoption of specific dress codes and daily practices, such as not smoking on the Sabbath or attending religious classes, goes hand in hand with an overall demeanor indicative of a deep internal transformation. In other words, the community expects consistency between the message women convey through their dress and religious practice and the serenity with which they carry themselves. When Efrat describes her husband's *hit'hazkut*, she dwells on his transformation into a calm man who becomes a contributing father, not on his sophisticated prayers or strict observance of Jewish religious codes. In fact, when women do not meet these public expectations, they can expect harsh criticism from those who are contemplating the path of *hit'hazkut* but have not yet made the actual move. Thus, for example, I hear, "That one, she's not really strong in her belief. She puts on a hat and long skirts, but then she goes around gossiping about everyone. What kind of *datiya* is that? It doesn't work that way."

The council of wise women spends many days discussing the set of expectations raised when a woman changes her dress code in accordance with accepted *datiya* behavior. Shula, a woman of about 25 who has a two-year-old daughter, brings this point home. Shula recounts, "It used to be that I would wake up in the morning and there would always be tension and shouting. All day, I would run around working, cleaning house, taking care of my daughter. Believe me, we were always competing with everyone: who has the nicest living room, pictures, kitchen. Today, I get up in the morning, wash my hands, say my prayers. I'm calm. I have peace of mind."

Shula describes here her deep yet gradual transformation as a result of her growing *hit'hazkut*. She does not define herself as *datiya*, and at this point in her life she dresses, in her words, in a "regular" way. But she repeatedly states that she plans to get rid of her fashionable clothes one day and dress "modestly." The rabbi told her, she says, that a "regular" (meaning immodest) style of dress not only is a personal failing (she uses the term *sinful*) but causes others (who look at her) to "fail" as well. God willing, she intends to eventually give away her stylish, immodest clothes to her niece, who is single—but not yet. At this point, Shula says, she does not feel that it "suits her" to wear modest clothing. One thing at a time. She now reads religious texts every morning and feels much calmer. "The only thing that's missing is the [modest] clothes," she explains. "And I won't wear them until I feel it inside. Not just because . . ."

Shula tells me that she has gone several times with a girlfriend to religion classes given by a young rabbi who calls her *tzadika* (righteous) and tells her that with God's help she will get stronger religiously. But she does not keep up with the classes because she is busy with her daughter. It is from the young rabbi that she learns about and begins to practice morning prayers, though she is not sure what the words mean or where they come from (she thinks they may be from the book of Psalms). She says, "I did not make up my mind yet" about the prayers, but she has taken to reciting a few phrases she has memorized each morning without referring to any text.

Shula's narrative makes it clear that she is waiting for the moment when her inner convictions support her dress code and her morning prayers. She is careful not to commit herself publicly to a religious position that she is incapable of maintaining.

Shula is not the only one who speaks of a gradual personal process whose goal is a life of tranquility. All the women on my council, even those who define themselves as "wild," want to have peace of mind of the kind Shula describes.

Teaching Calmness

During the animated discussions at our daily meetings, the women depict the process of *hit'hazkut* in terms of inner transformation, that is, a shift in their existing worldview. They speak about a change in priorities. The strongly committed *mit'hazkot*, for instance, talk about investing in their children's education rather than buying useless toys for them. Religious education for the children is considered a better alternative, and both *mit'hazkot* and those who hope one day to become stronger often opt to send their children to religious schools. As one of the women in my council explains, "I send my youngest daughter to the preschool of the Shasnikim [adherents of the Shas political party, which emphasizes Mizrahi religious pride]. And there's no comparison. She used to be in a regular preschool from the municipality, and she would come home cursing and yelling because that's how it was there. Now she comes and tells me that she was the Sabbath bride and did the candle lighting. It's so nice to hear her talking this way. No yelling. It's forbidden to curse there."

Calmness is widely valued and defined in stark contrast to rowdiness and disrespect for oneself and others. One woman (who does not define herself as a *mit'hazeket*) finds the tranquility of religious schools reminiscent of the peace and quiet of her parents' home: "The truth? I would like to have their education for my children. No yelling. It's calm, quiet. Like in my parents' home. Whatever our mother or father said, you would do. Not based on hitting or shouting, but out of respect. All that was needed was a look. They just gave you one look, and you did the right thing." In the old days, this woman asserts, parents had authority over their children and children were calm and well behaved, whereas the Israeli public school system today produces disrespectful, raucously behaved children. The kind of proper, respectful education that she received from her immigrant parents can be attained today only by sending children to religious educational institutions. But when women speak of the old days when proper behavior was the norm, they are expressing more than nostalgia. They are specifically criticizing Yerucham as a social space that breeds bad behavior and unrest.

One woman tells me of a family friend who has managed to leave Yerucham and move to the larger city of Be'er-Sheva. When the woman visits her friend in her new home there, she notices a positive change in the behavior of her friend's children, who used to "be wild and cursed often," like most children in Yerucham. Now, after the move, her friend beams, the children speak politely and behave well. The implication of this story is that Yerucham is an inferior, degrading social space that has turned those born to dignified Mizrahi immigrant parents into people who cannot properly educate their own children. In Yerucham, children who attend local public schools are wild; they curse and lack self-respect. One needs to escape from Yerucham if one wishes for a better education for one's children. For those who cannot leave town, religious education is the only available path toward a life of self-respect.

No Pokemon

The process of *hit'hazkut* involves more than achieving greater peace of mind or closer adherence to religious commandments; it often entails new patterns of consumption. One woman clearly sums up this aspect: "Religious women are different from us financially. They manage with what there is. They're more careful with money. They don't go to some boutique. They don't buy stupid things. No Digimon or Pokemon. No TV or PlayStation. They invest more in their children."

Another woman says, "They don't have it, that competition over money. Whatever they have is fine. In my home, you see modern art and knick-knacks. They don't have that. I'm talking about Shas women, not the Ashkenazi ones. The Ashkenazi women, they have money. They have their wigs and stuff. With the Shas women, it's modesty. When you're a secular woman, you look at others. What does she have that I don't?! She [the Shas woman] won't go to some boutique. She's not interested in luxuries."

The set of social expectations also changes when a woman proclaims her identity as a *mit'hazeket* and rejects the ostentatiousness of competition and consumerism. As Efrat's daughter Vered remarks, "Once upon a time, I would invest in a new outfit for every occasion. Whether it was a relative's or a close friend's event, I would put down 800 shekel for a dress and more on shoes and a hairdo—the works. If you insisted on a custom-made outfit, you're talking about something like 2,000 shekel for such an outfit. And it would hang in the closet. You're not going to wear the same dress to another function. Nope. Today I don't go crazy. I go buy a modest blouse and skirt. Something that I can use—not something that will sit in my closet. I don't have the hairdo and makeup and all that to worry about. Do you know what expenses I had then? And I have not counted in yet the cost of a suit for my husband or new clothes for the kids."

Precisely because the women who embark on the path of *hit'hazkut* and their families are from a lower socioeconomic class, this major change in consumption patterns has important ramifications for their potential to break free of the cycle of debt and poverty that many Yerucham families are locked into. And this path confers a new, locally legitimized sense of self-worth on those who follow it.

After long months of attending religious classes and after reflecting on the extended discussions I had with my council of wise women, I still struggle with one question: Does the acquired cultural capital of *hit'hazkut* have value outside Yerucham? In other words, are the changes in consumption and the sense of inner peace and self-respect that the *mit'hazkot* report or aspire to significant only in the local arena and only among those who are unable to escape from it? How constructive is *hit'hazkut* as a survival strategy in terms of breaking free of the concrete box that living in Yerucham dictates?

In an effort to consider this question, I return to Efrat and consider her effort to secure a position as a nursery school teacher's aide in Sde Boker. I suggest that the cultural capital gained through her *hit'hazkut* process translated into qualities that were marketable outside the limited physical space of Yerucham and that she was able to use her new dignity as a *mit'hazeket* to achieve meaningful social mobility.

Cultural Capital in Limited Markets: The Road to Sde Boker

Efrat tells me that there is a job available in Midreshet Sde Boker as a nursery school teacher and that she intends to try her luck at getting it. She had worked as a preschool teacher with the NA'AMAT organization in Yerucham for several years, and later she had opened a private kindergarten in her home. But over the past year she has realized that being self-employed is not profitable for her, and she decides to go back to being a salaried worker. She has scheduled a job interview in Sde Boker, and she asks me if I know the women who are going to be interviewing her. I answer that in fact I do know them. Several of my neighbors are members of the executive committee of the community's private nursery school. I offer to drive Efrat to the interview.

The morning of the interview, I arrive at Efrat's home, ready to critique her appearance and offer advice to help her make the right impression and secure the coveted job. She is wearing a greenish-gray dress custom-made by a professional seamstress. The elegant outfit emphasizes her slender figure and the quality of the material. The hat that she wears matches the dress and, I happily tell her, tops off her "attractive, respectable" look.

Efrat is nervous about the interview. The working conditions at the nursery school in Sde Boker are excellent compared to those in the preschools she has worked at in Yerucham. The number of children is smaller, the hours are convenient, and most important, Efrat emphasizes, "The parents there are really involved and educated." She does not talk about the salary but instead speaks highly about what "quality people" the parents of Sde Boker preschoolers are. The term *quality people (anashim ehutiyim)* has always made me uncomfortable. It is used in Israeli mainstream discourse as a euphemism for well-educated, secular (mostly Ashkenazi) people, distinguishing them from less worthy Others, those in the lower classes who lack cultural legitimacy. And it is precisely this social gap, hinted at by Efrat's reference to the "quality people" of Sde Boker, and her own position in relation to it that worries me.

On the short ride from Yerucham to Sde Boker, I try to lower Efrat's expectations. I try to gently suggest that the parents might not accept her for the position—not because she does not have the right skills but because they, my neighbors, are "very secular." Efrat listens to my words nervously and says, "But what's the problem . . . what's a little religious values . . . just lighting Shabbat candles . . . explaining a bit what Rosh Hashanah means." I try to offer her some support by agreeing with her—Shabbat and Jewish values are fine—and yet I suggest that she should emphasize in the interview that she is not a dogmatic *datiya* (I use her own terms, telling her to make it clear that she is "not some *haredi* woman") and that she does not intend to impose her religious opinions on the secular children or their parents.

My own discomfort and misgivings increase over the course of the short drive. I am not sure I am helping her with my advice. I am aware that I am overstepping my role as a researcher who is supposed to be dispassionately observing and documenting events, and I am not sure my views will be helpful to Efrat in her encounter with my own social milieu in middle-class, Ashkenazi Sde Boker. I simply cannot keep home and fieldwork spaces separate here. This is not the first time for me that the boundaries between these two realms have become blurred. Many of the women from Yerucham with whom I have developed ongoing relationships have visited me in my home, gotten to know my family, and of course spent long hours in my office. But in this situation I find myself caught between Efrat and the women of the bourgeois secular community that I belong to. I feel the need to protect Efrat. I want to help her get the job she so desires.

By the end of the day, it becomes clear that Efrat does not need my protection. What I learn from the experience is sobering on several grounds. When we arrive at the nursery school, located at the entrance to Sde Boker, I withdraw to my car, promising Efrat that I will wait there until the interview is over so that I can drive her back home. As we stand outside the school chatting among the swings and the sandboxes, a woman of about 40 comes up to us and envelops Efrat in a warm hug. The woman turns out to be Efrat's older sister, who has been working at the Sde Boker preschool for several years as a part-time cook and cleaner. The two sisters do not look alike. The older sister is obviously not a *mit'hazeket*, as indicated by her style of dress. She wears tight purple pants and a loose, faded sleeveless shirt. Black rubber roots, disheveled bleached blonde hair, and a lit cigarette held casually in the manner of a heavy smoker complete her characteristic lower-class Mizrahi appearance.

Efrat, with her tailored look and elegant hat covering her hair, exudes an air of almost bourgeois propriety that further emphasizes her sister's untidy appearance. As I watch the two of them hug, I remind myself that Efrat has no more formal education than her sister. Like her sister, she studied in a vocational religious school and married young. Yet Efrat radiates respectability, a term British sociologist Beverley Skeggs uses in documenting life among working-class women in Britain. As Efrat disappears into the school for her interview, I wonder whether this respectability will help her get the job in secular, Ashkenazi, middle-class Sde Boker.

When the interview ends, Efrat comes out with a huge smile on her face. The interview has gone very well, she reports to her sister and me. The parents who interviewed her have been "so nice" and really "loved her." On the way back to Yerucham, Efrat appears relaxed, smiling, and calm—very different from the way she looked on the way to Sde Boker. Gone is her earlier nervousness, gone her references to the "quality people" of Sde Boker and her apologetic remarks regarding her religious Jewish values. She states with a newfound confidence, "You should know, Pnina, all the drugs, all the crime and incest is found in secular society. The *haredim* are quiet. They're holy. So, you tell me: What's better—being a thief and a criminal, or wearing a *kippah* and keeping Shabbat?"

Cultural Capital, Limited Markets, and Respectability

The concept of cultural capital is distinguished in the sociological literature from the complementary concept of institutional capital. According to French sociologist Pierre Bourdieu (1986), cultural capital carries meaning in a local context and thus has worth only in limited markets. By contrast, capital that is rooted in large institutions, such as formal education, has practical value in broader markets. I propose that the kind of cultural capital accrued in the process of *hit'hazkut* by lower-class Mizrahi men and women on the Israeli periphery blurs the lines of the binary model proposed by Bourdieu. I contend that, contrary to Israeli conventional wisdom, the cultural wealth acquired through the *hit'hazkut* process can be and, in the given circumstances of life in Yerucham, is in fact the most constructive path to local upward mobility

I draw on two key feminist insights to establish my analysis. The first is the need to consider multiple lines of social marginalization. The second is the need to examine the intersectionality of social institutions that contribute to various forms of marginalization. Together, these insights ask us to consider the factors that shape one's life choices in real historical moments. At the turn of the twenty-first century, several factors combined to limit the options for escaping life in Yerucham's concrete boxes. The geographic remoteness of Israeli development towns like Yerucham meant that residents were constrained in their ability to travel to employment opportunities in major cities. Any effort to enter larger job markets was further blocked by the towns' second-rate formal education systems, which impeded people's ability to gain institutional tools, such as the matriculation diploma necessary to enter Israeli institutes of higher learning. To these obstacles one might add the association drawn in hegemonic Western-centered Israeli discourse between Mizrahi speech and behavioral patterns and lack of sophistication and backwardness. Against these mutually reinforcing downward-spiraling axes, *hit'hazkut* emerges as the best way out of the loop, perhaps because it grants respectability to its bearers and draws on the shared Jewish identity of its subjects.

I argue that *hit'hazkut* affords women who are trapped by limited employment opportunities and ethno-class stereotypes the best value within the limited range of options open to them in their life circumstances. Like the women at the center of Skeggs's work, the employment space available to Mizrahi women from Yerucham is limited to service professions, such as childcare or teaching. In this restricted labor market, an emphasis on a shared Jewishness with middle-class women who make use of their services is a marketable asset. Investment in one's Jewish cultural capital can translate into real economic gain.

Efrat's detailed story of *hit'hazkut* substantiates this argument. The process she has undergone leads to the construction of a power base that allows her to redefine her standing in the family and to draw closer to her daughters, who are undergoing similar processes on their own terms. Her *hit'hazkut* story yields not only personal empowerment but also professional options. All in all, the lesson gained from Efrat and the other women who opt for this path flies in the face of Israeli liberal conventional wisdom. According to this narrative, *hit'hazkut* is a debilitating option that reduces the chances of integrating into the national workforce. By considering the paths taken by other women in the multiply marginalized community, we come to realize that becoming stronger religiously offers the most constructive life option within the cement box.

3

RACHEL

Yerucham's "Ideal Resident"

RACHEL AND I often laugh about the first interview that she granted me a few days after I had called and introduced myself as a researcher from Ben-Gurion University. Our initial meeting, which took place on June 19, 2000, is documented in my first notebook. My notes are written with a blunt pencil, and the light gray handwriting is barely legible. I had to write quickly, because Rachel refused to allow me to record the interview on my portable voice recorder.

"I was born here and got married and had four children . . . a totally ordinary life," she begins, in response to my open invitation to introduce herself. "My parents were among the first people to settle here," she went on. "They came from Morocco straight to Yerucham in 1954." I wrote down that she loves purple (and, in fact, I noticed that she was wearing it that day and that the stairwell leading to her third-floor apartment was painted purple) and that she "does not like extremes in anything, especially the whole religious thing." I wrote that she was born in Israel, the eighth of 11 children, and that she was 38 years old at the time of the interview. She proudly informed me that she was studying at a special *beit midrash* (Jewish house of study) founded by two women activists living in Yerucham, Tami Bitton and Debbie Golan. "This is a creative *beit midrash*," she elaborated. "We create projects there. Every student creates his or her own project. This year, for example, the theme is the life cycle."

In subsequent years, whenever I come to Yerucham, I climb the stairs to Rachel's apartment and ring her doorbell. We both look back with amusement on that first interview, when she offered me an uncomplicated, picture-perfect version of her life story. "What did you expect?" Rachel giggles. "You asked for my 'life story,' and I wasn't sure I'd see you again after that interview. So I told you everything, you know, like it was perfect. I told it, you know, without the problems and the complications, without the pain and the hard parts. But you have to admit," she adds with a half wink, "that I insisted right from the beginning that you should not call me Kheli [an Israeli middle-class nickname for Rachel]." I sheepishly admit it.

"Go to Kheli. She's an amazing woman," Leah Shakdiel, an Ashkenazi teacher and activist who makes her home in Yerucham, had told me when I asked her to introduce me to local women who could guide me in the first steps of my research. To this day, I am grateful to Leah for her advice. Rachel opened up life spaces in Yerucham that none of the other women I met were capable of showing me. Through her eyes I saw the public side of life in the town: the Holocaust Remembrance Day ceremonies at the community center, the Tu b'Shevat parties, the PTA meetings at the high school, and the rehearsals of the local drama group. Rachel told me about the architecture students who held a weeklong workshop in Yerucham and about how proud she was to have hosted two of the women students in her home. Through her, I learned about the work of the Bamidbar Beit Midrash, and with her I went on day trips organized by the NA'AMAT women's organization for single mothers. By accompanying Rachel to her many social activities and meetings, I met the director of the local community center (who was later elected mayor of Yerucham) and was introduced to the members of the high school parents' committee.

Over the course of more than a decade, I have come to know Rachel well. Unlike the trouble-free story she wove in that first interview, her life, as I have witnessed firsthand, has been a continuous battle to break free of the poverty and lack of opportunity she faces in Yerucham. By the time I submitted the Hebrew draft of this book for publication in 2012, Rachel had secured a job as a secretary in a local factory. This was no small achievement for a woman with no high school diploma (she completed only two years in the vocational high school, in the hairdressing track), a woman who found herself, after a difficult divorce, responsible for raising four children in a town with few employment opportunities. Yet, when we met again in 2013, after the book was published in Israel and while I was presenting it in public and academic forums around the country, I learned that Rachel's success was indeed fragile: she had lost the coveted secretarial job, and the local employment office, to her great displeasure, had sent her to work as a cleaner in a neighboring kibbutz.

Rachel's fleeting success in breaking away from her dependence on the welfare system and her short-lived tenure in one of the few available secretarial positions in Yerucham might sound unremarkable to outside ears. Such achievement is even less impressive when one considers the position had *not* improved her economic situation a great deal. Her salary as a secretary at the factory did not amount to much more than the accumulated sum of welfare payments she received as a single mother and the part-time income she was allowed to earn as a welfare recipient. She complained that the money she earned as a full-time secretary did not cover her regular expenses, which included her young son's boarding school fees and payments for debts accumulated over the years. Her dream of buying a car, which would have made commuting to her workplace on the outskirts of town easier and would have freed her from dependence on irregular public transportation when she wanted to travel outside Yerucham, had not materialized. And yet, Rachel's success in breaking away from reliance on welfare and her ability to build a life of financial and personal independence, at least for a few years, is exceptional in Yerucham. The exceptionality of her story throws into stark relief the plight of most women who were born and raised in the town, who are unable to break out of the concrete boxes that limit their options for social mobility.

Leah Shakdiel and the founders of Bamidbar Beit Midrash describe Rachel as "an amazing woman." I concur. Rachel is indeed a woman of impressive intelligence, prodigious energy, and a great deal of charm. These qualities propelled her into an enviable work position (however briefly) in a place beset by unemployment and into a wide array of social activities in a small provincial town offering little in the way of stimulation. Rachel is one of the few local women to take part in the events organized by Bamidbar Beit Midrash. Her boundless energy and creativity convinced the organization's directors to designate her a group leader. Later, they offered her a part-time administrative job. But this position could not be made permanent because Rachel did not have the formal education and qualifications required for the job. A similar scenario had unfolded a few years earlier: Rachel had contributed her time and energy to organizing activities for single mothers, leading NA'AMAT's regional coordinator to offer her a part-time job as secretary of the organization's local branch, a position that lasted only a few months.

In the summer of 2002, after two years of ethnographic research in Yerucham, I began a sabbatical year in Canada. When I told Rachel of my travel plans, she referred me enthusiastically to her older sister, who had been living with her family in Montreal for many years. Meeting her sister made me realize just how much social setting shapes one's life. A well-groomed woman in her late forties, Rachel's sister works as the human resources director at a Canadian pharmaceutical company and lives in one of Montreal's nicer neighborhoods. The difference between Rachel's limited accomplishments and struggles and her sister's achievements highlights the question that stands at the center of the two chapters I devote to Rachel's life: How would her life have looked if she had lived in a social setting that did not place so many obstacles in her path?

Rachel's life story, like those of the other women described in this book, is not a tale of victimhood, but neither is it an account of heroic struggle against external forces of oppression. Her story has many elements in common with Nurit's and with the stories of other single mothers. Rachel married young, spent almost a decade outside the labor force as she took care of her children, and when her marriage dissolved, was left, like a growing number of women in similar circumstances, with no option other than welfare to support her family. Her story also briefly parallels Efrat's, as Rachel once considered the path of *hit'hazkut*, increased religious observance.

While aspects of Efrat's and Nurit's life stories echo in Rachel's, her story is uniquely her own. Unlike Efrat, Rachel rejects a life of greater religious observance, constructing her experience with the *hit'hazkut* path as a failed attempt to save her crumbling marriage. And, in contrast to Nurit and other single mothers on welfare, Rachel manages to escape the cleaning work offered by the local employment office and succeeds, at least for a short while, in securing white-collar office jobs. And yet, when Rachel's achievements are compared to those of her sister in Canada, a woman with similar skills and background, her success seems extremely modest. Tracing the contours of her life story over more than a decade brought me to the sobering realization that the potential to break away from the multiple marginalizations that life in Yerucham dictates, even for the most talented and ambitious residents, is virtually nil.

Rachel's story, then, addresses broader questions about the reproduction of class in Israeli peripheral towns like Yerucham.

I trace her story along two axes. First, I describe my encounters and shared experiences with Rachel beginning in 2000. Then, I present several brief essays that Rachel wrote at my request, in which she describes in her own words various issues that define her life.

Writing about Her Own Life

In 2001, almost a year after we first meet, I sit in Rachel's apartment one evening and suggest that she write about her own life. I promise her that I will publish her notes in my book and that I will pay her for each text she submits. Rachel wastes no time getting started; she takes out a pen and paper and quickly jots down several topics that she feels can serve as the basis for depicting her life story. Rachel writes seven texts in all. She types them on her home computer. She submits the first three essays in 2001, during the most intense period of our relationship. In the course of that year, I meet Rachel at least twice a week in Yerucham. She continues to write essays during my sabbatical year in Canada (July 2002 to July 2003). The final two essays are written in 2003, after I return to Israel and continue my field research in Yerucham.

By mid-2004 my visits to Yerucham become less frequent, and my interactions with Rachel are reduced to brief telephone conversations in which we update one another on what is happening in our lives. It is not until late 2008 that I return to Rachel's apartment one evening with a copy of the rough draft of this chapter. I leave it with her and ask her to comment on it. Rachel enjoys the idea that her story, incorporating her own texts, is to be published in a book. She asks me to make a few changes relating to specific details of her private life that she does not wish to reveal. She suggests that I use her real name but insists that I avoid mentioning her children's names. I decide against using her real name, but I otherwise modify the manuscript in accordance with her requests.

Writing did not come easily to Rachel despite her articulate speech. Still, she continued to write these texts and was openly happy for the chance to tell about her life in her own words. I have corrected only a few spelling and punctuation mistakes, but I have not otherwise edited or altered Rachel's texts; they are presented here verbatim and in full, arranged into three thematic groups.

The first group includes three essays that offer detailed descriptions of the main circles of Rachel's life. The first essay describes Yerucham as a community, a home, a life space. The second presents Rachel's family of origin and her place in a family of Moroccan immigrants that included 11 children. In the third essay Rachel depicts the more private spaces of her life as a mature woman coping with marriage, parenthood, work, and dependence on welfare. Rachel's explicit effort to put a good face on her life story is apparent in these first three essays. She is obviously aware that she is writing for an Israeli reader who, she assumes, is unfamiliar with life in remote Yerucham, particularly with the life of an Israeli-born Moroccan woman. Rachel writes these essays in a flowing, somewhat flowery style.

In the second set of essays (presented in chapter 4), I juxtapose two texts written by Rachel on the topic of religion. Read together, they reveal a change in Rachel's tone and mode of self-presentation over time. The earlier essay, which she titles "Religion and Me," has a declarative, public, almost apologetic style. The second essay, in which she describes her failed attempt to reintroduce religious observance into her life and the collapse of her marriage, is highly personal, reflective, and critical.

The essays in the third group (also presented in chapter 4) were composed by Rachel in 2003 and 2004. In these later writings she offers political commentary on her social status as a single mother coping with restrictive social frameworks. The tone of these pieces is vastly different from the tone of her earlier writings and suggests a reflexive critical thinking that might have emerged as a result of her intensive engagement in this study.

In the first essay, "Yerucham, My Home," Rachel describes the desert town where she was born and raised, enthusiastically representing her community to an outside audience. Rachel's imagined readers are middle-class Israelis living in the country's larger cities, and she invites them to learn about the advantages of Yerucham from a person who insists on emphasizing the positive: the beauty, the warmth, the friendliness of the community and the town. The essay opens with an almost touristic overview of what Rachel seems to assume is an unfamiliar reality for her readers.

Yerucham, My Home

I was born and raised in Yerucham and live here to this day. I wouldn't trade this quiet, friendly, peaceful town for any other place—in Israel or the world. Here, I know everyone, and everyone knows me. In Yerucham, it's all for one and one for all, in good times and bad. Everyone is there for you. At family celebrations, you can find half the town at the banquet hall. And in times of tragedy, everyone comes together and offers to help—each person as much as he can. The atmosphere here is very familial, warm, and supportive. Whenever a neighbor needs any kind of assistance, she knows that she has someone to rely on and that there will always be someone to help. In the same way, when a neighbor comes to her and asks her for help of any kind, she'll offer it without hesitation. Here in Yerucham, it feels like one big home. You can pop over unannounced for a cup of coffee at a close friend's, and you'll always get a warm welcome. Since the town is "compact," it radiates a sense of security. Almost everyone knows every pathway, the neighborhoods, the houses, the townspeople. Even little children don't get lost because they can easily find their way home and because most of the people who live here know everyone else's kids. So even if a small child strays very far from home and loses his way, chances are that someone will find him and know who he "belongs" to—and what's more, they'll even bring him home.

Since Yerucham is small, everything revolves around one major street, "the main road." That's where all the "action" takes place. This is a bustling street, crammed with parked cars, since it's close to the center of town where the various stores are located: clothing, shoes, vegetables, meat, photos, flowers, grocery stores, and a branch of Bank Hapoalim, our only bank (there used to be a branch of Bank Leumi as well, where I worked when I was younger, but it closed for lack of business). At these stores, you can buy things on credit and pay "when you've got the cash."

And the bank lets you have an overdraft until you need a loan to cover your "minus," because not everyone was born with a silver spoon in their mouth, and no one comes into this world with a nice fat bank account.

The road runs the length of Yerucham from the city entrance to the industrial zone, bisecting the town, with the post office, clinic, bakery, dentist's office, well-baby clinic, and supermarket on either side of the street. Further down are our beautiful community and cultural centers, the public library, the Magen David Adom first-aid station, the fire station, and a banquet hall. Up the street (as you leave town heading toward the Dead Sea) is the industrial zone, which is home to the Ackerstein cement factory, Negev Ceramics, Brand Steelworks, Phoenicia Glass, Tempo beverages, a hi-tech plant for manufacturing computer chips, a carpentry shop, a welder, a laundromat, and more. At the entrance to Yerucham (coming from Be'er-Sheva) is the Agis-Careline plant, which manufactures pharmaceuticals, cosmetics, and cleaning materials.

Most of Yerucham's residents, as well as those from the surrounding area, work in these factories, and their economic future is largely dependent on them. When any of these plants is facing closure—a situation that we've experienced in the past—the town's financial officers are called in. They launch an all-out war against the national government and its discrimination against development towns and try with all their might to prevent the shutdown from happening. At times, the residents need to get involved in demonstrations outside of town, primarily in Jerusalem at government offices (and I'm speaking from personal experience), with bus company owners from Yerucham donating free buses for this purpose. Kind people, even those not directly involved in the struggle, have given up a day of work and gone up to Jerusalem, out of pain and solidarity, to protest this injustice. It should be noted that they've done this in the most dignified way possible, without burning tires or cursing, maintaining their self-restraint and civility. Apart from these strikes, Yerucham does not get negative press coverage; on the contrary, it has been awarded a city beautification prize for the past five years for being a clean, well-kept town. In addition, our school system has exemplary rates of high-school matriculation. The percentage who take the matriculation exams has grown over the years, as a result of the belief, concern, and investment of the mayor and the director of our Education Division, who were wise enough to understand that the future of our children lies in their education. They spared no effort to provide each and every student with the opportunity to achieve matriculation (which a few years ago was only available to a chosen few). They brought the best teachers from around the country, offering them attractive salaries and living conditions so that they would agree to come to Yerucham. And it worked! The unbelievable happened! Thanks to this effort, many students stayed in the system and finished high school and can now go on to study at university.

Yerucham lies in the heart of the desert, surrounded by mountains, craters, cliffs, hills, and sand dunes. At the entrance to the town is a manmade lake that has seen better days. It used to have clear water with some fish, and people could even swim there. I remember as a little girl going down there with some kids from the neighborhood on Saturday afternoons and swimming there. Today the lake is closed by order of the Health Ministry due to pollution. What a shame. This place was part of the landscape of my childhood. Now my children have grown, and they find Yerucham boring compared with nearby Be'er-Sheva, which is full of job opportunities and leisure and entertainment options. They ask me why I stay in this "hole," and I tell them that here is where I feel the most secure and protected because of the special nature of the townspeople and the place. I know that here the residents are the family that I was born and grew up with. They're the ones who know me, and I know every one of them. In a different place, I'd feel like a guest, a foreigner, and it would take me a long time to trust people. And because I was part of the growth and development of Yerucham, I can't think of a better place to live. This is what I keep on explaining to my kids, because they were born at a point when Yerucham was a place that, as far as they were concerned, didn't move forward or develop. They're always comparing it to other places that are newer and that seem more advanced when it comes to jobs, places to live, culture, and leisure. This situation causes them frustration, disappointment, and despair, and it's no wonder that they're "doing [me] a favor" by finishing high school or being willing to work at the jobs offered them by the local Employment Office. When it comes time for them to do their army service, they ask themselves why they should contribute to the state if the state (and Yerucham) don't give them anything.

This reminds me of how people have lost faith in the town. They don't believe that things can work out anywhere with a little good will and motivation. It doesn't matter where you live if you always see the glass as half empty, or measure how much others have and you don't. People who live in big cities aren't always happy with what they have, and there'll always be something that they're missing in their lives. This is why people have to learn how to manage anywhere and to create something out of nothing. Everything depends on willpower. It's not the town that's "screwed up" but the people here who "screw up" their lives. If a person complains all the time about what he doesn't have, I'm sure he'll keep on doing it even if he lives in Herzliya Pituach [a wealthy Tel Aviv suburb]. The race to compare yourself to other people never ends. Here in this little place, there isn't much that can make the residents jealous of each other. There aren't extreme class differences here, with vast wealth in the face of abject poverty. Everyone here is from the middle class, with more or less the same houses and cars. Because of this, the solidarity is also more noticeable here than in a big city. With us, there isn't a situation of the grass is always greener on the other side;

everyone's grass is the same color. What's more, if the grass of one of the neighbors turns yellow, before you turn around a good neighbor will come over and offer to help.

But I'm mature and I understand life, more or less. My kids, like all kids their age, don't want to understand things based on our wisdom and life experience—that what you have is what you achieve on your own. No one's going to come along and give you anything for free, unless you were born to a rich father who freed you of the need to sweat and get your hands dirty. This generation has no idea how hard the previous generation worked to get as far as they did. They were born into the generation of Internet and technology where all they need to do is push a button to get things done. They're spoiled and lazy, and immediately look at the difficulties before they even understand what's going on. They don't have the patience for the process, and they want results right here, right now. Because of this, they often come up empty-handed and end up back at square one. It's the same broken record of anger, despair, and frustration. And again they blame the place where they live for not providing them with their basic needs.

How can one break free of this cycle? By having modest expectations, being satisfied with what I have, and never being jealous of my neighbors' drapes or carpets. I think of myself as the ideal resident for a humble place like Yerucham. In general, the more you have, the more you have to worry about, so who needs it?!

Rachel's essay, in which she proclaims herself "the ideal resident for a humble place like Yerucham," has a clear and consistent message: Yerucham is a small, warm, wonderful town and she "wouldn't trade it for any other place in Israel or the world." The piece reads like a public relations release showcasing everything beautiful and positive about a town that has a terrible reputation in Israeli public discourse. Only toward the end does Rachel make mention of the less pleasant perspective of Yerucham as an isolated, neglected town filled with frustrated people. This perception is mistaken, she hastens to explain, and she must therefore correct the misconceptions at the heart of this negative view of the town and its inhabitants.

The message Rachel's essay conveys, that Yerucham is a "quiet, friendly, peaceful town," a place of warmth, modesty, and family feeling, where people are satisfied with what they have, is precisely what those in the centers of power want to hear from residents of the periphery. Rachel's essay does not overlook any of these tropes. Like a practiced tour guide, Rachel leads the virtual visitor along the bustling main street and lists the variety of stores and public institutions that make the small town a pleasant place to live in bourgeois terms. Thus, she makes a point of mentioning the florist and the photo store—businesses that symbolize economic well-being and an urban standard of living—in addition to the necessary clinic and bank. There is only one bank in town today, but Rachel is quick to add that when she was younger, there was a second one that closed "for lack of business." A short time after she wrote this essay, the florist she mentioned closed and was replaced by a store selling Indian spices. It soon closed too "for lack of business."

Rachel's tour of Yerucham is not complete without mention of the factories located near the outskirts of town along the roads leading to the Dead Sea and Be'er-Sheva. Yerucham, she notes with pride, has won a city beautification award five years in a row—an official prize awarded to clean, well-kept towns—and the local school system has an excellent reputation.

Strikes? A filthy, useless lake on the edge of town? Isolation? Remoteness? Frustrated young people with no future? Angry people with no prospects? All are mentioned in the piece but are seen through rose-tinted glasses. The strikes by those who work in the factories on which "their economic future" depends are struggles waged "in a dignified way" in which the strikers are supported by "kind people" who express solidarity over (unexplained) "injustice." It is important to Rachel to emphasize that everyone maintains "self-restraint and civility."

The lake outside town is also presented in a positive light. Although it has "seen better days" and Rachel considers it a shame that the "landscape of [her] childhood" is in ruins, her reference to the lake's glory days gives her an opportunity to describe its once clear waters and abundant fish, details her imaginary readers (so she assumes) can appreciate. The poverty of the town's residents, who cannot afford to buy goods in the local stores, simply reflects the truism that "not everyone was born with a silver spoon in their mouth." Toward the end of the essay, Rachel cites the frustration and lack of opportunity for young people, noting that they have "lost faith in the town," but she dismisses this view as an error in judgment. The frustration, in her opinion, stems from improper comparisons between "humble" Yerucham and other, more affluent places.

At certain points, Rachel writes in an almost literary register. She sanitizes coarser language, such as *dfukim* (literally, "screwed up") by enclosing it in quotation marks. Her central message is that the key to living in Yerucham is contentment with one's lot, modest expectations, and love for the town. As one who has learned and internalized these concepts, Rachel has earned her self-ascribed title as Yerucham's "ideal resident."

The Ideal Local Girl Speaks to an Outside Audience

In her opening essay, as well as in the next one (about family), Rachel is engaged in an ongoing dialogue with an imagined external audience. She situates herself at the juncture between inside and outside, between "us" (residents of Yerucham) and "you" (people who are unfamiliar with the town and with life there). Rachel's imagined readers are assumed to subscribe to the concepts and logic of a bourgeois, liberal discourse in which the aesthetic reflected in, say, beautiful public gardens is appreciated. To such readers, Rachel needs to point out the official certificates of recognition awarded to Yerucham and its town council for developing a well-maintained public space. This imagined middle-class audience also expects a variety of services and stores, community centers, and a good school system. Rachel is clearly aware that a liberal outsider discourse does not encourage the use of terms such as *discrimination* or *injustice* and looks disapprovingly on labor demonstrations that are not "dignified." Outsiders, Rachel's narrative suggests, will be pleased to hear that people in this far-off town are happy with their lot—with the warmth, tranquility, and family atmosphere of their community.

Rachel sets her own "maturity" against the childish, immature, pointless feelings of anger and frustration that others, her own young children included, might express. She thus adopts and reflects back all of the expectations of the dominant discourse, ending her essay with the ultimate trope of self-help—the solution to all local problems, if indeed there are problems in beautiful, peaceful Yerucham. Local residents must buckle down and help themselves, she concludes: "What you have is what you achieve on your own. No one's going to come along and give you anything for free."

Rachel's ability to adopt the key tropes of centrist liberal discourse is not limited to her essays. In fact, in her daily life Rachel embodies the role of the amiable, gracious hostess who introduces Yerucham in a pleasant light to outside visitors. She is proud to tell me that each time a group of visitors, foreign donors, or Israeli officials arrives in town, she is summoned by the mayor to meet these people and present the "local perspective" on Yerucham. She frequently hosts visitors from the Jewish Agency, Israeli students, and volunteers in her home.

I experienced Rachel's bright hospitality firsthand when she invited my family into her home during the first year of my work in Yerucham. In an early field note I wrote on October 1, 2000, I describe her generous hospitality. I describe how impressed I am by the abundance of food she serves and by her insistence that she has not served spicy dishes because she knows that children and "visitors from overseas" are not so fond of such food. I note that Rachel is extremely gracious to my non-Israeli spouse, who does not speak Hebrew, and is amazed that my two young sons speak English with their father. During this early visit, I translate Rachel's comments into English, and I write how deeply touched I am by her warmth and pleasant manner. I realize that our visit to her home is not unique when we leave her apartment and one of her neighbors remarks, "You've got guests from abroad *again*?"

Following the meal, Rachel takes us on a guided tour of Yerucham. I later recall with a smile the sites she leads us to, places that I have never revisited in all the years since. Rachel guides us to a statue erected on a hill at the entrance to the town, to a public park at the southern end of town, and from there to a monument commemorating local war dead. She shows us a sculpted wall next to the public library, points out the music conservatory, and takes us to a square filled with palm trees not far from the refurbished commercial center. The spaces that Rachel leads us to are meant to convince us, the outsiders to town, that "there are things worth seeing" in Yerucham. These sites are markers of "high" art and culture in an otherwise marginalized landscape. In taking us to them, Rachel attempts to contest and undermine the hegemonic perception of Yerucham as a backward town, a space remote from Israel's national history and culture. Rachel works hard to redefine the space of her town for her outside visitors.

Throughout her guided tour with my family Rachel presents a flowing narrative. She cites the name of the artist who designed the relief on the wall of the public library and provides interpretive comments at various sites ("Here, in the commercial center of town, the idea was to maintain a uniform style, so the painted signs on every store front are of the same color"). When she shows us the dilapidated movie theater, she remarks nostalgically, "This is our old movie theater house. Oh, we have watched so many great movies here! Now it's empty. But our Heichal Tarbut [Cultural Center] fills the same role today." When we return to her apartment after the tour, Rachel shows us photographs of her daughter that she took days before the girl's bat mitzvah celebration. In these pictures the birthday girl is shown standing next to a statue or in front of a monument at some of the sites we have just visited. Rachel beams, "No one could figure out how I remembered all these places. There are people from Yerucham who themselves did not recognize the nice spots where I photographed my daughter."

In the next essay Rachel recounts her family history. She describes the dynamic in her large family, analyzing with great humor the balance of power among the children, who contend in their own ways with the responsibilities placed on them. But, as in the previous essay, here too a thread of romanticism is woven through the account of dramatic family events.

My Mother's House

I first saw the light of day in my parents' home, where I was brought from the maternity ward of Soroka Hospital in Be'er-Sheva. The date: August 12. The year: 1962. Construction had just been completed on a spacious new room in my parents' house to hold the many children in our family. As the ninth child, I was welcomed with great joy, in particular because I was a girl after four boys. When my parents immigrated to Israel from Morocco, they had brought with them my five siblings, born in this order: son, daughter, son, daughter, son. But in Israel, somehow the order got mixed up, and three boys were born in a row. When my mother became pregnant with me, my father was certain he had another son on the way and was already emotionally prepared for "disappointment." He claimed that girls weren't born in the Land of Israel, so he had already invited the mohel, stocked up for the celebration, and was awaiting the birth and the bris. When he was told that he had a daughter, he didn't believe it and insisted on seeing with his own eyes what was underneath the diaper. Only then was his mind at ease.

I don't really remember my childhood, but from old pictures that I found in the family album I can reconstruct fragments of time and past events. I was raised primarily by my second sister, who was 10 years older than me, because my mother was busy with everything else: laundry, cleaning, cooking, grocery shopping, and so on. My father was a civilian employee of the army, as a result of which he was absent during the week and would only come home on weekends. Even then, he had no time or energy to help with household matters or child-rearing. For this reason, the older children helped raise their younger siblings. My oldest sister didn't like helping with anything. She was only interested in her looks (she was, and still is, amazingly "put together") and in boys. She would stand in front of the mirror all day and ask: Who is the fairest in the town? And when she got no response, she would change her hairstyle, add more makeup, change her clothes—and this went on all day. This would drive my second sister (the one who raised me) crazy, because everything ended up falling in her lap. She was the one who cleaned the house. She was the one who ironed my sisters' and brothers' clothes and also sewed up the jeans that would get torn at every soccer game. She was the one who washed the clothing by hand because the washing machine was only half-automatic, and the clothing needed to be wrung out by hand. In short, I had a lot to be mad and complain about, but there was no one to hear it because everyone was preoccupied with their own things. My older brothers were busy with their ever-changing girlfriends. My mother was already tired and worn out from giving birth and housework, and I was just a little girl. I think that my sister got married early because of this; she preferred to get out while she still could. And when she did, just as I was getting a little older, her entire role was "handed down" to me, against my wishes and my plans. But no one asked me. Suddenly I found myself "doing a favor" for one brother who wanted his new pants hemmed, and ironing a shirt for a different brother who was rushing to a date with his girlfriend. And I, who was now responsible for four older brothers and two more born after me, didn't really have a way out. My older sister had already married much earlier and had two children, my second sister was just getting married, and me, they left behind.

When my father would come home from his work in the Sinai area, he would close himself up in his room and listen to his favorite Egyptian music: Farid al-Atrash, Umm Kulthum, Abdel Halim Hafez, Fayrouz, and Asmahan (the sister of Farid al-Atrash). Asmahan was murdered by a contract killer hired by a rival singer. Or so my dad told me at the time, when he felt like talking. Those black vinyl records and that old record player were his entire world. He would listen to them again and again until I knew all the words by heart, even though I didn't understand a thing. Egyptian Arabic is not that similar to the Moroccan dialect that was spoken in my mother's home. But despite this, I knew how to sing songs in Egyptian Arabic, though I couldn't answer my mother when she spoke to me in Moroccan Arabic. I couldn't even put two words together.

My mother, who didn't know how to read or write (apart from a few words of French that she had learned at the Alliance Israélite Universelle school in Casablanca), would use my help translating documents and letters from all over. These included letters from the schools where my brothers were "supposedly studying." Some of them had to do with their frequent lateness (no surprise after being up all night), and some with their many missed classes and absences in general. When such a letter came my way, I knew I held a treasure in my hands. Of course I didn't tell my mother what was really written in the letter; instead, I told her that everything was all right and that the teachers were pleased with her children, that they always came on time, with all their supplies, and that they could serve as an example to the other kids. Between you and me, isn't that what every Moroccan mother wants to hear? Why make her sad? Her life was bleak enough. And besides, by keeping the content of the letters from her, I could blackmail my brothers and come to them with all sorts of demands. For example, that they take care of their own clothes, buy stuff for me, or take me out with them, especially to see a movie at the fondly remembered Mira Theater, because that was basically our only entertainment in Yerucham, apart from hanging out on the main street every Friday night. So sometimes I would do really well, and sometimes they couldn't care less; it depended which brother it was, and how serious the problem in the letter.

One brother, who I'm still close with, was so cute and well liked. He never made trouble for anyone, loved to help everyone, was always smiling, always in a good mood, always surrounded by friends, was a member of the Boy Scouts, volunteered in the Civil Guard, just a sweetheart. He was the one I would always go to when one of my other brothers got on my nerves. And he, in his quiet, comforting way, would calm me down and tell me, "Don't pay any attention to them. They love you. You're our little sister. They just want to show off in front of their friends and show what big tough guys they are. But you know who the real hero is here? It's you, who shows them how strong you are by not acting stupid like them." His words worked like magic, calming me down until the next time. He was my anchor, my lifesaver, every time I felt I was going under.

Another brother was our "pretty boy," with his green eyes and blonde hair. Because of this, he was always surrounded by adoring girls. I remember he was always asking me to go to the home of one girl or another and ask her to come out, because in those days they didn't have cell phones (there were barely any landlines in the homes). And he was too shy to go into their parents' homes to ask them out. Sometimes he would ask me to introduce him to some of my friends; this was another one of my jobs. But ever the sly one, I could tell right away if there was something in it for me; like if I assured her parents that she was only with me and not "with some guy," God forbid, I could get myself a movie ticket out of the deal (because I was "responsible" for her). My brother had no choice but to drag me with him every time I "promised" the girl's parents that I was watching out for her. My older brothers already managed for themselves because they went out with older girls whose parents were already waiting for them to find a husband, so they didn't need me as an "alibi."

When I got a little older and grew from a little girl into a pretty teenager, things turned around and my brothers' friends asked to be introduced to me. At first, I was flattered that the "older boys" wanted to go out with me, but I quickly realized that they were in a hurry to grow up and already wanted to play "mommy and daddy" before getting married. Because they were my brothers' friends, I was caught in a dilemma: to tell or not to tell (like Shakespeare once wrote: "to be or not to be"). If I told my brothers what their good friends wanted from me, I risked ruining their friendship; and if I didn't tell, I would have to give in to their demands. And this, of course, I was unwilling to do. So I sat down and thought about it (I couldn't consult with my brother, my confidant, about this because it was somewhat intimate), and decided to announce that I was not interested in romantic relationships with my brothers' friends. This was also my message to anyone else who would listen. And that was the end of that.

My little brother was the apple of my father's eye, because he was the youngest child, born when my parents were older; for this reason, he always got extra pampering. Whatever he wanted, he got. My father never refused him anything. For this reason, we siblings would send him to Father whenever we wanted something and weren't getting it, because we were sure that he *would* get it. But we were also not "ingrates" who took advantage, and we knew how to "reward" him with sweets, games, or spending money (that he would get us from Father, of course). That's how it is in a big family: one helps the other "put one over" on the next one; each one looks out for himself, and everyone feels they're the smart one.

My father, may he rest in peace, was among the earliest immigrants to arrive in Yerucham (in 1954), and he built the town's first institutions and buildings with his own two hands. He died when I was just 17. I remember it was a Sunday morning. I went to work at Bank Leumi, where I was a clerk/mail girl (at the time, they would hire young people before their military service for light office work to instill a work ethic, responsibility, discipline, and to give them a way to support themselves and save some money for higher education; even today, some places still do that, but no longer the banks). So that morning I got to work as usual. An hour or two later, the head of the branch called me into his office. I didn't suspect a thing; from time to time, he would call me in to ask me to handle certain tasks. This time, he was flustered and shaking. I thought he wasn't feeling well and asked him what had happened. He asked me to sit down in the chair facing him, and said to me, "They just called from your house and told me that your father is very ill and that you should come home." Not liking to feel helpless, to see someone sick and know that I'm unable to help him or do something to ease his suffering, I told my boss that I would rather stay at work. Something in me was apparently protecting me from the possibility of facing some sort of trauma, so I preferred to remain in a "happier" place.

What I didn't know at the time was that he was not telling me the truth, that my father was already dead, because he didn't feel able to tell me. So he insisted that I go home. But the more he insisted, the more stubborn I became, because I already understood intuitively that the situation was much more serious. When my boss saw that he was unable to convince me to go home, he called in his second-in-command, who was more assertive, and it was he who told me the painful truth. He explained that he understood that I didn't want to be in a place of mourning with everyone around me weeping, and he told me that his own father had died not long ago and that he also hadn't known how to deal with it. But according to the Jewish religion, I had to remain home to sit shiva. Only then did I realize that I had no choice, because religion is religion and, with all my stubbornness, I couldn't argue with that. That same bank officer drove me to my house in his car, and when we got there I saw all our neighbors sitting in the yard and crying. "Go to your mother. She needs you now," he said to me. I got out of the car with trembling legs and went into the house. I found all my brothers sitting on the floor, wearing *kippot* and weeping. My mother was in a different corner of the room, and she was wailing and clawing at her face, as mourners do. I really didn't want to be there, so I did a U-turn and walked back to my place of work. When I walked into the branch, the workers saw me and didn't understand what I was doing there. I explained to them that I didn't want to go home because "it's scary there." But then they put me back in the car and took me home.

My father's body was sent for an autopsy to Abu Kabir [forensic institute] to discover the cause of death, since he had not been sick at all and had worked until his last day. He had simply gone to sleep Saturday night and planned to get up in the morning and travel to his work in the Sinai area. But in the morning, my mother had made him coffee as usual and gone to wake him. A short time later, she noticed that he hadn't gotten up. She went to him and touched his body and saw that he was cold as ice and wasn't responding at all. What a trauma for a wife to suddenly discover her husband, the father of her children, the man she has shared her entire life with, lying dead, and what's more, on the double bed in their bedroom. I don't know how I would have reacted under such circumstances. But my mother is a very strong woman who's always known how to deal with crises. This time too, she kept her composure and faced the situation with courage. After the shiva, we received the pathological report, which determined that my father had died as a result of suffocation. He had apparently eaten something just before going to sleep and fell asleep on his back out of sheer exhaustion. At some point during the night, he had wanted to vomit but could not get up, and then it all stuck in his throat and blocked his airway. He died such a foolish, unnecessary death that sometimes, later on, I would get angry with him for leaving us this way for no reason, without being sick or old, without giving us time, without saying good-bye to us. Because he was only 63 and was healthy to his last day.

I felt like he had abandoned my mother and me. My brothers, I wasn't worried about, because they were men and knew how to manage. Both my sisters were married and had husbands to take care of them. Just me and my mother were left. My oldest brother had died of cancer nine years earlier, when he was only 24 and I was eight. (When you lose a son, and especially a firstborn son, in a traditional Moroccan family, it's like losing your sight.) Another daughter, younger than me, died at the age of three due to medical negligence. She received a penicillin injection, though it was known that she was allergic to it and despite the fact that my mother had warned the doctor that the little girl should not be given penicillin. He thought that he was smarter than her and gave it to her anyway. Several hours later, her condition deteriorated. She was rushed to hospital and all of the efforts to save her life were in vain. My mother, who had already known loss, was experienced with pain. Apparently what didn't kill her made her stronger because it was she who kept the family on its feet and fought tooth and nail for our survival, especially after she was left with orphans and no breadwinner. And thank God, we all grew up and studied and worked and got married and had children. Life goes on.

Rachel constructs a narrative centered on a "traditional Moroccan family" for an imagined modernist reader. Throughout the essay she adopts an external perspective in describing her own family. For example, when she uses the phrase "between you and me," she is placing herself and her readers in a shared "us" category vis-à-vis her mother, an Other of whom she says, "Isn't that what every Moroccan mother wants to hear? Why make her sad? Her life was bleak enough."

While Rachel depicts her mother as a Moroccan woman with a "bleak" life (admiring her nonetheless as a "very strong woman" who always knows how to deal with crises), she portrays her father as a remote man who works away from home and consequently is not a significant figure for his wife and children, a familiar scenario for the middle-class reader with whom Rachel is conducting her implicit dialogue. Rachel is also careful to delineate her father's love of classical Arabic music, perhaps to make him a more complex, sensitive, parental figure to whom her readers might relate. Her father listens to *classical* Arabic music, not popular Arabic music, largely disparaged by middle-class Israelis. Her limited knowledge of Moroccan Arabic marks her as a sabra (Israeli born), yet she is aware of the newfound liberal Israeli appreciation for Egyptian Arabic lyrics, which allows her to express pride in her Arabic Jewish cultural roots.

Rachel describes her brothers with romanticized affection. There is the pretty one, the one she turns to in times of trouble, and the ones who use her to woo local girls. Like a skilled anthropologist, she explains the family dynamic as the product of a hierarchy resting on birth order and gender divisions. Thus, for example, she explains her sisters' need to get out of the house as a desire to escape their scripted obligation to provide free services for their brothers. She depicts herself as a rebellious girl who charms her way out of her expected gendered duties, as one who knows how to get along within the context of a strict patriarchic family.

When she describes her job as an errand girl and file clerk at the bank, she does so once again in terms drawn from the world of the middle-class reader. She feels the need to preface her story with a kind of sociological explanation, noting that "at the time, they would hire young people before their military service for light office work to instill a work ethic, responsibility, discipline, and to give them a way to support themselves and save some money for higher education." But her social and class background makes it clear that she is *not* working at the bank temporarily before joining the military (she never served in the army) or in an effort to earn money for higher education (this was not an option for her, even if she did have the full sum required for tuition).

Rachel's adoption of the language of the middle class only emphasizes how different her reality is from the life frame of her imagined readers. The act of rewriting her life course, which includes dropping out of school, early marriage, lack of formal education, and brief unskilled work experience, in terms of middle-class scenarios merely highlights the gap between Rachel's class position and life circumstances and the middle-class world she so ardently aspires to.

Rachel writes about a harsh reality of family deaths, poverty, and deprivation, but she does so in an almost fairy-tale language of courage, love, and romanticism. Rachel's effort to obscure the fact that she is a single mother on welfare and that she has no qualifications that might bring her solid work and upward mobility seems to navigate between two discourses that refuse to intersect. This juggling act, this ability to speak and see the world through two, at times contradictory, discourses, characterizes not only Rachel's written self-presentation but also, as we will see, the way she conducts her life.

The attempt to frame her life events in a way that will be pleasant to her imagined readers is well illustrated in the next essay, in which Rachel describes her employment history. Her text documents a cycle of brief, unskilled jobs before her marriage, years of pregnancies, the births of her four children, economic dependence on her low-income husband, and repeated failure to find a place in the labor market after her divorce. But here too Rachel's narrative glosses over the experience of deprivation and difficulty and is presented in middle-class terms as the pursuit of purpose. Framed in middle-class discursive language, the long line of brief low-level positions that she held before getting married is transformed into a search for a true vocation. The forced and prolonged absence from the labor market during the years when she needed to stay home and raise her four children is translated in this discourse into a necessary period of soul searching in a universal process of personal and professional development.

Work, Studies, and Other Pursuits

Ever since I remember myself, I have always loved to be around other people. I enjoyed broadening my circle of acquaintances and not staying in the same group all the time. It's nice to get to know different types of people, with different opinions, cultures, lifestyles, customs, ideas, and views of the world. So I have tried to go out to work even when I had small children at home. It was not always easy, but I would come home from work with great satisfaction. By nature, I'm a sociable person, and it's important to me to understand things differently than they appear at first glance. A good way of doing this is by being part of a diverse group of people. Each person teaches me something else, whether from an experience that he underwent or his own personal knowledge. I like learning new things from other people that can help me improve and correct mistakes so that I won't repeat them. As it is written, "Who is wise? He who learns from every person." There is no shame in learning from others. On the contrary, it's a great virtue for a person to recognize his limitations and be willing to listen to and learn from others. People also learn things from me—information or experience in a particular area that they're unfamiliar with—and I'm happy to help to the best of my ability.

I have worked at various jobs: I looked after elderly people for two years, working for the municipality. Or, more precisely, I helped them with housecleaning or shopping or running errands that they couldn't manage themselves because of their age or state of health. Some of them were very nice people whom I enjoyed spending time with, and others were annoying and behaved like babies. I understand that an older person who is ill needs a lot of attention and a sympathetic ear. But with all my patience, there were some who really crossed the line—actually not the patients that I was supposed to take care of but their wives, who thought that if the city was subsidizing their husband's care it was permissible for them to take advantage of the caregiver for other needs not directly related to the patient. In the beginning, I tried to explain tactfully to these women that I was there for their husband and not for them. But they weren't interested, and they continued to demand things over and above the usual housework. When I explained the situation to my supervisor, she claimed that this was a known phenomenon that had been going on for years in many homes and that there was no way to change it. I ended up leaving those families where I found the situation intolerable, staying on with the ones where I could somehow get through to the wife and win her over. With a little bit of attention to the wife (who apparently was jealous of the treatment her husband was receiving), I managed to break down the barriers of alienation and hostility, and even get them to the point where they sat and told me their innermost feelings, prepared tasty dishes for me so that I wouldn't be working "on an empty stomach," and gave me presents for the holidays. To this day, years after I stopped working for them, they still meet me on the street and ask how I'm doing and invite me over for a visit. With some of them, I'm in close touch even now.

I remember one elderly man who died a few years ago who was a really special person, exceptionally wise. He was a religious man of deep faith who had a strange hobby of collecting old newspapers, cutting out sentences and headlines containing sacred words or quotes from the Bible, and pasting them into ordinary notebooks. He had been doing this for many years since retiring, and this was his main pastime from morning till night. Over the years, he had accumulated thousands of these notebooks, much to the displeasure of his wife, who argued that he was busying himself with nonsense. This was what kept this man alive and gave him a reason to live another day. Knowing that many holy words in the daily press were thrown into the garbage, he saw himself as performing a mitzvah. I have no idea what became of those notebooks when he died. I was afraid to ask his wife. Maybe I was afraid of hearing the painful answer that they had been thrown out.

Another job I had—actually my first one—was as a clerk at a bank. This was before I got married. I was 16 when I got hired and worked there until age 18. It was an interesting, special job with a split workday, but I didn't mind. I loved the "stardom" of being close to so much money. I was the only worker from Yerucham at the bank; all the other workers came from Dimona, which was nearby. For this reason, the keys to the branch were placed in my little hands so that I could open the bank, turn on the air conditioning, and boil the water for coffee. It goes without saying that the head of the branch and the other workers had complete faith in me, and despite my young age I impressed them as a mature, responsible young woman. Over time, I was entrusted with more important tasks than filing the mail and answering the phones. I gradually became the favorite of the branch manager, who was like a second father to me after my own father died while I was working there. He treated me just like a daughter and at times would let me get away with chatting on the phone to one friend or another.

I remember there were times when young men would come to the bank to open an account, and they'd see a young, pretty girl and would usually flirt with me. If I was interested in the boy, I'd make coffee for the two of us and take a short break. If the break got a little long, I'd look through the glass of the manager's office and see if he was smiling at me, which meant I could stay a little longer; if his eyebrows were raised, I understood that I had to cut the "date" short. One time, a boy came in to the bank who wanted to get to know me, but I was really not interested in him because he wasn't good-looking enough for me to make the effort. So every time I saw his car parked by the bank, I would run right away to the manager's office and tell him to say I wasn't there. And in fact, when the poor boy came into the bank and asked about me, the manager would step out of his office and lie for me, saying that I hadn't come in to work. He was a great boss: a cool, easygoing guy. Sometimes he would say to me in a fatherly tone, "Racheli, what's going to be with you? You attract guys all over the place. Leave some for the other girls!" And I would smile and say, "How am I to blame if I'm so nice and friendly that all the guys who walk in here come mainly 'cuz of me and not because of their bank account?" By the way, the guy who became my husband, I also met there. I think I should have asked for a commission from the bank for all the guys who opened an account there. Thanks to me, a lot of new customers joined.

To get back to our story, after I got married and had the children, I didn't end up working anywhere else except for my job taking care of the elderly. But I kept myself busy with all sorts of activities and short courses, just for personal knowledge and so as not to be bored at home. I took a pottery course and made a lot of unique and beautiful ceramics that I keep in my home to this day. At the course, I helped the other women to decorate the items they made. Along the way, they became close to me and began to tell me their personal problems. I don't know how to explain this phenomenon that wherever I studied, worked, or volunteered, people felt the need to share their personal lives with me. Maybe because I would listen to them and identify with them. That's just how it was. And naturally, I would advise them and guide them as if I had a degree in psychology or sociology. I took a course in first aid and CPR. And all the young men there volunteered to be the "dummy" who lies on the floor. When it was my turn to perform mouth-to-mouth resuscitation, I did a funny bit and we would all roll with laughter. I'd pinch their nostrils as if to administer artificial respiration, but then I'd actually leave them that way so they couldn't breathe. At the end of the course, I got a certificate as a first aid provider. Every once in a while, when the security situation is worrisome like these days, they call me from Magen David Adom [the Israeli Red Cross] or the Civil Guard and place me "on alert" just in case.

Another course that I took was in hairdressing. It was given in Dimona by the Ministry of Labor and Social Welfare. The course lasted half a year, and I would travel there every morning, six days a week. I learned all these aspects of the theory of the profession: chemistry, biology. And I'm great at this kind of learning. I got 100 on all the tests! They called me a diligent, hardworking, serious student. And once again, I naturally found myself helping the weaker students. They were all older people who hadn't been to school in years, and their thinking and memory skills were a bit rusty. I completed the course with honors and received an official certificate as a hairdresser. The fact that I haven't done anything with it since then, well, that's another story. From time to time, when a friend asks me to blow-dry or dye her hair, I'm happy to do it. I also cut my children's hair when they were younger. Today when they want stylish, sophisticated haircuts, I send them—with all due respect—to a professional.

I mentioned earlier that since I like learning all kinds of things, I sign up for every course or activity that suits me at the time. But I have no idea beforehand if this will be the field that I'll want to work in for the rest of my life. So in the meantime, I'm branching out in several directions until I find my purpose in life—though something or someone is always pulling me toward community work. It's no accident that my next job was as secretary of the NA'AMAT women's organization in Yerucham. It was just part of my work for women in the community, which was done on a voluntary basis without payment from anyone. I did it because I felt it was the right thing to do. I realized that someone had to help them, and they didn't seem to be finding a sympathetic ear and genuine concern for their troubles. Maybe because I've gone through situations like theirs and have suffered what they're suffering, I was able to understand their feelings. I believed their stories—which a lot of social workers didn't do. I devoted as much time as they needed and didn't look at my watch to tell them that the session was over, see you next week. I sat with them until they were all talked out and their tears had dried, until they began to smile a little and to laugh at a joke I told them. When I knew that they were feeling calmer, I would say good-bye to them with a hug and kiss and keep in contact with them by phone to make sure they were feeling okay.

I worked at NA'AMAT for only one year. I actually liked the job, and it fit in with my work with women. It was an excellent opportunity to broaden the circle of women I knew. I had long-term plans for working with them. I wanted to do many things for them. I wanted to set up an organization for single-parent families that would give them information about their rights. I wanted to organize a special purchasing card for them that would allow them to buy goods or receive services from businesses in Yerucham at a 10% discount on each purchase. And I had already begun to work on it. I had written letters and personally delivered them to local merchants. And I should mention that the response was positive. A lot of them agreed to join this project and said they hoped it would succeed—not to mention the fact that it would also give businesses in Yerucham a shot in the arm. So it would have helped both the business owners and the needy families. But just before the idea of the cards became a reality, I was forced to leave my job. And so the rest of my plans were shelved. I still dream of setting up an organization for single-parent families and haven't forgotten it.

I was once a member of a group called Volunteer Community Leadership, an idea of the Jewish Agency's Partnership 2000 project. We were a group of people from Yerucham and

Dimona who would meet in the evening once every two weeks and think about projects for the community. Already at the time, I had this dream of setting up a group of single-parent families to make it easier for them to run their homes and take care of their children, given all the difficulties they faced as single parents. And then, when I came to this group, I realized that this was the right time and place to implement the idea. When I told the group about it, I managed to spark their enthusiasm, and everyone offered their help.

To begin, it was necessary to organize a general meeting of all the single-parent families in Yerucham. I had a list of women I knew from here and there, but I knew there were more such families whom I didn't know. I approached the director of the local welfare office, pointing out the importance of the matter, and asked for a list of additional single-parent families so that they too could join and benefit from the organization. To my surprise, my request was turned down without explanation. She was totally unwilling to work with me, using the excuse that this was confidential information and an invasion of privacy. Though I asked for a list of names only, without additional details, she refused to provide it. So, having no choice, I was forced to do it the hard way: I simply wrote up notices in Hebrew and Russian, preparing 1,000 copies with the help of the local community center, and handed out the flyers in every institution in Yerucham. I publicized the date and time, location, and purpose of the meeting and mentioned that their participation was very important.

On the evening of the meeting, I even made a few phone calls as a reminder. At the appointed time, one group after another started to arrive, and the hall filled up with a huge crowd. Many new-immigrant families came who had read the notices I gave out. Even the director of the community center and the chair of NA'AMAT, who were the guests of honor, were amazed by the number of people who turned out. The meeting was videotaped by a member of Partnership 2000 and was widely covered in the local press. It should be noted that no representative came from the Welfare Office, though they received invitations to attend the first event of its kind despite their lack of cooperation through-out the entire process. Even then they refused to acknowledge the meeting, perhaps because I had hit a nerve and proved to them that they weren't the only ones who could help disadvantaged people. But nothing came of the meeting.

The "Stardom" of an Errand Girl at a Bank

The attempt to translate her personal history into a narrative of self-discovery stretches Rachel's ability to reconcile her experience with the bourgeois ideal. Thus, for example, she transforms preparing coffee and opening the doors of the bank every morning into "an interesting, special job" that gives her a feeling of "stardom." Similarly, in response to the demands of the elderly men she cares for, her provision of services not included in her job description is presented as her generous way of attending to the unfulfilled social and emotional needs of these elders. She thus transforms herself from an unskilled, low-paid employee hired to care for the physical needs of impoverished seniors into a therapist.

Rachel's attempt to reframe her life experiences in terms of a middle-class value system is not limited to her recounting of her work experiences. Rachel seems to cross conventional boundaries that separate welfare recipients from professionals who make their careers by providing and managing state welfare services. One sees this, for example, in her volunteer effort to organize single mothers in town. As a single mother herself, Rachel tries to situate herself as a service provider, not a client. She insists that she is more effective in her ability to listen to and help these women than those she calls the "psychologists or sociologists." The ostensibly unexplained refusal of the social workers from the Welfare Office to cooperate with her initiatives makes it clear that they persist in seeing Rachel as a *recipient* and not a *provider* of services. They reject her creativity and thus stifle her attempts to shape a new boundary-blurring self.

In fact, not all of Rachel's efforts to position herself as an organizer and initiator, and not merely a welfare client, meet with failure. After several attempts at volunteer community work focused on single mothers in Yerucham, she succeeds in arranging a part-time job for herself as secretary at the local NA'AMAT office. On a certain level, Rachel is aware of the unique nature of her social activism, given her own position as a single welfare mother. She wonders out loud about the "something or someone [which] is always pulling me toward community work."

Rachel's aptitude for creating a space of activity for herself and for making connections lies in her exceptional articulateness and her ability to speak the language of those who can offer her resources, however limited. She is capable of juggling several codes of speech and make effective use of behavioral patterns that are not characteristic of her own class background. Her talent is vividly displayed in the following episode.

In August 2000 a group of architecture students came to Yerucham to conduct a weeklong study workshop focused on urban design. At the end of their visit, they held an open evening in the town library to present the projects they had devised. Only three locals showed up for the meeting. One was Rachel. This encounter between center and periphery, between the discourse of professionals and that of local residents, showcases Rachel's impressive ability to juggle, navigate between, and use the overt and covert codes of these different discourses. Rachel, I suggest, does not imitate the manner of speech and the thinking of the visiting students and their teachers; rather, she adopts them and makes them her own. Her conduct in the presence of these guests, with their distinctive cultural capital, illustrates her creativity in relation to what W.E.B. Du Bois called "a double consciousness."[1] I argue that all of the men and women in the town navigate between various cultural and class codes, though most do so with far less flair than Rachel.

Rachel and the Architects

I visit Rachel in the afternoon, and she tells me that a public meeting is to be held that night at the public library. Architecture students from several Israeli universities have spent a week in Yerucham as part of a community design exercise, and Rachel has hosted two "sweet" women students from the group in her home. The residents of Yerucham have been invited to the open evening to respond to the students' proposed projects. When we arrive at the library, we realize that, aside from Rachel, only two Yerucham residents have responded to the invitation. One is Shlomo Marcus, and the other is Eitan Shimkar, each of them a colorful character in his own way. Shlomo Marcus, in his eighties, came to Yerucham, Rachel recounts, with his wife, the painter Anna Marcus, 20 years earlier. Both were born in Germany, and their decision to make Yerucham their home was both personal and political.[2] Indian-born Eitan Shimkar is a small, fidgety man in his early fifties. He is an eccentric unemployed bachelor who manages to get by on a pension from the Ministry of Defense and occasional day jobs working for several stall owners in the local open-air market. He is a man with time on his hands.

Rachel and I take seats in the almost empty rows of white plastic chairs that face the large table in the center of the room. Around the table sit a dozen students and three advisers from the Landscape Architecture program at the Technion and from Tel Aviv University. The students take turns presenting their projects, a result of their weeklong stay in town. Their peers and their academic supervisors listen to each presentation and contribute their comments. The ostensible purpose of the event is to introduce the students' projects to the town residents and engage the local community in assessing them. Throughout the evening I record in detail what each student says and take rapid notes of the exchanges that ensue following the presentations. Rachel, who sits next to me, adds her brief observations, which she writes in the margins of my notebook. The next morning, going over my quick jottings, I highlight phrases the students used in introducing their projects. They say things like: "This project seeks to preserve local community values," "There is a desert landscape with unique topography here," and the proposed plan "is intended to integrate the town with its surroundings in a manner that will not detract from the natural beauty of the land." One student proposes setting up an "ecological college" to be surrounded by neighborhoods built in accordance with desert architectural principles and including shaded streets and protection from the wind. Another suggests building a bridge to connect Yerucham's lake with the center of town. A third, who stresses that "Yerucham is a place of 'ingathering of exiles' and [that] there is great local color here," proposes building a cultural center at the entrance to the town, featuring a rest stop, Bedouins, and camel rides to Makhtesh Ramon. Two women students draw a schematic representation of their project, which they call "Yerucham: Oasis or Desert?" It features camels, palm trees, and a blue lake.

The vulgar orientalism of the proposed projects is made even more explicit during these presentations by the sloppy dress of the young speakers. In T-shirts and shorts, sandals or flip-flops, they look like people on vacation in an exotic locale. The talk of the "natural beauty" of the remote desert town and the colorful inhabitants' embodiment of the "ingathering of exiles" does not even attempt to conceal the patronizing attitude underlying proposals such as the three-mile-long bridge connecting the lake with the town or the "cultural center" at the town's entrance complete with camels and Bedouins. None of the students gives any consideration to costs, feasibility, or the genuine, pressing needs of the town's residents.

When the time comes for "community responses," Shlomo Marcus is given the floor first. Sporting a black *kippah* and a white close-cropped beard, he begins by apologizing in a heavy German accent that he is not an "architectural expert" and that what he has to say is based on his having lived in Yerucham for 20 years. Marcus describes in detail a large number of architectural projects that have been carried out over the years in the town. Speaking slowly and hesitantly, he suggests that the students "read what was *already done* in the town and learn from history." The elderly man closes his long monologue by wishing the students good luck in their future work. The students and their teachers smile pleasantly but do not respond to Marcus's comments.

During his lengthy remarks, however, Eitan nods his head vigorously, blurting out, "That's right, that's right." As soon as the moderator thanks Marcus for his comments, Eitan jumps in impatiently: "Absolutely! Absolutely! Marcus is right. Where were the students all these years? What do they know about Yerucham? Do me a favor—tourism is a nice idea, but what good is tourism or the 'cultural center' you suggested if there's no work?" He is riled up and not entirely coherent:

"They're all corrupt here!"

"Everyone looks out for his own ass!"

"Everyone here is on drugs!"

"It won't help, whatever you do . . ."

And then he charges, almost screaming: "Education for the young people is what we need . . . I didn't learn in school, but I can teach everyone here a thing or two . . ."

The students look away from the agitated speaker. It is obvious that he has lost his intended audience.

One of the advisers tries to stem Eitan's restless flow, noting sourly that "the students didn't come here to speak about education; remember that they are architecture students." But Eitan is not listening; he launches into a lengthy diatribe about the nuisance of an alarm that goes off every night in the commercial center, where his apartment is located, and how, despite all his complaints to the town council, no one is stopping this annoyance that is keeping him awake. "I have not slept in days," he complains. The moderator becomes more and more determined to put an end to this embarrassment. He finally manages to cut Eitan off by insisting that the representative of the municipality has limited time and must be allowed to offer his remarks before he goes off to attend to pressing duties.

Rachel writes the name of the official who steps up in front of the gathering in the margin of my notebook. She notes that the man is the head of the municipality's Economic Development Unit and that he is indeed a Yerucham resident. The man faces the small group with the impatient manner of an overworked professional. He notes that he has already given his input at an earlier meeting with the students and that he can merely repeat here that the key issue in municipal planning is whether it is intended to serve a developing city with a growing population or to preserve the status quo. After these brief remarks, he excuses himself and leaves the room quickly.

Rachel then raises her hand and is given the floor. She speaks smoothly, introducing her comments with statements such as, "These are some preliminary ideas that I jotted down for myself. You can reject them, or perhaps consider them as possibilities to be developed further." Getting the attention of her listeners, she proposes rethinking what "you [the students] referred to as 'the town's major artery.'" Again, she prefaces her proposal with modest references to her position as a nonarchitect speaking to learned students and their teacher. "I am basing myself on my knowledge as a resident of Yerucham and as someone who has lived on this main street for 40 years" she tells them.

Rachel suggests turning the town's main thoroughfare into a pedestrian zone, closed to traffic, "so that children won't run onto a busy street, and there'll be a place to sit and talk with neighbors."

Rachel then goes on to comment on specific proposals made by the students during the evening. She likes the idea of building a cultural center at the entrance to the town, but she suggests "it might be preferable to allow Moroccan and Indian restaurants to open in the existing commercial center, and not to start building a new center far away at the town entrance." Strengthening the existing commercial center and closing it to traffic "will breathe new life into the center of town," she explains pleasantly.

The moderator responds with thanks, stating that he has found Rachel's comments "valuable." It is clear that it is time to end the "meet the public" event, and after a few more polite remarks, the guests pack up their presentation materials and leave the library. The weeklong urban planning exercise will be ending the next morning, and the students need to pack and prepare for their departure to their universities in Haifa and Tel Aviv.

As we head back to Rachel's apartment at the end of the evening, I consider her participation and wonder if she has noticed what I felt was the students' detached attitude toward the town. I am angry, but I decide to ask her simply what she thinks of the students and their presentations.

"They're sweet. They had nice ideas," she tells me. "I'm open to ideas."

I am taken back by her response and decide to tell her that, unlike her, I feel angry and frustrated by this entire encounter. Rachel seems not to understand my anger. "What do you have to be angry at them about?" she asks in amazement. I tell her that, in my view, the students were patronizing and had not even tried to understand conditions in Yerucham, that their ideas were superficial and bound by stereotypes, and, ultimately, that bringing students in for a week of "planning" was an exercise that demeaned local people rather than empowering them. I speak angrily, not trying to conceal my emotional turmoil. I tell her that the students and their teachers never intended to hold a genuine conversation with local residents and that the projects they presented only reinforced the preconceptions they brought with them. Rachel looks at me in open astonishment. I try to make my position concrete, asking her if the two "sweet" students she hosted in her home were ever going to invite her to their homes in Tel Aviv or Haifa. Rachel seems puzzled by my provocative question. She blurts out, "What does that matter? I enjoyed hosting them."

The Positioned Researcher

I digress slightly at this point from the encounter in the library to reflect on my obvious lack of objectivity in this situation and on my decision to share my opinions and feelings with one of my research interlocutors. Contemporary anthropological discourses encourage the ethnographer to explore and analyze her position within the research process and to examine personal reflections for analytical insights (see Anderson 2006). My intrusion into the episode I have just depicted was significant in two critical ways: First, my very presence at the scene clearly altered the unfolding reality that I have described; and second, my outburst articulating my anger at the event openly challenged Rachel to rethink her interpretation of her position vis-à-vis more privileged outsiders who enter Yerucham. The impact of my views on Rachel and the way she proceeded to develop a new and critical perspective on her life in town is reflected in the changing style of her essays, as we will see in the next chapter.

Let me say a few more words about these two interventions and reflect on the analytical and ethical implications they carry for my research. The nature of my presence at the small gathering that brought together architecture students and their advisers with a few members of the "local community" was not transparent. Although I tried to hide behind Rachel and was introduced to all present as her friend, the very fact that I took copious notes and that I was not invited to speak as a "local" underscored my position as an observer and recorder of the event and did not go unnoticed by the out-of-town guests. I am quite convinced that the students paid little attention to me, as they were more concerned with impressing their academic supervisors with their performance. The comment of the town's official that he had already made his input clear in his earlier meeting with the students suggests that the event in the library was a ritual of sorts, a politically correct event demonstrating "consultation with the local community." My presence might have made the teachers more self-aware, but I do not believe that it altered their conduct. The most significant impact of my presence was on Rachel, who was keenly aware that everything said and done in the room was recorded in my notebook. With or without my notebook, I had provided Rachel a sympathetic audience. Her relationship with me at that point in the research was part of a broader set of ties that she cultivates with people who possess distinctive cultural capital. People like me, I learn one day when Rachel introduces me to a municipal official, "study and study and study, and never stop studying in university." Rachel accumulates cultural capital by associating herself with outsiders like me, thus transforming herself into what French sociologist Pierre Bourdieu calls a "new autodidact."[3] She acquires books and brags to her girlfriends that she is interested in "psychology, philosophy, and music" rather than in the kinds of trashy novels she assumes they read. Rachel is highly aware of the world of middle-class educated women. She established social links with the two directors of the Bamidbar Beit Midrash, where she spent many months as a workshop participant and social activist. She describes these women as people who, having completed one academic degree, immediately went on to earn another. Rachel is keenly aware that, as a single mother on welfare who dropped out of the local high school's vocational track, she does not belong to this middle-class, academic-degreed professional stratum. But as we have seen above in her texts, she works hard to acquire the cultural capital of this educated class through her reading and her volunteer activity.

Rachel's performance in the library attests to her mastery of the vocabulary ("These are some preliminary ideas that I jotted down") of people who, like myself, "study and study." She is pleased to host "people from abroad" in her home and make herself available to play enthusiastic town representative when called on by the office of the mayor to speak to visiting potential donors. Her utter surprise upon hearing my angry reaction to the evening with the architects comes as no shock. In articulating a critical, angry position toward these privileged visitors, I introduce Rachel to an alternative perspective that challenges the dominance of the outside discourse she so ardently wishes to connect with. Rachel, a quick learner, begins to realize that she does not need to remain the "smiling, uncomplaining hostess" vis-à-vis these outsiders.

But is there an ethical infringement in this act of stepping out of my role as the observer and recorder of social events and in challenging the views of my interlocutor? After all, my class position and my temporary sojourn in her town placed me firmly in the privileged outsider category. Was I not imposing my views on her "authentic" articulation of the event at the library? I feel that if I had *not* shared my reading of the situation with Rachel, I would have been tacitly endorsing the paternalism of the visiting academics. I did not hesitate to share with her my anger and my critical perspective because I admired her intelligence and knew that she could deal with the challenge I posed to her interpretation of reality. Rachel was an interlocutor, not someone that I needed to position as a pristine Other in my "objective" research scheme. I could see how she had created her juggling act, and I allowed her to grow from our encounter. But, as I show in the next chapter, Rachel's juggling act and her ability to acquire new cultural capital have firm limits and are highly circumscribed.

4

RACHEL'S JUGGLING ACT AND ITS LIMITS

RACHEL CALLS ME up to invite me to her daughter's bat mitzvah celebrations. She tells me that her daughter will make an *aliyah* to the Torah—ascend the bimah to read a portion of the scriptures, an act normally reserved for bar mitzvah boys.[1] I wonder aloud about this decision. Rachel explains that the idea came up during her studies at the Bamidbar Beit Midrash[2] and that an *aliyah* at a bat mitzvah is common practice among the "*gar'in* people."[3] Leah Shakdiel, who introduced me to Rachel, is one of the more prominent members of this *gar'in* community, which is composed mostly of educated native speakers of English. The "*gar'in* people" organize a wide array of social activities around their neighborhood synagogue. Their approach to religion, Rachel says, aligns with that of the Conservative stream of Judaism in the United States. Women from the community set up the Bamidbar Beit Midrash, which offers workshops and interpretive readings that take a contemporary approach to the holy texts. Rachel has met a few of these women through the workshops. She insists it is her idea to have her daughter make the *aliyah* to the Torah, like other girls in the innovative *gar'in* community.

And so I find myself picking up Rachel and her friend Yael, who is also invited, and we make our way to the home of one of the *gar'in* women where the ceremony will take place. The spacious living room in the home is strewn with children's toys. Rachel arranges modest refreshments on a side table. About a dozen women stand or sit around the room. Apart from Yael, Rachel, and me, they are all from the *gar'in* community. The women are wrapped in embroidered prayer shawls—traditionally the preserve of male worshippers—and pray purposefully and loudly. Yael and I are also given prayer shawls and stand next to each other. Rachel and her daughter stand in front of a simple table, and next to them stands an American woman in her fifties with closely cropped silvery hair. She wears a loose dress and an embroidered cap on her head and appears to be the person leading the prayer and the ceremony. A young woman with a broad smile, blue eyes, and flowing 1960s-style hair—I have met her before on the Be'er-Sheva campus—is moving among the other women, holding a video camera. Rachel tells me later that she is there as part of a package deal with the owner of the local photo store, who will also film the main party planned for a few weeks later. Yael and I remain standing next to each other amidst the small group of women who pray, a few of them rocking backward and forward gently, davening like yeshiva boys. We exchange embarrassed glances and giggle and do not really know what to do with the prayer books we are given.

At the other end of the room, the bat mitzvah girl does not seem to be getting along with the text she is supposed to read from the pages handed to her. She mumbles a few phrases, stammers, and blushes. The entire improvised ceremony takes less than an hour, after which I drive Rachel, the mortified bat mitzvah girl, and Yael back to their homes. The girl apologizes for not knowing the prayer and for "totally" embarrassing herself and us. Rachel comforts her in short phrases that dismiss the importance of the ceremony. "It doesn't matter, let it go," she says. "What's important is the intention." She then adds, "They didn't care how you read it; you read fine." During the short drive home Rachel directs her attention to me and makes a point of explaining the background of her connection with the *gar'in* women and their idea of Conservative Judaism. She tells me about the trip she made to the United States as a guest of Conservative and Reform American Jews. Smiling broadly, she reflects, "So what, there's something you can learn from everyone. It was a very beautiful ceremony, and I really support being open to ideas and a range of opinions. I just really didn't connect with the American Reformists."

New Religiosity and Crumbling Marriages

Rachel wrote the essay "Religion and Me" at my request about a year after her daughter's *aliyah* to the Torah. The essay describes her encounter with American Jews and offers insight into the process that led her to articulate her ability to adopt ideas and opinions and assess the limits of such openness in her own life. "Religion and Me" is followed by an essay Rachel later wrote titled "Come

Back to Religion," which reveals a notable change over time in her approach to religion and religiosity.

Religion and Me

> Yerucham is a *masorati* town, most of its residents are observant. Because of the vast and unique variety of the residents (who immigrated from different countries), you can find a community synagogue in almost every neighborhood: Persian, Indian, Tunisian, Romanian, Ashkenazi, and Moroccan synagogues. There are some 22 synagogues in Yerucham, and each synagogue is maintained by the worshippers themselves. They collect contributions during prayer, and with this money they pay taxes, buy equipment, and celebrate *tzadiks*.[4] Our synagogues are Orthodox, even though the majority of residents are more Conservative religious, because the religious council in Yerucham does not allow even for a Conservative synagogue, not to mention Reform.

In her "Religion and Me" essay Rachel describes the tension that exists between American Jewish perceptions and her family's and her own perceptions of Jewish practices. She declares that she adopts some of the hybridism of Conservative Judaism (such as endorsing girls making an *aliyah*) but rejects other practices (such as lighting candles after Shabbat has already begun). Citing her experience in the United States raises Rachel's stature in the Israeli cultural economy. It makes her an informed observer of Israeli Jewish practices and positions her Moroccan family tradition as the proper, more legitimate Israeli religiosity. This is how she describes her visit to the United States.

> About two years ago, I was in the United States as part of a delegation organized by the Jewish Agency. The purpose was to reach far-flung places in which Jewishness has been growing weaker and weaker and there was fear that their next generation might not know anything about our forefathers' customs and about the tradition and values of the Jewish people. Part of the itinerary for our visit was touring synagogues of different streams in Judaism.

This was where I saw Reform and Conservative synagogues, for the first time in my life. I really liked the Conservative synagogues a lot because of the idea of equality between men and women. Men and women sat together in the prayer hall (unlike in Orthodox synagogues, where women sit in a "ladies section" behind a screen, lest "heaven forbid" a man sees them and gets distracted from prayer). I also loved the idea of including women in the reading of the Torah, which is considered until today to be a stronghold of the men, and I thought to myself that if we had such a synagogue in Yerucham I would visit it whenever I could. I would pray in it with even greater pleasure—because the ban on women from entering the hall during the prayer prevents them from feeling the full force of the experience up close, from feeling closeness to God. Because of this oppressive discrimination, I avoid going to synagogue, except on holidays.

The Reform approach I didn't like at all, because they do *kabalat shabbat*[5] after Shabbat has already begun. Which means, they light fire on Shabbat and bless the lighting of candles. When I saw this, I was shocked! For me, that was pure sacrilege. How can you light fire on Shabbat, and at a synagogue too?! Not only that, but they wanted to honor me, their guest, and offered me the "privilege" of lighting the candles myself. I froze where I sat and didn't know how to react. After a few minutes, when they understood that this wasn't possible for me, they apologized and lit the candles themselves. At this point, I covered my eyes with my hands, I just couldn't see the fire burning in the synagogue, and I waited impatiently for the service to be over so I could go back to my hosts' apartment. When I came back to Israel and told people about the Reform synagogue, they were all astonished. What kind of Jews are these? Maybe they're not even Jews, maybe they're some strange sect, maybe they are Christians pretending to be Jews. The speculations ran wild.

In Rachel's narrative, Reform Judaism's practices are defamiliarized. "What kind of Jews are these?" she asks. Here Rachel performs the classical anthropological exercise of translating between two different value systems: that of her imagined Jewish Israeli readers and that of the Jewish American Reform movement.

Rachel then changes registers and adopts a strongly nostalgic, romantic tone as she depicts the beauty and serenity of the Jewish Israeli religious space, which Yerucham is made to represent in all its Jewish glory.

> In Yerucham you can feel the atmosphere of Shabbat and of the holiday times, especially Yom Kippur.[6] In such holiday time, the roads are empty of travelers, places of business and entertainment lock their doors out of respect. People go to the synagogue, wrapped in prayer shawls and holding their little sons and daughters, with everyone dressed in Shabbat clothes. From every courtyard you can hear the songs of *kabalat shabbat*, each community with its own style and form, whether Ashkenazi or Sephardi.

Into this setting of beauty, serenity, and multiculturalism, Rachel inserts a description of her own Mizrahi family, which she also paints in idealized terms. She positions herself between idealized Mizrahi Jewish practices and American Jewish Reform and Conservative practices and emerges as a tolerant, multicultural subject.

> I, who grew up in a *masorati* home with a mother who baked challah and lit candles, I loved the difference between week days and holy days. First, there was the Shabbat-eve dinner, in which we all gathered around a carefully arranged table, with the fresh challah and a variety of salads made by my mother's hands. Then the kiddush, said usually by the father of the family, but as I lost my father early in our lives, said by my elder brother. During kiddush, there was silence, nobody moved or even squeaked, even if there were small children around the table; they knew this was a sacred moment. All the boys and men wore skullcaps, the married women (my sisters-in-law) covered their heads with head scarfs. After the round of sips from the wine (first the men from the older to the youngest, then the women from the older,

married ones to the single young ones like myself), the women would get up and go into the kitchen to help my mother serve the meal. When we were hosted [by] my married brothers and their wives, I would stay sitting at the table with the men and "let" my sisters-in-law do all the hard work (including washing the dishes after the meal). Simply because I wanted to feel spoiled and because I wanted to be served sometimes. Because at home, since I was the only one who did not leave home (my eldest sister married when I was 10 years old and my other sister left the country for Canada), I was always tasked with helping Mom serve the meal and clean afterward. During the high holidays this ongoing, never-ending work would be even harder, because each holiday lasts for several days, and for us Moroccans a holiday means meal obsession—you eat all day: in the morning you think what to make for lunch, and while you eat lunch you run a "staff meeting" to discuss the dinner menu. And as my mom thawed different meats from the freezer and began cooking them, I was assigned to make cooked salads. So it was an all-day-long process of cooking, eating, setting up the table, and clearing the table. So when the holiday is over and everyone goes to their own home, Mom would fall into sickbed for a few days because her entire body is aching, all her muscles are strained, the head, the back, the hands, the feet, everything hurts. And I? I'm happy that the house is finally itself again and the feeding frenzy is over. No more cooking alerts, peace and quiet through the land.

Even today, when I have my own family, this holiday madness repeats itself. You start with the crazy shopping, you break up savings accounts (if you have them), you mortgage the house (and I'm in social housing), and go raid the retail stores. You buy everything you can grab. You load up the shopping carts to the brink, because you never know if surprise guests will show up, and it's always better to stock up than to go wanting.

In my home, too, Shabbat and holidays are sacred. I'm even more strict than my mother. You don't turn on the television at mine, you don't switch off the light but keep it on until the end of the Shabbat or the holiday, you don't pick up the phone. You just don't do anything. Truly "on the seventh day he rested" [Exodus 31:17]. I use this time for complete rest and for peace for body and soul. After a tiring week of work my body simply demands it. And so immediately after dinner I dive into bed and don't leave it until the end of the Shabbat, when I look up to the sky every few minutes and look for Abraham, Isaac, and Jacob—the three stars separating the sacred from the everyday. Only then do I come out of bed and go back to the routine of housework, to the dishes piled up in the sink, to laundry I need to wash, to the children who need to eat, and I prepare myself for the new week that's coming for the best.

In the essay's next few paragraphs, Rachel turns to a new audience. It is no longer American Jews for whom she presents Yerucham as a picturesque town wreathed in beauty and magic on the Sabbath and on holidays. Rather, she writes for those secular Israelis who often question the seeming contradiction in the way Rachel and other Mizrahi women like her approach religion and religious practices. Rachel feels the need to explain her practices to those who sometimes ask how someone who does not look religious can insist on her faith and on strictly observing Shabbat. Rachel speaks to this imagined Israeli secular middle-class audience through clichéd references to the immensity of "the universe" and the need of every person to "believe in something."

Sometimes, when people ask me, how is it you keep the Shabbat and the holidays and adhere to it for so many years even though you don't "look" like a religious woman, I tell them that it's not the outside appearance that determines if the person is religious or not. True faith resides in the heart, not in the clothing; not every woman who wears a skirt and a head scarf necessarily believes more than someone who's wearing trousers. And not every man who puts on a skullcap is the great *tzadik* of his generation. People are measured by their relations with their fellow men, not in their proclamations or in their belonging to one stream [of Judaism] or another.

I, as a woman who grew up in a *masorati* house with a mother for whom God was the most sacred thing in the world, absorbed it, and I continue to believe there is a Creator for the world in this immense universe. After all, no human being could create such an awesome wonder. Besides, I think that every person needs to believe in something. There are many religions in the world, and each one believes in a different God. A person who has someone to believe in, to trust and to confide in, in difficult moments feels he's not alone in this jungle of life; even psychologically it affects the soul and comforts it. Sometimes, when a person goes through a crisis and he can't share or tell it to anyone, he can just sit with himself and imagine there is a great power managing the world. It's a great comfort, to tell this power what pains him and what is hard for him at that moment, and to hope that things will improve and change. By contrast, a person who doesn't believe that there is a Creator is usually a pessimistic person, who despairs easily and about anything. Such a person finds it difficult to believe in something he cannot see, and so he obviously will find it hard to believe in a positive future. The faith that there is a power supreme to our own is what helps me in my everyday life with the obstacles and difficulties that we people create in our chase for the material things supposedly meant to make life easier for us and instead making life more complicated.

In this essay one can see Rachel's ability to speak to different audiences and effectively use the conceptual framework most appropriate for each. Rachel makes a two-step move in legitimizing her world. She first constructs her firm national belonging by contrasting American Reform with Israeli Judaism. She then places Yerucham into the national arena of Israeli Judaism, presenting it as a religious space of charm and beauty on holy days, of multiculturalism and tolerance. The Jewish practices of her Moroccan family fit into this tolerant, multicultural space and emerge not only as legitimate but also as epitomizing liberal values. Toward the end of the essay, Rachel shifts her focus and directs her narrative toward the secular Jewish Israelis that she imagines her readers to be (she never imagined her words would be translated into English). For this audience she needs to explain what is often presented in Israeli secular discourse as a contradiction: a woman who does not look religious yet insists on complete rest during Shabbat.

This transitioning between different textual repertoires to address different reading audiences demonstrates Rachel's ability to juggle several discursive codes and use them effectively in different contexts. This type of juggling is highly characteristic of Rachel's world. Consider again Rachel's act of mining her trip to the United States as a platform that puts her on the same level as Israeli middle-class readers. As someone who has traveled abroad and has seen other ways of being Jewish, she can deconstruct the prevalent Israeli hegemonic discourse that tends to depict her Yerucham world as nonmodern, even inferior. Her American experience lends her authority to represent Mizrahi Jewish practices as liberal and tolerant and thereby to endow her traditional *masorati* cultural background with new legitimacy.

Come Back to Religion

Come back to religion,[7] said someone, a friend from Yerucham's ultra-Orthodox community, when I told her about the trouble in my marriage. Then you'll see, when your husband sees you dressing more modestly, he'll behave with respect and appreciation, because he is probably jealous about you and thinks you're dressing like this so that men [will] look at you and hit on you, and so he's angry. I thought to myself: What have I got to lose? I'm anyway a *masorati* girl; I keep to the commandments, the Shabbat and the holidays . . . maybe there is something to what she says? And so I find myself with a long skirt, stockings, and head scarf. I found it hard to get used to my new "uniform." I did, after all, give up denim and tricot and tight shirts and revealing dresses. The things you do for *shlom bayit*.[8] I soon earned the title of the family *tzadika*.

The change in clothes obviously brought also a change in habits; a modestly dressed girl can no longer speak to men on the street even if just the day before they were her best friends. And let's not even say anything about handshakes or a friendly embrace. I had to honor religion and behave accordingly. When girlfriends would meet me on the street, they wouldn't know what hit me, why I returned to religion; they thought maybe someone died in the family, or that I was looking for God. And when I told them the truth, they said: You lost your mind, nothing changes jealous men, not even if you become a nun and take up monastic silence. I said: I've got nothing to lose; I'm doing what the wife of the rabbi told me and let nobody say later that I didn't try everything I could to save my marriage.

And so days and months pass by, and I wait for my husband to follow my lead, to put on a skullcap, put on tefillin in the morning, say the blessing over the food, pray during the week. But except on Shabbat and on the holidays in which he already went to the synagogue, he would have nothing to do with religion. He went on walking around in sleeveless tops and shorts, even when I'd stew in my long sleeves and stockings at the height of summer. We'd go to events together—weddings, bar mitzvahs, and so on. People would stare at this "weird couple": she's religious, he's not. He'd get up on the dance floor, and I couldn't dance, because of the modesty. He'd go to the swimming pool whenever he pleased, and I had to wait for the special dates of segregated swimming, and who even wants to go to the pool on afternoons when the only view you can see is ultra-Orthodox women coming into the water in their pajamas and house dresses. I didn't have any common language with them. What could I even talk to them about? They only talk about pregnancy and labors, about husbands who spend all days studying in yeshivas and won't help them raising their kids. I didn't belong in this world; I felt like I went back a few decades, to the Stone Age. I found myself not belonging, neither here nor there; in secular circles I felt religious, and in religious circles I felt secular.

I went back to the rabbi's wife and told her my arguments. I explained to her that her theory failed to prove itself, that the gentleman did not change his attitude to me, and that I'm trapped between the two worlds. In response, she promised to come on a house visit and call my husband to order. And so, a few days later, she did. My husband knew her from before, as she was well known and highly involved in community life in Yerucham. We sat down in our humble living room. I switched off the TV, of course, and sent off the kids. She began talking and talking about how important it is to come back to religion and how God loves people who dress modestly and not in immodest [clothes], which, "God forbid," brings every natural disaster and hardship and diseases and poverty and drought and so on and so forth. And my husband sits there, nodding his head knowingly and tells her: I agree entirely; it's true girls shouldn't come out into the street looking like sluts. And this is one of the reasons why husbands fight with them and beat them, because a married woman should honor her husband and not irritate him in any way.

He pontificated away, and I was just barely holding myself back from turning the coffee table over him. But I didn't want to spoil the evening for the honored lady who came to my home in an attempt to install some *shlom bayit*, even though by now it was looking more like Shlom Hagalil.[9] I just sat there and listened to the speech of the chauvinist sitting in front of me and just waiting for him to shut his mouth, because not a single wise thing ever came out of it. And the rabbi's wife went on and on. As far as she was concerned, the more women covered their heads and the more men put on a skullcap, the better. Even if they're not very observant in everyday life, even if they have nothing in common, the important thing is they come back to religion. All my attempts to explain to her she was wasting her time, because he'll never come back to religion, fell on deaf ears. She was sure that she will eventually succeed in drafting him to the cause of the Lord.

After he agreed with everything she said in the beginning of the conversation and commenting how she was a very wise woman I should learn a lot from, we got to the point, and she turns the table on him, saying she didn't mean just me, but also him, and that he should also dress modestly, wear a skullcap and not just on holy days, and that it's not nice that he goes around in shirts and shorts while I'm wearing dresses and long skirts. And then he realized that he'd been snared and that he walked right into the trap set by this nice woman. He started squirming in his seat and looking for every excuse to end the conversation. But to no avail, because he was right in the spider woman's web. When he saw she wasn't going to let him off the hook easily, he offered to come to an agreement that he'll try to do what she asked of him but without any explicit commitment, because he didn't like promising anything. The hour was late, and all parties to the conversation were tired. And this is how the meeting ended.

After the rabbi's wife went home, I told him I really hope he'll take this to heart and that if he keeps behaving the way he did, our marriage will be over. He wasn't particularly fazed and said he'll keep doing what he feels like doing, and if I didn't like it, I could go and put some pants on. I spent the entire night thinking, What else could I do? After all I'm a housewife raising the children and minding only my own business. I don't cheat on him, I don't play cards, I don't drink alcohol, I don't smoke, I don't gamble. What more does he want from me? And then I realized that it didn't matter what I do or don't do; he simply will never change. I understood the problem wasn't with me, but with him. He's the one cheating on me. He's the one drinking. He's the one who mistreats me. It seems there's nothing for us to do together anymore. One day I went up to Tel Aviv to visit my cousins, who run a big and well-known hairdressers salon. I walked in there with a scarf on my head and came out with a new fashionable hairdo. From there I went to a clothes store and bought a new pair of tight jeans, and then to a shoe store where

I got a sexy pair of high heel shoes. I threw away the clothes I was wearing when I got to Tel Aviv that morning in the nearest garbage bin.

And this is how my return to religion ended, after two entire years. I went back to Yerucham, and heads started turning when I passed. I had long hair reaching to my waist (because I didn't cut it for two years, just gathered it in under the head scarf). So it was smooth and unbelievably beautiful. I went around like a peacock in a rooster house, and they didn't fail to pay attention. "How beautiful you are." "Where were you until today?" "Where was this body hiding?" And this is also what I was asking myself: Where have I been hiding? I went on keeping the Shabbat and the holidays, but I threw away all the modest skirts, dresses, and head scarves. I didn't want anything to remind me of these gray two years.

Today I know for certain that nothing will change a person's character unless they want to change it. And even if husbands keep saying, "if she does this or does that, I'll be better to her," that's just a lousy lie, because if the husband wanted to be better to his wife, he would be already from the start, and not wait until she felt bad about him. And so it's not her who needs to change herself end to end to cover up his deficiencies and to please him at any price. A woman needs to stay true to herself, to her character, to her principles, and to her desires, and not cancel herself out for the sake of anyone. I'd like women to be more assertive and more insistent, stand their ground and not need to let anyone else dictate their lives. Maybe this could prevent many cases of domestic violence and divorce.

In this essay Rachel's intended audience is clear. She directs her narrative to secular, mostly Ashkenazi Israelis, who, she assumes, can identify with and will support her refusal to adopt more stringent religious practices than those she already observes. Throughout the essay Rachel takes a critical approach to her failed attempts at piety and ridicules the process of returning to religion when it is presented to her as a guarantee of domestic bliss. Rachel's return to religion (known colloquially as *hit'hazkut*) contrasts with the experience Efrat depicts in chapter 2. Both Rachel and Efrat feel the tension that increased religiosity brings into a marriage when one of the partners (usually the woman) begins the *hit'hazkut* process by adopting more modest clothing and abiding by religious commandments, and the other partner does not choose a similar path. Whereas Efrat undertakes the process for religious reasons and finds the experience empowering, Rachel goes into the process to save a deteriorating marriage. Instead of attaining religiosity, Rachel achieves a quasi-feminist, secular understanding. She declares, a little formulaically, that a woman should stay loyal to herself, her character, her principles, and her desires instead of deprecating herself for the sake of someone else.

Blessed Be He Who Made Me a Woman[10]

Even at 16 I knew, from the looks from the boys in the neighborhood, that I look good and that I would never have any problems with members of the other sex. I didn't even have to make much of an effort. A bit of lipstick, a black line under my eyes. My hair was smooth and wavy and dropping to my waist, and there I am, ready for the ring. Who wants to fight? Many volunteered: schoolmates, boys from the neighborhood and the town, friends of my brothers (who probably befriended them for my sake to begin with). I always felt courted. There was always a volunteer to take me out to the movies, which is pretty much all we could do in the Yerucham of the time. We couldn't go out to Be'er-Sheva, because the boys didn't have cars, and neither did their parents. So all we had left to do was to go to the Mira cinema hall, may it rest in peace, and to make out a little bit when the lights were dimmed. When the lights came on again you could see the girls' lipstick smeared on the lips of their boyfriends. These were beautiful days of youthful innocence. Today every kid has a car, a cell phone, and a credit card, and there's no trouble at all to go to some hotel or some flat and to become parents at 17.

I married at 18. This can seem like a very young age today, but very common back then because women did not have much else to do. They couldn't join the army, because their parents wouldn't let them. They would say that the army is for the men, because only they know how to operate a weapon or drive a vehicle (which was true, because back then women didn't drive), and women would be better off marrying and having kids. I was a good girl then. I listened to my parents, and so I got married. Only later will I know that I would come to regret it for many years. I got married and gave birth to four children. I didn't do anything except change diapers and make bottles of porridge, running from the maternity clinic to the day care centers, to schools and to parents' nights. This is what I did for 13 years until I said, enough. This was just when my youngest son was born. I took him and his three siblings and broke the whole thing up. Actually, I defused a bomb, because I felt like I was about to blow up. The husband would get back from work, and the first thing he'd ask would be, What's for dinner? It wouldn't be, How was your day? How did it go with the kids? Do you need help with anything? None of that. He was only interested in my belly, and I felt I've been sold short. Because already then I knew I couldn't make peace with that, that I won't stay a housewife my entire life, that I won't keep birthing more children for this husband, and that the only way to make that possible was for me to separate from him. Actually leave home. Because if I stay there, the situation won't change for the better.

Only after four more years of separation did I get the divorce, and only then did I feel truly free. Only then did I feel I was 18 again, the age at which I married and effectively stopped living as an independent entity. And so I found myself alone, with four kids, starting from scratch. Renting an empty, unfurnished flat (except what I managed to get out of the house before I left), learning how to run my own bank account (I didn't have even that), starting to pay the electricity bill, phone, water and taxes, gas and rent. All this was completely new to me. But I very quickly learned the principles and everything worked out. The kids would go to their schools and day cares, and I went on with my business. For the first time in a very long time I could go and have coffee at a friend's without feeling stressed that if the husband comes home and doesn't find me waiting for him with a ready lunch, then woe is me. I felt like a prisoner coming out after a life sentence. I tasted freedom, and I liked the taste a lot. And since then I vowed that no other man would ever put a wedding ring on my finger. And I'm free and happy and feeling 18 (I don't count the years in which I was married to him, because this was when my personal life was stopped), and I decide to storm the market for available men once again. And indeed fate only brings up for me men younger than me by many years, as if to make up for the lost time. And I'm smiling again and glad again and feeling like a girl whose stolen years had been returned to her.

Today the men in a relationship with me claim they've won twice over. Once, by seeing a woman who's mature, not childish, has been through a lot in life, knows and understands their affairs, and twice because she also looks like a girl their age—where else could they find such a combination? Most of the young women today are spoiled and sensitive and like to argue about every little thing, spending more time pouting than anything. And with me they feel much more comfortable because I'm no longer at that stage of "take me to the movies or no kiss for you." Today they tell me I'm everything for them—mother, sister, friend. And I'm always the one who puts some sense into them because they are still young after all, and they always consult me when they face a problem, or when somebody wound them up. And I calm them down, cheer them up, and put everything in proportion. And so everyone is happy. I'm looking to enjoy without committing myself to anyone. I'm doing what I feel like with whom I feel like and when I feel like. I don't owe anyone any explanations. They get a woman who spoils them, doesn't intervene in their personal lives, and never throws a scene. I know that this is what men actually want from their younger girlfriends. But everyone knows you can't have the cake and eat it too. Because if you're someone's boyfriend, it's only natural she'll be jealous every time you talk to another girl. Not to mention men also feel when their girlfriend talks to another guy; they just don't show it, so you can't enjoy both worlds when you're committed to someone. But when there's no commitment, like in my case, then you can enjoy both worlds, because the conditions are mutual. Which is to say, you enjoy together and live apart.

Another advantage of that lack of commitment is that if I don't feel it anymore for a particular guy, I've no problem to send him nicely on his way. And then move to the next "nice guy." This is how I keep my adrenaline as high as I can. My soul feels young and I'm gaining a few more years overall. I suppose the saying that everything that happens for us happens for the best even when something definitely bad happens is true! Because if I was happy with my marriage and didn't get the divorce, I'd live until today with that same person. How boring that would be. To go to sleep every night and wake up every morning with the same person. After all love and romance die out with the years and what's left is the habit and convenience, the shared property and the kids, and you just keep pretending at holidays and family gatherings like you're a loving, loyal couple. And I anyway believe most married men cheat on their wives, and some women cheat too, but they are definitely fewer than the men. Honestly, how long can you stay with the same partner? It's like eating the same meal every day. It's disgusting! And so I warmly recommend to anyone with problems in her marriage but who is anxious about changes after the divorce, there's nothing to be afraid of. The opposite is true because it can't be worse than it already is and I'm a good example. There's life after divorce! Everything depends on a person's character and on her desire to recover and go on living. Everyone has a place in the world and everyone has

a right to live well. Everyone has air to breathe. You just need to
know to demand it. If you're shy or afraid, you lose. You live only
once and there's no second chance. And if we received this gift,
we should use it as best we can.

Here, Rachel develops a narrative whereby each phase of her life is a step in a
sequence leading to her liberation as a woman, a woman who has experienced
personal growth despite life's challenges. Accordingly, she describes her marriage as a life sentence from which she was freed only by her divorce. At the
time she writes this essay, Rachel sees the relationships she engages in with
younger men as compensation for the youth taken from her because she married at such a young age. In her wish to connect to an imagined middle-class
narrative, Rachel speaks about her early marriage as a decision made in an era
when "women [did] not have much else to do." With her generic reference to
"women," Rachel glosses over her particular class and ethnic circumstances.
Her early marriage, she suggests, is not a result of the economic and sociocultural constraints of her life but a general phenomenon familiar to all as part of
a bygone era when women had nothing better to do than get married. Similarly, Rachel feels the need to justify *not* joining the army, an expected step in
the life trajectory of middle-class Israelis. She had not done so, she says, in a
coy "I am just a woman, and not a militaristic one" tone, because "the army is
for men, because only they know how to operate a weapon and drive a vehicle."

The same flattening of class and confused feminist rhetoric are evident in
the way Rachel reports on the leisure activities of Yerucham's youth. Using a
modernist progressive lens, she says that *in her day* young men in Yerucham
could not afford to take the girls they courted to Be'er-Sheva, whereas *today*
they have money not just for mobile phones but for hotels. Emphasizing the
naïveté of her youth, explained simply in terms of differences characteristic
of the time, erases the ongoing class gaps between life in marginalized Yerucham and middle-class life in more central Israeli towns. The trite "universal
wisdom" declarations with which she closes the essay ("Everyone has a right
to live well. Everyone has air to breathe. You just need to know to demand it.")
reiterate the idea that her life experiences are not dissimilar to those of the
middle class.

What a Country[11]

For eight years now, I've been considered a single mother by the state. As such, I fall among the recipients of "guaranteed minimal income" by the National Insurance Institute (NII). At first I saw this as complementary to the alimonies given to me by the rabbinical court, because in my divorce agreement I agreed to a symbolic alimony, something like 1,000 shekels for the support of four little children, which is around 250 shekel per child per month.[12] This was enough precisely for a pair of shoes. But this was the only way he agreed to sign a *get*.[13] At the time it didn't bother me so much because I knew that the National Insurance Institute would complement this sum up to the national average wage. I also didn't have to sign in at the employment office once a week because I had a child under seven years of age, and the law doesn't oblige mothers of young children to sign in. This is why I found it more convenient to sit at home and get a monthly salary, even if it didn't really help me make ends meet. I needed peace and rest at home, especially after the rough period I had because of the divorce.

When the boy was seven years old, they called me to report to the employment office and told me that from now on I have to accept any job offered to me, otherwise I'll be labeled "work refuser" and denied my right to a monthly allowance from the NII. It goes without saying I really don't like being told what to do or to be subjected to such extreme changes in my life. Before that day, each of my days had a regular itinerary: On Sundays I would travel to Be'er-Sheva to a nonprofit that I volunteered with, on Monday I would thoroughly clean the house, Tuesday was market day, on Wednesday I attended a *beit midrash*, on Thursday I would run errands at the bank and shop for Shabbat. And then the state knocked on my door and said: Forget everything you've been used to until now, because from now on we tell you what to do, and if you disagree, you'll be left without any money. And how could I afford to be left without money? After all, I had four small children dependent on me. So I agreed to cooperate with them and started signing in at the employment office every week.

In their computerized database I was listed in the "unskilled" category, those who are not formally qualified to do anything and who have to accept any employment offer, even if it's washing floors in another city. I was begging the registration clerk not to place me in a job like this because it's just not me. I'm not on friendly terms with washing floors, and even my house can testify. I also told her about my routine and that I really don't want to change them around. But desires and laws are two things apart. The state pays and so the state decides. I didn't give in to the clutches of the government and immediately sent urgent messages to everyone I know: friends, neighbors, family; I asked everyone to find me a good job, because I will not be a cleaner in public institutions when I know I can contribute a lot more to the Israeli society and that I have other talents that will be squandered on chlorine and floor polish. And indeed my prayers were answered. I guess someone up there loves me. Or maybe because I was such a *tzadika* with all my volunteer work. So I became a secretary for NA'AMAT in Yerucham with a small, air-conditioned office.

I stayed in that job for just a year and left it for my current role as the secretary of the Bamidbar Beit Midrash. Obviously, as soon as I started working, I didn't have to sign at the employment office anymore, because I needed to go to work in the morning, and I continued receiving my guaranteed income. I couldn't go on volunteering in Be'er-Sheva, which has caused me great sorrow, but I had no other choice. This is not the only thing that weighs on me. According to their rules, I'm not allowed to get further education, I'm not allowed to own a car, even old and small and even if I was to get it as a present instead of buying it with my own money. In short, I have to lead a very primitive, subhuman life. I can only dream about going abroad every summer like all my friends who go abroad so often. And when I see them drive a car and take their kids to day care and to school, while I have to take my kids by foot from one place to the other in the baking summer and in the pouring rain, my heart aches. And when I need to run errands and go shopping outside town, I drag my feet from one bus to another with my heavy bags. And if I miss the bus even by two minutes, I need to wait around at the stop for another hour until the next one comes along. Not the greatest pleasure.

This is what our state wants apparently, to eternalize Israeli poverty and to eternalize the people as uneducated (actually, most recipients of alimonies and guaranteed income are women!). Because if they are not allowed to study or to acquire a profession independently, they will always stay unskilled and will not be able to find any work other than cleaning. Because clearly, no business owner will hire someone without professional certification. There is, I know, the possibility of some training through the Welfare Ministry; these classes are for free and do not impact on your welfare rights, but you can use that right for education only once every three years and the choices there are very limited and repetitive, such as hairdresser, makeup artists, and caretakers. How many hairdressers do we need in Yerucham? Besides, most people take these vocational training classes offered by the Welfare Ministry because nothing else was offered. Almost no one I know makes a living from the trade they were trained in.

In this essay, Rachel faces up to the limitations she encountered after her divorce and openly expresses resentment at her dependency on the welfare institutions of the state. The motif of a happy divorcée who takes on young lovers and enjoys her new liberty, central to the previous essay, is replaced here by one of rage and open political critique of what causes her everyday hardship. She recounts her struggles to make ends meet using the miserly alimony allocated to her by the rabbinic court and the supplementary benefit check issued by the state. Rachel is clear eyed in her description of the gap between her limited skills, which define her "in their computerized database" as a candidate for menial labor only, and her self-image as someone who can contribute much more "to Israeli society." She compares her lifestyle not to that of other welfare mothers in Yerucham but to that of her middle-class friends who drive their children to school and travel abroad. She is not less able than these middle-class privileged women, even if she is officially pigeonholed as an unskilled worker, for whom the only locally available job is cleaning. Keenly aware of this gap between her official classification and her abilities, Rachel draws on the connections she made during the first few years after her divorce as a volunteer and student at the *beit midrash* and transforms them into an economic resource. She mobilizes her connections to obtain a desirable position as a secretary at the local branch of NA'AMAT and escapes, at least for a while, the janitorial fate that the employment office has in store for her.

The way Rachel depicts her life in this concluding essay differs significantly from the way she speaks about her life in her earlier essays. If, in her first essay Rachel presented herself as the ideal resident of Yerucham, insisting that she makes do with what little she has and is happy in the warm town of her birth, in this last essay she speaks about a life without a car and trips abroad as "primitive and inhumane." In earlier writings she forcefully argues that those who complain about conditions in Yerucham are not doing enough to change their own situations, a responsibility that is theirs alone. In this final essay Rachel looks at the social and political context that locks her and people like her into a cycle of poverty and dependency on the welfare system. Shifting from the tone of affable spokeswoman for her peripheral community, Rachel uses her personal story to criticize a national set of social policies that curtail any effort welfare-supported women make to break out of poverty and marginalization. The approach here is systemic, not personal. Rachel understands her own life history in class terms. She now realizes that being taught a trade such as hairdressing or makeup has effectively limited her options for integrating into the job market and that this limitation applies to other women in similar positions.

The enjoyment she expressed at hosting the architecture students in her home is replaced here with a feeling of profound frustration at being defined as fit only for menial low-paying jobs and with direct criticism of social policies that do not allow her to free herself from economic dependency.

The Formation and Change of Self-Representation

The essays written by Rachel afford us complex, multifaceted insight into life in a marginalized Negev town. We learn about her Moroccan immigrant parents and about the internal dynamics of a large immigrant family. We are offered an intimate look into the limited local employment scene of the small town during the 1960s and 1970s and into the ways people in that era spent their free time. Rachel's narratives speak about religiosity and the ways it changes men's and women's lives. But more than anything else, we learn how Rachel, an intelligent, creative person, transforms her own understanding of her life and her town. What began with her relation of her life story over the course of one brief interview evolved, over the years of our relationship, into a long process in which her shifting interpretations shaped the ways she conceived her life and presented it to her readers. In the essays Rachel has written over the years, we can see her adopting a more complex, more critical narrative, reflective of her own evolving consciousness. From the smiling woman we meet in the first essay, who tells outsiders a positive story of life in Yerucham, Rachel becomes, in her later writings, a keen critic of the social system that defines her life.

This transformation took place over many years, and it may be partly linked to the relationship she and I forged and to her active participation in this study. But this is not the whole story. I developed long-term complex relationships with many other women in Yerucham who knew about my research and were willing, each from her own position, to play an active part in it. Rachel is what I termed earlier a juggler. Her relationship with me is part of a larger set of relationships she has developed with middle-class people who reside in Yerucham (such as the activist women who founded and run the *beit midrash* she attends and the *gar'in* women whose more open, Conservative Jewish practices she emulates) and with others who live outside the town, like myself. Rachel is able, as we have seen, to occupy two positions and articulate two narratives at the same time—she is a *masorati* Mizrahi woman but at the same time she is a liberal person who is open to learning from everyone (in her own words); she is a welfare-supported, unskilled single parent and she is at the same time an articulate woman who uses middle-class terms that have earned her jobs (for brief periods) that are often reserved for better-skilled people. Rachel's ability to juggle these two positions is spectacular, at times breathtaking.

Rachel is clearly a most able juggler of codes and social-class registers. But her juggling act is not unique. *Everyone* in Yerucham is a juggler of discourses and of ways of being in the world. My everyday ethnography of life in Yerucham has shown that most residents in this marginalized town are aware of discourses associated with centrist, hegemonic spaces. They do not live in a separate, isolated world—a distinct "culture" characterized by a set of unique codes of conduct. Rachel shows us through her texts and modes of behavior that marginalized, ethnicized people live their lives in a double register.

Speaking about life in the isolated transit camps (known as *ma'abarot*) that housed the masses of Jewish immigrants who flooded the Israeli state in the 1950s, Israeli cultural studies scholar Orly Lubin suggested that

> the margins are the site *outside the frame of the gaze*, outside the space of constructing morality as a byproduct of the penetrative stare of the higher class, the same gaze that constructs the subject and the community as moral (according to its norms) and as such as also ethnically marked . . . The margins are the site in which the otherness can construct a world according to its own measures. (Lubin 1991)

Lubin's thesis of life "outside the frame of the gaze," life that exists "in a separate space . . . *in parallel* to the historical hegemonic Ashkenazi narrative, and not in accordance with it, in contrast to it, or out of a critical perspective upon it" (ibid.), is an interesting one and in many ways mirrors Israeli public discourse that tends to refer to development-town, lower-class Mizrahi residents as belonging to a "Second Israel." Remote Yerucham, and its Mizrahi residents, as I note in the introduction to this book, are often presented as the quintessential Others to sophisticated high-tech Tel Avivites.

My thesis, best exemplified in Rachel's case but supported in the other stories presented in this book, is that there is no "separate space" or life "outside the frame of the gaze" in the remote desert town but rather an ongoing dialogue between local lives and, to use Lubin's term, a "hegemonic Ashkenazi narrative." Moreover, such dialogue cannot be reduced to a "reaction" to "external" hegemonic narratives, whether in the form of compliance or resistance.

Instead, it is an inherently complex mixture of codes and ways of being in the world that each person debates and resolves in his or her life. Efrat dealt with this gaze and with the material reality of marginalization by turning to the *hit'hazkut* path, and Nurit focused on her own social and economic survival, manipulating people with power over her life. One of the great benefits I have derived from knowing Rachel for such a long time and from encouraging her to write about her life at different points has been the understanding I have gained of her juggling, boundary-crossing performance. Another has been the opportunity to track her changing interpretation of her own life, her demonstration that there is no "fixed authentic subject." Rachel, like all of us, is a reflexive person whose changing circumstances and varied experiences shape how she views her life.

Another critical analytical point I take from Rachel's essays is that multiple narratives circulate in her world (not just a simple binary of local and external hegemonic discourses) and that she makes use of elements and fragments of various narratives in her effort to understand and write about her life. Recall how Rachel ridiculed the *hit'hazkut* narrative offered her and her gradual redefinition of herself from a woman who smilingly and uncomplainingly accepted her local situation to an angry social critic. Rachel's essays attest to her creativity in constructing not only her texts but also her life within a continuous, ongoing dialogue with multiple discourses. Rachel shows that she can juggle multiple discourses, adopting some and opposing or ignoring others, and forge her own new meaning within the unique individual mélange she creates. But can Rachel juggle her way out of her position of severe marginality? In the closing ethnographic vignette I show that there is a limit to Rachel's juggling act.

Juggling and Its Limits

Since my own reflexive article "You Have an Authentic Voice" (Motzafi-Haller 1997b) was published in Hebrew in the critical academic journal *Teorya VeBikoret*, a number of young Mizrahi intellectuals have published wonderful articles in which they explore their own Mizrahi identity within the context of hegemonic Ashkenazi Israeli discourse.[14] Take, for example, Yonit Naaman, a young student and peace activist who articulates her struggles as a Mizrahi woman in Ashkenazi-dominated Israel writing: "The longing to be welcomed into the Israeli space to bright applause has resoundingly failed. . . . In my frequent encounters with the undercover agents of hegemony, my attempts at camouflage in the struggle for belonging were exposed" (2007: 90). Vered Madar, a student of folklore, raises similar issues of situatedness and identity: "I myself am not mixed [race], but it seems as if I was born to a couple; to my Yemenite Jewish parents and to Israeli culture" (2006: 80). Madar asks pointedly, "We, the first generation to [be born in Israel to Mizrahi] immigrants, deal with behavioral patterns and dilemmas typical of mixed race individuals—which collective is it that we should listen to?" (80).

Although elements of her narrative resonate with these explorations of identity, Rachel, like other women in Yerucham, struggles with a much more restrictive material economy of alienation and exclusion than Naaman, Madar, and other second- and third-generation Mizrahi writers do. The elephant in the room in the more recent critical Mizrahi discourses of identity is class. I speak to the lack of a proper class analysis in Israeli sociology and public discourse in the concluding chapter of this book. Here I simply note that with no formal education or marketable skills, women in Yerucham are locked into the stunted economy typical of such remote development towns. It is a cement box not a glass ceiling that locks them in. Rachel's juggling act, I argue, cannot extricate her from her concrete box. The rigid limits of her multiple exclusions are poignantly revealed in the scene that closes this chapter.

"You're Bothering Everyone"

Rachel comes to visit me in Sde Boker for the weekend. She arrives on Friday, before the beginning of Shabbat, in her brother's car; he agrees to return and drive her back to Yerucham when Shabbat is over. During her visit, Rachel joins me for my irregular workout in the tiny campus gym. The gym is frequented by five or six regulars, mostly professors and a postgraduate student or two. In her tight purple tracksuit, sporting deep aubergine hair, and with a relentlessly ringing mobile phone always to hand, Rachel's presence provokes a sense of unease in the tightly packed gym that I become aware of as soon as we walk in.

We mount stationary bikes and begin pedaling. Rachel's phone does not stop ringing, and she engages in loud conversations with the callers while still pedaling intensely. I motion to her several times to keep her voice down, but she ignores me. I sense the tension building in the tiny gym and fearfully expect the inevitable explosion. I do not have to wait long. The men in the room exchange angry glares, and then one of them, an Ashkenazi professor in his fifties, stops his workout and walks up to Rachel, barely suppressing his anger. Rachel acknowledges him with a look and continues talking on the phone. The professor demands in an openly aggressive manner that she take her phone outside, because she is "bothering everyone." Rachel seems unintimidated, but I can see she blushes. She then informs her caller that she "can't speak now" because she is "being interrupted." She stares at the man standing in front of her and takes her time before suggesting we leave. "I am tired of this boring pedaling," she declares loudly. I follow her out of the gym, and we head back to my place.

In this closing scene, I observe the collapse of Rachel's flamboyant juggling act when it is transported outside the bubblelike space of Yerucham to a hegemonic setting. In this external space there is a strict penalty for unacceptable behavioral patterns. Loud vocal intrusion into the space of the Ashkenazi dominant male carries with it a real threat of being physically chucked out of that space. Despite her effort to seem dignified and her brief resistance to the demand that she leave the gym, Rachel stumbles and falls. Her creative juggling act has reached its limit.

5

ESTI

Subversive Interpretation of a Constrained Reality

BEFORE I LEARNED her name, I referred to Esti in my notes as "the small, funny one." She is a petite woman with closely cropped, dyed blonde hair and prominent, loose front teeth in urgent need of dental treatment. Every time she bursts out laughing, she covers her mouth with her hand. And she laughs a lot. She is a compulsive joke teller. She is the living spirit of the stealthy meetings the campus cleaners hold in my office. She never comes into my office hideout on her own but always with a friend or two. As soon as she enters the room, the atmosphere turns carnivalesque. Esti sings popular tunes, adjusting their lyrics with swear words. She twists her body joyfully as she sings and declares that she loves dancing. Underneath the gray-blue work gown marked with the cleaning company logo, Esti wears tight trousers cut off at the shin and minute, midriff-baring shirts. She flashes her breasts at her coworkers and me, feigning disregard for but clearly enjoying the sound of our embarrassed laughter.

Esti stands out in the group of women cleaners who come to my office in the late summer and early fall of 2001. The other women are all in their midtwenties and are mothers of at least one child. Esti is 34, single, and childless. She lives in Yerucham in a small public-housing apartment with her sister, who is a year older than she and is also single. I learn about Esti's life from the brief reports of her coworkers, who refer to her as "the poor thing." I hear from them that she was born in Israel, the youngest daughter in a large family that immigrated from Morocco in the early 1960s, that her father died when she was seven years old, and that her mother, who worked as a cook at the

Sde Boker campus to support her children through her years of widowhood, died of an asthma attack when Esti was in her early twenties. According to her friends, Esti cared for her mother devotedly, dropping out of school after only a few years of elementary education. Her fellow cleaners, who came to their campus jobs only after dropping out of high school or after stints in local factories, tell me that Esti has worked as a cleaner for most of her life. Later I hear more biographical details from Esti herself, but it is never easy to get her to talk about her life. She prefers to focus on the laughs.

Esti does not keep the cleaning job in my university office for long. After she is fired, we stay in close contact and she becomes one of my main inter-locutors for more than a decade. Every time I go to Yerucham, I seek her out and accompany her in her daily activities. Together we visit her bank, the local market, the Welfare Office. We spend long hours drinking coffee and sharing simple meals in her home or at her aunt's place, where Esti spends her week-ends. I see her in her private, intimate moments and observe her in her rau-cous public performances. I always enjoy my time with Esti, and I come to like her for her embrace of an unconventional spirited life that defies local social conventions. I enjoy the unpredictability she brings to our relationship, and I am openly charmed by her rebellious nature. At one point, I persuade Esti to write a number of short essays that describe her life in her own words. I pay her for each essay she pens. Esti is amused by the arrangement but is openly pleased with the unexpected income. She submits her handwritten texts on pages torn from an old school notebook.

Esti rebels against the major social norms that define life for a woman in Yerucham—she refuses to get married, to bear children, and to accept work that she finds humiliating and insecure. Within the limited possibilities she has in the town, Esti shapes what she openly defines as the good life. In this life she dazzles with her dress and hair, jokes with her many acquaintances, watches soap operas instead of working regularly, gambles, and maintains family relationships only when they suit her. By refusing a life of marriage, parenthood, and work, Esti challenges both local conventions and a wider middle-class discourse about how working-class women should live. Reject-ing local expectations allows her to experiment with other modes of being in the world, and as she tampers with social rules and conventions, she invents new rules, new patterns of behavior that suit her individual needs. Still, Esti's path is not an easy one. She is forced to deal with severe material hardship and with social isolation, against which she struggles and which she defiantly tries to reformulate.

To my mind, Esti represents an unusual option for female agency in a reality of multiple exclusions. Precisely because of its extreme anomaly, her life speaks to the limited space afforded to women like her in Israel's remote towns, and it highlights the few options for class mobility available to them. The defiant, carnivalesque way in which Esti celebrates her life is the most effective path for her to exercise her agency. The sheer spectrum of ways she expresses the subversiveness of her life is spectacular. And indeed, those around her are rarely indifferent to her. She does not behave like someone defeated by the "concrete boxes" shaping her life's struggles but like someone who refuses to surrender to them and who emerges victorious from her daily battles.

In a phone call with Esti in the early spring of 2006, I tell her that my students are reading and discussing a draft of the chapter I have written about her. "Oh yeah?" she counters in her usual raucous way. "And what *did* you write about me, Pniniyot?" she asks, using the nickname she has given me. "I wrote that you're a rebel of a woman and that I call you 'Esti the Rebel.'" Esti roars in laughter: "A rebel, eh??" and then she adds triumphantly, "'I'm a rebel, all right!'"

A Day with Esti

"What Do You Care about My Nonsense?"

It is a warm autumn day in 2001. I phone Esti from my mobile to tell her I will stop by. I have just concluded recording an interview with one of the elderly first-generation immigrant women whose life stories I have been collecting for some months. I am energized by the interview I have just completed and, as the recorder is still lying on the car seat next to me, I decide that I will record my conversation with Esti. I have known Esti for more than a year at this point and have been handwriting notes of our encounters as soon as they are over. But I have never really attempted to record our conversations. This time, I think, it might be nice to fully document Esti's crackling wit and the wacky dynamic she injects into our every meeting. I suspect that the act of recording our conversation will change our interaction. It certainly does.

I head to Esti's place, and even though I have been there many times, I find myself driving in circles, unable to locate the street where she lives. I call her again. "Your street is Yehuda Ha-Nasi, isn't it?" Esti bursts out laughing, declaring me the first person ever to manage to get lost in Yerucham. "What Yehuda Nasi? How would I know," she says in between giggles. "Who remembers his name. You need to turn left before the Hall. Did you turn there?"

When I finally make it to her street, I count three gray apartment buildings on the left and proceed to the fourth, parking in front of the second entry to the long three-story structure. Finding Esti's apartment has never been easy for me; the public housing complex she lives in has identical sets of buildings along the block. Municipal efforts to beautify the uniformly gray scene by planting tiny public gardens in front of each building have left small patches of dry grass strewn with sunflower seed hulls and plastic bags. I walk into the dark entryway of Esti's building and up a few stairs, knock on an unmarked apartment door, and open it without waiting for a reply. Esti is in the kitchen, wearing gray shorts and a white T-shirt. She is barefoot, and her bleached blonde hair is unkempt.

"Feeling like some spicy tuna?" she asks, by way of greeting, and, despite my protestations, she makes a sandwich of canned tuna and spicy sauce on fresh bread for me. She is in her usual animated and facetious mood and unleashes her teasing, lightning-fast punning, and antics the moment I enter her place.

"Say . . . this bag of yours . . . was it left behind somewhere by a bus driver?" she asks, winking toward the bulky black leather bag I have tossed into a corner.

I laugh. "I love these expressions of yours," I say. "Listen, I'm recording us just now. I hope you don't mind. It's because I don't remember all the expressions you use after I get home and make my notes." I produce the tiny recording device from my bag and show it to Esti.

Esti is unfazed. "What do you care about my nonsense?" she asks, but she seems flattered. "If you wanna do it, feel free."

We exit the kitchen and head for the living room. "So what's new, Pniniyot?" And then she adds in a singsong voice, "Pniniyot helmoniot," adding a reference to a Yerucham wildflower to the pet name she has given me.[1] I laugh, openly showing my affection for her, as I grab the spicy tuna sandwich. "Say, is this the most cooking you get up to?" I ask while chewing.

"Come on, what cookin'? I eat proper only on Fridays at my aunt's. Normally it's some bread, some olives, and *hopa* [voilà]. *La'avoda* [to work]." Esti starts humming "La'avoda ve' laMelakha," an old Hebrew song (by national poet Chaim Nachman Bialik), which calls workers "to the work, to the task."

Two simple sofas covered with brown faux leather are arranged in an L-shape; they face a color TV that plays soundlessly throughout my visit. The walls of the small living room are bare, aside from a small blurry watercolor hanging above the dining table. The face of a heavyset woman copied clumsily from an old photograph looks out at us from the unframed portrait. Two folding chairs lie on top of the dining table, placed there to free the floor for thorough cleaning. A foldable laundry rack is wedged between the back of one of the sofas and the half-shuttered window behind it. Esti perches on the edge of one sofa, and I sit down on the adjacent one. Our legs stretch over the coffee table, nearly touching.

Reading back through the transcribed records of that day's conversation, I realize just how much it was shaped by the presence of the tiny voice recorder. It is obvious that both Esti and I are speaking "for the record," in a demonstrative, contrived way aimed at invisible listeners beyond the little room we are sitting in. In this setting I am asking questions that are clearly shaped by an external, judgmental logic that challenges Esti to examine her world in terms I know she has rejected. Esti, who is aware of the external gaze framing my questions, plays the game according to her own rules. She decides which questions she will answer and which she will ignore. She makes clear that she has the power to decide what she will reveal about her life and what she will conceal. Keenly aware of the implicit rules of the game the recorder dictates, Esti deliberately toys with them from the start. In fact, she does not really wait for my questions. As soon as we establish ourselves on her living room sofas and begin to eat the food she has prepared, it is Esti, not I, who launches the first question. "So what's new, Pniniyot? I was thinkin', like, maybe I call you and you tell me a number. You dream something Pniniyot? What? Tell me."

Addressing me as Pniniyot, Esti overrides our expected positioning in an interview, in which I ask the questions and she responds. By asking the first question, she makes it clear that she will decide what is to be discussed for the record. When she asks me what I have been dreaming about, Esti makes a second move that brings me into her world, making me complicit in what outsiders listening to our conversation through the voice recorder might judge as inappropriate conduct or, at best, mischievous behavior. By inquiring about my dreams, she is hinting that I belong to her world, that my dream will provide her with a clue leading to a lucky number she can then feed into her gambling scheme. Esti positions me from the get-go as an ally in her world of dreams and gambling, thus stripping me of my assumed role as an outsider interviewer gazing at her life.

"That's How It Is in Yerucham. You Sleep, You Eat, You Buy on Credit, and You Don't Pay."

Esti feels comfortable drawing me into her world because she is confident of my friendship and compassion. At this point, we have known each other for more than a year, and she feels that I care about her, as I have often voiced my concern about her dire financial situation. So when I respond to her opening question by asking in an unconcealed judgmental tone, "Why do you want to hear about my dreams, Esti? Did you put your money *again* on the *mispar nosaf*?" Esti mocks my ignorance of the way gambling operates in Yerucham. "No, Pninit," Esti responds with ersatz patience. "That's on Tuesdays. Yesterday I bought a proper Mif'al HaPayis ticket. Fifty shekels I put. And that's it, I'm outa money. That's my last 50. I threw them on the lottery."

The *mispar nosaf*, literally the "added number," is the final digit of the national lottery number published each week by Mif'al HaPayis, the official state institute for betting, lotteries, and scratch cards. Gamblers in Yerucham, like Esti, place local, unlicensed bets on only the final two digits of the lottery number, spreading their bet locally without buying the Mif'al HaPayis lottery tickets themselves. Esti explains with mock patience that there are specific days of the week for each kind of bet—the *mispar nosaf* occurs only on Tuesdays, and "proper" national Mif'al HaPayis bets are made on other weekdays. She then talks about her gambling experience at length.

"What can I tell you, Pnina, I'm outa money. See, when I told you I bought them shoes in Dimona, I didn't really." As she speaks, Esti jumps out of her seat and grabs an old paper envelope from the top of her TV. She pulls some banknotes out of it and makes a show of counting them up. "That's it. Three hundred fifty shekels. I am out of money," she declares.

"What do you mean you're out of money?" I ask with real alarm. "When's your next unemployment payment coming in?"

"In two weeks. It's not coming 'til the 18th," she says flatly.

"And what will you do 'til then?" I cannot help asking like a doting mother.

"I'll masturbate," Esti says, illustrating her point with a rapid up-and-down movement of her hand. She laughs wildly. "What else have I got to do?"

I point to the food laid out on the table and inquire, "So who's buying you the Coke, the tuna, the bread . . ."

"I do."

"Well?"

"I ask him to put it down on my account. That's how it is in Yerucham. You sleep, you eat, you buy on credit, and you don't pay." She laughs loudly, evidently enjoying herself and my expected reaction to her.

"Tell me . . ." I begin, trying to break through her laughter.

"And say to me . . . is that the same?" she shoots back, repeating a common jesting phrase. I chuckle. But then I insist, "No, but seriously, do you know how much money you owe, all in all?"

"Me? Nine hundred ninety-nine." Esti sings the words to another familiar melody, one about an old train leaving Be'er-Sheva. This musical reference, like the earlier one, harks back to a quaint, out-of-context "First Israel" cultural grammar.[2]

"No, but really!" I protest, enjoying her puns.

"It depends," she says, becoming serious for one brief moment. "What can I tell you? All in all, altogether, it's some . . . 6,000 shekels."

"Wow. Do you have a bank account, and is it overdrawn?"

"Of course I got a bank account. From yeeeears back [she enjoys stretching out the word]. I had a credit line. But then the bank decided to close it down. And I persuaded them to open it back again."

"And what's your credit line?"

"Two thousand five hundred."

"And have you used it up?"

"Duh!" she says, laughing again.

"And you're paying interest on the amount you draw beyond that, right?"

"What interest? Who knows anything about their interest? What do I know? Yes interest, no interest? Two days ago I went to the machine that spits out a printout of your account, right? And I saw they charged me another 40 shekels on fees. A few days ago they rejected my online payment to the cable company. It was on direct debit and they refused to pay it. No problem, I'll make them pay it later."

"A direct debit? Do you have other direct debits set up in your account?"

"No, I don't. There might be this yeshiva I set up a direct debit monthly donation for."

"And what about electricity, water bills?"

"That's, like, my sister. She, like, pays it and we work it out."

"And when does your unemployment benefit period run out?"

"Two more months."

"And what happens then?"

"What happens? He'll probably shut down my credit again. For sure."

Esti evades my questions with a smile, bitter cynicism, and a medley of popular tunes. I keep asking her to answer seriously. I insist that she examine the scope of her indebtedness, and she laughs in my face and tries to shock me with lewd gestures, brushing off my moralist worries. She assures me that she knows her financial situation, but she also makes it clear that she does not intend to yield to the rules of the game. Her mocking tone is a response to the external, self-righteous voice behind my questioning. It is to an external audience that she speaks when she sums up the reality of life in Yerucham: "That's how it is in Yerucham. You sleep, you eat, you buy on credit, and you don't pay." Esti deliberately exaggerates the description *ad absurdum*, again, probably to mock the external, judgmental gaze my questions imply.

And so, once she has exhausted her spirited flipping of the mirror back at my middle-class moralist gaze by ridiculing my questions and painting an exaggerated picture of life in Yerucham as uncontrolled (maybe uncontrollable), Esti decides to move on to another subject. At this point, she turns the tables on me altogether. Instead of her being my interviewee, she makes me into the object of her attention. I become someone who falls short of acceptable standards of personal grooming. My eyebrows and my hair come under discussion, as Esti begins to critique what she insists is my lack of self-care, belittling me and thus effectively challenging my position as the powerful interviewer sitting in judgment of her life. It is my appearance and *I*, not her financial behavior, that stand to be corrected.

"Who Does Your Eyebrows?"

There is a long pause. Neither of us asks any questions. Esti and I stare at the shimmering, silent television screen. And then Esti starts drumming on her shins, humming a melody to the beat. She examines her bare legs, thrown across the coffee table between us, exclaiming, "Wow, look at the hair on my legs. I should go see Debby." Then she props herself up and leans over to look at my eyebrows. "Who does your eyebrows? Forget that Indian cosmetician you go to. She doesn't know shit."

I have gotten used to this particular kind of criticism from Esti. To her, my pants are never tight enough, my hair is boring ("Get them to put bright streaks into your dark hair," she advises me over and over, "It'll light up your face"), and my eyebrows are never plucked correctly, fashionably, or on time. Esti recommends her hairdresser, Debby, who has the best beauty salon in town. Esti's hair, like that of most of Debby's regular clients, is bleached to a light blonde, and her eyebrows are painted in the fashionable dark arrow shape. I giggle in embarrassment and then, remembering the voice recorder, I attempt to return to my line of questioning. "So really, Esti, what are you going to do when your unemployment benefit runs out?"

"What can I do?" she asks in a tired tone, and then she repeats with much less gusto her mimicking of male masturbation. I laugh. But I am deeply embarrassed, and I fall silent for a short while, not sure where to take the interview at this point. And maybe because she senses my genuine loss of direction, Esti becomes solemn and decides to explain more about her financial status in ways she has refused to do thus far.

"Look," she says, "I have my guaranteed basic income from the Welfare Office, and I'm allowed to supplement this by up to four hours of work. I'll work for old people. Two old people is a thousand, a thousand and something shekels per month. And with my guaranteed income of 12 hundred shekels, that's . . . well . . . a living wage." Then she shouts out, "What's wrong [*ma ra'*]?" copying a bit from a well-known Israeli standup group, a funny slogan that she throws at me from time to time with a broad smile. But at this point I do not find it humorous.

"What do you need to do at the old people job?"

"Depends on the old person. What's her state. Wash her up, do some shopping. Two hours a day each."

"So you're not worried," I state wryly.

"Come on, Pnina, do you think this is the first time? I've been like that for the past four years. That's tough. Twelve hundred [shekels; about US$300] is nothing. One spends that much on cigarettes."

"So what did you do? How did you manage?"

"What did I do?" She looks at me, and she is not smiling. "Well, good thing me and sister are single women, so we worked it out. It's not like we have to support children and such. But it's not easy. Look, the real difficulty is the rent."

"The rent? But I thought you inherited the flat from your mother, may she rest in peace."

"Inherited? This is *diyur tsiburi* [social housing]," Esti spits out the words bitterly. Then she proceeds: "When my mother was alive, she paid 70 shekels. Now they want 700 or a thousand every month. Depends on conditions. Because like now, when my sister is employed and I'm on the dole, they want their full rent, not like when my mother was alive."

"How much does the place cost, if you were to buy it?"

"Not much. My sister wanted to buy the flat, so the money doesn't get wasted on the rent. But where would she get the money?" There is another long silence. I do not ask anything further, and Esti does not volunteer more information about her financial situation. And then, her mood changes abruptly. "Forget it," she snaps happily. "*Hachol be'seder*. It's all fine. We're getting along." She flashes her big smile at me as she jumps to her feet without warning and then disappears into the bedroom. "Wait 'til you see what I bought yesterday." She calls out to me. "You wanted to see, right?"

When she decides to speak frankly, without her loud jests, Esti charts the limited options available to her in the face of chronic unemployment. This is not the first time she has experienced want. She is aware of the cyclicity of her situation in which short bouts of irregular employment are followed by long years of unemployment. She does not attempt to conceal the fact that life with no regular income, sustained only by meager welfare benefits from the state, is tough, and she is forthright about her dependence on her sister's income. Regardless of her dismissive "Don't worry, we're getting along," Esti actually worries quite a lot. Her rent is climbing because "they"—those who hold the power—have decided that two single women with no children must pay almost 10 times the rent their mother paid all her life as a widow. Esti mentions briefly her hope of finding a part-time job that would complement the meager income she receives from the Welfare Office, but she is doubtful that this part-time employment will materialize or that it will provide enough to support her modest lifestyle. But a narrative of a bleak future is not one Esti wishes to dwell on. She wants her listeners, whom she is aware of by way of my recorder, to hear about her blatant disrespect for the rules, the rules that block her ability to make a decent living and force her to live within her meager means. And so, with great fanfare, she insists on presenting her latest purchases—garments that she should not have been able to afford. Showing them off, Esti underscores her disregard for her financial limitations and emphasizes her ability to get along happily regardless.

"I Give Her My Word"

Esti emerges from her bedroom with a short embroidered denim coat and spreads it out before me on the couch. "It's beautiful," I marvel. "How much did you pay for it?"

"Four hundred shekels, but listen, there are gorgeous jeans at the market for 50 . . ."

"Esti, do me a favor, a 50-shekel denim is good enough for me, right? So why don't you buy that? Why do you buy a 400-shekel jacket?"

Esti pointedly ignores my question and turns back to the bedroom, only to return a brief moment later with two colorful pullovers. "I paid 170 shekels each," she declares. I make loud appreciative comments about the beauty of the pullovers, feeling the fabric through my fingers, "You're something else!" I say, and her joy at my reaction is palpable. But then, half-smiling and knowing all too well that she has no money to spend on clothing, I ask her, "But, really, Esti, tell me, this 170 . . . where did you get this money?"

Esti is unmoved. Not looking at me, she says flatly, "This money? I told her I'll bring her this money next week."

"How much do you owe her by now?" I continue, an unstoppable nag.

"This woman from Dimona?" Esti asks as she focuses her gaze on the pullovers. "I'm telling you, Pnina, she imports things only from Italy."

I watch her, waiting for an answer to my question, but she seems enthralled with her new purchase, and then, at length, she replies, "Aaah . . . well . . . so . . . all together? I think, maybe . . . a thousand shekels . . ."

"Wait a moment," I push her, "and she's not pressuring you to pay her?"

"Look . . . well . . . I give her my word?"

"And . . . ?"

"And the word doesn't work." We both burst out laughing at her pun. Esti hums another popular song, substituting her own funny words for the lyrics.

We stare again at the flickering TV screen. Esti fills my glass to the rim with more Coke. "Say . . ." I begin, sipping on the fizzy drink.

"What?" she counters in mock aggression.

"So . . . like . . . how do you see . . . your . . . future?" I take long pauses between each word, not sure what it is I am asking, not sure if I have exhausted her patience, feeling like a fool.

"My future? It's like that," Esti says emphatically. "*Mispar nosaf*, debts, unemployment, and welfare. This is about it. That's my life." She looks at me amused, waiting for my next question like an adult expecting another ridiculous, unanswerable "what if" from a child.

"And are you happy with this life of yours?" I blurt out, knowing that she is playing with me.

"*Ani merutza be'helki* [I'm satisfied with my lot]," Esti states in high Hebrew, making sure to use a strong mock-Ashkenazi accent, emphasizing a rolling, contrived *r*. She slaps her bare thigh and laughs wildly. And then, like a standup comedian, she repeats, "Tell me, Pnina. *Ma ra*? What's wrong? What's wrong, eh?"

I am painfully aware that Esti is toying with me, that I, with my dogged questions, am being ridiculed, dismissed. But I still cannot let go. "No, seriously, Esti. Be serious for a second." I plead with her. "Tell me . . ."

Esti leans toward me like a menacing teacher above a dull-witted student and says in a mock-authoritative voice, "Yessss????"

She then leans back again, with her legs thrust forward, and repeats her funny motto: "*Ma ra*? Nothin' is bad, nothing's wrong."

"And aren't you worried you won't have . . . that you won't have any money? How are you going to live? Seriously . . . come on . . . what about your teeth? They must be bothering you. Don't tell me they don't." Gum disease has caused Esti's front teeth to protrude, noticeably disfiguring her face.

At that, Esti becomes grave for a moment. "This . . . ah . . . yes . . . forget about it, that's a project! I'm scared. I went . . . I did X-ray, the checkups, everything. That's 6,000. He said they could let me pay it in installments, but I didn't want to."

"So you did not take care of your teeth because of money?"

"Money will come."

"How? From where?"

"Money will come. No problem. Pnina gives me a couple of numbers. Nice ones."

"You're thinking again about those lucky numbers?" I respond, surprised at the way she turns things around.

"I'm trying. If you don't try, you don't succeed."

"Have you ever tried adding up how much you spend on these 'numbers'?"

"It's like that . . ."

I see a merry twinkle reappear in Esti's eyes and give up. I know there's no point in trying to extract a more serious reply from her. I have pushed far and long enough, and I begin to doubt the value of the sober self-reflection that I am trying to pry out of her. After all, she has said what she had to say in her unique jesting way, with fanfare and cheer. She knows as well as I do that she is on shaky financial ground, and still she insists on living above her means. When she mischievously states that she gives her word to the shop owner, she is actually saying that she is counting on her social credit. Her word still carries some weight with her friends and neighbors. But we both know that its value is bound to run out. Still, Esti refuses to surrender to this glum conclusion and continues to purchase relatively expensive clothes for herself (not the cheap stuff from the market, which she says I should buy) as she pursues what she defines as the good life. And when I ask her time and again about the source of the money, she just tells me that "money will come." She is trying. She won't surrender, because "if you don't try, you don't succeed."

I am willing to laugh along with the contradictions that Esti celebrates before me, and I openly enjoy her rapid wordplay. But I keep oscillating between an accepting, inclusive stance from which I cheer on Esti's wild revelry and a middle-class, moralist, external positioning that asks her to be serious, that calls her to confront her never-changing material reality, to take up whatever employment she is offered in the local setting, even if it pays almost nothing. My movement between accepting and moralizing allows Esti to define her own space, to laugh with me about the questions that I pose to her. She rejects the bare moralism of my questions and cloaks herself in roaring cheerfulness. "What's wrong?" is not just a rhetorical question but a statement that challenges my interpretation of her life and offers an alternative to it.

Esti's cheerfulness carries through the interview, vanishing only for one brief moment when I bring up her urgent need for dental care. But even then she speaks about the situation as subject to her control, her decision. The dentist offered her an installment plan to pay for the treatment, but she declined the offer. "I didn't want to," she states, insisting that it is her choice not to use her money for the medical procedure but instead to buy expensive clothes. Esti makes clear that she has choices and thus that her life is of her own making.

But there is a barely hidden message in Esti's laughter. It is not just that gambling will give her the means to pay for a lifestyle she cannot afford; it is that *I* will provide her with the lucky numbers to make this happen. Beyond the larking, Esti communicates a call for help, for my financial contribution toward stabilizing her faltering situation. The call is not direct, nor is it explicit. But the message carries though, and its details are clearly communicated: Dental treatment costs 6,000 shekels, and only with my help Esti might be able to cover that cost.

The way Esti draws me into her world and maneuvers me into the position of the amused, affectionate, empathetic observer is not very different from the way she gets vendors to keep selling her goods on credit, even though they are aware of the difficulty she has paying. She engages us all in her carnivalesque, flamboyant game. She gives us a spectacular performance, and we become involved because we are touched by her courage and beauty.

During our long recorded interview, I am aware that Esti is avoiding my questions, redefining the stage through her raucous act. But I still wonder throughout, is this a performance she flashes to sympathetic audiences, or does this act constitute a strategy that Esti herself sees as effective in dealing with the reality of her life? I thus try pushing her just a little bit further—I want to hear what she says about not having children. At this point in our recorded encounter I do not expect her to pour out her heart to me. I expect more proclamations. But I want to document that proclamatory tone. I know it is an important layer in Esti's construction of herself. I want to give her the stage to articulate the profound choice not to have children.

"I'm Different!"

"Tell me one last thing, Esti, don't you want a kid?"

"Me? I need somebody to raise *me*!"

"Hand on heart, Esti. Everyone is talking about kids, kids, kids."

"Pnina, it's . . . I'm not up for that." She says this with apparent unease.

"So how is it that everyone here marries at 20 and immediately everyone's got kids and all that?"

She stares at me. So I hasten to add, "How is it that you're not like them?"

"I'm different!" she declares, immediately, without hesitation.

I feel that I have touched a sensitive, core issue, but it is too late to let go. "How? What makes you different?" I insist.

"How can I explain it to you? I'm . . . a lazy girl. I don't have the patience for it."

"Do you think about this, Esti? Do you see yourself like that, without kids?"

"I really don't know how it's going to be. I'm living for today. I don't know what'll come tomorrow. Believe me. Every day in its turn!" And then, as expected, she begins singing a popular song, this time by the Israeli singer Rita, "Every Day in Its Passing."

I understand that this answer is as much as I am likely to get from Esti on this topic, so I change track. "And do you want to get out of Yerucham?" I ask, knowing all too well what she will say, as I have heard her declare her love for the town many times.

"Me? I don't want to leave. I love this place! I love the peace and quiet here." And then she adds with a mischievous smile, "Although, y'know, people really suck these days. But what can you do? People are like that. They're jealous if you get a number right, if you're this or that. But I don't take it to heart."

I have asked enough. I decide to end the interview, and so I reach for my small voice recorder and turn it off. But, to my surprise, Esti is suddenly beaming with renewed energy. So I turn the recorder on again. When I read back through the transcript of the conversation that follows this pause, I understand the reason for Esti's new burst of energy. Gambling and other people's jealousy of her is a topic that, unlike the others I have raised, she enjoys talking about. In gambling she finds not only an escape from what seems to be a dead-end reality of loneliness and unemployment but also a space where people turn to her for advice, a space of hope, of meaning. So I turn the recorder back on and listen to Esti describe, in impressive ethnographic detail, a world of social connections and meaning, a world where she is not defined as a poor, unemployed, single woman but as someone in possession of knowledge sought out by an ever-growing number of people. Her joy when she talks about gambling is palpable.

The Added Number

"Yesterday I was visited by Batia and Rivka. The Givatroni[3] one. Y'know, the one who lives on the hill, at the entrance to Yerucham . . . and Pnina, let's see if you guess . . . what did we talk about?"

"About numbers?"

"A-s u-s-u-a-l!" Esti declares with shining eyes. "And . . . her . . . Rivka . . . she . . . *haval al ha'zman*.[4] Oh, there was a bombing? How many dead? How many wounded? And that's how it's gonna be. That number's what she's gonna put down. I tell her, enough of that, you can't put down terror attacks and such; that's not proper. But what can I do? That's how it goes."

"And you? What are you going 'to put'? What are you 'going for'?"

"Me? Tomorrow? I don't say until the very last minute!"

"So what are you looking at? You're not looking at bomb attacks? I heard a lot of people say they put how many years it's been since Rabin's assassination."

I'm proud of my ability to use the local gambling slang. I am happy I can answer Esti's opening question correctly (that the main topic of her conversation with her neighbor is gambling), and that I properly use the expression "numbers" rather than "gambling" to refer to the act. I also know enough to ask, *"Ma at sama?"* "What are you putting down?" and "What are you looking at?" My questions are informed by my knowledge of a local practice of determining the number placed on a bet by reference to a social event in the national arena, and I note, for example, that people place bets in reference to the nationally sanctified date of Israeli prime minister Rabin's memorial day. We both allude to the fact that this practice is probably deemed improper in hegemonic Israeli discourse, and Esti makes a point of noting that she too condemns such sacrilegious behavior, which is widely popular in Yerucham. Esti positions herself as somewhat more righteous than her friends and neighbors, but she does it with a wink. She has a different basis than they do for selecting numbers to bet on. Without much prompting on my part, Esti lays out the complicated knowledge system she relies on to place her bets.

> I'll tell you. I'm looking at the things I dream about. Take a bird. A bird is 4. The Indians[5] have a list. From 1 to all the numbers of the lottery. One is train, 2 is butterfly, a dead person is 3; 4 is bird, 5 is ship, 6 is horse. And Pnina! It's true, it's absolutely true! Listen, it works. You see, a rooster is 15; I dreamt it and it came up. A cat is 7. Listen well. Let me tell you how I first started playing the numbers. There was this dealer. I dreamt three cats: two are dancing and one is looking at me. She's looking at me like that [Esti opens her eyes wide to demonstrate], and I'm angry about it. Back then we didn't know about all this. So I told myself, I'll go and ask. I went to some Indian man and told him about my dream. So he tells me, "Cat means 7." And me, Pnina, you know how my head works. Don't see me like that, see me naked! [She laughs at her own Hebrew pun]. I came home, I thought to myself, there are three cats . . . that's 21. I went and I put down 50 and 50 . . . and, sure enough, it came up—21! And until today—just come here

on Tuesday, you'll see how many calls I'm getting. I used to tell everyone [what to bet on]. But now, forget it. I don't tell them anymore. They confuse me. Here's the one that came out yesterday. I'll show you.

Esti becomes extremely animated. She walks over to the chest of drawers at the end of the room and brings out a few crumpled envelopes containing water and electricity bills. She pulls out three elongated, rustling envelopes that once contained bills but that she now uses to write down her gambling numbers. She gives me the envelopes and sits down next to me. I see a long string of numbers written in a blunt pencil. The string, she says, lists the numbers on which bets are placed. Next to each number is another number, the sum of the bet placed on that number.

"I'll show you. You'll be shocked. You'll be stunned. Take a look: How many times do you see 1 here? Do you see it in the 30? In the 25? And believe me, I didn't put it down in the end! I put down 395 shekels and I didn't put on the 1. I didn't put it down! What was I telling you? They confuse me."

"I see you've put down a lot on 7 and 8—150 on each. Why? Did you dream about it?"

"Dream about it? Of course I dreamt about it! Listen. I dreamt [about] a mattress. A bed mattress. Folded out. And I'm pulling it out of the sewage. Sewage is black. And the mattress comes out red. And I'm about to throw it away and it opens up and inside was the number 7. And I saw the number and said I'll go for that."

"Right. Well? And then what happened?"

"So the dream here [laughs] was messed up. Because what can you do, you gotta understand, red? Red has nine numbers. So it's not at all simple. What can I tell you. Bracha [a neighbor] put down 1,000. And she started from 2 and put down 100 on each. Everything's gone! She put money like that for a long time. Rolling it every week. Recently she didn't get anything. What can I do for her? If I dream a number, it sometimes comes up and sometimes it doesn't." She looks down at the envelopes and the notes scribbled across them and says in a pensive way, "Me? Truthfully? I'm not investing now. Nothing. I don't go above 100 shekels. Twice a week, and some 50 shekels on a regular ticket lottery. That's it. What do you know, Pnina. Some people here, they put down thousands of shekels."

"And do they win anything? Isn't it a shame to lose all that money?"

"What can I tell you, Pnina? They're losing here like you wouldn't believe. It's a habit. A habit. I tell myself I'll stop. And then I walk by, and I see him [the dealer], and even if I don't have the money, I put [some] down. I tell him, put it! I once had a fight with him. I passed by and told him, put me down on 14. He tells me: I won't write it down [referring to the fact she has no cash to place her bet]. I tell him, 'What's the matter with you? I closed all my debts to you.' Honestly, Pnina, I paid him up. And he wouldn't take it, and in the end, you wouldn't believe it, it was 14. I told him, 'It's because of you, you son of a bitch.' But now—nothing. What do I ever put down? A hundred shekels?"

"So why not use this hundred? Why throw it away?"

"Pnina, what can I even buy for 100 shekels? You tell me!"

"Here's a hundred and then here's another hundred and you buy yourself a shirt. Or pay a debt."

"Forget about the debt. The money you see here," Esti says, pointing at the envelope, "I got this money here from the bank."

"But I thought you went over your credit line and you can't draw out money anymore?"

"Don't even ask, Pnina! I confuse him [the bank clerk]," Esti says with a broad, satisfied smile. "I go. I put a bandage on. I come to him and say, 'Do me a favor, Gideon [the bank manager]. I need to get to Be'er-Sheva. I got injured. What am I going to do, Gideon? I have to have 300 shekels!' So he agrees and says, 'Ok. Allow her that.' I go to Meir [the teller], and I confuse him, 'Hey, what's up? Gideon allowed me 500.' Or 1,000. And because he's so confused, he doesn't call the manager to confirm. And then I run off."

I watch her, speechless. She begins to hum another popular song, looking at me with immense satisfaction. "What can I tell you, Pnina, what can I recall . . ." she begins another pun and then, abruptly, she changes the subject. "Did you go to Batia? She has new boots [at her store], gorgeous ones."

I say nothing. I do not reply to Esti's question about the boots that Batia is selling. The story about her ostensible victory at the bank, putting on a display of misery before the manager to extract more money from her overdrawn account, is still settling in my mind. I am not amused by it. I do not applaud her ingenuity. I tell myself not to judge her, not to project my value system onto her. But I am also worried. I worry that her wild games will put her in so much debt that she will not be able to wiggle her way out of it. I am thinking about how I can help her, but I also know that even if I offer to cover her debt, I will not solve her problem. Esti will gamble with the money, incurring more debt. Aware as she is of her financial situation, she will not change her ways to fit the conservative solution I might offer her.

"It Is What It Is. I Didn't Study. That's It."

At this point in the conversation I am not smiling anymore. The questions I direct at Esti I now ask out of sadness, out of pain.

"Say, don't you have days in which you wake up and feel tired of it all? When you say, I'm worn out . . . I'm depressed?"

"No!" Esti declares defiantly, and then she relents and speaks in a softer tone. "Truth is, when there's work, the day goes by quicker. Like today, I went to the [employment] office. They tell me there's a complementary education course coming up, but I already did that. I can't do it anymore. And they have it all written down. I need guaranteed income, and if they have work with old people, I'll get into that. Got it? Today it's different. There's nothing. Nothing at all. Once, I remember, we didn't want cleaning jobs. There were all kinds of such jobs. Today, there's nothing. *Allah karim* [Arabic for 'God will provide']. Have you heard about [the layoffs at] Phoenicia [the local factory], Pnina? They weren't like me. It's families with kids. Today they promised them they will be hired back. And they didn't . . ."

She stops speaking, watching me, sensing my sad demeanor. "Did you know I worked at Phoenicia once?" she asks me. I say nothing. "Oh yes, I worked there about eight months," she adds.

"What did you do there?" I ask her gently.

"You sit on a chair and you mark bottles. If there's a crack you mark it. You know, anything that's not good, goes into the hole. I didn't do anything there. I worked until we all got fired. I'm telling you, it doesn't matter. If I like my job or if I don't like my job, they fire me at once."

"What kind of work *do* you like?"

"Look. The most important thing is that there isn't someone sitting on your head the entire time. Like Moshe, the one supervising us at your place, at Sde

Boker. He would run after the girls. Kept checking if you were working. Not sitting down. Had him up to here [with her hand she draws a horizontal line across her forehead]. When I was at the army base, no one told you do this or that. The driver who brought us over was in charge. You do what you have to do with peace of mind. But listen, it is what it is. I didn't study. That's it."

Her monologues become longer and more revealing, my questions short, sober.

"Would you like to study? To complete your education?"

"Me? No!"

"Why not?"

"I don't like studying. I did a course once, offered by the Welfare Office, to complete my education. But I don't like it. I don't like sitting on my ass."

"Maybe because you did not find something you were really interested in? Was there anything you liked studying?"

"Liked? Like how . . ."

"I don't know . . . composition . . . Torah . . . math."

"I did like math."

"Well? . . ."

"I did this math course three years ago, but I've forgotten everything. But what does it matter? Here, take Shula, she's so good at math and everything. She worked at the supermarket. Cashier. Lasted for three weeks, and just one day she didn't show up, she was sacked on the spot. Now she signs [for benefits] as well."

Esti moves here between accepting the fact that she "didn't study" as a legitimate cause for her current dead-end cycle of unemployment and short-term, unsatisfying, menial jobs and a deeper conviction that something is really wrong with the local job market because no stable, well-paying employment is ever to be had, not even by skilled workers (like Shula, who knows math). Moreover, when she looks back at her own employment history, Esti observes that the situation is getting worse and that the local job market is becoming increasingly limited. She remembers better times, when one could turn down a job as a cleaner. Cleaning, which Esti has pursued most of her life, is an undesirable job, something one takes only when there are no other options. Nowadays, she says, even cleaning jobs are hard to come by. Esti's analytical insights are profound. She goes on to insist that her own narrative of chronic unemployment is not unique, that hers is a prevalent experience in town. Many people, including heads of families, have recently been laid off, she relates, and their need for regular income is more crucial than her own. Being a single woman, Esti can get by.

Esti's analysis of the local labor market suggests that one's excellent performance on the job or one's skills are no guarantee against being fired for no cause, being paid an unlivable wage, or being denied the social dignity proper employment would confer. People with families to support are fired for no obvious reason, and promises to rehire them are not kept. Having outlined, in her own astute way, the larger social and political structure of Yerucham's labor market and its debilitating impact on local residents, Esti makes a point about her ability, limited as it is, to act, to make choices about how she behaves in such conditions. As a single woman with no dependents, she can decide to quit a job if she finds that her working environment is not to her liking. Thus, for example, when she is supervised too closely, she walks away from a job. A good job, Esti declares, is one that allows her to perform her duties peacefully.

I try to challenge Esti's analysis about the impossibility of keeping jobs in Yerucham by pointing out that her sister, Simcha, has been employed in the same job in the local supermarket for several years. I say to her teasingly, "Take your sister, Simcha, she's been working for six years now. Right? So what does she do that you don't?" Esti fires back, "She's smart. Not stupid, like me."

But she wastes no time in contradicting this statement, proceeding to question the choices made by her "smart" sister. She does not hesitate to pass judgment on women who, like her sister, hold on to humiliating jobs, are paid minimum wages, and have no employment security.

"I Do Have Brains"

"Really, Esti? You, lacking brains?" I ask her, smiling.

"I'm full of brains, but they're not working." She laughs out loud, enjoying her own witticism. Then she tries again. "Really, Pnina, how can I explain this to you? I do have brains. Of course. I could have done her job. That's not what it's about. My sister is more . . . how should I put it . . . serious . . . than me. I don't take anything seriously! She gets annoyed with me. She [referring to her work manager at the Phoenicia factory] tells me, 'You're not serious. You're lazy.'" Then Esti resumes speaking about her sister: "She's very serious. She's the one investing in the house. She changed the shutters. All kinds of things. She puts down the money. She gets loans." And then she adds, "But what *did* she get out of all that hard work? You see, she too was recently fired. Just like that. So, look at her now. She's looking for work in Be'er-Sheva. She wants to be an office clerk or something. Ha! She can't find anything. Nothing!"

There is a moment of silence as Esti contemplates her statement, and then, reflecting on her own past employment experiences, she recalls, "You know, Pnina, I used to work for Agis [a local cosmetics factory], but what can you do? They fired me too."

"Really? I didn't know you worked there. Why did you get fired from there?"

"Come on, Pnina, that's some question . . ."

"No, really—what did you do to them?"

"What didn't I do? I'll tell you . . . I'm not serious. Me and my silliness. I mess them up. I send on bottles with no corks [into the assembly line]."

"But why? Didn't you wish to keep that job?"

"I'm telling you, they don't let me work around here. I worked for nine months—and I got fired. I should have been there still and they simply fired me. She tells me, 'Come by my office at 2.' I told her, 'No problemos.' I'm fired . . . I know it. So I told myself—why should I work for her? So I really messed her up! I messed up all the labels. Everything. And when we were done with work, she goes, 'Listen, you don't fit in.' I says to her, 'No problem, hon. Just give me the dismissal letter.' And that's it. I went on benefits. And when that was over, I went on guaranteed income. I didn't find any work."

"And can you live on the guaranteed income?"

"I'll say it once again, Pnina. You can't. But one manages somehow." Esti uses an Arabic-derived slang word I have never heard before: *meharwedim*. It means you play a situation out, you improvise because you have no sense of what to do. I laugh.

"So tell me something, Esti: If you know it, if you know that it's so tough being unemployed, why don't you make an effort, try not to get fired?"

"Forget it. It's a lost cause. They'll fire me no matter what I do. Even Moshe [the work manager in Sde Boker] fired me, like, three times. He says to me, 'You got a job to do, be serious' and all that. But he keeps chasing me around. He'd catch me at something every time. Either sitting down or going to see my friend Shula at the administration building. Always something. Y'get it?"

Esti is convinced that keeping a job is a lost cause, that she will be fired no matter how she performs. For nine months she functioned as expected at the cosmetics plant, and then, when she knew that the boot was imminent, she salvaged some remnants of self-respect by sabotaging the production line. Esti stresses the sequence of events: She starts her "silliness" only when she knows, beyond a shadow of a doubt, that she is about to be dismissed. She is clear that she knows the rules of the game. She knows that she must have a dismissal letter to receive unemployment benefits. And she is painfully aware that the benefits alone are never enough and that another job will be difficult to find. But like the skilled Shula and like Simcha, her sister, who worked for six years at the same job before getting dismissed, Esti understands that earnest efforts and good behavior will not improve her odds of staying employed. She articulates a deep sense of hopelessness about the local job market and about any real chance of breaking out of it. Instead of the seriousness demanded of her from her employers, Esti engages in a defiant pattern of behavior, sabotaging the work scene. At the cosmetics factory, she sends bottles with no caps along the assembly line, and at Sde Boker she plays hide-and-seek with the cleaning manager, who chases after her in the office buildings to make sure she is never lax in doing her job. The cycle of dismissal, a short period of unemployment benefits, and prolonged stretches on a minuscule guaranteed income is inevitable. Within this inescapable cycle, Esti works to keep her self-respect, her human dignity.

I learn nothing new from listening to Esti's defiant words during our recorded session. At this point in our relationship, I am familiar with her stories and with her style and, to a large extent, I must admit, I agree with her analysis. But, always aware of the recording machine, I egg her on.

"Say, Esti, what would you tell someone who'd say to you, 'Oh, wow, those poor[6] people in Yerucham.' What would you say to that person?"

Perhaps in response to the unconcealed teasing tone of my question, Esti articulates what I think is the clearest statement yet of her social analysis.

"I'm Not Some Poor Thing"

"I'm not *miskena* [some poor thing]!" she explodes. "I am pleased with my life. What's wrong, Pnina?! What's wrong?! I tell you what. Just gimme a job! I don't want a lot, really. Some new clothes to flash a nice appearance every now and then. This is it. It's not like I got kids. I'm single so I afford it. If you get married, everything changes. Here, my friends who got married and all that, when I meet them, they tell me, 'Believe me, you were the smart one.' They say that if they knew then what they know now, they wouldn't have married. I'm good."

Esti rejects the patronizing outsider gaze that I have pushed into her face. All she needs is a proper job that will pay for her basic needs, her grooming as a single attractive woman. She made an unconventional choice *not* to get married. In fact, such a choice is rarely made by Israeli Jewish women of any class. To justify escape from the strict social dictates of marriage and children, Esti compares her lot with that of her women friends, putting in their mouths her assertion that her choice to remain single was in fact better than theirs to marry. I try to penetrate the declarative tone of her statement and broach a topic that Esti has not been ready to talk about in any of our earlier conversations—feelings.

"Say, and wasn't there anyone who you truly loved?"

"Yes, there was one guy."

"How old were you?"

"Twenty-four."

"Well . . . ?"

"You know what it's like. Can't be helped. We didn't hit it off. It didn't work."

She becomes serious for a fleeting moment, and then the twinkle in her eyes returns. And she comes up with another pun. "Pnina, you know what they say? If you don't click, you don't become a clique." I laugh warmly with her, enjoying her wisecrack. "I thought I loved him," she adds quietly, and then she raises her voice again. "Young and restless, that's what we are, Pnina. Ha?!"

"Who's 'we,' Esti? You're young, but I'm not."

"Why, how old are you, Pniniyot?"

"Me? Forty-six."

"So what's the big deal? Forty-six and 35 is the same thing. If you take the difference to the side . . . you move the 1 over here and the 0 over there . . . it doesn't make a difference," she juggles numbers, laughing wildly.

"Don't be silly, Esti. Let me ask you something else, just because. Tell me, so what is life for, tell me . . ."

"Life is to sleep, get into debt, and get rheumatic."

We both burst out laughing.

She comments on my age with her usually funny verbal acrobatics, and I follow up with a banal philosophical question about the meaning of life. Her humorous response is more intelligent than my preposterous question. And so I discover, rereading the transcript of our recorded conversation, that even though I am aware of how ridiculous my attempted interview is at that point, I still will not let it go. And when our laughter subsides, I try yet another line of inquiry, but I do not even get a chance to finish formulating my question.

"Say, Esti. Don't you have these moments when you say, I really want . . ." Esti cuts me off impatiently, clearly tired of my questions. She answers brusquely. "I really want cash. That's what I want!"

"Ok, fine. Fine. You know what? Great! Let's say I give you 2,000 shekels now, on the barrel. What do you do with them?"

"Two thousand shekels?" She does not lose a beat. "I buy . . . put a thousand on the numbers . . . and spend a thousand." She is snickering at me.

"But the thousand that you gambled will just be . . . gone."

"Honey! My life is gone! Why shouldn't a thousand shekels go also? Money comes and money goes. Do you know this song by Rita, 'I'm living from day to day, casting my days to the wind?'" Yes. I know the song. Esti is humming it now.

"That's it. That's my life in Yerucham."

"My life is gone," Esti sums up with piercing self-awareness and a sad smile. She is convinced that her choices are the best ones possible given the circumstances she lives in. She insists that she has made the right choice not to marry or have children. Time and again Esti claims that she is actually smarter than all the married women she knows, because she has retained her independence and self-respect. She rejects any attempt to define her as a failure; she does not apologize for getting fired or consider her frequent dismissals evidence of a character flaw.

When we reach the end of our long conversation and I start extending my hand to switch off the recorder, I ask her if I may pose one last question, for the record. Esti acquiesces with a tired smile.

"Last question, Esti, really. Tell me, where do you see yourself in 10 years?"

"In 10 years? If I live," chuckles Esti mirthlessly. "I don't know. Either I'll be here, or . . . same thing . . . Pninot-Pniniyot, what can I tell you, what can I say . . . there are some things you don't talk about. Understandos?"

I finally stop the recording. We have said enough. I invite Esti to come with me to the town center, to hang out, but she dismisses the idea. It's dead at the center today, she explains; everyone is there only on Tuesdays, on market day. We leave the cool flat and walk out into the street. Esti wants to call on her friend Shula, the one who's good at math. She does not feel comfortable moving far from her building when she is not immaculately dressed. She takes a few steps toward Shula's apartment building and begins shouting Shula's name from the sidewalk. But Shula is not home.

We sit down on the steps under a pleasant winter sun. We are the only ones out along the entire street, and I have no more questions to ask her that day. There is a long moment of silence, and then Esti turns to me and asks hesitantly about the years I spent abroad, in the United States. She is curious, she says, whether I had work over there. I tell her that I studied at a university and that I had a scholarship but that I also worked part-time jobs. I was a waitress in a restaurant, I worked at the university library, and I taught Hebrew. But then I start telling her about the later period, after I received my PhD and after I finished a three-year teaching contract at Harvard University. I was a mother of two small children, and I could not find work. I am suddenly so overwhelmed by emotion that I choke on my words. I thought that I had overcome that painful experience entirely. I am surprised by the depth of the emotions my memory has revived. Throughout the years I have been interviewing women and documenting the permanent instability in their lives, I have blocked my feelings about a difficult period in my own life.

I hear myself telling Esti that there were mornings when I would finish my breakfast, send my kids off to preschool, and start crying. I tell her that I was deeply depressed. But when I look at Esti, I see that she is embarrassed, that she is closing up. She does not want my tears. Throughout our long recorded conversation, she has insisted on telling me that everything is fine, that she passes the time, that her life is just what she says it is, that she lives day by day. And here I am, exposing the pain that she herself refuses to confront. Are her outbursts of laughter and her funny plays on words, the "I did what I want" proclamations, all part of a cover-up, a mask she has to put on because she has no other way to respond to my intrusive questions? Is it all a necessary defense for a woman who knows all too well that her life will not change, that no help will be forthcoming? That everything will be "the same" in 10 years, if she lives that long?

Interpreting Esti's World

Esti allows me into her world, up to a point. She decides what to share with me and what to withhold. She shares with me her deep frustration about her experience of what she views as inevitable dismissal from every job she has ever held. She tells me about her acts of sabotage against the forces that shape her life in Yerucham and about her refusal to be defined by those forces, which expect her to be a docile worker despite the reality of precarious, underpaid employment. Listening to Esti, to her pain and to her joy, to her keen social awareness and to her unconventional way of dealing with her ever-present financial insecurity, I develop my own interpretive narrative of her life. As I note in the opening pages of this chapter, I see in Esti a spirited rebel who develops creative means of survival, of existence, that allow her to cultivate self-worth in a reality that seems designed to deny her, and other women in her social setting, such dignity. I identify in Esti's narrative not only a sound awareness of the structure of the social and political reality that limits her ability to gain the education and skills that might clear the way to better-paying, white-collar jobs but also a defiance of the local codes that expect a woman to marry at a young age and juggle short-term employment as a cleaner or factory worker with pregnancies and the demands of motherhood. I see Esti's refusal to adhere to these social expectations and the limits imposed by the concrete box of her life in Yerucham as an act of rebellion, even if my middle-class logic fears her unconventional choices will have dire consequences. I have thus come to grasp why gambling is so central to her life.

When I enter Esti's apartment and request that we record our interactions on my small tape machine, I enter with that underlying interpretive model of her life. Esti's integrity and power during our long recorded session and our interaction when the recorder stops teach me about her ability to face her pain, loneliness, and lovelessness. I hear in her words and in her silences what I view as the triumph of her unconventional resolution to live in the moment in a social and material reality that offers no escape, no happy ending. I come to admire and enjoy her carnivalesque, unreserved humor, and I see it as part of her unorthodox social behavior. In the alternative model Esti has developed for her life, she will keep buying clothes because she enjoys dressing up, even if she does not have the means to pay for the clothes. She will ignore the accruing interest on her debts, gamble, and quit jobs that she finds humiliating, but she will maintain the basic tenets of what she defines as the good life for as long as she can.

I am keenly aware that this interpretation of Esti's life and her choices might make many of my readers uneasy. Students who read the original Hebrew version of this chapter and people from Yerucham and elsewhere in Israel who have heard me speak about Esti and my interpretation of her life often express great discomfort with my analysis. To them, Esti exemplifies irresponsible behavior. Her conduct challenges the basic convictions of the established liberal model in which hard work, building a family, paying one debts, and spending within one's means are necessary if one is to escape poverty and get ahead on the promised path of social mobility. This liberal model calls on the individual to act responsibly if he or she wishes to move beyond the limiting circumstances of social marginality. In these terms, Esti is a loafer who will end her days in dire poverty and loneliness. Esti, in this reading, is a classic example of a dependent, needy woman who, according to neoliberal concepts, exploits welfare benefits and must be made to take on productive work. If people like Esti stop gambling, work hard, and engage family life according to middle-class mores (two or three children; homework with the kids; a supportive family unit sustained by two salaries), they will escape the vicious cycle of poverty.

"I've come from a similar background," says Chemi, a student of public policy at the Israeli college where I was teaching when I was writing this chapter. He read about Esti as part of an anthropology class assignment. "I didn't get any help from my parents and yet I'm here, building my future with my own two hands, working hard with a desire to make something of my life." Chemi is passionate in his critique of Esti and her life. Adina, a young married student with a two-year-old child, says, "We live in a flat in the worst neighborhood in Sderot [a development town not far from the Gaza Strip in southern Israel]. My husband washes stairs in apartment buildings to make ends meet. We do this because we want to move ahead in life." And then she concludes with great passion, "This Esti of yours doesn't even try."

I am, of course, aware of this criticism. Moreover, when I reread my transcribed conversations with Esti and my many notes describing my other meetings with her, I realize how much the questions I posed throughout the recorded interview are shaped by these familiar liberal convictions. Even if I was not fully aware of it at the time, my insistence on asking these predictable questions was intended to make Esti confront the self-righteous, liberal narrative and respond to it in her own way. "And what will you say to *someone* who tells you you're a *miskena*, a poor, sad thing," I ask her, making myself the voice of that judgmental outside gaze, of that *someone*. Throughout the recorded interview we both know that we are playing our predefined roles— I am asking questions that I would never put to Esti in our other, unrecorded, more natural interactions, and she is allowed to respond to the pervasive logic of those Others who we both know are going to read the transcribed interview. Esti does not shrink away from the challenge. I am impressed by how emphatic she is in reacting to it. She feels no need to apologize or to explain herself in confronting the external logic that dictates my questions. She ridicules some of the questions. She responds to some questions and ignores others, and she stubbornly rejects any attempt I make to penetrate the shield she has erected around herself. She states, in an exaggerated imitation of an Ashkenazi accent, that she is happy with her lot or yells in a mock stand-up comic voice, "*Ma ra*? What's wrong?" Esti defines the rules and the manner by which she responds to my nagging questions, and I am impressed by her adroitness at turning the tables, at dealing with the external gaze without submitting to its defining power. And yet Esti knows that her wild game is not going to end happily. Her sober truth emerges loud and clear when she states sarcastically, "My future? The lucky number, debts, unemployment, and welfare. This, more or less, is my life."

But the long interview is not just a game we both play for the record, for consumption by the outsider steeped in liberal logic and neoliberal policies; it is also a process of self-reflection for Esti. How much can I, and my readers, learn from her summing up of her life in terms of more unpaid debts, gambling, and welfare? Can we take it to be a final pessimistically clearheaded acknowledgment of the impossibility of change in her life?

In chapter 6 I continue to explore Esti's life, following the old anthropological adage that to understand social reality we need to go beyond what our interlocutors *say* about their lives, nuanced and complex as their statements may be, and explore what they *do*, how they act in their world. I thus look at what Esti does, not merely at what she says, in a broad array of situations in her everyday life. I observe Esti in situations where our interactions are not fueled by the contrived need to make her confront an external, judgmental voice. Our ongoing daily meetings are characterized by mutual acceptance, friendship, and a simple, personal pleasure in each other's company. In these situations another voice of Esti's comes to the surface, more complex and less declarative than that heard in the above interview. I weave my depictions of these everyday situations into a string of short essays that Esti wrote at my request. Her writing and our daily fluid encounters constitute a more complex lens through which to view the life of one of the most original women I have met in Yerucham—or outside it. I also attend to the question of my ability to interpret or represent Esti's life, allowing Esti to react to my interpretation and respond with her own.

6

ESTI THE REBEL

No One Will Speak for Her

ESTI NEVER SAYS much about her childhood, although she does speak about her late mother. She notes with great pride how elegant her mother was, and I can feel how deeply attached she was to her. When I ask Esti to write about her life for me, she chooses to start with her mother. She writes her essays in an old school notebook she herself provides, and she seems to enjoy the task (and the 300 shekels I pay her for each essay). She writes about her home in Yerucham, about her working life, and about gambling. I reproduce Esti's texts here in full. I have tried to preserve her nonstandard Hebrew, keeping grammatical mistakes and correcting only obvious spelling errors.[1] In structuring this chapter around Esti's essays, I insert my own descriptions of everyday experiences relevant to each topic. I close the chapter with a theoretical reflection on Esti's ability to speak, describing a raucous scene in which Esti challenges my interpretation of her life and asserts, in her own way, an alternative way of reading it.

Gambling, Work, and Despair

My Mom Raised Us on Her Own

My mom died when I was 24 years old. She died of asthma. I used to care for her all the time. She had an asthma gadget, an inhaler, and she would also take pills. We bought them pills every month. It was very urgent for her. Without them, she would feel bad. The pills were private, costing 30 pills, 300 shekels a month.[2] My mom, she was clean, elegant. She looked good even when she was sick. She would dye her hair, do her face, take care of her legs.

She raised us on her own. She worked really hard in Sde Boker, in the kitchen, for 35 years. She would take us there when we were small. We would eat there, sleep there, play there. I grew up in Sde Boker, almost the entire time.

I was attached to her. I did the grocery shopping. I did everything. My mom, she suffered a lot. She didn't want to remarry on account of us. She had many proposals and we [her children] always said no. She had a stroke and was hospitalized in intensive care for two weeks. I went there every day. My sister slept there and I sat next to her until the very last day, when she died.

I took it really hard. I opened the window on the fourth floor and wanted to jump. My brothers grabbed me. I nearly fell out. After that I was depressed for an entire year. I've been keeping the Shabbat since then. I took it hard. I would cry a lot. I went to her grave, to the cemetery, a lot.

I am surprised to learn from Esti's essay that she actually spent her childhood days in Sde Boker, in the very place where we met, where my university office is located. She is the child of a kitchen employee, a single mother who brought her children to work with her. Esti's essay reveals that she spent little time in school and that she was severely depressed after her mother's death. Her laconic statement that she began to keep the Sabbath after her mother's death strikes a familiar chord, echoing the stories of many men and women who become stronger in their religiosity (see chapters 1 and 4) when faced with a personal crisis. Although her sisters and brothers went on with their lives after their mother's death, Esti was deeply jolted by the loss. She was 24 at the time.

For me, this self-testimony is a new, unfamiliar take on Esti's life. In our daily encounters, especially in my office when the other cleaners are present, Esti declares in her usual raucous manner that she never wanted to study, that it was *her choice* to drop out of school so early because she never *liked* school. She tells us loudly and repeatedly that she is single because she *chooses* not to marry. Her banter and her loud, extroverted behavior never fail to assert that she, unlike the rest of us, is a wild, unpredictable woman content with her life. When I read her essays, I am taken aback by her ability to articulate in writing what she cannot speak openly about—her immense personal pain and vulnerability. Her dropping out of school, it turns out, was necessary to enable her to attend to her ailing mother, a rather different account from the joyous, rebellious, celebratory tale she tells of opting out of school because she hated studying. In her first essay her mother looms larger than life; the rest of the family—the many brothers, sisters, nieces, and nephews—are mentioned only in passing. They too attended to the dying mother, but Esti was there all the time. The others went on with their lives after their mother's death; it was Esti who had to be restrained from jumping out a window in her despair. In fact, when Esti writes about "family," she refers to her local community, to Yerucham, a place she defines as "warm, family-like."

> Yerucham is a warm, family-like place. Everyone knows everyone. There are lots of gossipers in Yerucham. Whatever you do, everybody knows. If you leave the house in the morning, they ask you, What you up to? Are you working? Why aren't you working? All kinds of questions.
>
> Why don't I just leave? I'm used to Yerucham. They give you everything on credit[3] here. You can buy anything on credit. Groceries, nuts, I take clothes on credit. Anywhere else, you couldn't. Here, they trust me. What's good about Yerucham is that everyone helps each other, in any situation. If there's some family celebration event, almost everyone is invited, because everyone knows everyone. Even when you are grieving, people help each other.
>
> I'm used to Yerucham. It's a small place and, sure, there's nothing much to do, but the power of habit keeps me here. I don't leave Yerucham because my financial situation won't let me. And besides, I have family here that takes care of me. I mean, I spend Shabbats, holidays, and even weekdays with my family. People here love Yerucham. I mean, the old people who stay in Yerucham, because the younger ones all leave for the center of the country. Even longtime residents left Yerucham. We are only

a few now, about 8,000 people together with the Russian immigration that came to Yerucham recently.

People say that if they had the money, they'd leave Yerucham. Yerucham has very good people. They receive guests coming out of town well and will help with anything. It's a pity the place isn't developing like we would like it to. Maybe people wouldn't leave and Yerucham would develop, and people would stay in Yerucham. And maybe, who knows, today we could be a real city. What's good about Yerucham is that the place is quiet and safe and doesn't have crime like other places. You can go around freely, without fear. You can get by economically. There aren't many expenses. You save up on travel. It's a pity there aren't any jobs. Maybe people wouldn't leave, and stay in Yerucham.

Esti's message here is loud and clear. Yerucham is a safe space of warmth and mutual support. The only problem is the lack of local employment opportunities. Everyone can live cheaply in this small, family-like community. Not just someone like her—a single woman who spends holidays with her extended family—but anyone. According to Esti, the residents all love their quiet, safe community. And yet they leave because they cannot make a living locally. Her analysis is critical and grave: Yerucham suffers from a negative selection process whereby only the old and the weak segments of the population remain in the town. She puts her finger on the cyclical logic that effectively blocks Yerucham's growth—anyone who can afford to leave does so. Esti is deeply saddened by this process. Every week Esti reconnects with the communal love and warmth of her neighbors and friends. She patronizes the marketplace where merchants and buyers gather every Tuesday. She goes there to socialize, however, never to shop.

The Market Arena

One balmy Tuesday morning at the end of August 2001, I arrive at Esti's building shortly after 9 a.m. We plan to go to the market together, as we often do. On this outing I take careful notes of our expedition.

Esti meets me at the door of her small flat with a huge welcoming smile, holding a glass of sugared instant coffee with milk. We chat briefly, excitedly anticipating a day of socializing. On other days of the week, the town's small commercial center is rather quiet. It comes to life on Tuesday.

Esti disappears into her bedroom and reemerges wearing a colorful new outfit: a pair of tight jeans embroidered at the edges and a bright light-blue T-shirt. Her face is makeup-free. After running a comb through her close-cropped hair, recently dyed blonde, she is ready to lead the way "to the *merkaz*," to the center. The term *merkaz* reminds me of my childhood in Migdal Ha'Emek, a northern development town. We never referred to the assigned name of our "main street"; it was simply the *merkaz*, the center.

We drive the short distance to the small parking lot situated behind the newly refurbished commercial center, where the town's only bank branch, a small pharmacy, and a few stores are located. On market day the usually empty lot is jammed with pickup trucks from which merchandise is unloaded. Temporary stalls sell fruits and vegetables, cheap clothing is displayed on round carousels, and made-in-China trinkets are available throughout the parking lot. Having previously accompanied Esti on market day, I know we are not here to shop. Esti does not even look at the goods. She comes to meet with friends, to socialize, to enjoy the brief flurry of activity at the market. As she passes between the stalls, Esti exchanges hugs and kisses with shoppers and vendors alike. "How you doin', chief? Wassup? Full speed on reverse?" she fires off in her characteristic bantering way and, without fail, meets with warm, embarrassed laughter. The people Esti greets eye me quietly. I walk just a step behind her. But I am not part of the scene. I greet only those people I am familiar with. Otherwise, I just tag along.

Evidently, Esti likes this arrangement. I provide her with a supportive entourage. After she jokes with the vendors and the many shoppers, she tells me with a huge happy smile, "Everyone knows me here. Forget it. There ain't nobody I don't know who he is and who his daddy is." I listen attentively and continue to serve as backdrop, an attendant who adds bulk to her performance. As soon as we are out of earshot of the man or woman she has just talked to, Esti shares with me, "This one [referring to a well-dressed woman she has just conversed with]—don't be looking at her like that—her situation is real bad . . . her husband's a junkie" and "Him [referring to a man in his midforties whom she had spoken with at some length], he's the brother of Batia, the fat one who worked with us at Sde Boker. Poor guy . . . he was working many years in Phoenicia [a local factory], and now he's been laid off. Poor guy . . . he's got five kids."

It is hard to overlook the contrast between the lighthearted attitude Esti maintains in her conversations with the people she encounters between the fruit and vegetable stalls and the explanatory comments she shares with me, comments that reveal hardship, difficulties, pain. When she says of the woman she greets, "Don't be looking at her like that," Esti draws the disparity between appearances and realities to the surface. The woman's attractive, elegant dress hides a heart-wrenching story that is never mentioned in the amicable small talk she exchanges with Esti. Likewise, the man who was recently fired from his factory job does not mention his deep fear of never getting another job in the small town or the dire needs of his five children; he joins in the spirited greeting and banter Esti initiates.

"So what's up, Esti?" a woman asks. "Have you found work?" adds the vegetable vendor with a large smile. It is a habitual query. Esti grins: "Why, when did I ever work that I should start working now?" or "What work? This is Yerucham, ain't it? You ever seen any work 'round here?" This recurring bittersweet exchange, in which Esti plays the role of one who has never worked in her life, constructing herself as the ultimate out-of-work subject in a community of protracted unemployment, is a ritual of sorts. Esti is an odd bird among these family folks; she is a childless single woman with a sharp tongue. Her chronic unemployment, when exaggerated to an extreme, allows the bitter reality of their lives to turn carnivalesque, to be laughed at. Esti's banter turns the perpetual lack of employment in Yerucham into a gag, a grotesque fact of local life. There has never been work in Yerucham she declares and then deliberately overstates her own case: "I've never worked." Evidently, all know that Esti started working as a house cleaner when she was 14 and has continued to work all her adult life in a variety of odd jobs. By turning herself into a marker, a signpost of persistent community-wide unemployment, Esti communicates the message that failure to find a job is a systemic, not a personal, problem. And, as she writes in her first essay, unemployment is the main cause of local underdevelopment and out-migration.

Esti's insistent message—that being unemployed is not a result of personal failure—has a deeper local meaning. It communicates a critical take on the shattered sense of self-worth that afflicts many of Yerucham's residents. It says that employment or lack of it cannot be the basis for one's self-esteem. In the three encounters I describe below, Esti outlines an alternative source for self-worth and social esteem. The people she meets in these encounters are exceptionally well-off members of the community; they are shop owners and heads of thriving families. Esti reveals herself as a reliable counselor to these people— a trusted adviser on the local gambling scene. Her respectability stems from an altogether different basis of social value than conventionally recognized.

Bracha, Batia, and Maman—and Esti, the Respected Counselor

In a narrow back alley of the market, where the Bedouin vendors spread their wares, Esti meets Bracha. In her youth Bracha was a ravishing beauty. Now in her fifties, she still exhibits traces of this beauty. Bracha does not work, but she has a comparatively large income from welfare payments for her four children and other family support that she does not care to detail. After brief greetings, without much small talk and without any of the banter characterizing her interactions with others in the marketplace, Esti enters into a heated discussion with Bracha about the *mispar nosaf*.

"What do you say, sweetie," says Bracha. "What are you putting this week?"

Esti recommends "the orange and yellow" numbers and backs her assertions by referring to a dream she had the night before. Bracha says she has heard from Maman, an affluent shop owner, that she should bet this time "on small numbers," but she is rather hesitant to do so. Esti does not waver in her recommendation. The oranges and the yellows, she repeats emphatically. She has her signs, she says. Bracha gives Esti a searching look. "So . . . what . . . no small numbers then?" she asks in a soft, worried voice, and Esti replies resolutely, "I think 9, but orange 9, this is the best." Bracha says she put 3,000 shekels on Saturday's round of bets and nothing came of it. She seems perturbed and declares that she is definitely going to stop gambling. That's it. She is not going to put any more money into this. This is her last bet, she states, looking at me. Anyway, she goes on, there is no profit here. Only losses. But Esti does not seem impressed with Bracha's declarations. When we move on, Esti tells me with little compassion that Bracha is "burnt out," "a real addict." She tells me, "She will never stop."

I observe the dynamic between the two women with wonder. Esti, assertive and resolute. Bracha—a mother of four daughters, more than a decade older than Esti, with a nice income from her ex-husband on top of her welfare payments, a woman on much more solid financial footing than Esti—looks to Esti for guidance, for advice. Esti holds the upper hand in this delicate relationship. She has positioned herself as a keeper and dispenser of knowledge. At every turn of their brief and tense conversation in the narrow market alley, it is clear that Bracha counts on Esti's authoritative knowledge in the matter of numbers, that she needs and respects the advice offered by the younger, unemployed Esti. And, as it turns out, she is not the only one who seeks Esti's advice.

After making sure Bracha is on her way to place her bets in accordance with her advice, Esti leads us away from the marketplace and toward the end of the commercial center's cement plaza where the Bank Hapoalim, the only bank branch in Yerucham, is located. The bank's entry is only a few steps from Debby's popular hair salon. The salon's blue towels are hung out to dry, almost touching the deserted ATM machine outside the bank. At the other end of the plaza, a line of newly planted and already withering palm trees offers little shade at this blazing hour. A Tel Aviv architect who probably never set foot in Yerucham has recently redesigned this central arena, making sure all the shops carry uniformly designed signs, as though local people need to be reminded that one is a *makolet* (grocery store), another a *hanut yerakot* (vegetable stand). Several small, gray concrete pyramids and staircases leading to nowhere complete the renovated space. The exposed concrete staircases provide no shade in the large open area. A single bench is placed next to a shallow pool. But ever since the plaza was renovated, the water-spouting fountain in this single, seemingly desert-related feature has never performed properly. Several piles of candy and fresh buns exposed to the bright sun outside Maman's grocery shop are the only spots of color enlivening the large cement square. A few elderly Indian men crouch in one dark corner of the large open plaza that offers a little shade, watching shoppers carrying heavy bags full of groceries on their way home from the market.

We pass the bank and take refuge from the blazing heat in Batia's shoe shop. Esti calls the proprietress "Naalula," a playful name drawing on the word *naalayim* (Hebrew for "shoes") but also a reference to a popular children's TV show. Before we walk into the shop, Esti confides that she owes Batia almost 3,000 shekels and that Batia is "so nice" about it, not pushing her to pay back her accumulated debt. The store is cramped and gloomy. Batia invites us to sit down on chairs lining one wall. We prop ourselves up on the chairs and smoke cigarettes, chatting with the clients who walk into the store.

There is a constant flow of customers, mostly women. The women engage in a long string of greetings:

"How are you doing, Batia?"

"What's happening, Rina?"

"I have not seen you in a while . . ."

"I was at my mother-in-law's in Jerusalem . . ."

And on and on.

And then, in the midst of these ongoing personal exchanges, almost incidentally, they ask, "Batia, honey, do you have some slippers?" Batia quickly produces two or three pairs of slippers and presents them to the women with a few short comments: "I just got this merchandise. It's the best. Perfect for you." The women try the shoes on and quickly decide to take them. To my surprise, there is no bargaining; not one shopper disputes the prices Batia quotes. But neither do any of them pay for their purchases before they walk out of the store. One mutters something about paying tomorrow. Another murmurs, "Write it down" or "Put it on my account." When I ask Batia why none of her buyers actually pays in cash or by check for the merchandise, she gives me a sad smile and replies, "What can I do, hon? You're right. But I gotta put it down [give the women credit]. Otherwise I won't sell anything." I also notice that Batia does not have an organized record of what she is owed. Two dog-eared notebooks lie on the table, but she writes the prices of the four pairs of shoes sold while Esti and I are there on scraps of paper, which she then adds, in no apparent order, to a pile of such scraps.

Esti's presence cheers Batia up. Batia laughs along with everyone else at Esti's barbs and witticisms. When the last of the customers are gone, Batia perches on the chair next to us and lights up a cigarette. "How do you know Esti?" she asks me. Esti replies in my stead, "She's from work, back when I worked in Sde Boker." Batia does not press any further and from then on refers to me as Esti's friend.

Batia then probes Esti on the question of the added numbers. She has been told that they are going to be the "green ones . . ."; she breaks off, looking hesitantly at Esti, who is in no rush to volunteer her opinion. "Oh . . . yeah? You've been told?" Esti takes her time. Nothing seems urgent. Batia looks at Esti and then, in the silence that ensues, as Bracha had done a few moments earlier, she makes the expected declaration: She has to stop with this gambling; she has been losing all her money; her son wanted 100 shekels the other day, and when it turned out there was nothing in her wallet, he shouted at her, "It's all because of your gambling. When are you gonna stop?"

"My husband is also angry with me," Batia says, directing her words at me. "As soon as I sell a pair of shoes, I take the money to the dealer, and before the lottery results are announced, I'm nervous and sweaty and can't sleep a wink. So my husband says to me, 'You're losing your money *and* your health.'" Esti nods but does not look as though Batia's declarations—meant, perhaps, more for my ears than for Esti's—impress her much. I note that she has not shared her advice with Batia yet.

Meanwhile, Maman, a rotund man in his fifties, the owner of the grocery store located across the plaza, walks in. He looks at Esti and at me and seems amused by our presence. He has seen me in his store several times and guesses that I am an outsider to Yerucham, an educated woman, maybe a teacher. He points at Esti and asks me, "What do you have to do *with her*?" Without waiting for my reply, he turns to Batia and continues what seems to be an ongoing discussion involving a business offer. It turns out that he owns several stores in the commercial center and one is soon to be vacant. Would Batia like to move to that spot? "There's a lot of movement there," he cajoles. Batia says she will think about it. Maman lingers in the store. Before long, he too begins to talk about the weekly gambling on the *mispar nosaf*. I tease him: "Maman, you too play with these numbers?" He smirks at me like a naughty child: "Oh, my, I tell you, like you wouldn't believe." He, Batia, and Esti then continue their conversation, ignoring my presence as they discuss at length several gambling clues, maintaining, "This is what people told me." Just before leaving, Maman repeats his betting advice: "Only series of 3's. I am telling you. That's what's going to fall this time." But Batia seems not to understand, "What, what series of 3's?" she calls after him as he turns to go. Esti volunteers, "What he means is 31, 32, . . ." And then she adds with authority, "Listen to me, the best of all is the 34." "That's also good," Maman concurs as he walks outside into the blazing sun.

I wonder what happened to the "oranges and yellows" that Esti had insisted on with Bracha just a few minutes ago. Batia seems ill at ease. She tells us that a man they all know walked into her store earlier and insisted on the green numbers. He said that's what's going now for sure. Esti allows Batia to report the other views she has heard that day. She takes her time before stating in a decisive manner, "I don't think so, Batia. I still think it's the yellows and oranges."

Batia's attention turns back to me. "I know her," she tells me, looking at Esti fondly. "I know her since she was a little girl, coming with her mother to get a pair of shoes for the holiday . . . Why, her mother, God bless her soul, she was an elegant woman. Yes, she was." We linger in Batia's shoe shop until noon. It is time for lunch. Batia locks up the store, and the three of us proceed to the nearby supermarket. We buy a few warm bourekas from the shop's bakery. But the two women seem to pay little attention to what we eat for lunch. They are preoccupied with the evening's weekly bet. And they are not alone. Everywhere we turn in the supermarket aisles, people stand in groups of two and three discussing the numbers. A feeling of repressed joy seems to pervade these conversations. Maman's reply to my inquiry about whether he bet on the numbers—"Yes, I know, I am a naughty boy"—captures the way people interact, expressed in the lowering of their eyes, their giggles.

As we stand in line to pay for our baked goods, Esti moves aside, grabs a pen from next to the cashier, tears a corner of a paper bag and begins writing numbers on it, arranging them in a column. Next to each of these numbers she jots down the sum of money to be placed on that number. The sums range from 30 to 50 shekels. It takes a brief moment to complete the list. Esti hands the list to Batia without a word. Batia does not scrutinize the list. Her decision is made for her. She walks into one of the aisles where the bookie, a Indian Jewish man, stands holding a bunch of crumpled papers in his hands. The man does not ask any questions. He pulls a white piece of paper from his shirt pocket and copies Batia's listed bets onto it. He hands the original list, composed by Esti, back to Batia and money changes hands rapidly.

When this exchange is complete, Batia gives us a mischievous but worried smile. Her weekly bet is set. We walk out of the air-conditioned store into the bright sunlight, munching on our potato bourekas. Batia goes back to her store, and I invite Esti for a cool drink at the kiosk across the road.

Batia, Bracha, and Maman are all relatively affluent residents of Yerucham. Each expresses open affection for Esti, and, more critically, they all share an unquestioned appreciation for her opinion regarding the weekly bet. Younger, with far fewer material resources, Esti earns the appreciation of these better-off people because of her evident charisma in what are deeply insecure moments in the weekly act of gambling. She is supportive and offers her advice, and in the case of Batia, she makes the betting decision, freeing Batia from her fear and insecurity. Esti supports her symbolic knowledge by citing her dreams and by showing compassion for the weakness of others. By building and nurturing her betting network, Esti gains a sense of self-worth that does not hinge on her material or social accomplishments but on her warmth and the authoritative way she shares her betting advice.

Esti composed the following short essay about gambling with the same authority. She writes like a deft and practiced journalist, noting numbers (three times a week, seven dealers, and so on) and outlining an orderly sequence of events ("I now move on to the most important issue"). She volunteers her own sociological and economic insights ("Lottery is the talk of the day" and "Some sleep sad and some sleep happy"). Esti's essay documents a local gambling economy in which unauthorized bookies offer Yeruchami gamblers a chance to bet on the state-licensed national lotteries. The local betting network connects everyone, from the well-to-do to the paupers. It offers hope and excitement to those who gamble and bestows on Esti authority and power.

On Gambling

Three times a week you have the Pa'yis and the Lotto. There's a lottery on Tuesday. Everyone meet in all kinds of places at the center, at the bank, at home. They all talking about what's gonna come out. Neighbors come over. One says, I dreamt. Another does *gimatriya*.[4] If I dream about animals, they all have numbers.

Cat is 7, dog is 10, and there are 31 more animals like that. My other neighbor looks at license plates and bets on those.

There are seven dealers. He gives you 40 to 1. Say, 20 shekels, if I put that, I get 800. If I put 37 to 1, I get 740 shekels. Pa'yis is something else. This happens in the middle of the week. You bet between 1 and 100. You play on the numbers of the National Lottery. The last two digits—that's it. Say, if the lottery number is 116272, the added number [*mispar nosaf*] is 72. The bet is 70 to 1. So if I put down 10 shekels, I win 700.

Until now I spoke about the Sunday and Wednesday lotteries. Now I'll speak about Saturday night. On Saturday night all the people, they meet up again. The lottery takes place at 10:45 after the Shabbat is out. Everyone is only talking about the numbers. Everyone's guessing. One dreams about a color. There are colors, the five colors of the balls. There's green, red, yellow, orange, blue. Red is 1 to 9. Orange is 10 to 19. Yellow 20 to 29, green 30 to 39; blue is 40 to 45. There are six blue balls so people bet on them the most.

And this is how it is every week. Round and round. Lottery day is the talk of the day.

I'm moving on now to the most important subject, and that is the amounts that people place on their bets. Some bet 10 shekels, other bet 700 or a thousand. Each according to his pocket. Even those on guaranteed basic income and unemployment benefits are betting. Even kids bet. And this is how every lottery goes by. We are all in suspense waiting for the added number to come. Some sleep happy and some sleep sad, and hope to win next week.

Esti's depiction of betting in Yerucham is detailed. It explains how the local betting system operates in relation to the statewide National Lottery raffle as well as the local rules and the social setting in which the most common forms of gambling unfold. Before reading this text, I knew a bit about the local gambling scene. I often gave Esti a ride to the specific street corner where the local bookie stood. I observed how the bookie managed the gamblers' bets, and I recorded the conversations between Esti and other gamblers, some of which

I describe in chapter 5. But I had not realized that "everyone," as Esti writes, takes part in these weekly events. From Esti's written record I learn that the attempt to guess the *mispar nosaf* consumes everyone, young and old, penniless and well-to-do, and that it injects excitement and suspense, anxiety, joy, and sadness into life in the small town.

In the local weekly lottery scene people seem to be assigned specific roles according to their ethnic origin, and the bets Esti recommends draw on folk knowledge that transcends local ethnic boundaries. Thus, Esti, a daughter of Moroccan immigrants, adopts the symbolic system of a man born in India, Moroccans and Indians being the two larger Jewish ethnic groups resident in the community. The detailed knowledge she acquires from the local "Indians" provides her with a special authority within the weekly guessing frenzy. Most of the local bookies, themselves employed by outside bosses, are of Indian origin. A long-term familiarity and trust must exist between gambler and bookie for the local gambling scene to function smoothly. When Esti cannot provide the necessary cash, she can place her bet on personal credit. If her gamble fails, she owes the bookie the full sum. Esti reports above that when the bookie refused to allow her to place her bets on credit, she was furious. She saw it as a breach of her trust.

Esti prides herself on having built her sought-after knowledge about gambling from a creative mélange of signs drawn from her own dreams, the symbolic number and color map she adopts from local Indian Jews, and Jewish and national symbols. She offers this complex knowledge base to people who seek her advice. Her system is respectable, and her clues do not involve sacrilegious use of numbers such as the years that have elapsed since Israeli prime minister Rabin was assassinated. Esti positions herself as a serious counselor and her betting advice is widely respected. The authority she gains from her status as a trusted gambling adviser contrasts with her employment experience, characterized by frustration and discontent. This is how Esti writes about *avoda*, Hebrew for "work" or "labor."

Work

Since age 16 I've worked at the Ramon military base. I was a cleaner. I worked there for two years. I would clean the soldiers' quarters. Then I got fired. Then I worked in Nevatim. Also a military base. Also cleaning. And also household cleaning work for the officers. There I worked for three years. There, work stopped because they changed a contractor. Then I worked at the nuclear research place. On the buses. I would clean them. The buses. Offices too. I worked there for eight months. They fired me. Then I worked for Phoenicia. It's a bottling plant. I would sort the bottles. I would work in shifts, afternoon, overnight, morning. I worked there for a year. I liked it a lot. I liked it there. And then, contract ran out there as well and we all got fired. Then I worked for Agis, a cosmetics factory. I worked there for nine months, on the packing line. I worked with shampoos, soaps, body lotions, all kinds. I made them laugh a lot. Eventually they fired me. I didn't like working at Agis because of the discipline. You can't talk at work. Can't smoke. Can't do anything. It was like Gestapo. After they fired me, someone from the workers' committee got me my job back. But I didn't want to come back. I also worked in archaeology, at the Hazeba dig. I worked there for eight months. I would dig. Empty buckets. Sweep up. Working with a hammer. Once I dug a five-meter hole and found Roman coins. There was a Bedouin supervisor there and he fired me. He couldn't stand me.

Then I worked in Sde Boker. Four months. Also cleaning, There I meet you, sweet Pnina, in whose office I spent more time than I did working. And there I also got fired because I would skip work. Then I replaced someone close to home. Hostels. Cleaning again. I worked there in the cafeteria. Serving, clearing up. I worked as a replacement for a week and got 500 shekels. Now there's no work there because there aren't any tourists. I had a few offers since. I went with the bus to work with the foreman but I came back because it didn't suit me. I also had a three hours' job offer and I didn't go.

In this short essay Esti ticks off a long list of jobs from which she has invariably been dismissed. Even when she likes the work or feels she is making a contribution (finding Roman coins or making colleagues laugh), she still gets the sack. Esti recalls each workplace, cites the length of time she was employed there, and notes the reason for the termination of her employment, distinguishing between her individual firing and the collective discharge of all employees. It seems that Esti is trying to make sense of it all, to explain to her readers and herself, why she is fired each time. She makes the point of noting that she gets fired whether or not she satisfies her employers' requirements or explicitly disrespects the rules. The dismissals are unavoidable, and they seem to deeply humiliate her. Her only way to salvage any pride is to leave before she is pushed out or to decline an offer to return to a workplace after being fired there. "It's a lost battle," she says time and again in her recorded interview. "If I like my job and if I don't . . . they sack me right away."

When she composed this essay, Esti seemed depressed about the lack of any new employment prospects. She describes boarding the bus to a temporary position but turning back home moments after her arrival at the job site. Her report becomes more and more laconic: a few days of work as a cleaner in a hostel; serving food and cleaning again, at another local place. The positions that are offered her become less and less appealing. She is hired as a replacement for another worker. She works for one week, for one day, and eventually, for a three-hour stint. At the end of a long list detailing her recent frustrating experiences, Esti states flatly that when another short-term position was offered her, she rejected it out-right: "I did not go."

To understand the deep frustration articulated by Esti in this text about *avoda* and to grasp the dead-end situation she depicts, a moment when no employment is made available to her, we need to turn to several everyday situations in which Esti reveals her attitude toward work.

"That's a Great Job"

During the spring of 2002, I drive Esti several times to her dental appointments in Be'er-Sheva. My notes of the first visit to the dentist document a fleeting moment of self-reflection in which Esti expresses her deep, yet silenced desire to hold on to a "good job."

It is a beautiful morning on March 14 when I pick Esti up for the appointment. She is (uncharacteristically) ready to go and is happy and talkative throughout our 30-minute drive to Be'er-Sheva. To start the treatment, we need to go to a private X-ray clinic located on a side street in the old city. The technician, a young attractive woman with a strong Russian accent, treats Esti with professional courtesy. Unlike the office clerks at the central dental office we had visited earlier that morning, who seemed rather shocked at Esti's loud appearance and extroverted performance, the woman technician laughs at Esti's loud jokes, does not ignore her, and does not belittle her. When we leave the clinic, Esti observes, "That Russian gal, she's real nice, not like them makin' faces at ya cause of learnin' an all that." And then she asks in a much quieter, smaller voice, "Say, Pnina, how did she become a dental technician like that? That's a real good job." But before I can begin to respond, she strikes out her own question with the familiar cackle, "Well, sure, she gone and learned. And me . . . don't talk to me about learnin' . . ."

The X-ray technician offers Esti empathy and thus a bright, positive model of a person working efficiently and pleasantly in a "real good job." Esti, briefly rendered defenseless by this empathy and professionalism, expresses a yearning to take up similar work. But the world of those who have received a good education has always humiliated her and told her she is not worthy. She immediately shuts down the short moment of yearning, using the protective shield of self-deprecation. Esti preempts the anticipated external disdain, which often reminds her that she should have studied. By stating that she does not like studying, Esti makes her lack of education her choice, her decision, and covers up the history of frustration and feelings of failure documented in her essays.

The unlikelihood of Esti ever obtaining a proper job is made plain to me on another occasion, when I accompany her to the local employment office.

Signing Off at the Employment Office

June 16, 2002. I arrive at Esti's apartment unannounced and find her all dressed up and ready to go out. She tells me that this is the day she needs to sign in at the employment office. I ask to join her, and she is happy for the ride.

The corridors of the shaded building housing the local employment office are empty. I ask the clerk if I can step in with Esti; Esti introduces me as her friend. The little room at the employment office is bare except for a metal cupboard in the corner and a large computer on the clerk's otherwise empty desk.

"So wassup? What's happenin'?" Esti repeats the question several times over. The woman clerk smiles at Esti but does not respond, staring at the computer screen.

"Listen, Esti. Nothing here."

Esti waits quietly, giving the clerk time to check the flickering screen in front of her. And the clerk says slowly, without moving her eyes from the screen, "There's something at the tap factory."

"Whadaya mean, taps?"

"It's one month. In Mashabei Sadeh [a kibbutz about a 20-minute ride from Yerucham]."

"Whadaya mean, one month?" Esti asks, staring into space, not trying to make eye contact with the clerk.

The clerk looks away and says nothing.

"And what else? Anything else?"

"No. Nothing."

"All right then." Esti bends forward and reaches into her back pocket for a folded, faded piece of cardboard for the clerk to sign. Her signature confirms that Esti has reported to the office, that no suitable job was found for her, and that she is therefore eligible for her guaranteed basic income. Esti places the card on the clerk's desk, and the clerk duly adds another signature to the column of signatures already there.

We get up to leave. The necessary ritual of signing in at the employment office is complete. The clerk played her role, and Esti did not have any expectations to begin with. Another week without a job.

We walk out. My car stands in the empty parking lot by the building. We sit on the curb to smoke a cigarette, and I try to figure out what has actually taken place in that brief ceremony. The rapidity of it all has taken me by surprise. I ask Esti why she didn't agree to take the taps job in Mashabei Sadeh. "You told me you really want to find work," I say. "So why didn't you ask for some details about that one?" I keep pushing, and eventually Esti replies impatiently,

"Come on, Pnina. What details? What else do I wanna know? It's a one-month job. Didn't you hear her? And no transport either. Where am I gonna find transport? How will I get to Mashabei Sadeh?"

I smoke my cigarette quietly, looking at her. It is clear that Esti is extremely upset. She feels the need to go on explaining, even though I have not said anything. "And even if I got that . . . that's minimum wage, that is. My social security card, it gets all complicated, 'cause she says I took a job. And then I come back a month or two later and she needs to reopen the card. And then I need to go bring all them documents and shit."

"But you really wanted a job," I repeat, sensing her rage and her pain.

"Let off," she says, unsmiling. "I know how it is. You know how many times that happened? When I agree to work for two weeks, everything gets screwed up with my files and I don't even get my guaranteed basic income."

She falls silent. Her exasperation and hopelessness are profound. She is trying to explain to me the disappointment, the frustration, the fact that she knows the dynamic of the system and that she does not have any hope left, because bureaucracy traps her, prevents her from taking even a temporary job, shoots down every chance she has of ever clambering out of the trap. "Forget about it, Pnina," she says again. "Didn't you hear the news? They said the government is making cuts to the welfare budget, especially on guaranteed basic income. I'm telling you, I'm gonna lose a few hundred shekels on this. Ain't nothing you can do. It started with 800 shekels a month. I used to get that. Then it came up a little. And now it's gonna go down again."

I keep quiet. I have never seen Esti so distressed. So angry. No laughs. No banter. Only a painful awareness, carved out of years of exasperating experience that have taught her just how firmly all the roads ahead of her are blocked. Esti is entirely dependent on her meager social security payouts. She is anxious that even these are at risk. A few weeks later, this apprehension reaches its peak when Esti hears that she has been summoned before a medical commission at the employment office. She understands that this time she will need to defend her very right to her tiny welfare income.

The Medical Commission

Sunday, February 8, 2004. Esti tells me that she has to appear before a medical commission at the employment office. I offer to drive her, but when I get to her apartment, she is already gone. I drive to the employment office. The small place, often deserted, is now teeming with people. A few young men stand outside, smoking. The small reception room is packed, and I cannot find a vacant seat. Men and women, newly arrived Russian immigrants and Yerucham natives, Moroccan and Indian, fill the room from wall to wall. Esti laughs in embarrassment when she sees me walk in. I compliment her on her appearance. She has made a special effort to look elegant. She wears tight cream-colored trousers and a matching sweater, with orange fake fur around the collar. Her usual bright blonde hair is complemented with shades of brown. "I went to Debby's," she informs me. "I got 'the full 10,000 treatment' [referring to a car's 10,000-mile mechanical maintenance]—brows, mustache, hair dye, the works!"

The atmosphere in the overcrowded room is bleak. A heavyset man in his sixties is complaining loudly: "Who's gonna give me work now? With my health all screwed up like that? What kinda work them going to have for me anyway?"

"Forget it, they don't have any jobs to give," a younger man replies. "We're not here for any reason. It's all bullshit."

The door of the inner office opens and a woman comes out. She smiles at the waiting crowd and says, encouragingly, "They don't ask you anything. Took me two minutes!"

"What two minutes?" asks Esti in her usual bantering tone. "You were there for half an hour at least."

The woman chuckles. "Come on, Esti. It's really nothing. Look, he goes, 'What d'you work in?' So I go, 'I don't work. I got small kids and I am divorced.' That was it. So he goes, 'We'll let you know on Wednesday.'"

The older man next to me says resolutely, "It's always Wednesday!" and then he turns to the young woman and adds, "By Wednesday you'll hear from them if it's a yes or a no. Dead straight: they'll tell everyone on Wednesday."

Esti shows me the slip of paper listing her number in the queue: 7. I know what will come from that. Esti never overlooks the potential for every number she encounters to determine her weekly bet. "Seven," she muses out loud. "I always get a 7," but she adds immediately and disappointedly, "But this week they got 15 . . . half Yerucham was raking it in."

A thin woman walks into the reception room. I notice that like all the other women there, she is dressed particularly well for her appointment.

"Go, take a number from him," Esti instructs her, gesturing toward a Russian man in his twenties sitting behind a low table in the corner and holding a perforated roll of paper tickets. The woman who has just left the interview says reassuringly to the new arrival, "Don't worry, hon. It's nothing. They don't examine you or anything. He asks two questions and that's it." The newly arrived woman examines her number and announces that it is 43. Esti beams at her and declares that she can go home, take a nap, and come back in time for her turn. The woman gives Esti a tired smile: "What nap? I need to take the kids out of day care. I'll take them to my mother and I'll come back." She leaves.

When Esti's turn arrives, I slide out for a smoke on the steps. But she comes out and joins me before I even finish my cigarette. I am surprised—such a short interview! "Don't ask," Esti explains. "He didn't ask me nothin'. He says to them, 'So this is Esther then?' And he says to me, 'Esther, how you doing?' I says, 'All right.' He says, 'All right? Then what are you doing here? You look great. Look at her body . . .' So I says to him, 'No, you don't get it. When I say I'm all right, it ain't about my health. "All right" is in the general. You don't see what's inside of me. Inside I got heart palpitations. I'm sick, I am.' So that was it. He looks at me and says to them, 'OK. We'll give you an answer Wednesday.' And that's it."

"That's it?" I ask. "So what makes that a medical commission? Wasn't there a doctor there?"

"Of course not," Esti explains patiently. "They got all my medical files, and it says I went to hospital and all. But forget it. Who cares? They want to cut down my guaranteed basic income? They're welcome. Let them cut it down. There's nothing left anyway. Let them!"

Back inside, people try to calm each other down, to offer each other some support in the face of their complete vulnerability before the obscure criteria that shape the decisions of the all-powerful committee members. Esti's defiant proclamation—"There's nothing left anyway. Let them!"—comes out of exasperation and helplessness. Does Esti choose to dress her best for this humiliating interview simply to feel that she is a person of value? And yet, when she faces the degrading gaze of the committee member marveling at her healthy, attractive appearance, she feels the need to scream, "You can't see inside of me. . . . I'm sick."

Months later, Esti is still subsisting on her small guaranteed basic income, but she makes no secret of her exasperation. She still shows glimpses of the woman who will not despair, but the pain is now out in the open. The following is a transcript of a recorded conversation I had with her in May 2004.

> I'm always home, on my own. My sister Simcha is so mad at me. She says, "How can you stand doin' nothin' the whole day?" Life is a bore, Pnina. What can I tell you? But really, I don't give a damn. I never despair. What does my poor sista get outta her being employed? Two thousand? Ha! So she's got 800 shekels more than I get [from welfare]? What's 800? And she works, Pnina. You wouldn't believe how hard she works. And after a long day of slaving, she doesn't even come home. She goes straight to my aunt's place. This is where she eats. I don't go there, to my aunt's. It's boring. I don't need that food. I drink my coffee and cookies, and if I am hungry, I make a tuna sandwich and that's it. I wake up at 12, and I play these games on the TV and I sit outside with my neighbors. And I'm good. Nothing's bad! Bracha, my neighbor, you know her, she doesn't even get up to sign up [at the employment office]. But me, I say you must do that. You must go there once a week.

> Me, I show my face there every Sunday, like clockwork. Yesterday she goes, "There's some work fruit picking, Esti." I says, "Go on, put me at the top of the list." But now they're still waiting for enough people to sign up. I dunno why. Here, Baruch Elmakias [the former mayor], he tells me, "I'll fix you up with a job at Agis [the cosmetics factory]." I told him, "Forget it, I don't want Agis. I can't stand the people there." I'm telling you, Pnina. I can't stand 'em. I don't know what to tell you. There simply ain't no jobs here in Yerucham. There ain't nothing. What can I do?

This recorded monologue captures one of Esti's more exposed and bitter reflections on her life at that point. She still declares in a tone of bravado that she never despairs, that she does not give a damn, but her isolation and lack of hope are tangible. Her daily routine of sleeping late, socializing with her neighbors, and watching TV is "a bore," she says openly. Her sister, her last tie to the rest of her family, is no longer really part of her life. Although they share the apartment, the sister works long hours and disappears every evening to their aunt's home. Esti refuses to maintain any link to her extended family. Giving up on her aunt's cooked meals, the last sign of an organized home life, Esti opts for minimal nourishment from coffee and cookies, bread and canned tuna. The limited menu reflects her social isolation and at the same time is a statement of her independence from conventional frameworks of family and its routines.

Unlike the defiance she displayed during the interview recorded in chapter 5, in the above statement Esti does not frame her life as a victory over her social circumstances. She mentions her refusal to be reinstated in a job from which she had been fired, giving as her reason her dislike of her coworkers at that job, not the exploitative labor conditions. Esti compares her choices to those of her sister, who accepts what is offered her. She presents her sister's choice to work long hours for little pay as ridiculous. Still, Esti abides by some rules, and unlike her neighbor Bracha, who does not bother turning up at the employment office to have her card signed, Esti makes sure to perform the ritual of reporting to the office every Sunday.

In contrast to the swagger she projects during our walks through the town center on market day, Esti exposes here her pain, confusion, and utter, unqualified helplessness. "There ain't no jobs here . . . What am I gonna do?" she asks in closing.

Helping Esti

Wednesday, January 14, 2004, is a gray, rainy day. The week before, Esti calls several times and sounds so desperate that I promise her I will visit her soon. It is clear that she does not simply call to say hello but to ask, in her desperation, for my material support. She repeats that she has no job; she speaks about her loneliness at being home all day, and then she informs me that she is sick. She sounds depressed. I am worried. On the national news that week there is a horrifying story of a man who pulled out a gun and killed himself during a meeting with welfare officials. A few days before Esti's call there are reports of a woman who threw herself from the 11th floor of a building—all because of financial hardship. Esti's semiovert pressure on me to provide her with material support because of her dire financial situation is not new. Neither are her recurrent pleas for "loans" from her family members and friends who know all too well that she has no way of paying back.

Over the years, I have tried to help her as much as I can. I have no qualms about paying her from my research budget for her research help. I have paid several of my interlocutors small sums budgeted for that purpose in my grant. Esti receives direct payments for each essay she provides and as many direct cash payments as I am able to arrange for her, more than any of my other interlocutors. At one point, I have the idea to make her into a formal research assistant and thus provide her with a small but regular monthly income. After all, I reason, I do spend many hours with her and what I learn from her enters my field notes regularly. She is thus, in my eyes, a research assistant, and I have the available funds for such a role in my research budget. But when I approach the university official responsible for managing those funds and ask about arranging such payments, I am told that the university cannot pay Esti as a regular research assistant. The administrator is supportive when I explain the context. No, Esti does not have even a high school education, I explain. And, no, she does not conduct interviews on my behalf. The administrator listens attentively to my description of the nature of ethnographic work, but then, empathetically, tells me that there is no "slot" in the university payroll for the kind of post I envision. Only students with clear "research assistance" skills can be enrolled. Esti cannot receive more than three small payments from my research budget.

When I tell Esti about my efforts to hire her into a secure if part-time position as my research assistant, she is amused. But then she makes it clear that she does *not* want the post, even if I manage to arrange it for her. "They will ask me to sign all these forms and shit and then you, my dear Pnina, will go [finish your research] and the papers of my social security will be all messed up for a long, long time again." I can see her point: The insecure, part-time position I am trying to organize for her is not a solution. She knows better than to place her welfare income at risk.

At one point I decide to pay for Esti's dental treatment. Esti's teeth are in a horrendous state, and every time she smiles, she covers her mouth with her hand. I decide that paying for her dental treatment could be the best way to deal with her relentless, semicovert efforts to manipulate me into providing her with money. I know that if I hand her cash, she will gamble away most of it or shop for extravagant outfits. I know all too well that Esti will not pay her debts, which continue to grow as the interest on her bank overdrafts accumulates. I offer to pay for Esti's dental treatments out of my own pocket. No research funds can be justified for that purpose. I want to help Esti, but I know that my contribution will not make her change her ways. I also feel that I have no right whatsoever to preach to her. Reflecting on this decision now, as I write this chapter, I realize that I wanted to compensate Esti for bringing me into her life because I wished to offset the inherent imbalance of our relationship. I allowed her to take advantage of me materially, aware that she was manipulating me to give her money because I felt guilty. I wanted to muffle the feeling that I was spying on her life by writing about her world. I knew that I would make a professional profit from writing and publishing her story.

Esti at the Bank

Over the years, I have accompanied Esti to the local bank branch on many occasions, and I have had many opportunities to observe the protracted process in which she deploys all her powers of persuasion to get authorization to withdraw money from her overdrawn account. Esti is by no means unique in attempting to get permission to go beyond her credit limit. The local branch of Bank Hapoalim teems with people on the days when social security payments are issued. On all other days, people queue in long lines in front of the personal teller windows asking for a special signed permit to withdraw money. The ATM booth outside the branch door is almost always deserted. To withdraw money using the ATM, customers need a positive balance in their account. And because most people overdraw their account and go beyond what the bank has defined as their credit limit, they need special authorization from a clerk.[5]

Esti speaks often about her maximum credit limit of 2,500 shekels (more than twice her guaranteed basic income of 1,200 shekels). Esti has long gone beyond this limit, and she spends many hours at the bank asking for special authorization to withdraw even more. To withdraw money she does not have in her account, Esti must convince the bank teller of the unique and urgent circumstances that make her need for the money acute. She has perfected these bargaining stories. She often pleads with the teller that she needs to pay for necessary utilities like water or electricity. At other times, she dwells on the shared cultural understanding of the teller about the need to attend a family event—a wedding or a bar mitzvah—and the expectation she must meet to provide a small gift in cash. I try several times to convince Esti that these specially authorized withdrawals involve high interest rates. Esti gives me a glazed stare and says she neither understands nor cares about "their interests."

I recall once pointing out to her that her monthly statement of account showed the bank charging her a 49-shekel commission for a rejected cable company debit in addition to interest accruing on her accumulated debt at the exorbitant rate of 16%. Esti was unmoved: "What's 49 shekels? They take what is due to them," and she waved my alarm away. "I have several direct debit lines, one for cable, one for electricity, and I even have some 150-shekel monthly payments I made as a contribution for some yeshiva," she informs me. If the bank does not honor these payments, "I need to come over here and speak to them and they fix it up, no problem." Whenever I propose that her overdraft is growing because of service fees and interest charges, or if I try to explain to her how to read the lines on her bank statements, she declares, "Forget about it. Only winning the lottery gonna help." And then, with a smile of joy, she adds, expressing perhaps the humiliation she feels when she pleads with the bank clerks, "And when I have won my hundred grand, I'll come here and laugh in their faces. I'll go one by one and I'll laugh in their faces."

One day, Esti insists that I join her at the bank branch because she needs my support with one particular bank clerk whom she describes as "real mean." "Do me a favor, Pnina, just you tell her, like, that I'm a good person and all that. That's all I ask you." She tells me she desperately needs 450 shekels. She convinces me that the need really is urgent. I go with her. And as we sit in front of the bank clerk, I hear Esti request special authorization to withdraw 1,000 shekels. Then she tells the clerk, who is as embarrassed as I am, that she should authorize this withdrawal despite the lack of funds in her account because "tomorrow on the dot, this woman here [pointing at me] will deposit 2,000 shekels into the account." The young clerk lowers her eyes. I am paralyzed with shock at Esti's audacity. We are all silent for a short while. But Esti goes on relentlessly: "What, you don't believe me? Look at her." She points at me. "She's a serious woman. She is, she is from the university, y'know." The clerk does not ask me if indeed I intend to deposit money into Esti's account, and I do not say anything. After a long embarrassed silence, the clerk says quietly that she can authorize only 500 shekels. But Esti is not completely satisfied and she haggles for another hundred and then another. Eventually she gets 700 shekels.

When we walk out of the air-conditioned bank branch into the open square, I am too stunned to speak. I do not know what to make of the scene I was just manipulated into. I keep my silence. When we reach my parked car, I ask Esti if she wishes to be given a ride home or if she has other business and plans to stay in the small shopping center. I declare coldly that I am going home. Esti assures me that she does not need the ride. She plans to stay in the center. She eyes me curiously, leaning through the open car window, and says, "Listen, Pnina. I lied to her. I know that. But I had to. What can I do? I used to never lie or cheat, but now life made me like that." I watch her and say nothing. And then she adds, unsmiling, "You, too, have to lie and cheat sometimes. There's nothing you can do. This is life." I smile at her meekly. And just as I am pulling the hand brake and getting ready to leave, the cackles return: "'Cause you know, Pnina, what can you do, what's life without money . . . money oils the wheels, inside and out."

And still, even in such difficult moments when I cannot contain Esti's choices, when I am conflicted about my ability to remain nonjudgmental, I continue to see Esti's behavior as boundary-breaking subversion. I read her wild, reckless revelry as a flamboyant challenge to the system that shackles life on the Israeli periphery. There is something about Esti that enriches my own life. On some level I feel like I am applauding her, this woman who will not accept her limitations, who refuses to squeeze into frameworks, and who insists on celebrating her life. But on many other days I am less tolerant and speak my mind openly. I try to tell Esti that she cannot refuse a new job offer, and I tell her she has to repay her debts. Thus, for example, when I hear that she was offered work at the local health clinic as a cleaner and that she rejected the offer outright, I abandon my nonjudgmental stance and try to coax her into taking the job. "Esti, come on, give it a go. What do you care? You have to." I offer to set her up as a cleaner with my middle-class neighbors in Sde Boker. But Esti seldom keeps her commitment to show up for a day of cleaning work. So, I stop making such arrangements for her, chiding her that she will never get work if she does not commit herself. And whenever I speak to her about work and commitment and about the need to pay debts, she responds with short dismissive sentences: "Yeah, yeah, sure, you're right." And I know that she is not listening, that I sound like a schoolteacher, that I am losing her.

The Subject Interprets Her World

One of the more common arguments in anthropological scholarship since the 1990s is that the subject has the right to be a part of constructing what is written about him or her. Returning the written text to the subject is a way to develop more democratic cooperation between researcher and research subject. By reading and responding to the text, the argument goes, the subject legitimizes the interpretation offered by the researcher/author. The practice of having subjects read our written texts is also said to be a way of empowering the subject, making that person part of the study's conclusions. But what happens when the subject has no interest in the researcher's written text?

I want to know what Esti thinks about my interpretation of her life, so I give her the chapter I have written about her, urging her to read and comment on it. But the typed pages I put on the table just lie there gathering dust. "Forget it," she says. "When there's money in it, let me know." I decide that her feedback on my interpretation is essential but that it does not have to come as a response to a *written* text. In my many notes about my encounters with Esti I discover the following record of one fascinating evening in which Esti had in fact responded to my interpretation and had offered, in her inimitable way, an alternate narrative. On that evening, I had brought a visitor into Esti's small apartment—a young student about to begin her own research project in town. By turning to that evening and by outlining Esti's response to my view of her life, I engage with larger epistemic questions that stand at the center of the very act of representation in ethnographic research.

Esti on a Rampage

In January 2002 I introduce Reut Bendrihem, a graduate student in anthropology, into "the field" in Yerucham. Reut is interested in Mizrahi women's experience of motherhood, and she wants to explore this issue in Yerucham. It is the first time I have come to Esti and Simcha's flat with a guest. I introduce Reut as "my student" and briefly explain her research interests.

"Where are you from, honey?" Simcha asks, with a gentle, welcoming smile. Reut, an attractive, shy young woman, is understandably terrified. Here she is with her academic supervisor, about to plunge into the ultimate anthropological experience: fieldwork. She smiles at her hosts and at the neighbor women who are also present and declares that she is from the same place as Pnina, from Migdal Ha'Emek. I note that Esti looks Reut over but does not take part in the polite exchanges in which Reut is the center of attention.

Reut's presence, I realize only when the evening is over and I turn to write my notes, makes explicit my distinct class position, a position that my years of ongoing interaction with Esti and her sister have somewhat ironed out, muted. In our encounters—during our shared visits to the market, to the employment office, and elsewhere—Esti has often introduced me as "Pnina, my friend from work." The fact that I entered her life alone, without social connections that might have underscored my higher social status, did not make our respective positions irrelevant, but we were able to interact in an easy manner that hid these gaps, that allowed them to be glossed over. Thus, for example, when Esti met my two young sons on our way to a dental treatment in Be'er-Sheva, she always made a point of simply ignoring their presence. She spoke incessantly, effectively monopolizing my attention. At the dentist's office Esti related to the staff by relying on my friendship and emotional support. Esti's insistence that I accompany her to the bank to convince the "mean clerk" to authorize her cash withdrawal underscores her awareness of my higher status and willingness to use it to her advantage. She knew that I was someone "from the university," but she could play with my status to suit her needs, offering me her used clothing and allowing me to tag along after her in the market, on the one hand, and drawing on my status to legitimize her claims for cash in the bank, on the other hand.

When Reut walks into Esti's flat and is introduced as my student, my social status becomes tangible in ways Esti does not control. While Simcha and the other women play their expected roles, greeting Reut in a manner befitting an educated young woman from the university, Esti refuses to join in. Reut's presence has threatened the comradeship she and I have created in our encounters. The intensity of Esti's reaction to Reut's presence takes me by surprise.

As Reut plays her expected role as the polite guest, introducing herself and her research interests to the women gathered in the small room, accepting their invitation for a cup of coffee, and responding politely to their many questions ("No, I am not married"; "I am studying at the Hebrew University of Jerusalem"), Esti silently watches from the corner of the room. But then, without warning, she breaks into the polite small talk, turning to her sister and declaring, "Simcha, you know, actually, who *she* reminds me of?" The conversation comes to a halt as Simcha looks at Esti, baffled. Esti, who does not wait for any answer, declares in an excited manner, "She's, like, a copy of Larisa! That Russian woman, when we were little kids and she helped me at math." Esti does not look at Reut. She speaks of Reut in the third person and directs her attention only toward her sister. Simcha asks, "Larisa? Who?" and Esti goes on exuberantly, "The one who'd help me with homework. She's exactly . . . same face. I tell you, I was sure it was Larisa who turned up in our place just now." Reut blushes and I laugh out loud. I detect yet another attention-grabbing, characteristic, Esti-style performance. "What Larisa, Esti?" I interject. "Give me a break. Reut is Moroccan, just like you." Esti is not impressed. She is out to challenge the intrusion into her space by this student, Moroccan origin or not. She is openly agitated.

Over the course of the evening Esti's behavior and her stories get wilder and ever more provocative. When I tell Reut that Esti and I know each other through our work in Sde Boker, Esti draws on this shared reference and asks me if I remember Beber, "the old guy, who also worked with us at Sde Boker." She adds a few details that might help me place this mutual acquaintance. She tells me that he was a maintenance man and that he's now retired. And before I can confirm that I do remember Beber, Esti goes on excitedly: "This Beber, well, don't be seeing him like that [a pun in Hebrew]. We used to work together at the Ramon army base. He was old but had eyes for all the young girls. And

I was friends with one of 'em, a soldier girl, and I would go in her room. Hide there, like I did in your office, Pnina. And one day I says to Beber, you know, this soldier girl, she's so hot for you."

Esti describes in detail how she convinced Beber that the woman soldier was waiting for him in her room and how Beber rushed there straightaway. Esti laughs loudly, declaring that foolish old Beber was up for a great disappointment but that she did not care so long as he paid her 50 shekels. When Esti concludes what she calls "the funny story" about Beber, there is a long, embarrassed silence in the small crowded living room. One of the neighbors asks, "What d'you mean, Esti? What 50 shekels?" Esti seems pleased with herself. She ignores the woman who posed the question and directs her answer at me. She looks at me and announces with great relish, "Sure, like . . . I need my cut." Grinning from ear to ear she goes on, "I got my share!" Ignoring our stunned reaction, she adds, "But check this out, that Beber, he goes to that gal all hot and, like, she throws him out of the room screaming!" Esti is the only one in the room who breaks into loud laughter. She is evidently enjoying being the center of our attention and the shock she has created when we all grasp that she took money for prostituting young women soldiers. She does not obfuscate or apologize for her role. On the contrary, she openly calls it "my cut." And in case her listeners might have missed the point, she clarifies that although this one soldier threw Beber out, other women soldiers had indeed accepted Beber's advances. She concludes with a large, smug smile, "And I would always take my cut."

Reut is pale. The neighbors giggle in embarrassment. It is clear to me that Esti is doing everything she can to shock everyone present, to carve out a space of her own by reporting and celebrating her illicit behavior. And, as it turns out, the Beber story is only the beginning. Throughout that evening, Esti comes up with more and more stories that illustrate her provocative behavior in various workplaces.

She describes working with a group of young Bedouin men and several other women from Yerucham who were all sent by the local employment office to help excavate an archaeological site located on the outskirts of town. One time, Esti says, she and the Bedouin men were in a room that had been uncovered on the site. The room was low ("like a basement, like") and isolated, and she was there with another young woman from Yerucham. That woman was "totally wild, even more than me," Esti pronounces with great delight and a broad grin. "And we were mad, the two of us. So we were dancing like that with the broomstick between our legs [she illustrates] and the Bedouins . . . they just went wild . . . thinking they were going to get something out of it. But there was this other woman with us. She was married, and she watched us and she started crying and she begged us to cut it out, saying she'll get fired for this and that we should be working, not playing. That poor gal."

After Esti tells a few more wild stories like these, I turn to Reut and in my professorial tone explain that Esti always acts out at work and is never afraid of getting laid off because the jobs she gets are invariably boring and unsatisfying. My comments sound out of place in that small room, but I feel the need to explain to the shocked young student why Esti's chaotic behavior is understandable. Listening to my comments, Esti decides not to allow me "interpret" her in this manner. She is openly furious at my attempt to "explain" her life. When I tell Reut that the cleaning foreman in the university offices in Sde Boker was a strict man who micromanaged his cleaning staff, Esti is quick to counter my apologetic narrative with its implied empathy for her and the other cleaners in such a labor relationship. Esti rejects my interpretation, insisting, "But the problem is, Pnina, we really did *not* do the work. We just played hide and seek with the poor guy." And to convince us all that her behavior was indeed out of bounds, Esti goes on, "I was there working [at the university offices] for only three months but I knew it all. I knew that to get an outside line you need to dial 9, and I made long-distance calls from all the offices. I told all the girls about this. There were those who were scared even to call their mother or get in touch with their children at home. I would show them: 'Come on, what's wrong with you? Dial 9 and you got an outside line.'" And as though to dismiss any lingering doubt that it was she using the system rather than the other way around, Esti tells us about "one of them researchers there in Sde Boker," this one old guy, who was "hot for her" and had defended her against the foreman. Esti hints that the old professor might have expected favors in return for such protection, but she remains deliberately opaque as to whether she ever fulfilled these expectations.

Esti's claim of having played a game of seduction with an elderly researcher is consistent with the way she uses her sexuality in other settings. She wears provocative attire and is known for teasing, wild, incongruous behavior—flashing her breasts in the company of other women and putting a stick between her legs while dancing in front of Bedouin youths. However, her playful, boundary-crossing act always seems to be under her control. She brandishes her sexuality but makes it clear that the performance serves her needs. Fully aware of the power of her defiant sexuality over men, she makes it clear that she fully controls her use of her body and her provocative behavior. In the ultimate act of control, she depicts herself as a person who profits from other women's sexual services.

In her wild no-one-can-explain-my-life performance, Esti exhibits her desire to represent herself, to establish her own extravagant, provocative self-interpretation. She rejects my protective, somewhat paternalistic narrative that offers to justify and thus maybe legitimate her unconventional life choices. Esti makes herself into an agent who openly violates accepted rules of proper conduct. In her narrative she gets fired again and again because she does *not* fulfill the work ethic expected of a normal employee. She plays with her sexuality in overtly provocative ways and refuses to become stuck in a job she does not like. Esti ridicules everything—the army system, the young women soldiers' sexuality, the old man's desire, and my efforts to interpret her life. To break free from my sympathetic interpretation of her life and to fashion an independent narrative in which she alone sets the rules, Esti opts to depict her life as a series of acts of sabotage. She thus crafts a new space where *she*, not powerful, moralizing others (including me), sets the terms. In such a narrative of self she emerges victorious.

In her classic essay "Can the Subaltern Speak?" Gayatri Spivak (1988), the feminist postcolonial theoretician, poignantly questions the ability of the subaltern woman to speak, to express herself in an independent manner. Spivak points out the inherent problematics of any attempt by "intellectuals from the center" to represent women on the margins of society. I offer my analysis of this encounter with Esti as a way of engaging with Spivak's question. I argue that positing the question in terms of two distinct narratives, that of the intellectual from the center and that of "the subaltern woman," is a conundrum that can be played with, explored, and unpacked within specific social settings that emerge within the ethnographic encounter. I propose that there might be a way to bring together "the intellectual" and her interpretive frame, on the one hand, and her interlocutor and her interpretive frame, on the other. In the scene I have just depicted, Esti is clearly not the quintessential silent subaltern woman. Esti speaks incessantly, refusing to let others speak for her. In this encounter, more than in our many other, less tense encounters, Esti is clearly able to reject any attempt to make her an object of observation and is determined to control her own representation.

During the long recorded interview presented in chapter 5, Esti plays an active role in redrawing familiar boundaries that separate interviewer from interviewee, observer and observed. She not only makes clear what she wishes to speak about but she also unequivocally draws the line at the "things you can't talk about." When she allows me to record her and pose my questions to her, Esti is keenly aware of the outsider gaze that is focused on our interaction and she controls the tone and dynamics of the interaction with that gaze in mind. She mocks the underlying liberal logic that calls on her to become a docile worker in precarious underpaid jobs. When I pry into her emotional and deeply personal decision not to get married or have children, she responds with proclamations that render my questions ludicrous. Esti is able to perform in such a forceful and creative manner because she is, as she says, "different"; she is a person who refuses to accept social norms and oppressive frameworks.

In the following closing short scene, I place my ethnographic encounters with Esti within the broader political and social reality in which they unfold.

"So What Do You Say about the Situation?"

It is already past two in the afternoon and the market is emptying out. Esti and I are seated at a small café at the edge of the square, facing the main street. A few young Bedouin men sit on white plastic chairs around a table next to us, smoking and sipping from small glasses of black coffee. Esti ignores them and keeps her eyes glued on the road. The proprietor of the kiosk-café turns off the radio that is blasting the hourly news, and in the relative quiet that ensues I can hear bits of the conversation he carries on with the Bedouin men. They are commenting on a terrorist bomb attack that took place that morning in Tel Aviv. The radio report says that several people were killed and that many were wounded in the blast. The men exchange a few commonplace phrases that express their dismay over the tragic and senseless deaths and the futility of terrorist attacks, which are reported almost every day now in the Israeli media. "*Haram* [Arabic for a forbidden shameful act]," says one of the Bedouin men. "*Zeh lo beseder* [this is not good]," he adds in Hebrew. "*Betakh haram* [for sure, *haram*]," concurs the proprietor in his heavy Moroccan-accented Hebrew. "They were mostly women and children," he adds, referring to the morning's reported casualties. The conversation lingers in the heat of the day. I do not take notes. I am tired and emotionally drained. But I do remember that at one point the proprietor declares, "The Arabs, in Morocco, they used to love us, the Jews."

"So what do you say about the situation?" Esti asks me lightly, as if asking someone how he or she is doing without expecting a comprehensive reply. I throw the question back at her. "What do *you* say about the situation, Esterika?" I ask, using my affectionate nickname for her.

"Situation's chill," she replies in her familiar frisky manner. I smile at her and sip on the cool drink in front of me. We remain silent for a long while. We watch the rapidly emptying street. Market day is over, and everyone is hurrying home with full bags and baskets. And then Esti says, with uncharacteristic gravity, "Forget about the situation this, situation that. It's quiet here, in Yerucham. I never go to Tel Aviv."

7

GILA

A Story of Success

I FIRST MEET Gila in 1996, when I move with my family to Sde Boker. Gila is the Bible teacher and deputy principal at the only elementary school in our remote, elitist campus community, known to its residents as the Midrasha. Even before we meet in person, I learn from my sons that "no one messes around in Gila's classroom." By the time Gila becomes school principal, we are already friends and I congratulate her on her promotion. Gila's appearance exudes authority. She is an attractive woman in her midforties, with a round face framed by meticulously groomed honey-colored hair. She is always dressed in a careful, dignified manner.

Gila is not the kind of person to open up easily, and our friendship developed slowly. In the first two years of our acquaintance we would run into each other at events organized by the school and greet each other politely along the narrow footpaths of our shaded campus community. Our connection grew stronger when we discovered that we share somewhat similar personal histories. Like me, Gila broke out of the development town where she grew up by attending a boarding school that guaranteed acceptance to a prestigious high school (she in Jerusalem, I in Kfar Saba). Like me, she married a non-Israeli man, and like me, she was a single parent when we met. Her son is about the same age as my own two boys.

Native Yeruchami, Friend, and Research Adviser

When Gila learns about my research in Yerucham, she is fascinated and wants to hear more. I tell her about my encounters and share with her my initial interpretations of what I have learned in her childhood hometown. Gila listens earnestly, contributes her own interpretations, and asks pertinent, thought-provoking questions about the aims of my research and its method. Many of our conversations are informal—we exchange our ideas as we meet next to the small post office or on our way to the grocery store. But then we schedule more formal meetings, held in my house or hers, and I record our exchanges. I tell Gila that our discussions are critical to my work and that I might use them, with her permission, in my published work. Gila is flattered. She enjoys her role as my research adviser and the fact that I find her challenging questions deeply invigorating. Rereading the transcripts of our recorded exchanges makes it clear that many of the essential insights offered in this book were formulated and honed during these meetings with Gila over the years. What also emerges from these transcripts is that traditional boundaries that separate researcher from interlocutor were erased in our exchanges. As two Mizrahi women who were raised in underprivileged development towns and made it to middle-class adult life, we are both subjects of this study, and we are both engaged in the interpretation of the social reality in which we grew up. And still, eventually, it is I, and not Gila, who writes this text.

Our collaboration started when I introduced my project to Gila, saying, "Listen, Gila, the idea of this research is to document what I call 'the life worlds of Mizrahi women.' I want to really listen to them, to depict their lives using their words, without being judgmental about their values, their ways of being. I don't think that they are 'a problem,' as so commonly maintained, and I don't want to 'fix' them. They fascinate me. I want to understand and then write about how they see the world, how they understand their lives, and why they act like they do. The key here, Gila, is not to be judgmental, not to begin the research with a set of benign preconceptions of what is 'wrong' about their way of life."

Gila replied, "Yes, Pnina. This is all very interesting, not to be judgmental and such. I wanted to ask you about your methodology and so on. But first, tell me, I understand that you're investigating *only* Mizrahi women, that you didn't include other women in your study. You're specifically focusing on this section of the population of Yerucham. Why is that?"

I give her a rather long answer.

> Absolutely. Yes. My focus is mainly the Mizrahi women. You are right, this is not a study of Yerucham and will not include all the people who live in Yerucham, or all that is happening in Yerucham. It's not even a

study of all women in Yerucham. I am particularly interested in the lives of working-class Mizrahi women. You see, I began my research with the cleaning ladies who came to clean my office at the university. They were all from Yerucham, bused in every morning. Most of them were Moroccan, a few were Indian. And obviously they were women with very little formal education. They were young women, mostly in their twenties and early thirties. And I began talking to them about their lives and learned about their struggle to manage family, work, and personal ambition. I've been thinking for years about this group of working-class women, residents of development towns. There's very little research about these women. You and I both came out of this same social setting. We both know about the quality of education in places like Yerucham and how its isolation limits employment options for men and women. This is true of most development towns. Yet in my literature review I found that Israeli feminist scholarship has almost nothing to say about these women and that social workers, journalists, and various well-wishers often begin with the question of what's *wrong* with these women. Why do they fail school, get married and have children at a particular age, speak non-standard Hebrew, become welfare mothers? Whereas I wanted to ask: How do they cope? Do they walk around feeling like "failures"? What motivates them to make the decisions they make in their lives? And Gila, I have to stress that my study begins with the women but that I'm interested in the relationships between these women and the men in their lives, their families, the people that employ them.

Gila replies:

I understand. You want to document their lives. But tell me honestly, who will be interested in that? You're a professional. You're a doctor of anthropology . . . maybe for you this is all very exciting. But who will really care about what you write? And, honestly, people like me, if we read your book, do we get to learn anything new from it? When I listen to you, Pnina, there is nothing new in what you say. I know these women and I am so familiar with their lives. Oh-ho, how well do I know the stuff you put down in your notes. And, this documentation, which you say doesn't exist in the academic record, well, it might seem new to someone from Ramat Aviv, some rich Tel-Avivian who'd never been to

Yerucham and who knows nothing about the lives these women lead and their far-from-the-center everyday reality. For such a man, it will be like reading about some exotic African tribe, like the people you wrote about in your doctorate, right? But if you asked me, I'd say, "Sure, it's a research topic; but who's going to care?"

Gila's open and sustained challenge of my research and her questioning of its importance in the Israeli setting are not surprising. Every time I mention what I am working on to family and friends, I encounter a particular look implying that my interlocutor knows all about the subject of Mizrahi women of lower socioeconomic background. My friends and family volunteer their observations about their Mizrahi housecleaner or hairdresser, offering insights that range from downright racist to barely disguised paternalism. But Gila's comments and observations are different. Her insights are sharper, and her willingness to listen to how I see my research subject seems more sincere. My conversations with Gila make me sharpen my own thinking about the multiple audiences for the book I am planning to write. They make me more aware of the slippery path that could lead to exoticizing my subjects if I try too hard to dismantle the mainstream Israeli public discourse that stigmatizes and patronizes them. I have been keenly aware of this danger from my first effort to speak to Efrat's daughter, Einat, as I describe in chapter 2. Einat agreed to take part in the study and to bring in her mother only when she realized that my interest focused on the process of increasing religiosity, of which she and her mother were proud. I need to explain to Gila why my research is not going to exoticize its subjects, to clarify who my target audience is, and why documenting the reality of my subjects' lives is worthwhile:

> With all due respect to the man from Ramat Aviv, he's not my main audience. I don't want to amuse him with descriptions of "exotic Mizrahi customs." I don't write about the downtrodden life of Mizrahi women to entertain the man from Ramat Aviv. I want to document the lives of Mizrahi women in Yerucham because it is a social reality which, as I told you earlier, had never been properly understood in Israeli academic sociological work and because I believe it offers a unique and useful prism through which I wish to analyze Israeli society as a whole. I am interested

in studying gender relations, but I want to understand them from a particular ethnic and class setting, and for that purpose the Mizrahi multiply marginalized women's lives are absolutely interesting. I ask very specific questions about Israeli social reality. What I ask through this study is why do we witness a reproduction of social marginality and poverty in the *third* generation since the Mizrahi migration of the 1950s? Because, Gila, just think about it: These are women who were born in Israel. Their mothers arrived here as little girls and went through the Israeli socialization process. The mainstream argument has it that the generation of Mizrahi immigrants who arrived from Morocco or India in the 1950s and 1960s were the "desert generation," that they didn't have the proper skills or education to be part of modern Israeli society, and that this is why they ended up at the bottom of Israeli class hierarchy. Even if we do accept this narrative—and I can show you studies that reject it—the question must be asked, Why has the second and then the third generation, born and educated in Israel, fallen into the same multiply marginalized social position? The question becomes particularly acute when you consider that the women I focus on in my study are mainly the *third* generation of Mizrahi emigration. Why have more than 50 years of free public education and numerous policies intended to promote the "development" of marginalized communities like Yerucham been unable to cause change, to enable upward mobility for the majority of these women? You and I, women who were born in development towns and made it to college and a secure middle-class lifestyle, we are exceptions to this rule of class reproduction. And why, I want to ask, are the majority of these impoverished women Mizrahi? Is that a coincidence, this correspondence between class and ethnic background? Is the fact that these women were born in Yerucham a defining factor in shaping their life chances and their opportunities for social mobility?

Gila interrupts me. "Hold on, hold on. Look, my question is, Is this life part of being Israeli? You have to see this movie called *Mimi's Hair Salon*. It's exactly like Yerucham! A day after I watched the movie, I read a review in the paper by Orna Landau. She said that for Mizrahim, the wedding celebration is much more important than the marriage itself. This really was infuriating. It was outrageously patronizing."

I reply, "If you ask me whether life in Yerucham or in Shlomi [where the eponymous salon of the film is located] is part of Israeli reality, or what you call 'Israeliness,' then yes, absolutely yes. The question is not if it is part of Israeli society. Clearly it is. Obviously, the margins, the bottom, the periphery are part of society too. The question I pose is, How can you see Israeli society, its values, its policies, from the perspective of those who were effectively marginalized? Now the issue of depicting life on the margins in a patronizing way . . ."

Gila agrees. "I know, I know. Landau's patronizing tone made me furious. However, she did say something I agreed with. She said that the reality depicted in the film suggests that Mizrahi women 'manage' their men, that they control them like puppets on a string. Like, a Mizrahi woman could lead her man by the nose and he'll do exactly what she wishes, thinking all along that he is the real boss. And that's true, Pnina. These Mizrahi women do whatever they like with their men. Most of the women—and I'm not talking about violent men here—are world champions at letting their man think that he makes the decisions, that he's the king, when in fact, the man wouldn't take the smallest step without his wife."

I reply:

OK. I like your interpretation. I have not seen the movie, but your interpretation is a good example of what I am talking about when I say that looking from the perspective of the margin can be interesting and can tell us a lot about Israeli society in general. If I take your interesting analysis of gender relationships in the Mizrahi periphery as something that suggests that Mizrahi lower-class women are powerful and not submissive as the general view has it, then I suggest that you offer a different take on Israeli feminism: not the flag-waving Feminism with a capital F, feminism defined by the bourgeois middle-class Ashkenazi women. As I'm listening to you, I think that what you propose here is that there is a pattern of gender relations and a reality of everyday female power that has been overlooked by studies of Israeli feminist accounts, causing them to completely miss out on its significance. The common discourse is steeped in orientalist perceptions of the reality of Mizrahi lower-class life, speaking about it as deeply chauvinist due to its "lack of progress" and so on. And this is precisely my point. Who decides what "feminism" is? Today when we read about feminism in Israel, we always refer to the political activism of the few women MPs like Yael Dayan or about the struggle to achieve equal pay for women on corporate boards. What I insist on by documenting the lives of women in Yerucham and by examining the larger social forces that shape their marginalization is not an exotic study that is entertaining for those at the "center." I use the reality of life in Yerucham as a critical entry point to any discussion of feminism and ethnicity and power and class and how these shape each other at the same time in Israeli society.

When I listen to this recorded conversation with Gila—one of many we had over the years—I notice that both of us speak of the women of Yerucham in the third-person plural. We say "these women," "them," but never "us," even though both of us are Mizrahi women and even though both of us came out of a social setting similar to the one that shaped the lives of "these women." I also realize that I have invited Gila to share my position of analyst, not that of a native of Yerucham, despite the fact that she grew up there. It is obvious that we both speak from a solid middle-class perspective, harboring no doubts that we do not belong to the social reality of "these women." I also note, however, that in my long answers to Gila's questions and challenges I take up the tone of a lecturer, using sociological terms that set me apart as "the professional," the "social scientist." Gila, for her part, allows me to explain myself in full, without interrupting me. Her questions are sharp and targeted, but she voices them with an open appreciation of what she perceives as my undisputed professionalism. Listening to these tapes, I notice that our exchanges use polished, refined Hebrew and that we are equally articulate. We also seem to share a disdain for the shallow, patronizing tone of the public discourse that diminishes the people of Yerucham in general and Mizrahi women in particular.

In our later recorded exchanges Gila breaks away from the sociological tenor of our earlier conversations and begins to speak at length about her own experiences, maybe because she seeks to substantiate her analytical insights: "Yes, I really know what you're talking about. I've seen this paternalistic outlook toward 'people of Yerucham' from up close. When I lived in Yerucham, I was a trustee for the local community center. I met those people who came to Yerucham, and for all their good intentions and sincere desire to help and volunteer for Yerucham, they never hid their open and complete contempt for the uneducated local population. They thought these people were failures, that only they could 'save' these people."

Family, Career, and Conflicted Identity

For almost four years, Gila was my empathetic listener, adviser, and interlocutor. At some unspecified point, however, she emerged as a key figure in the research and one of the five main characters in this book. It is difficult to say precisely when and how this happened. As Gila's friend, I come to know bits and pieces of her life story. But when she suggests that I include her story in the book in its entirety, I immediately propose a long recorded session. "I need to have your precise words. I need full quotations," I tell her. But a calm and complete recorded session never materializes. We meet several times with the recorder at hand, but each time our interview is interrupted after a short while—a visitor appears or we simply get sidetracked and decide to stop the recording. Thus, instead of the comprehensive interview I try to procure, I end up with several tapes containing almost 10 hours of conversations that took place over the course of five separate sessions.

By the time I get these tapes transcribed and begin to outline the chapter that will focus on Gila's story, it is 2007. After much trimming and editing, I organize Gila's narrative around three main themes: family, life trajectory, and reflexivity. The first locates Gila within her large and exceptional natal family, the Aboutbouls. The second deals with Gila's personal life and her career. The third revolves around Gila's candid ruminations about her relationship to the town of her birth and her ethnic identity. The chapter closes with what I call an "ethnographic drama" that brings together three protagonists, Gila, Esti, and me, and confronts us with our interwoven positionalities. "These moments of going back to Yerucham," Gila concedes after an eventful day with Esti and me in the town market, "are never easy."

After conducting the first recorded interview with Gila, I write the following in my notebook:

> Only now do I grasp the uniqueness of Gila's family in Yerucham. It is an extraordinary story of a well-to-do family that had considerably more material and cultural means than the rest of the Moroccan immigrants

sent to Yerucham. The family manages not only to survive in the remote little town but also to propel all 10 children into higher education or trade. Within that larger family story, Gila's quest toward upward mobility begins with her repudiation of both her Moroccan origins and her association with Yerucham. Her coming to terms with these two components of her identity becomes possible only years later. But Gila's reconciliation with herself remains incomplete. She still is deeply at odds with her background, and this continues to cause her much pain. She is not proud of her demeanor toward the people of Yerucham. There is a recurring tenet of self-inflicted failure in her behavior, prone to erupt particularly in her moments of triumph. In every stage of her professional career where her success becomes recognized and commended, she flees, entrapping herself. Does Gila's story imply a social dynamic representative of people who emerge from the social and geographical periphery of Israel? Gila's story can also teach us about the true probability of the town's age-old hopes of being bolstered by those who "made it."

Is Gila's persistent fear of success representative of a broad social dynamic among those who emerge from Israel's social and geographic margins? Israeli literature has little to say about this fear among middle-class Mizrahi Jews in general or among Mizrahi women from the marginalized spaces of development towns in particular.[1] Gila's story is also instructive in pointing to a process of interpellation of upwardly mobile Mizrahim from these marginalized spaces. After delving into Gila's story, I present relevant statistical data that document this internal "brain drain" from Israeli development towns.

The Aboutboul Family: "My Father Was a Remarkable Man"

Our first recorded session is also attended by Leah, Gila's older sister. Like Gila, Leah lives at the Midrasha, but she is less articulate and her body language is less sophisticated than her younger sister's. Leah was educated in Morocco and attended an Alliance school;[2] her speech carries clear traces of a French accent. When I tell Leah that I have come to record Gila's life story and that I want to begin with the story of the family, it is she, not Gila, who tells the story of the family's immigration experience.

"They brought us to Yerucham on a Shabbat night. I still don't understand why. They knew that we keep the Shabbat, so why send us to this remote settlement knowing we won't arrive at our destination before Shabbat began? That was my father's first shock. He told me, 'This is no Jewish country. This is heretic country.' And when my mother begun to scream loudly that this is not right and that she does not want to be on the truck during Shabbat, the driver giggled and turned the radio up. It was shameful. They ignored our religion. They deliberately insulted us."

Gila listens respectfully to Leah's story and then she adds in a staid tone, "Pnina, this is, of course, the classical story . . . like all the stories of that experience of the first arrival in Yerucham. I'm not even sure how real it is anymore. It became a collective story. It's a story they told each other again and again and so it became 'their story.' Take, for example, my mom, she tells it like that: From Morocco they went by boat to Marseille and from there they took a plane to Israel. But the plane was delayed because of a storm and we made a forced landing on Cyprus. My mom would always laugh about how we all started to kiss the ground [of Cyprus] and my dad shouted at us that this wasn't the Holy Land."

"How old were you then? Do you yourself remember anything?" I ask Gila. She replies:

I was just five years old, but I certainly do remember that day of our arrival in Israel. I recall how we entered the passenger terminal, where they gave us oranges and cheese. One of these melted cheeses. I still remember the taste. A few hours later we got to Lod, and there were these immigration officials there. My dad tried to negotiate with them and insisted about the place he wanted us to be sent to. Naively enough, he asked them to send us to "a place with water," because he was a swimmer. I remember that element of "a place with water" rather clearly. I've heard other versions of what happened that day, but I'm not sure of their veracity. At any rate, as the story goes, they told him, "Sure, sure," and sent us to Yerucham. My parents had with them 10 children, my dad's unmarried sister, and our grandma. And again, there are the recurring stories that my dad, who could read Hebrew, saw the signposts on the road and asked them where they were taking us. And then there's the familiar story of their protestations that they're not getting off the truck . . . and the usual repeated twist about the driver who got angry and was yelling at them. I've heard about their insistence not to get off the truck; some speak about staying put on the truck for hours, demanding to be taken back to the center of the country. And then there is always this closure with, at some point, one of the kids needed to pee and my mother took him off the truck. And then, as she was waiting for the child to relieve himself, she recognized someone from her hometown of Morocco. And this man recognized her too and told her that her sister, Hannah, already lives here, in Yerucham village. You see, my parents had no clue where other members of their extended family were sent to. So, obviously, my mom immediately ran to her sister's place. And sure enough, she went back to the truck and told my father, "I'm staying here with my sister."

The Collective Story of a Remarkable Family

Gila is a bit playful in her rendering of the familiar family story. She presents it like a scholar reporting undocumented oral history, implying that one cannot sift the true facts from the different versions. By suggesting that it has become a "collective story," Gila also hints at other Mizrahi stories of migration and forced settlement in the remote desert, the arrival on Shabbat, the ridicule of their Jewish religious practices. She is a well-read person and is aware that these stories are currently being documented and debated in the literature. And yet Gila makes clear, despite this familiar collective story, that her family and their experience are unique.

"You do need to understand, Pnina, that my family was always special, unlike anyone else. You see, my dad was the principal of a Talmud Torah school and a rabbi. He ran a Jewish school in the town where he was a rabbi. He was an extremely scrupulous man. I remember that he taught all of us Hebrew already in Morocco, including me, even though I was only five years old when we made *aliyah*."

After a short break, and after we all have enjoyed coffee and some refreshments, Gila makes sure to recount the family story "properly," for the record.

We were all born in Morocco. My younger sister was three months old when we arrived. I remember my father teaching us Hebrew phrases like,

"If one says, I have labored and found, you may believe him."[3] My father was continually testing our Hebrew reading skills. He was a very, very remarkable person. He was religious, but he wasn't a religious extremist. You see, he sent Leah to a secular French school, not a religious one, because he insisted that she get the best education. In Israel, he insisted on sending all of us children to secular rather than religious schools. He said that the local religious school was of a lower academic quality and he would not have his kids poorly educated. But the sad part of this story is that he himself did not manage to regain his status in Israel, after the *aliyah*. He tried getting a teaching job and failed. He briefly worked as the secretary of the [local] religious council and gave it up, because he did not like the political aggravation the post entailed. Eventually he opened a grocery store. He arrived with some money, not a lot, but enough to buy a store. My parents had earned enough from that store to raise us in relative comfort. Childhood friends tell me it was always clear that we were a "rich" family. We would come to school with sandwiches lined full of cold cuts and clementines. Other kids would come with red bean sauce on a slice of bread. But Pnina, what's "rich"? It's all relative. I remember I never owned even a single toy. But again. The emphasis on taking initiative and achieving excellence was very strong in our house. I remember I would lend books to kids in the neighborhood. I don't know where these books came from. I guess my dad brought a collection with him from Morocco. I don't know where they came from. But just imagine a little girl running her own private borrowing library. With reader cards. . . . Amazing!

Gila breaks off her monologue and gives me a pensive look. She takes a deep breath and then offers an unexpected self-revelation:

I listen to myself tell you all this about my family, and I still cannot understand how it happened that I grew up to be ashamed of them. I will be honest with you and with myself. I remember clearly that I was ashamed of my parents' particular use of the small house we were given as a large family by the authorities. You see, relative to others, my family did not suffer much. We moved into a house fairly quickly. In fact, they gave us two semi-detached units for our use. And even if these were very small spaces, each contained two small rooms and a kitchen. We fared much better than many who lived in tents or corrugated iron shacks for long months and even years. But the way my parents organized that space strikes me today as strange. In fact, I remember being angry even then, at the time. You see, my parents lived in one unit of two rooms and all the 10 of us were clustered into one of the rooms in the second unit. The other room was kept as a living room intended for guests only, it was kept closed and empty. It irritated me tremendously. I'd tell them so indignantly. I also had a lot of anger toward my mother—not both my parents, just my mother—for having so many kids. How did I get this idea as a young girl? I have very early memories of such bitter resentment, and I lashed out at them. I was furious they did not fit the model of a family I somehow internalized as the "proper" family.

And the funniest thing of all was my anger at their choice not to emigrate out of Israel when they were offered the option. Consider this. In our second year here, my dad had an interview set for him in Jerusalem. I recall that we all made a day trip and joined him for that day in Jerusalem. I don't know for sure what organization it was, but they had offered my dad a post as a rabbi in Canada. But for some reason, and I still don't know why, he turned it down, told them he wasn't interested. My mother, I remember clearly, really wanted to go. She felt imprisoned, like a deposed queen. But he made up his mind. He wasn't an easy person. He was prone to anger, not a man to listen to others. And so he was simply stuck in Yerucham, in his little grocery store.

Yes, I was furious. But this is the kind of man my dad was. He'd make a decision and that was that. And he was a respected man. His former students were spread far and wide across Israel. Many of them came to visit him, pay their respects, and kiss his hand. They worshipped him. For a while he toyed with the idea of garnering local political power, and he was, for a short while, the local party secretary of Mizrahi, a religious party. He was one of the first in Yerucham to own a car. Yes, he was an exceptional man. But, on the whole, he didn't really use his skills. And when he was ill and lost his eyesight, he stayed at home. When it became known that he went blind, many people—former students and people who admired him—came to visit. There were always people at the house.

Gila dolefully narrates the decline of her admired, charismatic father but also criticizes him for his tyranny and his disregard for the needs of her mother. She reveals her earlier feelings of rage and shame toward her family. She wonders aloud about the social mechanism that made her resent her parents for having too many children, for allocating a separate room for guests while cramming all 10 of their children into a single tiny bedroom. She bemoans the missed opportunity of emigrating to Canada.

Gila forewarns me she is going to be brutally honest. She marshals her memories of her family's accomplishments as well as what she feels today were their shortcomings. She tries to grasp the complex strands of the family story and offers her interpretations of it. It is clear that the small recorder I place in front of Gila encourages her not simply to piece together the family story but also to reflect on it and on her own changing interpretive frameworks. And then she turns to the place of her mother in this larger story.

A Mother's Joy in the Education of Her Children

My mom, she is the only one who remains living in Yerucham. If you see her today, she goes about Yerucham as if she has a halo. She is totally proud of her children. People in Yerucham have a lot of respect for her. She's an impressive woman in her own right, but it's also because of her kids. My mom's pride and joy are the accomplishments of her 10 children. Our education and success makes her happy. The fact that she had remained alone in town is not easy for her, but it is somewhat bearable because we, her children, had all "made it." She had contributed to this, no doubt, even though much of the achievement-oriented atmosphere at home was due to my dad's influence.

Pini, my older brother, is also very bookish. I actually followed in his footsteps. Pini attended the teacher training seminar at Sde Boker, and I followed. Pini became a school principal and so have I. My other siblings are also very successful, each and every one, even if along different tracks. Everyone attended high school here; all completed their army service. One brother runs a community center, the second is a personnel manager here at the local Phoenicia factory. One of my brothers is writing his PhD thesis on urban planning. Three went into entrepreneurship and trade. They followed in my mother's footsteps.

You see, my mother was not one to spend all her days at home. A couple of years after we arrived in Yerucham, she opened her own clothing store, and she ran it separately from my dad. She clothed generations of people in Yerucham. Her shop offered clothes and a range of accessories no one was selling in remote Yerucham of the 1950s and 1960s. She'd take a bus to Tel Aviv, go to every shop there, pick the best Tel Aviv fashionable items, and have them delivered to her in Yerucham. And she did everything in her business: choosing, pricing, orders, bills, coordinating deliveries, everything. And she did pretty well. Two years after she opened the first shop, they bought another shop, this time in Netanya. But somehow the one in Netanya didn't take off. Then they bought a third store, in Yerucham, on the main street. Today my mom rents this store out and lives off the rent. This is the store that she wanted me to run when I came back to Yerucham after my army service and was out of work. But I never was any good in business; I was not connected to trade like the rest of the family. Today, one of my sisters owns and runs a clothing store in Tiberias. My brother owns a chain of 16 stores, men's clothes, spread across the country.

And as feminism goes, it is clear that all of my sisters fit into the feminist model of being independent career women. We are five sisters and all of us went on with our education and developed careers. I have only one sister who doesn't work right now because she gave birth recently and couldn't find another job. We all feel very strongly about this. We're all well educated, and we all worked hard on our careers.

"I Always Liked Studying"

I ask Gila if she is the most educated among her five sisters.

You could say that. I always liked studying. And my family supported my scholastic success from the very beginning. I always had it easy in school. Part of it is because when we moved to Israel, I was only five years old and I already spoke some Hebrew. So I came into preschool in Yerucham without any of the difficulties that many immigrant children have. And when, at the end of elementary school, I was invited for an interview at the Jerusalem boarding school, because I was picked out as a "gifted student," the entire family celebrated with me. The difficulties, emotional as well as academic, began only after I had left Yerucham for that boarding school. Oh, the big shock I got then.

I really crashed in ninth grade. I had no preparation for the level of knowledge expected of me there, and I found myself struggling alone with a style of teaching I wasn't used to in Yerucham. But, reflecting on that experience now, I think that the problems were more emotional than scholastic. I had a really racist teacher. I still remember her remarks about how we, Mizrahi kids, will never amount to anything. She actually told us that Mizrahi kids like us don't invest in their studies and that it was such a shame that all the money the state invests in us is going to waste. It was all in the open. No one questioned her right to say these things. But, you know, we let it pass over our heads, and we did enjoy the social life the boarding school offered. It made up for such racist comments, for missing home, for everything. I loved the wonderful landscape of Ein Kerem in Jerusalem (even though I really wanted to go to Boyer, and the Ein Kerem boarding school was the default option). There was a rose garden, a swimming pool, and lots of extracurricular courses. It was a formative experience. The people were great. I lived with the same girls for four years.

But the price for all that was detachment. Emotional detachment from home, from our families. We were allowed to go home for a short weekend once every three weeks. But I had often decided against going home and preferred to go and stay with a friend instead of going back to Yerucham. And so I would regularly be away from home for six, seven weeks. It didn't bother me. I didn't want that connection. I was ashamed of it, ashamed of everything that was linked to my family and to Yerucham. I remember how one time I asked my mom to buy me a pair of jeans. And she did indeed send me a package, but when I saw the pair she had sent me, I started crying. I remember myself sitting on a rock and crying my eyes out. Why? Because the jeans she picked for me weren't up to my new standards, because I was ashamed of her. Of myself.

When school ended, I returned home but stayed there only a short period of time. Soon after graduation, I began my teacher's training seminar in Sde Boker. And when I completed that training, I joined the army. I wanted to go to a kibbutz during my army service, but I was sent to be a military schoolteacher in Dahab, in Sinai. My God, that place was a mess. I served without a uniform, no clear supervisor, nothing. The two years I spent in Dahab were the wildest times of my life. I'd teach in the small local school by day, and work as a bartender by night. When I completed my army duty and had returned to old Yerucham, I did not know what to do with myself. I rented a small flat in town because I didn't want to live with my mom.

I was a certified teacher so it was easy to get a post in the local school. I taught two classes. And I did really well. But then, at the peak of my success, when everyone was pleased with my performance, I decided to quit. I'd had enough with education. I was bored. I was just tired of it all. I went to the principal, who really liked me and told him about my decision. He tried his best to convince me to stay on. He offered to let me run a new project that he was initiating in school; he offered me a better contract. He said that I will manage this school-wide project and not teach classes. But I wanted nothing to do with it. I felt like I was suffocating there in small Yerucham. I had an urge to leave. To just get up and go.

I had some friends from Canada whom I met when they came on an exchange program from Montreal. So I decided that I'd drop everything and fly to Montreal. Just like that. Without plans or any idea about what I was going to do in Montreal. I took all my savings and for a few months I hung out with these friends and then left them and traveled from coast to coast for another six months. But when all this was over, I returned to Israel, penniless, with no money even for cigarettes. So I ended up living with my mom, who supported me financially. I refused to go back to teaching, so we decided that I would try to run her local clothing store in Yerucham. I was really stubborn in my refusal to go back to teaching. But as I told you earlier, I wasn't very good at running a store, and I didn't enjoy marketing. So after a short while I found a post at the Yerucham employment bureau. That job lasted three months. I was unhappy and I was looking to get out of Yerucham. And then I heard that a position of a youth guide was open at the Sde Boker boarding school. Funnily enough, and despite my higher qualifications as a certified teacher, it took a long time until I managed to get that job that others get with a basic high school diploma. I worked at that job for three long years. You're laughing, Pnina, wondering why I had taken on that job and kept it for so long, and yes, I never mentioned this to you until today because I have tried to wipe this entire chapter out of my memory. I didn't like this period of my life.

I was eventually offered a job as a cultural coordinator for students on the campus in Be'er-Sheva. I was happy to leave Sde Boker. Although I lived in the student dorms in Be'er-Sheva, I enjoyed my new job tremendously. I initiated this idea of coordinating students' cultural and social activities from scratch. And I made good money. I looked after myself, and I was well dressed. When, after two years, they asked me to set up a similar program in Haifa, I was happy to move. Change of place, change of luck. I just turned 30 and I was also thinking about marriage. There was all this social pressure: "Single? At your age?" So I moved to the student dorms in Haifa. It was a great place. This was where I met John. A nice English guy, a Zionist, a committed lover of Israel. His idea of serving the country was to join the police force and, using his native English in special missions, he'd work undercover. We got married. I was the main breadwinner, since he hardly earned anything in his job. We took a large mortgage and bought a flat in Haifa.

Gila repeatedly comes home to her family and to life in Yerucham as different stages in her life end. She returns to Yerucham after graduating from boarding school but does not stay long. She lives "the wild life" during her army service, attends teacher training, and flies off to Canada on an unplanned trip, but in times of need she always comes back to Yerucham, where she can find work and rely on her family's support. And it is this pattern that she falls back on when, after marriage, she and her husband find themselves on shaky financial ground. As Gila puts it, "The family took us under its wing." She describes the rapid disintegration of her marriage with a sad smile.

The idyllic phase was over very quickly. When my son David was born, I quit my job and for the first few months I was unemployed. I will tell you the honest, if bitter truth of it, this is one amazing story. I put David into day care when he was just three or four months old. I just couldn't be like, like all those mothers, who want to stay at home with their kids. I've had it up to here. So I sent him off to day care when he was just a few months old. But the real problem was that for a long time after that I couldn't find work. And day care cost money. And expenses just kept piling up. I remember getting a call from the bank—John was on some of his police training at the time, and anyway he didn't really care about what was going on. I guess he never really understood that life costs money. So they called from the bank and said we were something like 13,000 shekels overdrawn. Which was an enormous amount of money. You can't even imagine it today. Just think that at the time John was making 2,000 shekels a month, and I wasn't making anything at all. And after the most humiliating six months of my life, living on welfare with debts that grew and grew, I decided our economic condition was so bad that I took up cleaning. I cleaned houses.

"You say that with a lot of pain," I remark.

Listen, it's not a simple thing to do; it came out of overwhelming despair. I decided I wasn't going back to teaching even if I had to starve. I remember applying for some job in cultural organizing that was advertised. But—nothing. They wouldn't take me. I guess this rejection hurt my ego so badly that I stopped applying for jobs altogether. Humiliated and depressed, for three or four months I washed floors and cleaned private homes. My parents didn't know. But my brother, who lived in Haifa, saw that our financial situation was bad and deteriorating and told my mother. And then, just like that, on Saturday night of that very same week, my mom and Haim, my brother-in-law, appeared at our door with loads and loads of food. And they pretty much decided for us on the spot that enough was enough, the Haifa chapter was over. The family took us under its wing, you could say. They immediately found work for me in Yerucham, where my brother was a school principal. And John? They decided it wouldn't be a problem for him if he'd move to the Be'er-Sheva police station.

But John, he took it really hard. The problem was I never really understood why, what bothered him so deeply about the help we got from the family. I saw how he took it. He said he was humiliated; he had no say in the decision that affected his life and his family's. I tried to soothe him, saying, "Look, they are doing everything they can to help us. What are you talking about? What humiliation?" He never grasped the fact that the entire family pitched in their own money to pay off our debts and close our overdraft. They found a job for me, they found us a new flat.

But looking back on the whole thing, I realize that such help came with a price. They never consulted with me as they secured this teaching position for me. They knew very well how unenthusiastic I felt about teaching at that time. And they got us a flat right next to my brother's and my mom's place. Keeping us close by. And Yerucham, by the way, is an amazing place . . . [she smiles wryly].

So at first John would drive down from Haifa every weekend, because he couldn't just get up and leave. But then Esti, my sister, came up with the idea of John becoming a youth guide here, at the boarding school at Sde Boker, because the benefits attached to his job were considerable: We could get a rent-free apartment and free childcare for our son David.

"And did he do that, did he take the job?"

He did. We didn't have much of a choice, really. He realized that our small family's income was now dependent on him. So he resolved to take a leave of absence, a kind of sabbatical, from his police job. Yes. But the real story was that John was really unhappy about this change. He viewed his undercover police job as a calling, his way of promoting Zionism. He thought his new position as a counselor was less meaningful, less prestigious than his glorified days in the police. And he became bitter and accused me of destroying his career. We'd have a lot of arguments, and he became increasingly depressed. And it all affected his health. One night he fell asleep with the gas heater on, and it caused him severe lung damage. His deteriorating health then put an end to his prospects of going back to his old police job. It was all very bad. He wanted to go back to England, and I, of course, decided that I stay here, so we got a divorce.

Then Gila shakes her head and switches to a more cheerful tone.

Be that as it may, I recovered from the whole divorce crisis pretty quickly. I adjusted to the new situation of being a single mom and raising David on my own and put my energies into building my life. Perhaps I never dealt with the pain, with the loss. Now I think I simply suppressed my feelings. And anyway, John and I maintained a positive post-divorce relationship. I went to visit him in England with David a few times. At one point we even played with the idea of getting back together, of rebuilding our shared life. Because, you see, the divorce wasn't acrimonious; we parted with a kiss and a hug. But life took its course. After his return to

England, John joined a private investigation firm and then another firm. At some point he was sent to Jamaica, where he built himself a new life.

And me? I was doing well. I took educational management training, and when our school principal left, I found myself taking up her position. But you know all this. We were already friends by then, right?

"Giving Up at the Height of My Success"

Gila was the school principal in Sde Boker, and as the parent of two sons who attended the school, I shared the general admiration for her tireless performance. What I did not realize at the time was the emotional and physical price she paid during the three years of her tenure as the acclaimed, perfectionist principal.

"Yes. They all loved me," she recalls. "I worked with a team of fantastic teachers and organized all these events the parents valued and enjoyed. I was so obsessed that I would get to school at 6 a.m., making sure that the chairs were in place, that the secretary knew what she needed to do because I outlined it for her every morning on a colorful board. I wrote personal notes and followed up on the progress of each and every pupil. When I came back home, I had no life. I planned the semester ahead, I sent notes to each teacher. I worked late into the night. And I was under tremendous stress. Everything had to be perfect. I knew that these overeducated parents, professors teaching at the university campus here, were watching me. But the intensity of 20 hours of work each day was simply unsustainable. I started having terrible headaches. Then I ended up having a cardiac episode, and I spent five days at the cardiology department."

"What caused such stress, Gila?"

Look, this place is not simple. It's the very epitome of Ashkenazi-hood, if you can coin such a word. All these Ashkenazi doctors and professors had sky-high demands and expectations for the education of their kids. But, clearly, it was also due to my own relentless perfectionism. The problem with my management was that I was unable to delegate responsibilities. I had to do everything myself. I mean, I'd make sure that every classroom was ready for the new day by moving the desks and chairs in perfect lines, collecting paper strewn in the hall. I reached a point that, without warning, I announced that I am leaving. They did not understand why. But I knew that I should leave with my head held high, that is, when the appreciation and admiration of my performance was at its highest. It was not only the parents, I also was ranked extremely high by the Ministry of Education. The District Committee came to inform me that they had decided to skip the next step of assessment of my work and grant me tenure. And they were all so pleased with their exceptional decision they could not believe their ears when I announced on that very same day that, instead of being tenured, I had decided to quit. I thanked them for their compliments and handed them my resignation letter. They couldn't understand. Then they became angry. They figured it was a ploy I was running to present further demands. They told me they were willing to consider accommodating all my "demands." But I didn't play along. I could not explain myself to them. I just couldn't do it anymore. I wanted out.

Gila pauses in her long emotional monologue. And then she begins to reflect on that moment and other moments like it in her career.

"You know, recently, I started thinking about it. Why? Why do I always sabotage myself like that? Why do I give up and escape it all precisely at the zenith of my success? Hearing myself tell you about my life, I realize that the same pattern was evident with my divorce. When John said for the first time, 'I want to go back to England,' I reacted with a 'So you want a divorce?' I didn't talk to him. I didn't ask why. I did not let things settle down, negotiate with him. Believe me, the very next morning I ran to the rabbinate. I wanted to be there before him. Maybe, just maybe, I could have saved that marriage. But, no. I could not take something that might smack of . . . ? Of what? Me not being an angel? Why this pattern? Search me."

"Umm, Gila, this is tough. I'm not a psychologist you know, it's not my field, but I listen to you, and I think maybe it's because you kinda . . . umm . . . want to preempt the failure."

"Yes, yes, yes, exactly. As if I am convinced that I'm not that good after all, that I am going to mess things up, so before I actually fail, I just tap out . . . yes . . . definitely . . . and I feel horrible about it . . . and I tell myself not everything has to be perfect, and I see how many much less talented people who do go on become successful, rise up and up. I know I have a very serious issue here of self-confidence. And evidently, I can't cope with even a single word of criticism. It was enough for one student's parent to make one critical remark, some little offhand comment, to make me uneasy for two whole weeks."

"Look, Gila, I don't think it's all a personality flaw or something that is confined to psychological explanations. From my perspective, as an anthropologist, I know that the pattern you're describing is not unique, not something linked only to your way of handling life, but a social, structural pattern found among minorities, blacks, women, Jews—people who feel a tremendous need to excel, because they grow up with an explicit or less explicit but powerful message that questions their—I should say 'our'—abilities, skills, talent. The overwhelming feeling that we have that maybe we are not good enough stems not from intrinsic doubts but is structural, it is a result of power relations . . . of actually being under perpetual scrutiny."

"Yes, you're using your professional terms now, Pnina. But I agree. It's precisely that place of . . . of always being placed under a magnifying glass, a feeling you're constantly tested. It might not be nice for me to say this, but here, of all places, in Sde Boker, I often felt as if they were asking, 'Who is this Moroccan woman who presumes to educate our children?'"

"And this is why you felt that you had to be the best."

"Exactly, exactly. I needed to be flawless . . . and so even one word of criticism . . . could undercut my confidence, my self-assurance. I don't know about you, but I, I can't cope with even one word of criticism, even the most simple and straightforward, no matter from whom. It's astonishing. This need, to always be the best . . . it takes a toll. No doubt. And as soon as I realized that this whole state of mind was taking a grave toll on my health, I said, enough, I'm not going to go on with this. What do I need it for? I quit. Still, I always have that nagging doubt that maybe that health thing was just an excuse. Maybe I really wasn't good enough."

"What about all the unequivocal praise you got from everyone? I recall the huge farewell party the teachers threw for you, how much love they expressed toward you in what they said. And, Gila, really, I heard with my own ears that several parents came to talk to you and to ask you to reconsider your decision. They literally pleaded with you to go on as school principal."

"True, true . . . the teachers made me such a beautiful album . . . and, sure, all that love sure makes you feels good . . . but . . . I never walked around with a feeling that I deserved all of it. I always questioned it, asking, 'Why would they do that for me?' I think about this a lot, Pnina. This is no false modesty. It's a deep sense of self-doubt. You see, I could never deal with compliments. And when someone gave me a compliment for my work, I would depreciate my own accomplishment. I would say things like, 'Oh, come on, what are you talking about? What did I really do? It's nothing.' I never took it easy. It was always a struggle for me. And even if everyone was supportive, I never felt that I have done enough. So I worked even harder. But that's it. I am glad it is over now. Today I am focused on taking care of myself, you know, as our retired politicians say, 'I am doing for my home.'[4] Now I'm thinking about going on with my academic education. I am focused on me. I don't want to teach others, to contribute to society, to be a good Zionist . . . you know."

Gila does not need my sociological analysis. She is aware of the pattern in which she undermines herself again and again. She is articulate in her depiction of the debilitating effects of her constant self-doubt. Gila made up her mind to quit the job that made her anxious and caused her health to fail. But as our conversation continues, she offers another angle on her self-aware story of her pattern of failure. She links it to her early upbringing as a Moroccan immigrant girl in Yerucham.

"Going Back to Yerucham Is Not Simple"

"I never liked that name, Aboutboul. I gladly took John's last name and I stayed with it even after our divorce. Only one of my brothers, the one with the PhD, changed this name when he married an Ashkenazi woman. The others stayed with theirs. But what you don't know, Pnina, is that I deeply hated my given name—Gila. I found it to be old-fashioned, not stylish enough. So when I entered high school, away from Yerucham, at the boarding school, I became Galit. I came back to Gila only after my military service, when I began my college education. Today I can see that changing my name from Gila to Galit was a blunt effort to hide my ethnic roots. Think about it. I was so ashamed to be associated with Yerucham that when people I met in Jerusalem would ask me where I was from, I'd say, 'I live in a small place near Be'er-Sheva . . . you probably never heard of it? If you would ask any of my high school friends who is Gila Aboutboul, they wouldn't have guessed who you are talking about."

Gila sighs deeply. She says she is telling me these things because of who I am, because I understand. Then she pushes her reflection even deeper, linking it to the present:

> It's not easy for me today, going back to Yerucham. I admit. It was never easy for me. I'll give you an example. A few weeks ago a good friend and I went to see a Moroccan play in Yerucham. You know, the play that they speak in Moroccan the whole time. And there we were, two girls from Yerucham—she is of Moroccan origin like me—sitting there, making snotty comments about people in the audience.
>
> And now, now that I am thinking about the two of us, flesh of the flesh of the community, sitting there criticizing everyone, considering ourselves of a higher league . . . I am embarrassed. But, really, [she giggles] they were acting weird . . .

"What was weird about the people of Yerucham? What do you mean?"

"Their appearance, for example. You should've seen their clothes. You'd expect people to dress up properly when they come to the theater. And people came looking . . . just horrific. Wearing cheap clothes, in bad taste. Unkempt hair. Incessantly calling out to each other from one end of the theater hall to the other. I know it sounds patronizing, but I couldn't help but get this feeling that they didn't care, that they couldn't care less. Odd people . . ."

"I think I know what you're talking about, Gila. I too have that constant need to deal with my complicated feelings about Migdal Ha'Emek, where I grew up. I remember being a young student in Kfar Saba, and on one of my weekend visits home, I went to see the film *To Sir, With Love* at the Tamar Cinema, the only cinema hall in Migdal Ha'Emek. I went with my two older sisters, who were schoolteachers. And during the break—you know how they used to have a break in the middle of screening these films, and they did this of course so we will all dash to the tiny internal cinema kiosk to buy drinks and falafel—and during this break, a young man came up to us, the educated sisters, and with the utmost reverence, he said that this film really touched him, that it spoke about 'people like us, who were giving our teachers hell and refusing to study.' The guy said, 'It's like here in Migdal Ha'Emek,' and I remember now with great shame how I rudely cut him off, saying something curt along the lines of 'It's not the same,' as if I was denying his very effort to compare himself to the reality depicted in an English film. It's been years since that brief incident, and I'm still deeply ashamed of myself and what I did at that moment."

Gila listens to me attentively, and then she connects our similar experiences to a widely known scene in a film by Moroccan filmmaker Hannah Azoulay-Hasfari. "Do you know that scene in *Shkhoor* when the kids sent to boarding school from a background similar to ours were humiliated by the Ashkenazi teacher? I really identified with that scene."

Gila tries to figure out which boarding school I was sent to. She assumes that I attended the well-known Jerusalem Boyer high school. I explain that the same educational association behind Boyer, the Society for Advancement of Education, had established another boarding school in Kfar Saba, in central Israel—my alma mater. "My brother went to Boyer," I tell her. "And my sister who was two years older than I stayed at home and attended the local Migdal Ha'Emek public secondary school." And then I reflect on the price paid by those who, like my sister, stayed in local second-rate schools.

"You know, when I think about it, she, my sister, completed her matriculation exams, despite the fact that the local school was by all accounts not as good as the school I attended . . . She could have entered university based on her grades, but she opted not to do that and went to a teachers' training college. I think that what the school at Kfar Saba gave me was the feeling that I *deserve* college education. Somehow, I never had doubts that once I am out of my army service, I will continue my education at the best university in Israel. My sister, on the other hand, never really internalized the idea that she 'deserves' to get an academic education. It took her years. I think she was in her thirties when she finally mustered the courage and began her bachelor's degree in special education at Haifa University. And I tell you confidently, she's every bit as talented and as hardworking as I am. She was stuck in a lower educational nonacademic rung because she was socialized to think that she does not deserve better. It's the low self-esteem anchored in a development town setting you spoke of earlier."

Leah, Gila's sister, who is listening in on our conversation, adds, "It's not just your confidence. It's the social stigma. It's society telling you that you're worthless because you come from a place like Yerucham. Take my daughter, for example. If you ask her where she is from, and she says she's from Sde Boker, people treat her completely differently to how they would treat her if she said she was from Yerucham. If you're from Yerucham, people immediately think that you're a *frecha*.[5] And once you are associated with such a place you need to prove you're not worthless."

Gila nods in agreement and says:

> When I was in boarding school, I hitchhiked to get home, and I suddenly realized that people would ask me where I was from for a reason: They wanted to "place" me socially. Only later, when I achieved some success in my life, was I able to proudly respond to such questions with "I'm from Yerucham" because now I have nothing to be afraid of. I'm a fact. I've established myself. It's not like a 14-year-old girl coming to the big city school with her straight A's from Yerucham only to be shocked that within two months her grades dropped to the C level. I recall my first shock in the boarding school when the teacher is talking, but you have no idea what is being said, because it's not your language, not your codes.
>
> And of course, my sister is so right about the stigmatization. It's still no great honor to say you are from Yerucham. It brands you. It's much nicer to even say you're from Dimona. [The sisters giggle loudly.] Even that! The best fun is to say, "I'm from Sde Boker." It rolls off one's tongue so beautifully.

Leah and Gila are clearly having a laugh. Leah says, "When you write a check with a Yerucham address on it, people give you this long look as if it's sure to bounce." I share their half-bitter laugh, telling them that "with everything we know about the stigma attached to Yerucham, I am still rather shocked when women from Yerucham tell me about applying for working-class positions as cleaners or supermarket cashiers in Be'er-Sheva and writing down on their application that they reside in Yerucham (only 20 minutes away by car), only to be systematically denied the job. Just like that. Not even an apology or an explanation for their rejection is offered." In response to my comment, Gila sobers up and adopts a "sociological/analytical" tone, discarding the emotional, personal introspective tone she has used thus far. She begins to talk about the social cost of internalizing the stigma that defines Yerucham's residents, and even those who work in Yerucham, as worthless. She says that the problem is not solely the creation of the "outside" world that stigmatizes the community and its people. The people of Yerucham, she asserts, also bring failure and lack of social development on themselves. Her prognosis for the future of the town is bleak. "Nothing, nothing will help here." I ask her to explain, on the basis of her own experience.

"Yerucham's Reality Cannot Be Changed"

Gila tries to explain. She is sorry, she says, but she is convinced that the problem does not lie only in a lack of resources, stigmatization, and so forth. She says that the failing educational system, for example, is not shaped solely by "external factors" but also by the attitude of local Yeruchami residents themselves.

"I told you earlier that I worked in Yerucham for two years after my army service. The truth is, I simply ran away from that post. Someone said to me, 'What are you going to do, working so hard here? Even if you become a principal? A school inspector? A mayor?' It's still only Yerucham. Whatever you achieve, it will never be valued. It's not like making it in the city. The people here don't know how to appreciate hard work. Whatever I did, no matter how hard I worked, I was put down, criticized, suspected for having too big of an ego. Look at my brother, who was a school principal, and look at what he's gone through. The parents were appalling, made his life a complete misery."

Gila sighs deeply.

> It's my hometown and all, but I tell you, one simply can't change life there. There's a core group of people there who just don't want to see you succeed. There's this feeling of "a prophet is not without honor except in his own town." Like, who do you think you are? Are you patronizing us? So people like me, born and bred in Yerucham who try to make it in this town, are always burned out and leave. Paradoxically, it's easier for people from outside the town. My brother is really gifted and so driven. And he ate dirt throughout his time as the school principal. He left and

continued his career elsewhere. I don't know how this negative process can be diverted. Once I thought that a good solution might be to go with the flow and rely on a good contingent of teachers and educators that will come from outside the community. But these people must be lured in with larger salaries and offered personal contracts. I believe it was tried but never in full force. In fact, there are serious tax breaks offered to people who are employed in Yerucham, but the local teachers never accepted that their salaries will be lower than the outsiders'. So the really good educators and administrators never came, and this is why Yerucham remains the way it is. This is why school graduates from Yerucham can't break out and really integrate in society.

"Is that what you think?" I ask gravely. "That the only hope to 'uplift' Yerucham should come from the outside? Intuitively and based on all my teaching about international development projects, this is never a good solution. I am surprised that you suggest this."

OK, OK. Listen, what I said is that it's a combination of factors. There are all these external limitations, of course, no proper budgets, remoteness, etc. What I was speaking about is the general atmosphere in the town. The overall feeling is that there's no support. It begins early on, long before you're grown up and try to live and work here. It begins with a supportive atmosphere in the family, at school, in the street, making the child feel he or she is expected to make something of their life, that they are expected to spread their wings, to grow. True, basic resources are essential. You need good nutrition, a proper shelter. But all this does not require that much money. All you need is a solid place that supports you and believes in your very right to spread your wings.

Look, compare the kids in Yerucham today to our kids here in Sde Boker, mine and yours. They speak and behave differently from the kids in Yerucham. It pains me deeply. These Yerucham kids are my own flesh and blood. Why do they fail so miserably in school? Why do they end up without proper skills and get jobs, if they even get jobs, in a local factory for minimum wages?

And then she refers to her own lapsed commitment to her hometown.

I know, I know. What right do I have to be saying this? After all, all of us have left. Only my elderly mother still lives there. But it still is my hometown. And I do care about what happens there deeply. I go there to visit my mom, but that's about it. I don't even go to the local market. If I go to the market, I go to the stall with the most expensive fruit. And then, I admit, my entire behavior is geared toward never being taken for one of the "natives." I won't ask for the price, because what do I care about the price? I'll demonstrate that I'm not looking for any favors or discounts. I don't need them. These poor people need them, not me. But again, I'm aware of my position vis-à-vis Sami the greengrocer when I tell him to pack for me a basket of fresh strawberries or exotic fruits like annona that other people don't buy, because they're so expensive. And after all that, I am appalled when he charges me 90-something shekels for just those few items. And it pains me to pay it, but I won't say anything. I won't even make the obvious comment about how high the prices are. This is the place where my way of treating Yerucham is embarrassing, where I like myself a lot less.

From her position of relative middle-class affluence, Gila struggles with a deeply contradictory attitude toward her hometown. She knows the grocer by name—she may even have taught his children—but she carries herself, in her own words, as an outsider who buys the most expensive fruit. Gila is painfully aware of and ridicules her own conflicted behavior. She is enmeshed in a love-hate relationship with Yerucham; she feels a sense of deep belonging to the place that was once her home but at the same time has grown away from and deliberately distanced herself from it. And still, her conflicted identity is deeply tied to this place.

"I Went through a Process"

In another recorded interview, Gila elaborates on the contradictory feelings she has toward her hometown.

I'm torn. On the face of it, I'm out. But I'm not really free, either. I see all these impoverished people when I come to visit my mom. And I can't stop thinking to myself, "Well, I made it." I hate being in this position. And I'm attuned to it. When I get out of my new car, it is as if I feel an old, not entirely healed scar itching, hurting. It's as if, just the way I move and act, I never stopped telling them, these poor people, "Look here, I made it, I run a school, I have a successful kid, I have a life, I have a career, I don't need anyone's help." It's pathetic, really. It's like I never completely freed myself from this ongoing conversation. And more than that, I begin to detect in my attitude the very patronizing perspective toward them that I had always despised when it was directed at me, the Moroccan girl from Yerucham.

Look, ostensibly, I moved on. For years, I would say, "I'm from Yerucham *originally*," but I always added that no one from the family lives there anymore. Today I can tell people that my mom still lives in Yerucham, and I say this confidently, without any need to apologize or explain. But on a deeper level, when I am candid, as I am now, I'm still not entirely at peace with it all. Take my attitude to the Moroccan language, for instance. For years I'd exclaim that I couldn't speak a word of Moroccan. And then, suddenly, it all came back to me. Today, there's not a Moroccan play out there that I haven't seen. And all of a sudden, I understand it all. And I can speak. Not fluently, but I can converse. My older sisters are amazed—"How do you know all these words?" Suddenly I tell jokes in Moroccan! It became a great source of joy. I knock everyone at family gatherings dead with my Moroccan jokes. And believe me, I never told jokes, in any language. It's as if a hidden block was removed, something that had effectively choked my joy at Moroccan culture, language, anything. And as you know well, Pnina, I've been organizing these elaborate Mimouna parties[6] at my house for the third time now, inviting all the neighbors. In Sde Boker, at the very center of Ashkenazi-hood!

So clearly, I went through a process. Before my wedding, I was scared of anything that so much as smelled Moroccan. I remember that my mom gave me this original, very elaborate Moroccan woven blanket as a wedding gift, and believe it or not, I simply gave it back! I didn't want *that* blanket in my house. I carried it back to her with undisguised contempt. What is this blanket? But, note this: I did insist on a *henna* ceremony, maybe just to spite my English in-laws. I could imagine how this proper English Jewish family would feel about all this "ethnic screaming." And I insisted on a small Moroccan all-female ceremony at the mikvah too.

"But you know, Gila, it seems that you speak about your Moroccan identity and your Yerucham identity as one and the same. Did you evolve, through that process you describe, on both these axes at the same time?"

"Well, as you well know, it's not easy to distinguish between these two. I didn't like the fact that I'm Moroccan, and I didn't like being from Yerucham. On both fronts I acted in denial, in obfuscation, and in shame. I feel more at ease with both parts of my identity now."

The growing ease with her origins that Gila displayed and articulated in these recorded interviews and during the many informal discussions we carried out over the years indexes her growing engagement with the issues that stand at the center of my research. She spoke often about her evolving self-acceptance, and she eagerly requested to see my written field notes. I was glad to share my notes with her. One evening, after reading about my encounters with Esti, Gila said that she was really intrigued by this woman I depict at such length in my notes and asked me if she could accompany me on my next visit to Yerucham so she could meet Esti in person. I was happy to have Gila join me and invited her one early Tuesday morning to accompany me on my usual market-day visit with Esti. What unfolded turned out to be an extremely complex ethnographic drama.

The Making of an Ethnographic Drama

I call Esti to let her know that this week my friend Gila will be joining us. She wastes no time making this news into a playful exchange. "Who's that? Gila? What Gila? I know not of anyone by that name. Is she another one of them Ashkenazi friends of yours? Who's this Gila?" I laugh at the rapid set of questions and assure her that "this Gila" is originally from Yerucham and is not the Ashkenazi woman Esti would make her out to be. I say that my friend Gila wants to meet her and that we will be picking her up from her flat on our way to the market. But Esti does not seem to want to let this new guest enter our usual routine easily. She keeps on inquiring who Gila is and who her family is only to conclude that she does not know this woman I claim is from Yerucham. She then relents by saying, "She wants to see me? . . . ha ha ha. She can come, sure, no problem." And so, on Tuesday, October 19, 2004, Gila, Esti, and I set out to spend a day at the Yerucham marketplace.

Gila plays it safe. She insists on driving her own car and meeting me in Yerucham, instead of riding from Sde Boker with me in my car. She says she needs her independence and might go to see her mother later, so she does not want to depend on me. She agrees, however, that we will take my car to Esti's place, and so she parks hers in the lot next to the bank. Esti opens the door with a toothbrush sticking out of her mouth, wearing crumpled shorts and an oversized T-shirt. It is clear that she has only just woken up. She offers Gila and me something to drink, and when we decline, she disappears into her bedroom, leaving us in the living room. The shutters are half-closed, and the house seems prettier and more thoughtfully arranged than I recall. I call out to Esti to express my impressions: "Hey Esti, your place is so pretty. What did you do to it? Changed anything? It's very nice. Is this picture new?" The little living room looks brighter and more elegant than I remember it, but Esti insists nothing has changed. "Maybe it's just clean," she guffaws self-deprecatingly—unjustly so, because the house is always spick-and-span.

Gila is reserved and takes no part in our loud, exuberant exchange. She closely examines a small faded painting on one of the walls and says to me that she recognizes the woman in the picture; it's Esti's mother. "She worked in the Sde Boker kitchen for years," Gila says, and then, raising her voice for Esti's benefit, she comments, "Your mother was a beautiful woman. Always elegant. I remember her." Esti does not react to this comment.

Despite our protestations, Esti goes into the kitchen to make us coffee. I follow her there, leaving Gila in the living room. Esti uses this opportunity to ask me in a whisper, "She a teacher, this Gila?" I suggest that she ask Gila directly. But when we return to the living room, Esti ignores Gila. Instead, she launches into her usual laughs and banter. She presents me with a flashy shirt and insists that I try it on because she wants to give it to me. I can see the game Esti is playing, making me into a candidate for her hand-me-downs. But I am happy to go along. I stand in front of the mirror in the narrow hallway and try on the shirt, which is two sizes too small. I look ridiculous, as the shirt squeezes my breasts and reveals my belly. I laugh and tell Gila and Esti that I never wear clothes that are really tight or revealing because my Ashkenazi boyfriend already thinks that I dress too provocatively. Esti leaps at the chance to laugh about my boyfriend "who probably wears trousers up to here," indicating her chin. We laugh. Gila looks at me embarrassed, but I continue talking about my boyfriend. I tell them about using some of Esti's language on him. The other night, I relate, as we stood in front of the box office at a movie theater, I asked him, using Esti's lingo, if he "releases" (the Hebrew word is *le'shakhrer*, which means both "to release" in a monetary sense—to release funds or to be generous—and to allow one freedom, that is, not be possessive). I recall the shock on his face, until I made it clear that the expression was drawn from my "fieldwork" life.

"Come on, you ain't serious," Esti says. "What's a ticket? That's nothin'! That's what you call 'releasing'?" And then she adds, "These men . . . I ain't gonna even start talking to a guy who wants to take me out before he puts a hundred, two hundred shekels up front." Gila shoots me a quick look that says she is a bit shocked. She coughs in an embarrassed chuckle. I notice that Esti is shooting her usual string of witticisms at a rapid, somewhat overwhelming speed. Her manner is worked up a bit, not relaxed. She stands very close to me, and whenever she cracks a new joke, we share a light affectionate touch. She eyes Gila but never looks at her directly or addresses her in any way. After I try on the shirt and we drink the coffee, Esti puts the final touches on her look: Her hair is nicely combed, and she perks up her outfit with high-heel shoes. Gila generously compliments Esti's appearance. She asks whether she has her hair done at Debby's or at Jacqueline's. A direct conversation ensues between the two as they debate the relative merits of the two main hairdressers in Yerucham. Esti turns her attention back to me and makes her usual comments about my uninspiring hair. "You have to put in some highlights," she says. "That black really doesn't do you any good. Some highlights oughta bring some light to your face." Gila smiles but does not comment on my hair.

I can see that Gila is making a real effort to be pleasant. She asks Esti if she knows this woman or that man, placing herself and Esti in the same familiar local social networks. She then declares that even though she does not really remember Esti, she remembers her elder sisters well. "Who was your teacher in school?" Gila asks. Esti states she does not remember the teacher or the principal all that well, because she "didn't really study after sixth grade." When Gila presses on, Esti declares with her usual flair, "The teachers, the principal, they were all fine. It's me that was wild and wouldn't study none."

I find myself trying to defend Esti, who cannot and does not wish to respond to Gila's inquiries. I mention that Esti dropped out of school because she was looking after her sick mother. But Esti cuts the conversation off, announcing that we need to head for the market now, before it is too late and everyone goes home. We walk out of the apartment building. My car is the only vehicle parked on the road. I take the driver's seat and invite Esti and Gila to get in. There is a brief moment of hesitation: Who should take the front seat, next to me, and who should sit in the back? I sit there in silence, awaiting their decision. Esti takes the front seat. It is a statement, no doubt: Esti claims her right to the more prestigious seat and leaves Gila, "the teacher," to sit in the back.

Throughout that day Esti repeatedly shows Gila, "the teacher," her power. She places Gila in the category of people who always wanted to "improve" her, to "help" her, those who made her feel like she was a failure. When she refuses to name her teacher, stating provocatively that "the teachers ... were all fine. It's me that was wild and wouldn't study none," Esti rejects the framework in which Gila has been, perhaps unwittingly, trying to place her. By making herself the wild one, Esti displays her alternative base of strength and her ability to define her own life. She rejects my meek attempt to explain her failure in the education system, to justify her dropping out of school as a response to her mother's illness and death. Esti accepts pity from no one.

Throughout the day, Esti plays up her wild, boundary-crossing persona to an extreme. She uses me unhesitatingly, knowing that in me she will find a supportive audience. And she is right—I find her wild act inspiring. When she makes me look ridiculous by insisting that I try on her clothes in front of the mirror, Esti announces her power over me. She knows full well that I earn more than she does and that I can buy my own clothes. But this little game, in which I am happy to take part, declares that Esti has wonderful clothes she no longer needs and that I occupy an inferior position, however fragile and fleeting, as a person who would like to receive her secondhand clothes. When she sits next to me in the front seat of the car, Esti declares her privileged position loud and clear. The relegation of Gila to the back seat is repeated metaphorically throughout the day.

At the Yerucham Market: "Full Speed in Reverse"

It takes a few minutes to reach the marketplace. The normally empty lot behind the commercial center fills up on market day, and it is difficult to find a parking spot. The colorful weekly market takes place every Tuesday. All around the small plaza are stalls loaded with fresh produce, cheap clothing, and other items (usually made in China) spread out on the ground. After some hard maneuvering between makeshift stalls and trucks unloading goods, I manage to park. Esti shoots out of the car, exclaiming, "Wai wai wai . . . Lots of people today, not like last week. It was dead then." Gila takes her time joining me. Esti is already way ahead, weaving in and out of the crowd. I have learned not to expect Esti to wait for me. We have been to market days often, and we have developed a familiar routine. Esti walks a few steps ahead of me, and I stay close enough to listen to her loud exchanges with the vendors, but I am not part of the conversations.

Esti's joy at meeting people is palpable. I think of a female version of the protagonist of the Israeli film *Kazablan*, which depicts a Moroccan youth, a leader in the neighborhood. She moves with confidence, and her delight in the scene is contagious. She never introduces me to the people she hugs and exchanges long, warm greetings with, but it is obvious that they notice me and that my presence elevates her status. I enjoy tagging along, being part of Esti's celebration of her social connections, listening to her comments. When Esti bolts out of the car and begins her foray into the market this time, she does so knowing that Gila is part of our small party. For a long while, I walk with Gila a few steps behind Esti, witnessing Esti's performance, stopping to buy a small basket of fresh strawberries. But Gila soon has enough of this. She mumbles that she needs to get something for her mother available in another part of the market, and before I can react, she leaves our small procession, promising to join me later.

I stay with Esti. I play my assigned role. Esti, I know well, does not come here to shop. She comes to socialize and to celebrate the many friends who enjoy her witticisms.

"Hey, Esti. Wassup? How'ya doing? How's it going?" they ask with big smiles. And Esti, never missing a beat, replies, "Hey, not bad, not bad, y'know, going forward in reverse." Or, "Sure everything's moving along but the damn brake's on." Each time she repeats these phrases, she is rewarded with a burst of warm laughter, as though the listener, ever so familiar with her twists of phrase, still eagerly anticipates them. Esti's interlocutors peek at me. Some repeat, in a tone reserved for privileged outsiders like me, "No, seriously, Esti, did you find work?" and others say, "No, man, there's no work here. It's tough going." But Esti refuses to cooperate with this joyless narrative flung in the face of outsiders and maintains her carnivalesque tone: "Who? Me? Work? Like, for real? Since when did I ever work that they'd give me some now?" and then she engages in a bit of Hebrew wordplay, pronouncing the word *karagil*, meaning "as usual" or "as always," as *kharagil*, a reference to *khara*, an Arabic-derived word for "shit," her own creative rendition of the sentiment "same shit, different day." Her listeners show their joy at her playful, dirty talk by laughing out loud before throwing me a quick apprehensive and embarrassed glance.

Esti's market-day banter is all very familiar to me by now. I wonder where Gila has gone. I can still feel her resentment at being part of Esti's entourage.

"Are You Rabbi Baruch's Daughter?"

And then Gila is back. She is holding two bags of fresh produce. She declares that she has done her shopping for the day and inquires about my plans. I decide to spend some time with her, calling out to Esti that I will see her later. Esti nods briefly and goes off in a different direction. During our short walk back through the market and toward the parking lot, several vendors look at Gila and me inquisitively. We are clearly not part of the usual crowd. But then one bearded man in his fifties, his head covered with a large black *kippah* examines Gila closely and exclaims, "Hold on, don't I know you?" Gila smiles bravely and stops to make conversation with the vendor, who says with great reverence: "You're Rabbi Baruch's daughter, aren't you?" Gila confirms his recognition of her, saying pleasantly, "Yes, I am the youngest. You knew my dad, God bless his soul."

We stop next at a stall selling trinket jewelry. "Every item for 10 shekels only," the heavyset vendor informs me, noticing my interest. Gila looks at the jewelry and says, "Pnina, what's wrong with you, this is really a waste of time." She insists that the items on sale are worthless and will disintegrate after the first use. I argue back that one can find good deals if one looks hard enough and that a necklace I once bought here was really nice and elicited many compliments. Next to the jewelry stall is an open space, shaded by a large canvas.

Colorful tracksuits, glitter-covered denim for 50 shekels, and cotton dresses hang from large, round carousels. We examine the clothes briefly and move on to Hanna's fruit stall. Hanna knows me from my frequent visits to the market and greets me warmly. I compliment her on her long hair and the fact that she is slimmer since the last time I saw her. Hanna asks where "your friend, the little funny one," is, and I say she is around. But our pleasant small talk is drowned out by the bellowing of a man with a face swollen by alcohol and disease, advertising Hanna's goods. "Ladies and gents, price is down, just a shekel, just a shekel." "Does he work for you?" I ask Hanna, as I have not seen her employ any help in her stall before. "Not really, he just attaches himself to me," she says pleasantly. It is clear that the man is a wreck and that she is generously allowing him to earn a few shekels and maybe a few free pieces of fruit from the stall in exchange for his "help."

It is hot. We reach the end of the line of stalls. A large truck is parked there, its back open toward the market displaying a variety of herbs—bunches of parsley, coriander, fresh mint. I want to sit for a moment and rest, and the vendor, a heavyset man with a skullcap, offers me an overturned crate as a seat. As he is also offering me one of his cigarettes, Esti appears and briefly jokes with the man, whom she knows, of course. The man realizes that Esti is my friend, and he asks her if I am "available for a ride" (i.e., unattached). "Yeah, sure," Esti says with great relish. "She's as available as it gets." Gila sits down and watches the scene with disbelief. "You're not from around here?" the man asks politely, serving me a slice of the grapefruit that he has just peeled for me. I begin to respond that I live in the Midrasha (I never say Sde Boker when asked in Yerucham about my place of residence). But Esti jumps in: "I tell you, she's my friend. She's *not* a teacher." The man looks at Gila and offers her a slice of his fruit. "You were a teacher here, I recognize you," he says. Gila smiles, abashed.

"Sure, don't you know me? I'm Aboutboul's daughter."

"Oh man, I didn't recognize you," the man says. He uses the Hebrew word *zihiti*, which literally means "I identified you," in a grammatically incorrect manner common among lower-class Mizrahim, saying *ziheti otekh* (instead of the proper *zihiti otakh*). Gila and I exchange a quick look at his grammatical mistakes. Gila declines the grapefruit. "No thank you, we must be leaving," she announces, and gets up to leave. I follow her. Esti watches us and declares she will join us later.

Gila and I are silent as we walk toward our cars. It is hot and we are both rather tired. But before we reach the parking lot, we are stopped by a man who has been trailing us for the last few minutes. His red swollen face and sloppy appearance suggest that he wants to beg some money, so I have tried to ignore him. The man then blocks our path, calling out to Gila, "Aboutboul, yo. I know ya. Gimme something. I need a cigarette. Give us a coin or two." Gila is livid. She tries to ignore the man, but he continues his loud pleading, insisting that he knows her and addressing her directly. Eventually she opens her wallet and gives him a coin, and he disappears without a word of thanks. Just before we are about to pull away, Esti materializes again. "What? Already leaving? Wait! I need to pop into the bank for a moment." Gila and I look at each other and decide to follow Esti to the bank.

"Al Ha Panim: My Situation Is Really Shit"

At the local branch of Bank Hapoalim, the only bank in Yerucham, there is always a crowd of people waiting in long lines in front of the few teller windows. Gila and I sit on chairs facing one of the windows, and Esti walks briskly toward the bank clerk, who watches her approach with tired eyes. We listen in, feeling like a captive audience for an impending drama. Esti speaks loudly. We hear her ask the clerk to authorize an over-the-limit withdrawal from her account. "I need only 200 shekels . . . no big deal, yalla [Hebrew slang, from the Arabic 'come on'] just put a little signature here and I go." The teller is familiar with the script and evidently knows Esti well. He says in a quiet tone, "Listen, sweetheart, no way. You know the state your account is in. I simply cannot do this." But Esti, expecting this rejection, escalates with "OK, OK, you can't. Maybe the branch manager will let you?" Then she has another try at pleading with the clerk, "I really, really gotta have this money. There's a wedding tomorrow and . . . you know what? Gimme a hundred shekels. Okay? Just a hundred. They'll let you authorize a piddling hundred shekels, right?"

Gila and I watch the exchange from our comfortable seats in silence. It is clear that both Esti and the clerk are aware of our presence and that they are acting out a familiar scene. This is not the first time I have watched Esti request special permission to overdraw her account. And she is not the only one who does this. Most people waiting in line will engage in the same scenario. The ATM located outside the branch is seldom used, as it allows withdrawals only from one's available balance. People need special, personalized approval from a bank clerk to withdraw beyond their credit limit.

The scene is a painful one for me to watch. Several times, when I have accompanied Esti to the bank and watched her plead for cash, I have felt the urge to just take the desired sum out of my pocket and hand it over to her. But at this point, I know that Esti must have her way. Gila's presence seems to make the scene more unwieldy. Gila sits frozen in her seat next to me, avoiding any eye contact. And Esti? She seems joyful, unfazed by the predictable refusal of the clerk. She walks toward us, flashing a huge smile and declares, as though to rub it in, "Eventually he'll give me a 50. He'll get the authorization. No problem." And then she adds teasingly, "I'm gonna put that 50 on the *mispar nosaf* today because, me, my situation is really *al ha panim* [Hebrew slang for 'really bad,' literally 'on its face']. Maybe I'll get something out of this bet today."

When Esti returns to the teller, I turn to Gila and explain in a hushed tone that I have been in this situation so many times before and that this is just how Esti's life is. There is nothing Esti or I can do about it. If Esti gets the money, she will use it for her gambling or her shopping sprees. I can feel Gila's horror. She stares at me, speechless.

I feel that Esti has stepped up her usual performance as part of her reaction to Gila's presence. Instead of concealing her financial difficulties and trying to get the money she needs with the least possible fanfare, Esti seems to be waving her situation before our eyes. She is enjoying the fact that the two of us, women who evidently do not need anyone's permission to withdraw money from their bank accounts, are her audience that day. I am painfully aware of Esti's game and that she is brandishing her subversive power to shock Gila. I am not going to interfere in her game. I make sure to clear the stage for her.

As I see it, Esti's performance is an intentional raucous act of crossing discursive boundaries for dealing with acute material want. She throws the fact that she is penniless in Gila's and my complacent, confident bourgeois faces. She is not going to lower her eyes and pretend to be a docile subject. Her bawdy behavior is intended to shock us, and she pushes it to excess, by insisting that she is not trying to wrench money for necessities but for her gambling. By insisting that the money is for gambling, Esti turns the tables on what could mark her as a needy, weak, disadvantaged subject. Esti's show makes a mockery of our judgmental, middle-class world.

Esti plays the bad girl to the finest detail. When the clerk insists that he needs the bank manager's authorization for even a 100-shekel withdrawal, Esti joins us only to insist: "Let him go . . . I know I will get my money in the end. They always do this. I know them all. This [branch] manager never says no to me . . . my bookie is waiting . . . this time it's a good omen." Brandishing her wild, unconventional behavior, Esti celebrates her way of life, her social connections, her wit, and clearly, on this particular day, her open defiance of the value system of teachers and social workers who call on her to mend her ways. Esti refuses to lead her life according to terms set by judgmental outsiders like us; she holds on to her own reading, her own subversive plot.

When we walk out of the bank, Esti's bawdy performance continues. She declares that she is going to have a chat with the shop owner next door. "I owe her a lot of money," she says gleefully. And without any prompting from either Gila or me, she adds, in a somewhat reflexive, sociological-analytical manner, "Of course I have no money to pay back my debt. I am going to calm her down like, 'cause she needs to see me every so often when I owe her and don't pay her."

At this point, Gila decides to make her farewells. She turns to Esti and says the brief polite "it was nice to meet you." She announces she must see her mother, and we agree to meet shortly at the bus stop on the main road so I can drive her back to her car. I follow Esti to the trinkets shop, which she enters with a great fanfare of kisses and exuberant talk about the good old days when she and the shop owner worked together as cleaners at the Ramon Air Force Base. Throughout our brief stay in the shop, not a single word is said about Esti's debt. The purpose of this visit, just as Esti had announced, is to solidify the mutual trust she has with her creditor. The long banter about their shared history of cleaning work reflects personal connections based on mutual respect and a common humanity and seems to reassure the shop owner that Esti is trustworthy and that her (unmentioned) debt is secure.

Toward 3 p.m. I finally drive Esti back home. On the short ride, Esti comments calmly, "That Gila, she was always so frigid . . . like . . . never laughs . . . kind of a mean woman you might say. I never saw her say hello to anyone. Her whole family, I know them, they're all like that, with their noses up . . . But, Pnina, I tell you, today she's, like, so nice all of a sudden. I dunno what happened to her."

I rush back to meet Gila. She is sitting on a bench at the empty bus stop on the main road at the edge of the town. I apologize for making her wait, and she reassures me that she hasn't been there long. She has spent time with her mother, she says, and has just arrived at the bus stop. There is a long silence between us. Then Gila says, "You probably felt it, Pnina . . . but this has been a really difficult experience for me," and before I can ask what she means, she hastens to say that she cannot really talk about it now. She invites me to come for a cup of coffee later that night at her house, where we will talk about "this whole day."

Anthropologists, Subjects, and Departed Village Girls

I make my way over to Gila's later that evening, crossing the narrow road linking my neighborhood to hers. Walking along the narrow, shaded footpaths crisscrossing well-kept lawns and gardens, I stride between children's bicycles and toys left on lawns unattended, "like in the old days on the kibbutz." It's true, I think to myself: living in a community that unequivocally respects private property does inspire a sense of well-being.

I use the short walk to Gila's to organize my thoughts and process some of the complex experiences we shared that morning in Yerucham. I had written extensive notes detailing what had transpired as soon as I returned to my office earlier that day. My notes suggest that a drama has taken place, an ethnographic drama with three key players: Esti, Gila, and me. I tinker with an outline for analyzing the many scenes of that drama. In my notes I reflect on my role throughout the day as "the anthropologist," the one who participates but also observes from the sidelines. My role entails what I call, with a deep sense of self-cynicism, a "Teflon experience"; that is, I participate but I am never rendered deeply vulnerable. I write that Gila's position is more complex.

Having initiated the event after reading my notes about Esti, she enters the scene, at least at first, in the role of an observer. But delving back into the local market and being exposed to Esti's bawdy behavior, Gila is thrown again and again into another position, that of native girl, the daughter of Rabbi About-boul. Esti, the third participant in the drama we perform, is no passive player in the company of two articulate women with greater cultural and material capital. Quite the contrary: she carves out a central and active role for herself as lead actor, operating on her own terms and directing Gila and me in our supporting roles throughout our encounter. In my notes I make the following observations about Esti:

> Her "*Kazablan*-like" strut along the market, which I have seen on many previous occasions, was today infused with new ceremony and prowess. Esti was the driving force throughout, and Gila and I were her captive audience. All Gila could do to get away from Esti's power was to occasionally retire from the stage dominated by Esti; but she returned to the stage again and again. Gila was shorn of her established higher status vis-à-vis a girl who was not even a proper student in Gila's dominant domain, I mused, because of Esti's relationship with me. And so, the stroll across the local marketplace was a site for ongoing celebration for Esti and a tormented, painful experience for Gila.

Esti achieves her final victory during the short ride to her home at the end of that eventful day. She speaks of Gila and her family as people who snubbed her all her life and delights in, as she sees it, having put Gila in her place, at least on that day. In Esti's fragile value system, where dignity is based on warm, personal, and supportive relationships with others, Gila is dubbed a "mean woman," someone who does not greet other people on the street. Throughout the day Esti renders Gila a captive observer of her strength, a strength based on connections, intimacy, and humor. Esti's social power posits Gila's "aloofness" as hollow by comparison. Esti is making a life for herself in Yerucham, and she proudly flaunts her social connections. Whereas Esti says hello to everyone, Gila bristles at the mention of her family name.

Walking toward Gila's place that evening and mulling over my recorded observations and analysis, I realize that I have focused entirely on Esti's perspective, on her needs, on her triumph. Esti's actions and her open observations supported and corroborated my interpretive framework. But I am not quite sure about Gila. She said so little throughout the day. I resolve to listen to Gila tonight and have her speak about why she found the experience so difficult. What did she think about Esti? How does she interpret the morning's drama?

And then I wonder, what about my place in this drama? Was I being manipulative? Did I put people in unpleasant situations for the sake of my research? I walk toward Gila's place with a nagging sense of self-doubt about my own performance. To calm down, I remind myself that it was Gila who asked to meet with Esti, that I did not invite her to do so, and that I made all my notes and interpretations available to her. I did not lure her into this difficult experience. She was an ally and a friend, not an object of observation.

And still, I am acutely conscious that Gila has gone through an excruciating experience and that her deep discomfort with it is significantly greater than mine. I recall her silence, her inability to fit in during the protracted situations at the market and the bank. Her conspicuous vulnerability forces me to confront my own relative imperviousness to the same situations. When I examine my behavior at Esti's flat, at the market, and at the bank and when I compare it to Gila's obvious unease, I come to question my comfortable role as the anthropologist: observing, accepting, nonjudgmental. Despite all my claims to being, like Gila, a Mizrahi woman from a development town, my positioning is much easier and much less emotionally taxing than hers.

Thus, for example, I do not perceive the courtship by the parsley vendor as an act that might have real consequences. Although I am, in Esti's terms, available—that is, an unmarried woman of the right age—my amicable, ostensibly welcoming behavior signals, above all, the futility of the market man's advances toward me, the university lecturer, a woman who for him is out of bounds. The ease with which I accept his cigarette and sit down on the overturned vegetable crate by his truck and my open, easy friendliness stem from the clear and unambiguous knowledge (which Gila and maybe Esti share, though the generous parsley vendor himself may not) that I am not really available to his courtship, that my social position is not compromised by a fleeting marketplace flirtation. This unshakable awareness of my class positioning offsets all the other lines connecting me to my naive would-be suitor. Gila's position is less solid, more fluid in that scene. Being addressed as Aboutboul and recognized as Rabbi Baruch's daughter put her back in a space of belonging that she has long sought to leave behind.

"This Uneasy, Complicated Day"

When I enter her immaculate little house in Sde Boker, Gila serves coffee but makes little small talk. She is evidently emotionally stirred up. "Pnina, I understand that you, somehow, as a professional, portray 'this Esti' as something special . . . what did you call her in your notes? A rebel? But I have to tell you, after watching her this whole day, I really wasn't impressed with her, to put it mildly."

"I'll tell you straight," she continues. "After I read your notes about this girl, I was genuinely curious to come with you to Yerucham. I didn't remember who she was. But after this uneasy, complicated day, I have to tell you that she's just . . . a bum! And she . . . she . . . she is everything my mom raised us *not* to be. I'm sorry, but I didn't see any of that . . . what did you write . . . her 'subversiveness'? I didn't see anything 'glamorous' about her. She's just a failure. And she brags about it!"

I am taken back. I can see how shaken Gila is. "You said in the car, on our way back, that this was a very difficult experience for you. What was so difficult about it, Gila? Can you explain?" I ask.

"Definitely. Definitely. Yes. How to begin? Well, look: That stroll through the market . . . stopping at every stall . . . I don't remember the last time I did that. I told you, my rare appearance in the Yerucham market was—how did I describe it?—in the manner of the ultimate Ashkenazi. You know, doing what I had to do as quickly as possible, not spending a minute more than absolutely necessary, buying only the most expensive fruit. And today, this walking from stall to stall . . . And that man: 'Aboutboul, gimme a shekel!' That absolutely killed me. You clearly don't know this man, Pnina. But I . . . well, I knew him well. He was in my brother's class. I remember him as a healthy, handsome youth. And now . . . just look at him now, he's a junkie and a wreck. And seeing him like this was so painful. I don't know . . . this entire day wasn't simple, wasn't easy for me. Maybe to you all this is 'anthropology.' I'm not criticizing you. But for me it was hard. Really, truly difficult."

I listen to Gila quietly. I had suspected that the encounters with people in Yerucham's marketplace and the slow, protracted walk in Esti's footsteps were not easy for her. But Gila is revealing an angle here that I had not considered. She knows the people we encountered today not merely as players in an "ethnographic present" but through their full, complex personal histories. I have invited Gila to give her interpretation of the scene, and she reveals an agony stemming not from the present but from the sad process of decline and impoverishment of people she grew up with. For her, the drug addict who demanded a shekel is not a colorful extra in what I have been considering an ethnographic drama. Gila's unease is not limited to the fact that the man marked her as a local woman, calling her by her maiden name, a name that she openly admits she despises because of its stigmatic association with the community she has worked so hard to escape. Gila's horror speaks to a collective and personal process of deterioration, of a history of humiliation experienced by people who, unlike her, are trapped in Yerucham—to become market vendors at best or impoverished drug addicts at worst. Gila remembers Sami, the greengrocer who packs the expensive produce she buys during her occasional appearances in the market, as a young man in her brother's class, and she notes that she also knows him as the parent of a student when she taught school in Yerucham. I can relate to Sami only as a vendor. I cannot share Gila's perspective.

When I listen to Gila that evening, I realize that her engagement in my project both as a reader of texts and as a subject who enters the ethnographic scene to meet with other interlocutors is not a simple matter for her but rather a complex, nuanced, and at times excruciating experience. Trailing Esti on a market morning and facing familiar people whom she has avoided meeting or thinking about for many years, Gila is confronted with the contradictions of her life in ways she has tried hard to ignore. We both realize that our academic or intellectual conversations over the years have not prepared her for the whirlpool of emotions and conflicting identities and spaces that such a day evokes.

Gila never again offers to join me in Yerucham. But she clearly has taken the lessons of that day to heart. Gila now not only speaks about her Moroccan identity and her Yerucham roots but she also acts on them in new ways. She seems to have developed a greater acceptance of her Moroccan heritage. For the third year in a row, she has hosted the "Ashkenazi professors" of Sde Boker for Mimouna celebrations at her house. Gila's parties are held on her front lawn, where long tables offer not only typical Moroccan sweets but also little handwritten signs explaining the cultural meaning of each food item. Gila is out to educate the Ashkenazi professors about the significance of her Moroccan Jewish heritage. We speak often about her coming to terms with and reclaiming her formerly hidden and despised roots. She tells me with glee that she has recently discovered that she understands a good amount of Moroccan, the language she claimed for years that she did not know. She speaks about her ability to tell jokes in Moroccan at family gatherings, to the open amazement of her siblings.

Gila's process of self-acceptance is not unique, nor did it emerge in a social vacuum. In recent years a more accepting Israeli public discourse has emerged around Mizrahi culture, and Mizrahi music has made it into the mainstream. Gila knows of my own wider social activism. I share with Gila my published work, in which I explore Mizrahi-focused social critique of Israeli mainstream scholarship.[7] Her growing acceptance of her Mizrahi roots, however, does not cancel out another critical lesson that emerges from Gila's story—her inability to build a life as a middle-class person in her own hometown. Gila is a representative of what in policy-making discourse is known as a "strong population," and her inability to reconnect to her hometown speaks of a larger social phenomenon: internal brain drain—the inability of peripheral, underdeveloped towns to retain those who would make their populations "strong."

Those Who Succeed and Those Who Are Left Behind

A study released in 2006 by the Bank of Israel puts Gila's story in wider context. The study focuses on what authors Kobi Braude and Guy Navon (2006) describe as trends in "internal migration" within Israel's Jewish population. Alongside suburbanization, which sees "strong populations," that is, better-educated and skilled people, leaving the city centers of Jerusalem, Tel Aviv, and Haifa in favor of suburban communities, Braude and Navon document a parallel, nationwide "weakening of development towns." Despite official policies designed to attract people into development towns, Braude and Navon record a 17% decline in the population of these towns from 1983 to 1995.[8] This decline is particularly significant when we learn that those who departed were better educated and of higher socioeconomic status than those who remained. The total population of Yerucham in 2004 stood at 8,700 residents (Local Authorities in Israel 2004: 474–76). Data from that year show that the town lost 419 residents to emigration and gained only 267 new ones, despite concerted efforts to increase the local population by resettling new arrivals from the former Soviet Union there by providing them with special financial support packages. Throughout my fieldwork in Yerucham, my interlocutors made it clear that people with a solid education or marketable job skills do not stay.

This nationwide exodus from Israeli development towns is described as a "polarization" of the Jewish population, with economically strong populations clustering in the center and older, less educated, dependent populations in the periphery. The debilitating impact of this emigration, Braude and Navon stress, "is qualitative, not merely quantitative" (2006: 26). Not only do development towns suffer a net loss of population through emigration but they also lose the most prosperous members of their communities. The literature suggests that there is a close link between the characteristics of a town (such as size and geographic isolation) and the scope of out-migration. The smaller and more remote a town, the greater the likelihood that people with the resources to leave will do so (Alfandari and Sheffer 1992; Khazzoom 2002). Government efforts to stem the outflow over the years have focused, somewhat half-heartedly, on "encouraging" professional people to move into these towns by defining them as national "priority areas," offering those who move there tax breaks, affordable housing, and investment incentives. These policies have had limited success. As Gila suggests in her narrative, the investment incentives and tax breaks that have brought in outsiders are resented by local professionals who no longer feel welcome in their own communities. Moreover, studies show that people who hold skilled and senior positions in development towns opt not to live in those towns (Alfandari and Sheffer 1992), put off by their isolation, negative social image, and limited public services. Meanwhile, research has seldom focused on the perspective of the people who leave. Gila's narrative is an entry point into such a perspective.

Gila's story raises important questions about key issues germane to the process of development-town brain drain. It speaks to the complex experience of people who manage to pull themselves up by their own bootstraps and are made to leave their native town rather than stay and contribute to its betterment. One of the key effects of this brain drain is the negative image peripheral communities acquire. Gila and her sister Leah speak about the shame of being associated with Yerucham. Gila describes how she understood, with the keen social instincts of a 14-year-old, that her reputation in Ein Kerem would suffer if she disclosed that she was from Yerucham. It is this shame, and not a lack of employment opportunities or a failing educational system, that seems to be most salient for the people I spoke with in Yerucham. Recall my interview with young Adi, Nurit's daughter (see chapter 1). Adi speaks about her friends who have moved to Tel Aviv as "success stories." Their success does not hinge on any concrete economic or professional gains they may have made but simply on their ability to escape the trap of living in Yerucham. Gila takes this view a step further when she depicts how her local accomplishments are ridiculed and diminished because they occur in the context of a peripheral community.

And there is a deeper level still to Gila's story, one that reveals, for those who leave, a legacy of self-doubt and, for those who remain behind, hopelessness in the face of institutionalized dead-ends. Can this two-pronged destructiveness be overcome? As we have seen, Gila's efforts to hide from her complex class and ethnic background produce only a sense of self-defeat and pain. The cultural humiliation and self-denial that she suffers raises critical questions about the price paid more generally by Mizrahi sons and daughters in development towns who manage to break out of their concerete boxes and make their way into hegemonic cultural centers. It also raises poignant questions about the meaning of success.

Conclusion

IN HIS BOOK *Dreams from My Father* (1995), former president Barack Obama recounts his work as a community organizer in a poor area of Chicago. In his recollections, he makes several perceptive observations that would serve an ethnographer well. Obama goes from house to house in African American neighborhoods and listens to the stories of the residents. He attends their church services, dances with them at their Christmas parties, talks sports with the men whose wives become community leaders, and helps their children fill out their college applications.

Throughout this period Obama does not interview his subjects; rather, as he puts it, he "swaps stories" with them. He tells them about his African father, who left his white mother in Hawaii and went back to Kenya when his son was only two years old. He tells them about being raised by his white grandparents and about his life with his mother in Jakarta, after she married an Indonesian man. People smile and shrug, wondering why someone who could be sunbathing on a Hawaiian beach has chosen, of his own free will, to settle in windy, cold Chicago. But then, Obama writes, they tell him stories of their own, tying their seemingly disparate experiences to his with a frail common thread.

After listening to a great many personal stories, Obama observes that "beneath the small talk and sketchy biographies, . . . people carried within them some central explanation of themselves" (1995: 183). These explanations, he notes, transcend the particular details that compose the bulk of their stories. They instill meaning in the lives of those who tell them and embed their actions within constructive frames of meaning.

Like Obama in Chicago, I find the partial, fragile stories that people in Yerucham have shared with me over the years full of beauty and poetry, humanity, and strength but also of significant social insights that go beyond the ephemeral details of the everyday lives they describe. Their stories do more than feed the interest of a persistent interviewer or a well-meaning ethnographer. Like Obama, I am convinced that the stories people tell are "explanations of themselves," with the power to motivate action and shape lives.

French sociologist Pierre Bourdieu (1993) makes a similar observation when he notes that people engage in forms of "self-analysis" in recounting their subjective narratives. Bourdieu goes further than Obama, proposing that such self-analysis makes people grapple with the contradictions in their lives in fundamental ways. He contends that some people, more than others in their community, are particularly attuned to the meanings not only of their own individual life stories but also of the larger reality they live. These people are "practical analysts" (Bourdieu 1999: 511) who offer insights into the social forces that structure their everyday world.

In many ways, my five key interlocutors fit the role of practical analyst or "spontaneous sociologist" described by Bourdieu. The women I selected (and who, no less, selected me) offer rich, textured accounts of fashioning a life in a reality of multiple marginalizations, my metaphorical concrete box; each is uniquely disposed to develop insights into the larger forces that affect her life. I chose these five women, as I explain in the introduction to this book, because they arguably embody five distinct paths for dealing with life on the margins.

I have been deeply influenced in my work by feminist scholar Patricia Hill-Collins's (1990, 2005) contention that disempowered women's self-knowledge should be integrated into social research. Hill-Collins claims that knowledge produced by underprivileged women bereft of social power is no less legitimate than academic or hegemonic forms of knowledge produced for and consumed by elites. Following Hill-Collins, I have tried to treat the women whose lives I have documented not as predefined entities who constitute objects of research but as subjects, as knowledge-producing agents. Yet considering this self-knowledge as a "hidden transcript" deliberately concealed from the powerful (Scott 1990) is only a first step in the analysis I offer. My challenge has been to develop my own capacity to listen to my interlocutors' accounts and enable them to produce these narratives on their own terms. The analysis I present in *Concrete Boxes* is predicated, therefore, on a distinction between the "knowing subject" and the notion of the "known subject" (Vasilachis de Gialdino 2006: 473). In other words, I believe that the stories presented in this book are worthwhile not just because they are fascinating or colorful but precisely because they have interpretive autonomy that should be attended to and given center stage.

Unlike proponents of realist writing, who present life stories as original, untarnished truths disclosed by "authentic" research subjects, I consider such narratives to be the negotiated outcomes of the relationship between the ethnographer and the subjects of her research. To borrow Ruth Behar's apt phrase, "It is in translation that women find out who they are" (1993: 276).

Recall, for example, the scene depicted in chapter 1 in which Nurit actively constructs her life story during the course of our recorded session. She does not simply produce a ready-made narrative upon request. Instead, her narrative is an outcome of her effort to simultaneously grasp and then explain her actions and choices to herself, to her daughter, to her ex-husband, and to me in the "local moment" (Moore 1993) that unfolds one evening in her small living room. As she leafs through the photo album and plays the videotape documenting her son's bar mitzvah, Nurit articulates her fears (that her son's party would be poorly attended) and her ongoing struggle for social recognition (despite the disintegration of her nuclear family unit) in ways that lend her strength to persevere in the face of a difficult reality. Her story emerges as more than a form of self-explanation that affects her capacity for future action. It also offers significant social analysis that deserves recognition and consideration alongside, not subordinated to, discursive academic knowledge and interpretation.

Nurit's story is first and foremost her individual life history, but it is also strewn with insightful knowledge about the larger social forces that shape her life. Take, for example, her insights about the deep contradictions of the Israeli state welfare system and the ways it reproduces marginality and dependence. Professional literature documenting impoverished single-parent families in Israel is still scant (Herbst 2009; Swirsky et al. 2007). Nurit's struggles to pay the cost of her son's bar mizvah speak about a parallel economy that is rarely documented, an economy of unrecorded, underpaid labor shorn of the benefits required in the mainstream economy. But rather than justify blaming Nurit and other women welfare recipients like her for "cheating" the system, her story enables an understanding of the social forces that give rise to such unrecorded economic activity and to an understanding of how policies affect lives in marginalized spaces.

Taken together, the stories outlined in *Concrete Boxes* offer critical insights into the nature of contemporary social marginalization in Israel's understudied and little-understood periphery. Consider Esti's account of the cumbersome system that disrupts the monthly welfare payments she depends on if she dares accept a few days' employment. Similar testimony regarding the inherent contradictions in the system can be found in the stories Rachel tells about her post-divorce years and in Esti's narrative and performance in the marketplace and at the employment office. By focusing on textured individual life experiences rather than abstract sociological observations, I am able to capture the dignity of my interlocutors as they struggle to make lives for themselves and their families as well as the ethnicized and gendered ways in which class injuries are experienced. Rachel's, Nurit's, and Esti's dealings with the cumbersome bureaucracy of the Welfare Office are not coincidental, unrepresentative, or particular. They reveal a structural dynamic that *fosters* dependence and *reproduces* it. Nurit's, Esti's, Rachel's, and Efrat's accounts speak clearly, authoritatively, and comprehensively about everyday life in development towns. They provide evidence that labor markets in these multiply marginalized communities do not allow for a dignified existence, and they point to structural mechanisms that reproduce the exclusion of the Mizrahi working poor from mainstream Israeli economy and society. The individual stories and the larger analyses they invite suggest how difficult it is to escape the concrete box, which is reinforced not only by material deprivation but also by entrenched ethnic and gendered bias. The story of Gila, who gains middle-class status only by dissociating herself from her Moroccan and Yeruchami identity demonstrates that the social stigma associated with this ethnicized space continues to inflict injuries on all, even on subjects who manage to escape the town's physical constraints.

Ethnographic study focused on the margins is analytically valuable in yet another sense. Not only does it depict a reality of life not familiar to those who hold power but it also opens the way, in the words of sociologist Deborah Bernstein, "to examine the center differentially" (2008: 11). In what follows, I consider the critical importance of studying the periphery as a prime vantage point for understanding Israeli society at large. I am particularly interested in exploring the process of Israeli class reproduction using this ethnography.

I then attend to the significance of the process of *hit'hazkut* and the emergence of new Mizrahi religiosity as part of a larger process of ethnic, class, and gendered reformulation. I conclude with reflections on the power of auto-ethnographic writing.

The Center and the Margins

> We cannot understand the margins without studying the center that operates on them, but we also cannot understand the center without studying the margins, which subvert the notions of self-evidence that it creates.
>
> Deborah Bernstein, *Women on the Margins*

In Israeli public discourse, Yerucham is the quintessential remote, peripheral, and thus unsophisticated social space. People who live there are said to be devoid of cultural and symbolic capital, and their lives undermine Israel's self-image as a Western, liberal society. People in Yerucham often speak bitterly about the stigmatization of their town. Older first-generation Moroccan women express their anger at what they call the *shtigma* that drives their children away from them. None of this is surprising. Social theory has long shown that individuals with symbolic and cultural capital are able to dominate public discourse and define spaces as prestigious or unworthy. And yet, as Slovenian philosopher Slavoj Žižek (1998) forcefully argues, the role of the critical intellectual today is to problematize dominant stories, like that told by the Israeli center about Mizrahi Others. The most profound lesson I hope to convey with this ethnography is that stigmatizing stories about life in marginalized social spaces such as Yerucham are manufactured, "unnatural" stories rather than given, suprasocial truths. Still, the ostensibly simple act of exposing the patronizing, reductive narrative that dominates hegemonic Israeli discourse toward residents of marginalized peripheral spaces, most of them Mizrahim, is subject to pitfalls. One is an apologetic tendency to present what is constructed as the "authentic" voices of marginalized Others. Such discourse tends to represent subaltern subjects as warm and wonderful and, thus, in need of "help" or "development" by well-meaning people at the center. This narrative underlies the many well-meaning projects designed to "uplift"

Yerucham. The outreach programs of the *garin* groups who settle in the town and the community design projects of the architecture students depicted in chapter 5 reflect this narrative. An alternative narrative posits that people who reside in Yerucham and other marginalized Israeli spaces of the *periferya* are warm and "authentic people" with a culturally "traditionalist" way of thinking who need to be documented by a classical anthropological gaze.

To avoid reproducing either of these narrative traps, I show throughout this book that there is no "First" white, modern Israel that is desired or resisted by people in a "Second Israel." *Concrete Boxes* shows that there is no "culture of poverty" or local world completely divorced from centrist values and modes of being. Rachel, who performs a spectacular act of juggling social codes of behavior and speech, vividly illustrates this theoretical observation. Rachel is not the only juggler of codes in Yerucham; all of my interlocutors are keenly aware of how they are perceived by the Israeli center, and all of them are engaged in an ongoing conversation, at once yearning and resistant, with hegemonic Israeli discourse. The individual life narratives presented in this book show how each woman in her own way forges a path to deal with the objectifying forces emanating from the center.

Nurit, who, among the five women, inhabits the most disadvantaged social and material position, confronts representatives of Israeli power—social workers, welfare personnel—by hiding her illicit income from unreported part-time jobs. When she defines me as part of the social class that has power over her life, she exercises her limited control over our unequal encounter by refusing to surrender the one thing she knows I want from her: her life story. Gila stands at the other end of the spectrum from Nurit in terms of her relationship to local stigmatization and hegemonic external discourses. She manages to leave Yerucham and break into the middle class, as evidenced by her higher education, late marriage, and professional career. But even in such exceptional cases of success, the paralyzing power of hegemonic discourse is still felt. Gila cannot break free from her drive to excel and prove herself to those who forever judge her an unworthy development-town Mizrahi woman.

In between the two poles marked by welfare-mother Nurit, on one end, and successful Gila, on the other, stands Esti, who rejects the tyranny of the outside gaze and insists that her life is centered in Yerucham and not dictated by middle-class liberal values. But even Esti makes a point of dressing up when she is summoned before a welfare official, as though paradoxically she too wishes to be accepted by the representative of the powers that be.

The story of the religious strengthening of Efrat and her daughters is, I argue in the next section, the most constructive avenue for dealing with both the judgmental patronizing gaze and the material deprivation that structure local life.

New Religiosity as the Most Constructive Strategy

The process of *hit'hazkut*, or growing religiosity, is clearly revealed in the stories of Efrat and her daughters. But it is a structural option—that is, it exists as a possibility in the lives of most Yeruchami men and women. Every member of my "council of wise women" has considered the religious path, and many have participated in one or more of the evening religious classes offered in town. Of the five key paths depicted in this book—survival (Nurit), juggling (Rachel), rebellious subversion (Esti), conflicted success (Gila), and religious strengthening (Efrat)—religiosity strikes me as the most constructive life option for a resident of Yerucham. Indeed, the religious theme surfaces to varying degrees in the stories of a number of my interlocutors. When Rachel's marriage starts to fall apart, she tries to save it by going the *hit'hazkut* path, only to eventually reject it. When Shula and other women I meet in the religious classes I attend feel overwhelmed by the materiality of their everyday lives, they look at those who have committed to greater religiosity and comment on the calmness of such a life. Even Esti, the rebel, becomes more religious after her mother's death, and she describes her relatively observant sister as her moral superior.

Going back to religiosity (*hazarah bit'shuva*) entails rejecting the secular lifestyle that the Zionist state imposed on immigrant parents, including most of the Mizrahi first generation, who were religious believers. The children of these immigrants, such as Efrat and her husband, cast off their parents' religiosity, adopting secular clothing and practices. As Efrat makes clear, she did not *become* religious, because from the time she was a child growing up in her parents' home she was a believer. The process of *hit'hazkut* led Efrat and her daughters on a path not of new religious beliefs or dogmas but of social practices that have profound implications in terms of redefining both gender relations in the family and economic standing within and outside the community. Efrat's detailed description of adhering to religious practices and facing down her husband (who calls her a moron and drives his car on Shabbat while she and the children walk in the rain) is a story of a struggle that culminates in Efrat redefining her relationship with her husband, who takes up the religious path and becomes part of a functioning family. He becomes a better father (warming bread for the children's breakfast instead of sleeping in), is more attentive to his wife (making her coffee in the morning), prays every morning, and joins a group of other observant men while on reserve service.

Increased religiosity, for men and women alike, is defined in opposition to the weaknesses of a secular lifestyle. The consumerism and greed of those who do not embark on the process of *hit'hazkut* are contrasted with the modesty and minimalism of those who do. Vered, the former clothing store manager, exemplifies this contrast, giving up her rampant consumption of fashionable clothes and adopting modest attire that does not threaten the family's tight budget. *Hit'hazkut* is associated with new patterns of consumption and a life of greater inner peace. Modest attire and behavior that stresses inner calm bestow cultural capital on a *mit'hazeket* woman, lifting her out of the vulgarity attributed to women of her class, giving her an advantage in the job market. As we have seen, in the context of the extremely limited job market in Yeruham, Efrat's respectability, associated with her increased religiosity, lands her a job in the middle-class community of Sde Boker.

Material reward, expressed in increased social and economic mobility, is only one positive outcome of embarking on the *hit'hazkut* path. A second is a significant transformation in gendered relations within the family.

Changing Gender Relations

Four of the women whose stories are depicted in this book are not married. Esti has never married, and the other three (Rachel, Gila, and Nurit) are divorced. The narratives presented in *Concrete Boxes* speak to a generation of Mizrahi women who shape their lives knowing that they can end bad marriages. "I can't accept him," Nurit says of her drug-addicted husband, despite her love for and loyalty to him. And Efrat, who takes her family down the path of *hit'hazkut*, faces stubborn, at times abusive, opposition to her life choice from her husband.

These women's stories cannot be construed as simple articulations of feminist consciousness. They must be understood within a specific socioeconomic context. Early marriage, as we see in Rachel's case, is not a personal choice but an outcome of her desperate wish to escape her restrictive life in her family of origin. When their marriages collapse, women like Rachel and Nurit cannot economically support themselves and their children and they become dependent on the state welfare system. And, as their stories show, the Israeli welfare system curtails any attempts by women like them to wean themselves from such dependency.

Another important phenomenon that these stories bring to light is that gender relations are rapidly changing in the Israeli periphery. Where are the Mizrahi working-class men in these women-centered stories? The men are not absent; we see them through the eyes of their wives and mothers: the drug-addicted husband who cannot live up to his role as a father and a spouse, the good friend, the bank manager, the partner who becomes more religious under the influence of his wife, and the husband who refuses to be a part of the *hit'hazkut* process his wife undergoes in an effort to save their marriage. These narratives add up to a picture of Mizrahi masculinity in crisis. The place of men in second-generation family life is quite different than it was in the patriarchal structure that prevailed in the first generation of Mizrahi immigrant families. The lives of the women who immigrated from North Africa (predominantly from Morocco) and Asia (predominantly from India) are different from the lives of their daughters who were born in Israel or were raised there from a young age. The daughters' experience of romantic relationships, parenthood, and family is articulated in distinctly new ways. The number of children in Mizrahi families has dramatically declined from the first to the second immigrant generation. Rachel's mother raised 11 children, whereas Rachel gave birth to four; Nurit has two children, and Gila one. Rachel's father was expected to provide for his family, and such an expectation is also directed at Nurit's husband. But second-generation Mizrahi women expect more: that fathers will take an active part in raising their children. Rachel depicts a life of feeding children and changing diapers as unfulfilling. Efrat notes with great joy the changes in her husband's behavior after he becomes stronger in his religiosity, her account focusing on his growing participation in family life. Women who take courses to expand their job skills expect their partners to take on childcare duties. These developments are new, unfolding in second-generation families.

This recent restructuring of gender relations is an understudied social phenomenon in Israeli scholarship, and it needs more careful exploration. Rachel's story illustrates this transformation. Her family immigrated to Israel from Morocco. She describes a breadwinner father, dominant and aloof, and a family in which only the daughters were expected to do household chores. This patriarchal family model is shattered with the crisis that consumes Rachel's marriage when she refuses to follow the template of the wife who produces baby after baby, cooks, and waits on her husband when he comes home from work. Nurit's story affords another important insight into the reshaping of gender relations in the family. When her drug-addicted husband fails in his obligation to support his wife and children, Nurit becomes the family breadwinner. Her appropriation of the role is beautifully illustrated when she stands alone (her father supporting her in the background) to welcome guests to her son's bar mitzvah.

Beyond the details unique to each story, we learn about Mizrahi working-class women born or raised in Israel who see work outside the home not as a burden but as a way to achieve a more complete sense of self. These women emerge as central pillars of support in their families. Thus Efrat's increasingly religious daughters do not think of quitting work after marriage. Vered becomes a teacher in a religious day care center, Chen works as a dental assistant, and Einat cleans offices for a living. Likwise Nurit's daughter, Adi, plans to marry but also aspires to one day have an office of her own.

What of third-generation women? Do the daughters of the Mizrahi women depicted in this book stand a better chance than their mothers of extricating themselves from the poverty and marginalization set for them by life in Yerucham? How different is their social positioning from that of their mothers? The story of Nurit's daughter, Adi, raises several key questions regarding the processes of class reproduction and calls for a more complete study of the third generation growing up in the Israeli periphery. Although Adi rejects her mother's life model and yearns for an office of her own, she expresses loyalty to her hometown. Success, as embodied in moving to Tel Aviv, rings hollow to her. A decade after we first speak, Adi's aspirations to develop professional skills that will allow her to work from an office, not as a cleaner or a factory hand, seem to have vanished. When I meet up with her again in 2013, she reports with great pride that she had enlisted in the Israeli army and that she had delayed her marriage to her childhood sweetheart until the age of 24. But she had not secured a stable job in any of the local factories. Commenting on the interview she had given me a decade earlier, she laments, "When you are young, you have big dreams. But Yerucham is Yerucham. There are no jobs here."

Class: An Intersectional Analysis of Social Positioning

Israeli gender studies scholars have taken to the idea of intersectionality only recently. Before I examine the several axes of inequality evoked by the term *intersectionality*, I briefly review the unique way the idea of class has been treated in mainstream Israeli studies.

Although social inequality has been at the center of sociological studies since the 1950s (Jerbi and Levi 2001), Israeli sociologists tend not to address the concept of class, preferring instead to speak of "social stratification" or "obstacles to social mobility" (Yaish 2004). The literature of social inequality tends to be limited to quantified measurements of income gaps among clearly delineated economic categories. The empirical evidence used for such economic categorization is derived from large-scale statistical data collected and made available by government institutions such as the Israeli Central Bureau of Statistics and the National Insurance Institute.

This economic approach to studying class relations has clear advantages. It engenders an important debate on the phenomenon of poverty and provides hard data for social planners (see Achdut and Bigman 1987; Dahan 2009). But it also has several crucial limitations. First, it tends to ignore the place of women in class analysis, because women are assumed to hold the same position as their husbands in the family unit. Second, it focuses on quantifying existing gaps instead of explaining the mechanisms that produce and replicate social inequality. And, most crucially, a narrow economic framework seldom considers ethnic, religious, and national affiliations, even though these identities interact and cut across class differences.

In a scathing critique of the political implications of the prevailing model of Israeli inequality, Iris Jerbi and Gal Levi (2001) note that, contrary to official rhetoric regarding governmental redistribution, the state *contributes to* rather than helps diminish Israeli inequality. Political economists Momi Dahan and critical sociologists Shlomo Swirsky and Deborah Bernstein analyzed the process through which Israel's economic growth contributes to expanding socioeconomic inequality (Dahan 2009; Swirsky 1995; Swirsky and Bernstein 1993). Important as these more recent critical analyses are, Israeli scholarship still has no established tradition of examining class formation as a social phenomenon rather than as a narrow economic construct. Israeli sociology remains focused on the material aspects of class, leaving the issues of ethnicity and culture to anthropologists. Even less empirical work has focused on how groups and individuals experience forces of exclusion and oppression.

In this book, I have modeled my thinking on what American sociologist Diane Reay calls "the new sociology of class analysis" (2005: 911). Feminist sociologists Beverly Skeggs, Angela McRobbie, and Julie Beattie have also been my guides in this analysis in two important ways. First, their work directs me to explore how class is experienced and how subjects cope with their positioning within the social hierarchy. McRobbie (2000), who studied young working-class women in Britain, inspired me to explore how my subjects articulate their class position through family, language, body, community, and sexual conduct. McRobbie does not begin by defining class and then looking for evidence of her subjects' place within that category; rather, she explores how they create the category in their lives. From Beattie I take the notion that "various gestures of class performance never exist outside of race and gender meanings" (2003: 191). Below I provide two examples to illustrate the imprints of these theoretical insights in my work.

The first example takes us back to Gila, whose path is the exceptional—that is, "successful"—one in the larger pattern of class reproduction. Whereas my other main interlocutors remain in Yerucham and reproduce their parents' blue-collar positions, Gila crafts a life course typical of the Israeli middle class, including military service, a long trip abroad unrelated to future plans, delayed marriage and childbirth, and an uncompromising commitment to developing her career. To understand Gila's unique story, we must consider her exceptional family, which arrived in Yerucham with more cultural and material capital than other Moroccan immigrant families, and we must also note her early departure for boarding school outside Yerucham. Her immersion in a hegemonic environment propelled Gila onto a path of upward mobility not shared by her siblings.

Avi Shoshana (2006: 131), whose work focuses on this unique boarding school project, argues that extricating children like Gila (and me) from development towns might offer social mobility to a few, but it also strips the towns of their most talented students and stifles development of local educational systems. Shoshana highlights the political implications of this policy, which followed popular Mizrahi unrest in Wadi Salib in the late 1950s. Gila's story can be seen as symptomatic of the broader social and economic neglect of the periphery. To succeed, Gila must leave Yerucham. Yet her story also demonstrates that she continues to experience the debilitating effects of her past even in her new middle-class life. Material success does not eradicate the other components of her class position, and Gila feels that to prove her worth she needs to work harder than anyone else. Her conflicted personal identity leads her to repeated acts of self-sabotage. To use Beattie's terms, Gila's class origin does not cohere with her class performance. Her painful attempts to reconcile the two mutually constitutive axes of the experience of class are illustrative of the complexity of class formation.

The second example—Rachel, who excels through her ability to move between different discourses—highlights the limits of class performance in the absence of material support. Despite her spectacular juggling skills and her obvious interpersonal talents, Rachel does not manage to move beyond the constricted spaces of her life in Yerucham. When her charisma impresses the middle-class women who run the local NGO for which she volunteers, they consider her for a position in the organization, but her lack of the required professional credentials bars her from securing it. When she frees herself from a failed marriage, she becomes dependent on the local welfare office. Rachel's story of class reproduction is made more poignant when compared with the story of her sister, who manages to break out of Yerucham and build a life in Canada. Canada offers the sister not only material support and social mobility but also a release from the stigmatizing ethnic labels that are always attached to her social background in Israel.

A Southern Mizrahi Feminist Ethnography

Barack Obama describes his urge to work among poor black communities in Chicago as akin to that propelling "a salmon blindly swimming upstream to where it was conceived" (1995: 131). From the outset, my ethnographic research in Yerucham has been driven by more than an effort to document life in a little-studied Israeli social reality or to test or refine narrow theoretical frameworks, exciting as these projects may be. Writing *Concrete Boxes* after years of intensive work in Yerucham has been a deeply personal and political journey. In many ways my research in Yerucham has been the fulfillment of my goal when I decided to make anthropology my life's vocation. My work in Yerucham began more than a decade after I earned my doctorate, for which I undertook ethnographic study in Botswana. My African research, as I describe more fully elsewhere (Motzafi-Haller 1997b), equipped me with professional tools and, most critically, the confidence to tackle my own burning questions of identity as a Mizrahi daughter born and raised in a development town not very different from Yerucham.

I opened this book with a moment of connection to my own childhood memories, when on a Saturday night I strolled along the central street of Yerucham with an elderly interlocutor. I was able to explore my own emotional vulnerability in that and many other moments I depict throughout this book. Virginia Dominguez writes beautifully about the value of the researcher's emotional openness, calling it "a condition of fieldwork and a consequent tool of data gathering" (1989: 13). She argues that developing an introspective analysis of our own reactions, of love, hate, fear, and other feelings, toward the society we study "may ironically allow us to approximate 'reality' *better than* the perennial attempts to maximize objectivity by minimizing subjectivity" (14; emphasis mine). I hope that *Concrete Boxes* illustrates the wisdom of this insight, which has not been widely recognized in Israeli academic discourse.

Since I wrote my 1997 essay, originally published in English in Deborah Reed-Danahay's *Auto/Ethnography* (Motzafi-Haller 1997a) and then translated into Hebrew and published in *Teorya VeBikoret* (Theory and Criticism) (Motzafi-Haller 1997b), there have been only a handful of reflexive, experimental works by Israeli researchers that make use of an intersubjective research and writing style. Tamar Hager's *Malice Aforethought* (2012) is an inspiring example; not only does the author examine her own life and perceptions, fears and emotions, but she also introduces fictional characters to further explore intersubjective dimensions, blurring realist and fictional genres. Israeli cultural studies scholar Orly Lubin contends that "accountability for my position in the research becomes part and parcel of the alternative research mechanism itself" (2003: 95). For me, *Concrete Boxes* has been, at one and the same time, a political, personal, and epistemic journey.

Notes

Foreword to the Hebrew Edition

1. The Shas Party is an ultra-Orthodox religious political party. It was founded in 1984 under the leadership of Rabbi Ovadia Yosef, a former Israeli Sephardi chief rabbi, who remained its spiritual leader until his death in October 2013. The party primarily represents the interests of Haredi Sephardic and Mizrahi Jews. See en.wikipedia.org/wiki/Shas (accessed November 2, 2017).

2. For a review of Israeli academic studies of Mizrahi women at the time I set out for field research in Yerucham, see Motzafi-Haller 2001. The last decade or more has seen very little empirical research documenting the life of Mizrahi women in the Negev. Sigal Nagar-Ron and Reut Bendrihem, who worked in Yerucham and Ofakim, have produced MA and PhD theses, but these have not yet been published.

3. See my introductory chapter to the anthology *Mizrahi Voices* (Aboutboul et al. 2005).

Introduction

1. NA'AMAT is an acronym for Nashim Ovdot U'Mitnadvot, the Movement of Working Women and Volunteers, a women's organization affiliated with the Labor Zionist Movement.

2. I began fieldwork in January 2000. From July 2002 to July 2003, I was on sabbatical in Canada. During that year, I corresponded with Rachel and Esti, two of the central figures in this book, who sent me their own notes documenting their lives. I also met with Rachel's sister in Montreal. Upon returning to Israel, in July 2003, I resumed intensive fieldwork in Yerucham, which continued until late 2004. Since 2005, I have maintained contact with the key women in this study and have followed up on their lives. The Hebrew version of this book was published in 2012. Two of the five key interlocutors joined me for several public events at which the book was discussed. I still travel to Yerucham to shop and visit friends, but I do so less frequently now than during the research period.

3. Some of the material appears in published articles. See, for example, Motzafi-Haller 2005, 2006, 2014 and Nagar-Ron and Motzafi-Haller 2011. I am currently writing a critical analysis in the form of a series of essays provocatively titled *Shkhordiniyot* (literally, "black-blondes"; a pejorative term directed at lower-class Mizrahi women). In this new book, I incorporate some of the empirical data I could not include in this ethnography as well as autoethnographic essays that go beyond the Yerucham story.

4. I have changed all personal names to protect the privacy of the women and their family members.

5. See, for example, Stacey 1988 and Haraway 1988. I also engaged with the work of Kamala Visweswaran (1994) and Beverly Skeggs (2001). For a more recent review of feminist ethnographic methods, see Schrock 2013.

6. Despite several essays that had laboriously tried to define "Mizrahi feminism" (see my review of this work in my 2001 essay), there is still no empirical work that documents the lives of lower-class Mizrahi women. Smadar Lavie's recent book (2014) poses extremely important questions but offers regrettably little ethnographic description of everyday life for marginalized Mizrahi women.

7. Mei-Ami 2003.

8. Data are from the National Insurance Institute, Planning and Research Administration (Toledano 2007: 57 [Table 35]).

9. In 2002, Ofakim and Kiryat Malachi, two development towns in the northern Negev region, registered a slight population growth of 0.5% and 0.3%, respectively, whereas Dimona and Yerucham experienced a de facto negative rate of growth. Dimona lost 0.4% of its population, and Yerucham suffered a 1.2% decrease (CBS 2003: Table 3).

10. Data from the National Insurance Institute, Planning and Research Administration (Schmeltzer and Koren 2002: 33 [Table 1.0]). More detailed data can be accessed in the records of the Israeli National Insurance Institute, Planning and Research Administration (NII 2007: 8 [Table 1]).

11. In 2001, when Yerucham's population stood at 8,900, natural growth (births minus deaths) yielded 155 new residents, and there were 49 new immigrants. That year, 322 residents left the town. For a complete record, see Table 2/b, "Sources of Population Growth," at www.negev.co.il/stats.html (accessed January 13, 2010).

12. These Central Bureau of Statistics figures appear in Table 2/c, "Population Data," available at www.negev.co.il/stats.html (accessed January 13, 2010).

13. Rapoport 2005, citing Yosef Bitan.

14. This image is astoundingly resilient. See, for example, the November 2015 *Haaretz* essay depicting Yerucham as a "dark, godforsaken place on the most remote margins of Israeli society" (Gilad 2015). The author expresses his doubts that this place will ever transform itself into a tourist attraction.

15. The site has since been removed and cannot be accessed.

16. See www.ynet.co.il/articles/0,7340,L-3989077,00.html (accessed March 11, 2014).

Chapter 1

1. The phrase is Hebrew slang, a kind of throwaway line, like "you know," "I mean it," "no kidding," and so on.

2. The Hebrew slang she employs uses the verb "to do" instead of "to say."

3. In the early 2000s, prices ranged from $17 a plate for dinner in the local hall to $35 or more in halls in Be'er-Sheva. Minimum wage at the time stood at $4–$5 per hour.

4. A *henna* is a pre-event celebration that takes on "traditional" overtones. Only family members are invited, and the outfits worn are often exotic and richly embroidered. The word *henna* refers to the coloring of the hands with natural henna dye, a practice often followed by a bride and her guests.

Chapter 2

1. *Masorati* denotes a certain type of religious practice often associated with Mizrahi families. See Yonah and Goodman 2004 and Tzabari 2015 on the problematics of this hegemonic definition of Mizrahi religiosity. As Efrat's narrative unfolds, it becomes clearer who makes and upholds such definitions and how these categories intersect with ethnic and class positionings.

2. Tamar El-Or writes lyrically about this stringency: "Every morning, a religious or haredi woman is required to carry out a precise process of declaring her identity. With each item of clothing, she . . . signifies acceptance, rejection, objection, or dalliance with the familiar dress code that belongs

culturally to a specific group. From the tip of her covered head to her toenails, her body serves as an organic substrate for the presentation of her preferences and repudiations" (2006: 57).

3. This attitude lies at the heart of El-Or's analysis in *Reserved Seats* (2006). El-Or notes that in weekly lectures to a local Mizrahi community, Rabbi Zer, who heads the neighborhood *haredi* education project, stresses the expectation that everyone will ultimately experience a process of *hit'hazkut* and that their place is reserved for them when they finally decide to take the first step.

4. The term *rabbanit* refers in this case to a knowledgeable woman who gives religious talks or classes, though in other contexts it is a term of respect for a rabbi's wife.

5. The *mikvah* is the bath used for immersion to achieve ritual purity.

6. In other words, what we find in Yerucham is not religious feminism as expressed in a call to broaden the circle of students, as described by El-Or in her book *Next Year I Will Know More* (1998). But neither do we find a framework that "supports the women and frees them from the burden of their day-to-day existence," as in the Pardes Katz groups of *mit'hazkot* she presents in *Reserved Seats* (2006: 39, 43), which center on survival and outreach. An English translation of the latter book can be found at the author's website (www.tamarelor.com/books/reserved-seats).

7. The adjectives in this sentence are presented in their masculine forms. The feminine forms are *masortiya, datiya, ma'amina, mi'thazeket,* and *harediya.*

Chapter 3

1. Du Bois describes "double consciousness" as follows: "It is a peculiar sensation, this double-consciousness, this sense of always looking at one's self through the eyes of others, of measuring one's soul by the tape of a world that looks on in amused contempt and pity" (1903: 3).

2. The Hebrew Wikipedia entry on Anna Marcus relates the following: "In 1988, the Marcuses moved to Yerucham following a dream of Anna's in which she heard a voice telling her to move there, without her having known of its existence previously." See he.wikipedia.org/wiki/ (accessed March 12, 2017).

3. Bourdieu applies the term *new autodidact* to individuals who attempt to acquire a cultural connection to fields of discourse that are inaccessible to them because they lack the requisite academic degrees. In his article "Some Properties of Fields," Bourdieu describes the struggle between "the newcomer who tries to break through the entry barrier and the dominant agent who will try to defend the monopoly and keep out competition" (1993: 72).

Chapter 4

1. After the publication of the Hebrew version of this book, I learned that when the ceremony is held in a private home, not a synagogue, Jewish Orthodox laws allow the bat mitzvah girl to step up on a platform for the Torah reading.

2. *Bamidbar* means "in the desert." Here it is a pun alluding to Yerucham's geographic location as well as to the Hebrew name for the book of Numbers, in which is found much of the revelation of Jewish law. A *beit midrash* is a place for the collective study and discussion of religious texts, often but not always attached to a synagogue or seminary.

3. *Gar'in* means "nucleus" or simply "seed." It is a common term used for groups delegated by Zionist youth movements to start new communities or to undertake volunteer work in existing ones.

4. A *tzadik* is a righteous man. *Tzadik* is an honorific title for spiritual leaders, usually rabbis, venerated by communities long after their passing.

5. *Kabalat shabbat* is the welcoming of the Sabbath. The ceremony of lighting candles, reading prayers, and blessing the wine and the bread demarcates the holy day of the Sabbath from the rest of the week.

6. Yom Kippur, the Day of Atonement, is the holiest day in the Jewish calendar; in Israel, even in secular communities, traffic largely stops and no commercial activity is carried out.

7. The phrase Rachel uses is *chazara b'tshuva*, the process of becoming *baalat teshuva*, "a master of return"; the term is used mainly to denote secular Jews who adopt Orthodox observance.

8. *Shlom bayit* means "domestic peace or harmony." The phrase encodes a detailed notion of what the ideal relationship between a husband and a wife should look like.

9. Shlom Hagalil is the code name for the First Lebanon War (1982). Rachel plays with the two terms in a cynical manner.

10. In the title, Rachel subverts a well-known and controversial blessing repeated by many observant Jewish men in the morning: "Blessed be He who has not made me a woman." Women who observe the ritual conversely say, "Blessed be He who has made me as He will."

11. "What a Country" is the title of a popular protest song by Mizrahi pop singer Eli Louzon.

12. For a complete guide to the legal rights of single-parent families in Israel, consult www.newfamily.org.il/.

13. A *get* is a divorce statement given by the husband, without which no Israeli court can recognize a divorce.

14. See Madar 2006, Naaman 2007, Shimoni 2007, and several articles in issue 16 of the journal *Due East* (2008).

Chapter 5

1. *Helmoniot* is a subgenus of desert crocus (*Sternbergia clusiana*).

2. The term "First Israel" references the hegemonic society of the center, against which underclass, ethnicized Israelis, who make up a "Second Israel," are measured.

3. Givatron is a kibbutz choir that was prominent in the 1950s and 1960s; the name is a portmanteau made up of *giv'a* (hill) and *te'atron* (theater), which is the basis for Esti's pun.

4. *Haval al ha'zman* means, literally, "shame for the time" (wasted on further elaboration). Depending on the context, the English equivalent would be "Outta sight" or "You don't even wanna know."

5. The local Jewish immigrants from India. About 10% of Yerucham's residents are of Indian heritage.

6. The Hebrew word *miskenim*, translated here as "poor," is not the same as *aniyim*, which connotes material poverty. I could have translated *miskenim* to mean "wretched" or "miserable," but these adjectives are too strong in this context.

Chapter 6

1. The English translation of Esti's Hebrew narratives produced several challenges that were not easy to resolve. Attempts to find parallels to Esti's speech in nonstandard English were not always satisfactory, and many of her puns and some of her street talk were lost in translation.

2. By "private" Esti means that the medication was not covered by Israel's national health insurance scheme. Three hundred shekels would have been about one-tenth of her mother's monthly income. At the time, Esti was making 17 shekels an hour as a cleaner.

3. Credit on personal terms, not on the institutionalized terms determined by a credit card issuer.

4. An arithmetical system that assigns a number to each letter of the Hebrew alphabet.

5. In contrast to American practice, Israeli banks allow a person to overdraw his or her account, often to a sum roughly equivalent to a month's income. Most middle-class and lower-middle-class Israelis live in a rolling state of overdrawn accounts, as permitted by the bank. The people in Yerucham who line up at the teller's window request special authorization to go beyond this credit line. The interest on these special bank debts is particularly high, reaching, at the time of my research, more than 16%.

Chapter 7

1. The work of Avi Shoshana (2006) is a significant exception.

2. "Alliance" is short for Alliance israélite universelle, an international Paris-based Jewish organization founded in 1860. Among its projects is a chain of some 60 schools across the Middle East and North Africa.

3. A proverb praising hard work as the only path to success, based on an extract from the Talmud: "R. Isaac also said: If a man says to you, I have labored and not found, do not believe him. If he says, I have not labored but still have found, do not believe him. If he says, I have labored and found, you may believe him" (BT *Megillah*, ch. 1).

4. Coming from politicians, this phrase signals the intention to enter the private sector. For Gila, it means focusing on her personal welfare.

5. *Frecha* is deeply charged Hebrew slang for a Mizrahi woman. Derived from the Arabic first name Freha (joy), it implies loudness, vulgarity, and a tendency toward promiscuous clothing and behavior.

6. Mimouna celebrations mark the end of the Jewish Passover and the return to eating leavened foods. They are associated with Moroccan immigrants.

7. I have analyzed my dual, simultaneous positioning as a researcher and as a native in my article "You Have an Authentic Voice" (Motzafi-Haller 1997b).

8. The number of those departing during that period is smaller when offset by the number of new arrivals; but even when the number of new residents is taken into account, net emigration was 8%, which Braude and Navon describe as "significant."

References

Aboutboul, Guy, Lev Grinberg, and Pnina Motzafi-Haller (eds.). 2005. *Mizrahi Voices: Toward a New Mizrahi Discourse on Israeli Culture and Society.* Tel Aviv: Masada. (Hebrew)

Achdut, Leah, and David Bigman. 1987. *Indexes of Poverty and Measuring Poverty in Israel.* Discussion Paper no. 40. Jerusalem: Bureau of Research and Planning, National Insurance Institute. (Hebrew)

Alfandari, Tovi, and Daniel Sheffer. 1992. *Migration to and from Development Towns in Israel.* Haifa: Shmuel Ne'eman Institute, Technion. (Hebrew)

Anderson, Leon. 2006. "Analytical Autoethnography." *Journal of Contemporary Ethnography* 35(4): 373–95.

Beattie, Julie. 2003. *Women without Class: Girls, Race, Identity.* Berkeley: University of California Press.

Behar, Ruth. 1993. *Translated Woman: Crossing the Border with Esperanza's Story.* Boston: Beacon Press.

Ben Simon, Daniel. 2001. *A Shady Deal in the South.* Jerusalem: Keter. (Hebrew)

Ben Zadok, Efraim. 1993. "Oriental Jews in the Development Towns: Ethnicity, Economic Developments, Budgets, and Politics." In Efraim Ben Zadok (ed.), *Local Communities and the Israeli Polity: Conflict of Values and Interests,* 91–122. Albany: State University of New York Press.

Bernstein, Deborah. 2008. *Women on the Margins: Gender and Nationalism in Mandate Tel Aviv.* Jerusalem: Yad Ben Zvi. (Hebrew)

Bitton, Michael. 2011. "I Discovered a Serious Financial Crisis in the Yerucham City Council." *Maariv,* January 5. www.nrg.co.il/online/54/ART2/197/015.html (accessed March 24, 2014).

Bourdieu, Pierre. 1962. "Célibat et condition paysanne." *Études Rurales* 5–6: 32–136.

———. 1986. "The Forms of Capital." In John C. Richardson (ed.), *Handbook of Theory and Research for the Sociology of Education,* 241–58. Westport, CT: Greenwood Press.

———. 1993. "Some Properties of Fields." In Pierre Bourdieu, *Sociology in Question,* trans. Richard Nice, 72–77. London: Sage.

———. 1999. "The Contradictions of Inheritance." In Pierre Bourdieu et al., *The Weight of the World: Social Suffering in Contemporary Society,* trans.

Priscilla Parkhurst Ferguson, Susan Emanuel, Joe Johnson, and Shoggy T. Waryn, 507–14. Stanford, CA: Stanford University Press.

Braude, Kobi, and Guy Navon. 2006. *Internal Migration in Israel.* Discussion Paper Series. *Jerusalem:* Research Department, Bank of Israel. www.boi.org .il/deptdata/mehkar/papers/dp0607h.pdf (accessed March 23, 2017). (Hebrew)

CBS (Central Bureau of Statistics). 2003. *Population in Settlements and Broad Geographical Divisions in Israel, 2003.* Jerusalem: Government Publishing House. www.cbs.gov.il/population/new_2003/tab_3.pdf (accessed April 4, 2017). (Hebrew)

Dahan, Momi. 2009. *Third-Generation Poverty.* Jerusalem: Israeli Democracy Institute. (Hebrew)

Dominguez, Virginia R. 1989. *People as Subject, People as Object: Selfhood and Peoplehood in Contemporary Israel.* Madison: University of Wisconsin Press.

———. 2000. "For a Politics of Love and Rescue." *Cultural Anthropology* 15(3): 361–93.

Du Bois, W. E. B. 1903. *The Souls of Black Folk.* Chicago: A. C. McClurg.

Efrat, Elisha. 1994. *The New Town of Israel: A Reappraisal.* Munich: Minerva.

El-Or, Tamar. 1998. *Next Year I Will Know More: Identity and Literacy among Young Orthodox Women in Israel.* Tel Aviv: Am Oved. (Hebrew)

———. 2006. *Reserved Seats: Religion, Gender, and Ethnicity in Contemporary Israel.* Tel Aviv: Am Oved. (Hebrew)

Geertz, Clifford. 1973. *The Interpretation of Cultures: Selected Essays.* New York: Basic Books.

Gilad, Moshe. 2015. "Yerucham: From a Godforsaken Town to a Touristic Pearl?" *Haaretz,* November 4.

Hager, Tamar. 2012. *Malice Aforethought.* Or Yehuda: Dvir.

Haraway, Donna. 1988. "Situated Knowledge: The Science Question in Feminism." *Feminist Studies* 14(3): 575–99.

———. 1997. *Feminism and Technoscience.* New York: Routledge.

Herbst, Anat. 2009. "We Support the Single Parent Families Law—Poor Things: A Survey of the Single Parent Family Law." *Social Security* 80: 25–58. (Hebrew)

Hever, Hannan, Yehouda Shenhav, and Pnina Mozaf-Haller. 2002. *Mizrachis in Israel.* Jerusalem: Van Leer Jerusalem Institute; and Tel Aviv: Hakibbutz Hameuchad. (Hebrew)

Hill-Collins, Patricia. 1990. *Black Feminist Thought: Knowledge, Consciousness, and the Politics of Empowerment*. New York: Routledge.

———. 2005. *Black Sexual Politics: African-Americans, Gender, and the New Racism*. New York: Routledge.

Jerbi, Iris, and Gal Levi. 2001. *The Socioeconomic Cleavage in Israel*. Jerusalem: Israeli Democracy Institute. (Hebrew)

Katan, Yosef. 2002. *The Problem of Poverty: Components, Causes, and Strategies*. Jerusalem: Henrietta Sald Institute. (Hebrew)

Khazzoom, Aziza. 2002. "Becoming a Minority, Examining Gender: Iraqi Jewish Women in the 1950s." In Hannan Hever, Yehuda Shenhav, and Pnina Motzafi-Haller (eds.), *Mizrachis in Israel*, 212–44. Jerusalem: Van Leer Jerusalem Institute; and Tel Aviv: Hakibbutz Hameuchad. (Hebrew)

Krumer-Nevo, Michal. 2006. *Women in Poverty*. Tel Aviv: Hakibbutz Hameuchad. (Hebrew)

Lather, Patti. 2006. "Paradigm Proliferation as a Good Thing to Think With: Teaching Qualitative Research as a Wild Profusion." *Qualitative Studies in Education* 19(1): 35–57.

Lavie, Smadar. 2014. *Wrapped in the Flag of Israel: Mizrahi Single Mothers and Bureaucratic Torture*. New York: Berghahn.

Leon, Nissim. 2009. *Soft Ultra-Orthodoxy: Religious Renewal in Mizrahi Jews*. Jerusalem: Ben-Zvi Institute.

Lieber, Stella Korine. 2015. "How Do You People in Tel Aviv, Live with Such an Outrageous State of Social Inequality?" *Globes*, April 5.

Lister, Ruth. 2004. *Poverty*. Malden, MA: Polity Press.

Local Authorities in Israel, Israel Central Bureau of Statistics. 2004. *Census 2004*. Publication 127. www.cbs.gov.il/publications/local_authorities2004/pdf/474_0831.pdf (accessed March 23, 2017).

Lubin, Orly. 1991. "From the Margins to the Center: The Subversiveness of Transit Camp Films." *Zmanim* 39–40: 140–50. (Hebrew)

———. 2003. *Women Reading Women*. Haifa: University of Haifa; and Tel Aviv: Zmora Beitan. (Hebrew)

Madar, Vered. 2006. "Searching for a Feeling of Home." *Eretz Aheret* 36: 81–86. (Hebrew)

McRobbie, Angela. 2000. *Feminism and Youth Culture*. New York: Routledge.

Mei-Ami, Naomi. 2003. *Development Town of Yerucham*. Report supervised by Dotan Russo. March 13. Tel Aviv: Knesset Research and Information

Center. www.knesset.gov.il/mmm/data/pdf/m00502.pdf (accessed April 5, 2017). (Hebrew)

Mohanty, Chandra. 2003. "'Under Western Eyes' Revisited: Feminist Solidarity through Anticapitalist Struggles." *Signs* 28(2): 499–535.

Moore, Sally Falk. 1993. *Moralizing States and the Ethnography of the Present.* Washington, DC: American Anthropological Association.

Motzafi-Haller, Pnina. 1997a. "Writing Birthright: Native Anthropologists and the Politics of Representation." In Deborah Reed-Danahay (ed.), *Auto/Ethnography: Rewriting the Self and the Social,* 169–95. Oxford: Berg.

———. 1997b. "You Have an Authentic Voice: Anthropological Research and the Politics of Representation." *Theory and Criticism* 11: 81–99. (Hebrew)

———. 2001. "Scholarship, Identity, and Power: Mizrahi Women in Israel." *Signs: Journal of Women in Culture and Society* 26(3): 697–734.

———. 2005. "New Challenges in Historiographic and Sociological Research of Oriental Jewish Women." In Tova Cohen and Shaul Regev (eds.), *Women of the East, Women in the East,* 267–83. Ramat Gan: Bar Ilan University Press. (Hebrew)

———. 2006. "Religiosity, Gender, and Class in a Desert Town." In Yossi Yonah and Yehuda Goodman (eds.), *In the Whirlpool of Identities: A Critical Look at Religion and Secularity in Israel,* 316–45. Jerusalem: Van Leer Jerusalem Institute; and Tel Aviv: Hakibbutz Hameuchad Press. (Hebrew)

———. 2014. "Work, Family, and Life at the Margins: How to See from Below." *Hagar: Studies in Culture, Polity and Identities* 11(2): 127–38.

Naaman, Yonit. 2007. "Black on White: Mizrahi Women as Photo-Negatives." In Nir Baram, Naftali Shem-Tov, and Mati Shemoeloff (eds.), *Echoes of Identity: The Third Generation Writes Mizrahiness,* 88–94. Tel Aviv: Am Oved. (Hebrew)

Nagar-Ron, Sigal, and Pnina Motzafi-Haller. 2011. "'My Life? There Is Not Much to Tell': On Voice, Silence, and Agency in Interviews with First-Generation Mizrahi Jewish Women Immigrants to Israel." *Qualitative Inquiry* 17: 359–71.

Narayan, Deepa. 2000. *Can Anyone Hear Us?* New York: Oxford University Press.

NII (National Insurance Institute, Planning and Research Administration). 2007. *Settlements in Israel: Number of Residents and Number of Welfare Recipients.* Jerusalem: Government Publishing House. www.btl.gov.il/Publications/yeshuvim/Documents/2007-1.pdf (accessed April 5, 2017). (Hebrew)

Obama, Barack. 1995. *Dreams from My Father*. New York: New York Times Books.

Rapoport, Meron. 2005. "All-Out War against the Ashkenazi Enemy." *Haaretz*, May 28. (Hebrew)

Reay, Diane. 2005. "Beyond Consciousness? The Psychic Landscape of Social Class." *Sociology* 39(5): 911–28.

Salzberger, Lotte. 1995. *Socio-Familial Deprivation Over Time*. Jerusalem: Academon. (Hebrew)

Sambol, Sarit, and Orly Benjamin. 2006. "Motherhood and Poverty in Israel: The Place of Motherhood in the Lives of Working Poor Women." *Social Issues in Israel* 1: 31–64. (Hebrew)

Schmeltzer, Miriam, and Ira Koren. 2002. *Recipients of Benefits by Settlement*. Jerusalem: Government Publishing House. www.btl.gov.il/ SiteCollectionDocuments/btl/Publications/seker_184.pdf (accessed April 5, 2017). (Hebrew)

Schrock, Richelle D. 2013. "The Methodological Imperatives of Feminist Ethnography." *Journal of Feminist Scholarship* 5. www.jfsonline.org/issue5/ articles/schrock/ (accessed April 17, 2017).

Scott, James. 1990. *Domination and the Arts of Resistance: Hidden Transcripts*. New Haven, CT: Yale University Press.

———. 1994. *Poverty and Wealth*. London: Longmans.

Shayo, Moshe, and Michael Vaknin. 2002. *Ongoing Poverty in Israel: First Results from Cross-Reading of Population and Housing Censuses, 1983–1995*. Jerusalem: Institute for Economic Research. (Hebrew)

Shimoni, Baruch. 2007. "Ethnic Demonstration and Cultural Representation: From Multiculturalism to Cultural Hybridization—The Case of Mizrachi-Sabras in Israel." *Hagar* 7(2): 13–34.

Shoshana, Avi. 2006. "The Invention of a New Social Category: The Deprived Gifted." *Theory and Criticism* 29: 125–45. (Hebrew)

Sinai, Ruth. 2007. "Who Even Wants an Elected Mayor?" *Haaretz*, October 28. (Hebrew)

Skeggs, Beverly. 2001. "Feminist Ethnography." In Paul Atkinson, Amanda Coffey, Sara Delamont, John Lofland, and Lyn Lofland (eds.), *Handbook of Ethnography*, 426–42. Thousand Oaks, CA: Sage.

Spivak, Gayatri Chakravorty. 1988. "Can the Subaltern Speak?" In Cary Nelson and Lawrence Grossberg (eds.), *Marxism and the Interpretation of Culture*, 271–313. Urbana: University of Illinois Press.

————. 1990. *The Post-Colonial Critic: Interviews, Strategies, Dialogues*, ed. Sarah Harasym. London: Routledge.

Stacey, Judith. 1988. "Can There Be a Feminist Ethnography?" *Women's Studies International Forum* 11(1): 21–27.

Stier, Chaya, and Aliza Levin. 2002. *Poor Women in Israel*. Jerusalem: Women's Caucus. (Hebrew)

Swirsky, Shlomo. 1995. *Seeds of Inequality*. Tel Aviv: Breirot. (Hebrew)

Swirsky, Shlomo, and Debbie Bernstein. 1993. "Who Worked Where, for Whom, and for What? Israel's Economic Development and the Emergence of the Ethnic Division of Labor." In Uri Ram (ed.), *Critical Aspects of Israeli Society*, 120–47. Tel Aviv: Breirot. (Hebrew)

Swirsky, Shlomo, Itay Connor-Atias, Vered Krauss, and Anat Herbst. 2007. "Single Mothers in Israel." In Matat Adar-Bunis (ed.), *Families in Sociological and Anthropological Collections: Readings, Part Two*, 208–37. Raanana: Open University. (Hebrew)

Tamir, Shlomo. 1978. *Chapters from a Lifelong Calling*. Tel Aviv: Culture and Education. (Hebrew)

Toledano, Esther. 2007. *Recipients of Unemployment Benefits*. Jerusalem: Government Publishing House. www.btl.gov.il/SiteCollectionDocuments/btl/Publications/Skarim/seker_208.pdf (accessed April 5, 2017). (Hebrew)

Tzabari, Einav. 2015. "Tzion Golan vs. Rabbi Kook, an Ethnic Duel in the Corridors of the Ulpana: Ethnic Belonging as a Formative Factor in the Definition of Identity for Formerly Religious Mizrahi Women from the Periphery." MA thesis, Ben Gurion University.

Vasilachis de Gialdino, Irene. 2006. "Identity, Poverty Situations, and the Epistemology of the Known Subject." *Sociology* 40: 473–91.

Visweswaran, Kamala. 1994. *Fictions of Feminist Ethnography*. Minneapolis: University of Minnesota Press.

Yadgar, Yaacov. 2011. *Secularism and Religion in Jewish-Israeli Politics: Traditionists and Modernity*. London: Routledge.

Yaish, Meir. 2004. "Israel's Class Structure." *Megamot* 43(2): 267–86. (Hebrew)

Yiftachel, Oren. 2001. "The Consequences of Planning Control: Mizrahi Jews in Israel's 'Development Towns.'" In Oren Yiftachel, Ian Alexander, David Hedgcock, and Jo Little (eds.), *The Power of Planning: Spaces of Control and Transformation*, 171–88. The Hague: Kluwer.

Yiftachel, Oren, and Erez Tzfadia. 1999. *Policy and Identity: The Influences of Planning and Development on Immigrants from North Africa, 1952–1998.* Be'er-Sheva: Negev Development Institute and the Ben Gurion University of the Negev. (Hebrew)

Yonah, Yossi, and Yehuda Goodman (eds.). 2004. *In the Maelstrom of Identities: A Critical Look at Religion and Secularity in Israel.* Jerusalem: Van Leer Jerusalem Institute; and Tel Aviv: Hakibbutz Hameuchad Press. (Hebrew)

Žižek, Slavoj. 1998. "A Leftist Plea for Eurocentrism." *Critical Inquiry* 24(4): 988–1009.

Index

Gila's evaluation of day, 286,
289–91
at market in Yerucham, 279–83,
287
Motzafi-Haller's analysis of day,
286–89
panhandler in Yerucham market,
Gila's reaction to, 283, 289–90
self-presentation and treatment of
Gila by Esti, 277–80, 284–85,
287
Golan, Debbie, 109
gray economy, 47–48, 297

Hafez, Abdel Halim, 125
Hager, Tamar, *Malice Aforethought*
(2012), 309
hair, covering, 66, 72, 73, 84, 90, 157,
161, 314n2
HaKeshet HaDemocratit HaMizrahit
(Mizrahi Democratic
Rainbow), x
Hamakhtesh Hagadol (the Big
Crater), 11
HaMizrahit HaMeshutefet, x
Hanna (fruit stall keeper), 282
Haraway, Donna, 9
haredi (ultra-Orthodox), 12, 74–79,
85–87, 99, 100, 157, 311n1,
313–14nn2–3
Hebrew, political reasons for initially
writing in, xi, xix, 10
Hebrew slang and wordplay, 18, 281,
283, 284, 313nn1–2, 317n1,
318n5
henna ceremony, 48–50, 275, 313n4

Hill-Collins, Patricia, 296
hit'hazkut. See religious observance
hooks, bell, 5–6
hozrim bitshuva (newly observant),
82–84, 88
hybridity and its limits, 4, 109–75
architecture students, Rachel's
encounter with, 141–48, 170,
300
Conservative and Reform
Judaism, Rachel's exposure to,
149–50, 151–53
double consciousness, 141, 314n1
ideal resident, Rachel's self-
presentation as, 119, 121, 170
jugglers and juggling, 8–9, 171–
73, 300, 307
liberal middle-class audience,
Rachel' essays addressing,
121–22, 131–33, 140–41, 155,
156–57, 161, 166, 170
middle-class educated women,
Rachel's awareness of, 147,
171
Motzafi-Haller's impact on Rachel,
146–48, 171
multiple class-based exclusions,
Rachel's struggle with, 173–75
new autodidact, Bourdieu's
concept of, 147, 315n3
quasi-feminist stance taken by
Rachel, 161, 162–66
Rachel as epitome of, 110–13 (*See
also* Rachel)
social setting, lives shaped by,
112–13

Rachel's awareness of world of middle-class educated women, 147

Rachel's essays addressing, 121–22, 131–33, 140–41, 155, 156–57, 161, 166, 170

life narratives, self-analysis contained in, 295–99

Lister, Ruth, 37

Louzon, Eli, 316n11

Lubin, Orly, 172, 309

Women Reading Women (2003), xiii

Luk, Chaim, 83

ma'aminot (believers), 98, 99

Madar, Vered, 174

Maman (confidant of Esti), 215, 216, 218–19, 220

Marcus, Anna, 142, 314n2

Marcus, Shlomo, 142, 143

marriage, divorce, and gender relations, 302–5

Efrat, 65, 67–73, 99, 100, 302, 303, 304

Esti, on being single and childless, 178–79, 186, 198, 201, 202, 204

Gila, 262, 265, 266, 268, 275

Mizrahi periphery, gender relationships in, 250–51, 303–4

Nurit, 28–37, 41, 44–45, 49–50, 302–3, 304

Rachel, 110, 112, 136, 157–62, 163–66, 167, 303–4

religious observance and spousal attitudes, 67–73, 81–82, 157–62, 301, 302

sexuality, Esti's use of, 238–41

Vered (daughter of Efrat), 77, 80–87

work outside the home, attitudes toward, 303–4

masorati, 64, 65–66, 75, 87, 151, 153, 155, 157, 313n1

McRobbie, Angela, 306

medical commission, Esti required to appear before, 227, 228–31

menstrual blood, ritual purity laws regarding, 91–94, 95

meshumada, 99

middle-class viewpoint. *See* liberal middle-class viewpoint

Mif 'al HaPayis, 182

mikvah (ritual bath), 94–95, 275, 314n5

Mimi's Hair Salon (movie), 249–50

Mimouna celebrations, 275, 291, 318n6

Mimran, Yair, 2

miscarriage of Efrat, 66–67

mispar nosaf, 182, 188, 215, 218, 221, 222, 284

mit'hazkot, 98, 99, 102, 103

Mitzna, Amram, 14–15

Mizrahi activist and cultural florescence, ix–x, xvii

Mizrahi versus Ashkenazi. *See* Ashkenazi versus Sephardi/ Mizrahi

consumption patterns and, 81,
85–87, 88, 103–4, 302

"council of wise women" on, 89,
97–104, 301

datiya, 74, 75, 78, 81, 99, 100

dress and clothing reflecting,
65–66, 76, 81, 83, 84, 85, 86,
90, 98, 100–101, 157–59,
160–61, 313–14n2

education and, 63–65, 74–75, 86,
87, 102–3

Esti and, 210, 301

as free choice, 84

hair, covering, 66, 72, 73, 84, 90,
157, 161, 314n2

haredi (ultra-Orthodox), 12,
74–79, 85–87, 99, 100, 157,
311n1, 313–14nn2–3

hierarchical scale of commitment
to, 64, 66, 75, 98–100

hozrim bitshuva (newly
observant), 82–84, 88

intergenerational, 73–77

kippah (skullcap or yarmulke),
wearing, 69, 72, 79, 83–84,
107, 153, 155, 158, 159,
160

ma'aminot (believers), 98, 99

masorati, 64, 65–66, 75, 87, 151,
153, 155, 157, 313n1

meshumada, 99

mit'hazkot, 98, 99, 102, 103

mutual acceptance of individual
process of, 76–78, 79–80

as ongoing, gradual process, 73,
84, 101

poverty/debt cycle, breaking out
of, 104–8, 173, 301–2

pride and self-worth associated
with, 61–62

ritual purity laws, 91–95, 99

sense of purpose, well-being, and
calm attributed to, 81, 85, 86,
87, 98, 101, 102–3, 302

spousal attitudes and, 67–73,
81–82, 157–62, 301, 302

as strengthening process, 62–63,
68–73

women, religious classes for,
89–97, 101, 109, 314n6

Revakh, Ze'ev, 25

Rina, xiii–xiv

Rita (singer), 191, 202

ritual purity laws, 91–95, 99

Sa'ar, Amalia, xix
Economic Citizenship: Neoliberal
Paradoxes of Empowerment
(2016), xx

"Second Israel," concept of, 172, 300,
316n2

Sephardi. *See* Ashkenazi versus
Sephardi/Mizrahi

sexuality, Esti's use of, 238–41

Shabbat chatan, 48–50

Shahaf (son of Nurit), 30, 51, 53. *See
also* Nurit, on bar mitzvah
of son

Shakdiel, Leah, 110, 111, 149

shampoo, halakhic rulings regarding,
94–95

Shas Party, xvi, 102, 103, 311n1

www.ingramcontent.com/pod-product-compliance
Lightning Source LLC
Chambersburg PA
CBHW051949270326
41929CB00015B/2593